TARTAN

TAR

TAN

Revised and Updated Edition

JONATHAN FAIERS

BLOOMSBURY VISUAL ARTS
LONDON · NEW YORK · OXFORD · NEW DELHI · SYDNEY

BLOOMSBURY VISUAL ARTS
Bloomsbury Publishing Plc
50 Bedford Square, London, WC1B 3DP, UK
1385 Broadway, New York, NY 10018, USA
29 Earlsfort Terrace, Dublin 2, Ireland

BLOOMSBURY, BLOOMSBURY VISUAL ARTS and the Diana logo are trademarks of
Bloomsbury Publishing Plc

First published in Great Britain by Berg 2008
This edition published by Bloomsbury Visual Arts 2022

Cover image: Jun Takahashi for Undercover "Melting Pot" Autumn/Winter 2000/1.
Photograph by Mamoru Miyazawa courtesy of Jun Takahashi and Undercover.

A catalogue record for this book is available from the British Library.

A catalog record for this book is available from the Library of Congress.

ISBN: PB: 978-1-3501-9377-2

Typeset by Integra Software Services Pvt Ltd
Printed and bound in India

To find out more about our authors and books visit www.bloomsbury.com
and sign up for our newsletters.

CONTENTS

PREFACE TO THE REVISED EDITION

The world is a different place since the original publication of this work in 2008. Appearing at the same moment as the beginning of the global recession as well as the election of Barack Obama as the 44th President of the United States, the theme of contradiction that is explored throughout the book and which understands tartan as 'an indeterminate textile sign', seemed serendipitously appropriate. Writing this preface to the new paperback edition at the close of 2020 the world once again faces economic collapse, greater than the recession of 2008 due to the Covid-19 pandemic that is wreaking global devastation on a previously unimagined scale. The glimpse of spring following America's four-year long winter, provided by the recent election results suggest signs of thawing the prevailing atmosphere of isolationism that has become the all too familiar global default setting, not least evidenced by the United Kingdom's opting out of the European Union. Climate change, the growth of politically motivated terrorist acts, social media's universal ascendency and the upsurge of nationalism leading to global conflicts and humanitarian crises have become all too familiar features of the years since first writing this book, disasters with little or no redress nor long-term solution.

Global culture during this time has also faced unprecedented challenges with the arts and design attempting to reflect these fundamental shifts while simultaneously surviving in a climate where funding is diminished, and more recently venues are closed and businesses failing. Of particular relevance to this book and its new chapter, the fashion industry has had to radically rethink its possible future and understand the pandemic as having imposed a necessary interruption, an enforced

1 (Facing Page) Georgia Russell, *The Clans and Tartans of Scotland*. Cut paperwork print, plastic wire, perspex and board, 2002. Courtesy of England & Co. Gallery, London

cessation of the unsustainable, ceaseless round of production which has characterized it throughout the twenty-first century.

During this same period, tartan, however, seems to have faced no such similar diminution in its popularity nor its application within the design industries, and established history of rallying supporters of a common cause behind its declamatory has indeed gained a newly rediscovered political potential. As a textile with an grids, tartan continues to be the cloth of resistance against oppression, of unity amongst dispossessed and geographically disparate groups or simply as an expression of originality. While much of the focus of this book is on tartan's globalization, recent developments within the United Kingdom concerning Scottish devolution and renewed calls for its independence largely as a result of the decision to withdraw from the European Union, has made tartan once more a visual reminder of past and present antagonisms between England and Scotland. Interest in the textile has been reawakened as both representative of indomitable Scottish independence by its adherents, whilst for others it remains forever implicated in the Scottish capitulation to English rule. Indicative of this renewed awareness and critical attention is the major exhibition devoted to tartan scheduled to open at V&A Dundee in 2023.

At the time of writing the book, tartan was enjoying one of its regular moments of fashionable popularity with a number of key designers utilizing it for collections that expanded tartan's sartorial language and which, in turn, have since become part of its accumulated aesthetic resonance. These tartan moments have occurred with increasing regularity since 2008, so that the old adage that tartan is never in nor out of fashion would now be more accurate declaring that tartan *is* fashion. Tartan's long history as a cloth that can express resistance, a subversive textile that offers a challenge to sartorial hegemony has made it the favourite of a number of radical designers that have come to prominence in recent times. Its contradictory history and associations, its ability to speak both conservative and revolutionary languages, and its potential to represent a number of ideological perspectives have led to its ascendancy on global fashion runways. Most noticeable perhaps has been tartan's deployment by designers, and indeed wearers, who are committed to expanding - and in some cases dismantling - received notions of masculinity, a phenomenon that prompted the writing of the chapter 'Tartan Undecided' for this new paperback edition.

It is of course entirely apposite that tartan should be so highly regarded by those who refuse fixed gender identification. Tartan as a cloth worn and loved by both men and women throughout its complex history, in turn bestows this fluidity and possibility of choice on today's wearers, who respond to its historical duality and contemporary multiplicity. The contemporary undecided tartan wearers, who celebrate the cloth's multivalency, its assertiveness and its performative potential, are the successors to the 'swell' and 'fast' gents discussed in 'Tartan Toffs' who wore their tartan as a badge of swaggering fashionable self-esteem. Continuing their sartorial mission, today's tartan disciples relish in the cloth's ability to transform, to enable and to challenge. Tartan's seductive patterns, so redolent of pride, resistance and passion, continue to offer both collective and individual modes of expression, a cloth forever timely and inimitable.

INTRODUCTION

Tartan: the immediately recognizable symbol of a fiercely independent nation. A ubiquitous pattern that has been commodified into a super brand signifying all things traditionally Scottish. The badge of rebellion and nonconformity worn with pride throughout history, from Jacobite sympathizers to punks. The cloth beloved of royalty. The global messenger carried by Highland regiments and football's Tartan Army, inspiring architects, artists, film-makers and contemporary fashion.

Tartan has developed from a Highland craft to a mass-produced, globally consumed textile. Its use in both 'traditional' Scottish dress and high fashion, and its sociocultural significance as a pattern, is at once complex and in a process of continual development. What becomes immediately apparent from the most cursory list of its associations is that, above all, it is a textile of *contradiction*. The subject of fierce academic debate concerning its origins, tartan's subsequent history has been shaped by periods of revulsion and reverence. It has been employed as a textile that can both honour and repress its wearer, and is simultaneously regarded as quintessentially traditional and rebellious. Apparently simple in construction, tartan is also capable of staggering complexity; it is multivalent and dichotomous.

The structure of this book is shaped by the complex relationship that a specific textile's use in both historical and contemporary dress has with its much broader sociocultural and historical significance. From the earliest studies of tartan at the beginning of the nineteenth century, it has been at the centre of a number of academic and political debates. Tartan and its study has been both applauded and vilified, generating heated debate from those who see tartan as the visual symbol of an ancient Scottish clan system, and those who regard its role in that same system as primarily a nineteenth-century sociopolitical invention. The majority of work undertaken prior to the mid-twentieth century was concerned with establishing and defining tartan as a textile tradition, and identifying specific patterns or setts, as they are more properly known, with the Scottish clan system. Most published works on tartan, from the nineteenth century to today, devote much space to listing and illustrating tartan patterns and attributing specific clan associations to them. Tartan research continues to be concerned with establishing the origin and first recorded evidence of the alliance between a specific clan and its associated tartan pattern. The ability to check a tartan against a family name has proved an essential component of the heritage industry both within Scotland and abroad, and generates equal amounts of genealogical reassurance, financial reward and critical controversy.

Other studies have attempted to locate the textile in broader anthropological and topographical contexts, suggesting parallels between tartan patterns and other cultures' weaving traditions. In many cases these similarities are unmistakable, and are often cited as 'evidence' of ancient Celtic global migration and domination. More specific assessments of tartan's relationship to location attempt to replace clan association with that of district, arguing that tartan patterns developed out of a combination of local production methods, available dyestuffs and topographical, rather than dynastic, alliance; in *District Tartans*, Gordon Teall of Teallach and Philip D. Smith Jr. present fascinating and convincing research in this field.[1] Other studies have been concerned

2 Young competitors in a Highland dancing competition, 2007

with establishing an accurate weaving notation for named patterns and thereby maintaining and continuing the uniformity of those same setts, and Donald C. Stewart's *The Setts of the Scottish Tartans*, first published in 1950, must be considered as the pioneering study in this particular area.[2] In this work, Stewart presented for the first time a systematized and accurate collection of the thread counts of a number of popular and lesser-known tartan patterns.[3] Historically, a variety of methods have been used to record tartan patterns, some of which will be considered in this study, but for reliability and accuracy the contemporary weaver will find James D. Scarlett's *The Tartan Weaver's Guide* and his *Tartan: The Highland Textile* invaluable.[4]

Military tartans have generated specialized studies, often found within the histories of specific Highland regiments, as has the history of what have become known as 'forged' tartans, both areas which will be returned to later in this book. For the contextualization of tartan production within a tradition of Highland crafts, Isabel Grant's seminal *Highland Folk Ways* of 1961 remains a classic study, and provides many insights into tartan's relationship to Highland traditions before industrialization.[5] The following year, 1962, saw the publication of what was the first attempt to unite many of these hitherto discrete areas of tartan study in one work: John Telfer Dunbar's impressive and painstaking *History of Highland Dress*.[6] Dunbar's work includes sections on the technical processes of pre-industrialized tartan manufacture, clan and regimental associations, the development of Highland dress, forged tartans, tartan in portraiture, alongside a host of other fascinating and insightful detail; and all subsequent, broader surveys of tartan are indebted to Dunbar, this present work being no exception. More recently, Hugh Cheape's *Tartan: The Highland Habit* is pioneering in its scope and one of the few studies to assess tartan's impact both historically and in the present day.[7] Finally, Hugh Trevor-Roper's essential and ground-breaking reassessment of tartan's implication in eighteenth- and nineteenth-century constructions of nationalism, set out in his 'The Invention of Tradition: The Highland Tradition of Scotland', remains vital to any serious interrogation of tartan's history.[8] All of these works and many more will be referred to throughout the course of this study and to their authors I remain deeply indebted.

> Some Scots decry the tartan image of their country since they feel it impedes a proper appreciation of the technological achievements of modern Scotland. Wiser counsel, however, generally prevails, since tradition and modernity need not conflict but can complement one another.[9]

Teallach and Smith's invocation of the spirit of modernity, and their advocacy of using tradition to inform the present, can act as an indication of the aims and approach of this book. Tartan will be positioned within broad philosophical, political and cultural contexts, and its impact assessed domestically and globally. Naturally, considerable emphasis will be given as to how tartan was shaped by – and in turn periodically influenced – the fashion industries both historically and in the present day. Tartan's manifestations will also be considered in arenas as diverse as popular entertainment, art, design and cinema, and it is hoped that this more interdisciplinary and inclusive approach will make *Tartan*, as well as other titles in the 'Textiles that Changed the World' series, both accessible and useful to a wide readership. All textiles, including tartan, have had a profound impact on the cultural, economic and political history of society, and yet very few works have attempted to explore the extent, diversity and richness of these histories. *Tartan's* pioneering approach will attempt to redress this, and alongside the others in the series will finally give textile studies the same critical breadth of enquiry that has long been applied to its related field, fashion theory. In order to achieve this, an a-historical and heterogeneous approach will be adopted which, whilst utilizing previous studies of the subject, will provide an alternative, more inclusive and interdisciplinary assessment of tartan as a highly complex and persistent cultural phenomenon.

Introducing the concept of the collision between tradition and modernity automatically invokes the work of Walter Benjamin, and his investigations of the complementary interconnectedness of the past to our conceptualization of the modern, is of acute relevance to this project. This study will be an attempt to analyse particular aspects of tartan's history, its production and use, whether they be technical ones such as its development from hand-woven to fully mass-produced textile, or its implication in specific sociopolitical events. In addition, its association with a host of biographical, fictional and other constructions will help to assess tartan's impact on a variety of cultural institutions and products. Benjamin's methodology is set out in his *Arcades Project,* which states that: 'The first stage in this undertaking will be to carry over the principle of montage into history. That is, to assemble large-scale constructions out of the smallest and most precisely cut components. Indeed, to discover in the analysis of the small individual moment the crystal of the total event' provides the inspiration for a more inclusive and simultaneously less rigid conception of tartan and its history to be assembled.'[10] Following on from Benjamin's 'small individual moment', the notion of the fragment, and its significance to historical tartan research, will be considered and its significance assessed.

Through sections that consider tartan's relationship to traditional dress, to fashion, to textile production, alongside broader concepts such as colonization, historicism, rebellion and fabrication, an appraisal of tartan will be produced that will expand – and in some cases dispel – many of the assumptions previously placed upon it. These sections will then be extended by reference to a range of critical and theoretical positions directly or indirectly related to tartan, and illustrated by a similarly diverse range of material. As a result of this method, a model will be constructed enabling the study of a specific cultural production to be used to investigate critical territory outside of its immediate context.

This book avoids any strictly chronological development of tartan, in acknowledgment of the fact that the early history of the cloth is often shrouded in myth and speculation, and therefore any attempt to establish a definitive chronology will always remain inconclusive and somewhat strained. Similarly, its subsequent development both practically and culturally is characterized by periods of intense progression and decline, or rather disfavour, making the examination of its contradictory sociocultural construction more urgent than yet another attempt to 'fix' it chronologically. However, certain navigational landmarks will remain constant throughout this study: an assessment of its imbrications with the fashion industry, for example, its essentially fictive historical development and, visually, its function as a grid that disrupts and constrains. These and other theoretical formulations will be revisited and reassessed in a number of different contexts, the intention being to demonstrate tartan's ability to adapt, absorb and survive shifting economic, cultural and political trends. And so, whilst this account of tartan may often appear ambiguous and even conflicting, hopefully this will present a truer reflection of tartan's contemporary complexity as a cloth of contradiction and a pattern of possibility.

> Clothing, like language, always happens somewhere in geographical and social space. In its form, colour, material, construction, and function – and because of the behaviour it implies – clothing displays obvious signs, attenuated markings or residual traces of

3 John Galliano, Autumn/Winter 2000–1

struggles, cross-cultural contacts, borrowings, exchanges between economic regions or cultural areas as well as among groups within a single society.[11]

Philippe Perrot's declaration concerning clothing, from his work *Fashioning the Bourgeoisie*, is equally germane when considering how to approach the study of textiles. Textiles too, especially patterned textiles, display perhaps even more strongly than clothing 'signs', 'markings' and 'traces' of political, economic and cultural transformations. Textile studies is dominated by traditional ethnographic, economic or technical considerations, and more recently gender studies and psychoanalysis, but tends to remain firmly embedded in the terrain of traditional academic research, where one particular hypothesis and critical framework is adhered to. However, with a textile such as tartan, which is at once pattern, cloth and garment, there is an opportunity to integrate textile studies more closely with other methods of cultural critical enquiry, expanding the field of research into a number of territories simultaneously.

To limit the study of tartan to one particular critical model would run the risk of establishing parameters that might prove too inflexible for interrogating its unique position. Simultaneously occupying the spaces of fashion, historical costume, subcultural and military uniform, as well as being a globally consumed pattern applied to a bewildering variety of products, tartan deserves a more fluid approach. Textile studies is particularly suitable to a broader, but no less critical reading, an approach similar to that taken by art criticism, which broadened its scope via philosophy, literary criticism and psychoanalysis. This work will utilize a variety of methods, thereby reaffirming textile studies as an independent field of enquiry rather than, as has often been the case, an occasional adjunct to fashion theory, art history, or cultural studies. By considering tartan in a variety of forms – as clothing both on and off the runway, in subcultural and mass-produced garments, in popular entertainment, art, design, literature and film – we can construct a textile study that is egalitarian, less reified and genuinely sociocultural in its scope and popular appeal. A study that will treat the tartan uniform worn by Eddie Murphy (illus. 61) in the film *Coming to America* (John Landis, 1988) with the same degree of relevance as a tartan suit from Nicolas Ghesquière's Autumn/Winter 2006 collection for Balenciaga (illus. 118). An enquiry that can trace a tartan line of descent from the excesses of Balmoral's Victorian interiors to the tartan carpets beloved of innumerable contemporary pubs and guesthouses.

Ever since tartan was banned in the eighteenth century and excised from its original cultural significance, it has been able to infiltrate a myriad of cultural arenas. The Act of Proscription released tartan from its impending ossification as an exclusively national textile and allowed it to occupy a space that is at once elusive and yet connected to other spaces, imbued with the memory of triumphs and tragedies as well as the potential for future development.[12] Its relationship to clothing, fashionable or otherwise, and other cultural products is closest to two spatial models, one structural, the other literary. Michel Foucault describes the *heterotopia* as 'capable of juxtaposing in a single real place several spaces, several sites that are in themselves incompatible', whilst the *chronotope* originally discussed by Mikhail Bakhtin can be thought of as 'a fictional setting where historically specific relations of power become visible and certain stories can "take place"'.[13]

A condensation of these two theoretical models provides a method by which to understand how tartan operates across a number of sociocultural spaces. For example, when used in clothing, tartan can register as historically specific or vague, nationally defined or global, handcrafted or mass-produced, conservative or revolutionary, vibrant or muted, and so on. Add to this host of signification the layers of meaning inherent in the actual garment under discussion (jacket, trousers, shawl etc.), plus details of cut and fabric, and we can begin to account for tartan's endurance and the particular resonance underlying stock phrases such as tartan being 'a staple that moves in and out of the fashion focus but never entirely disappears'.[14]

Rather than being in or out of fashion, tartan should always be considered alongside fashion; it can never be fully contained within one system as it is too rich a signifier, too mythic in proportion, and so this study will only refer to tartan *and* fashion, for example, rather than tartan *in* or *as* fashion, for as Roland Barthes reminds us: 'What must always be remembered is that myth is a double system; there occurs in it a sort of ubiquity: its point of departure is constituted by the arrival of a meaning.'[15] Therefore what follows will take the form of a series of materializations of

4 Teddy Johnson, Eve Boswell, Pearl Carr and Bruce Forsythe at the London Palladium, 1957. Photo: Harry Hammond, 1957

tartan which will take examples of tartan and dress, tartan and art, tartan and film and so on, with which to consider broader issues and contexts. These fictional constructs, the products of designers, artists and film-makers, will be considered not only within their immediate spheres of influence, but historically contextualized by events and figures that will recur at regular intervals throughout this study. At times, these materializations will necessarily encompass much larger philosophical, political and economic considerations; at others remain specifically focused on particular aspects of a garment, film or other artefact: Benjamin's small moments. It is hoped that by adopting an inclusive rather than exclusive method, a greater understanding of tartan's resonance will be reached, and some of the complex trajectories tartan traces temporally, politically and economically will be revealed.

Since its proscription, when tartan was prohibited for certain sectors of Scottish society and in effect pushed underground, it has functioned *rhizomatically*, to utilize the term of Giles Deleuze and Félix Guatarri. The ban ironically allowed it to flourish elsewhere, to find new wearers and new surfaces to cover, and since the ban tartan has followed a pattern of lying dormant for periods of time, only to erupt with renewed vigour in different contexts and locations. The spread of tartan into so many diverse sociocultural spaces, forming dense concentrations as well as unexpected outcrops, prompts the use of a horticultural metaphor by which to understand textile history and development. Just as plants can be tended and encouraged to grow in certain directions, or left to run wild or go to seed, textiles also go through active cycles of growth and decline. Like plants, they can be repositioned or left to flourish in their natural habitats; similarly, they are often imported, nurtured and hybridized. The similarities between tartan's development and Deleuze and Guatarri's model of the rhizome, an underground stem that sends roots downwards (historically) and shoots upwards (future developments) are unmistakable:

> Every rhizome contains lines of segmentarity according to which it is stratified, territorialized, organized, signified, attributed etc., as well as lines of deterritorialization down which it constantly flees. There is a rupture in the rhizome whenever segmentarity lines explode into a line of flight, but the line of flight is part of the rhizome. These lines always tie back to one another.[16]

Thus the various manifestations of tartan encountered in this study, on a variety of garments and products ubiquitous and rare, domestic or global, current or dated, will be seen to 'explode into a line of flight', subsequently crossing other lines from other tartans, before returning to their original setts valorized by the traces of these encounters.

5 'Tartan', a decorative, dark red and white, bi-coloured variety of dahlia

Part I

TARTAN AND HISTORY

6 Loom from South Uist, now in the collection of the Highland Folk Museum, Kingussie. Early 1700s

1.
TECHNICAL CONSTRUCTION
Sett, Weave, Colour

The starting point of any history of tartan, as with all similar traditional textile histories, must be selected from a number of possible positions. It could commence with the tried and tested historical method of trying to establish tartan's first recorded references. Alternatively, it could be contextualized within broader terrains of sociocultural and, in particular, national significance. Tartan's unique ability to occupy and transcend both traditional and fashionable dress could furnish another opening that would lead to a consideration of its global dominance. Likewise, its relationship to geographical location and the notion of clanship, alongside its significance as both proscribed civilian textile and its incorporation into military uniform, promotes discussion of its paradoxical historical status. Yet whilst all of these possible beginnings are relevant, and are indicative of the complex historical, social and economic issues underpinning tartan, it is perhaps simplest to start with the actual construction of a tartan pattern. However, although opting for the most fundamental aspect of tartan – its construction – some of the broader territories tartan inhabits will inevitably be encountered and acknowledged, but more detailed analysis of these aspects will be reserved for subsequent chapters.

SETT

Weaving is the process of forming cloth by interlacing two sets of yarns. The yarns parallel to the long edge of the cloth are called warps; the opposite yarns are termed wefts (also woofs, fillings, or picks). The warp yarns are stretched under tension between two beams – a warp beam and a cloth beam – and the wefts are introduced one at a time. A woven tartan pattern is produced by a relatively straightforward process whereby bands of different colours and varying width, depending on the number of yarns used to produce them, are employed in the weaving of the cloth. The number of yarns of each colour required to produce a particular sequence is known as the sett. The sett is the identifying sequence of each individual tartan pattern. This sequence, or sett, is repeated across the loom as many times as necessary until the warp is completed. Then exactly the same sequence is interwoven at right angles, horizontally from left to right, to form the weft and produce the finished tartan. The repetition of a sett horizontally and vertically is the basis for all tartans, from the simplest such as the MacGregor variation known as Rob Roy, which consists of equal-width bands of red and black forming an all-over uniform two-colour chequerboard pattern, to highly complex tartans such as Ogilvie of Airlie, with its 182 colour changes (illus. 8).

7 One of the simplest of all tartans, the variant of MacGregor known as Rob Roy

The sett can be repeated in one of two ways. Either the sequence is repeated in reverse order, which will result in a symmetrical tartan pattern (typical of the majority of modern tartans produced today), or the sequence is repeated from the beginning each time, forming an asymmetrical tartan. The point where the pattern sequences ends and begins again is known as a pivot point. In a symmetrical tartan, there are typically two (sometimes more) pivot points around which the sett is reversed, so that the sequence of stripes continually repeats and reverses across the whole width of the cloth. In an asymmetrical tartan, however, there will be only one pivot point where the sequence ends and begins again. Whilst the majority of older tartans still in production today (and certainly nearly all contemporary designs) are identical warp and weft, and symmetrical about the pivot points, this has not always been the case. Some of the oldest surviving examples and historical representations found in portraiture are asymmetrical; this is partly due to the types of loom used to produce the cloth, which will be discussed in further detail in the following section, Weave. In these cases, the whole sett is repeated from beginning to end without reversing around a particular point.

As long as the sett is maintained, it becomes a relatively simple operation to scale a particular tartan pattern up or down; for example a larger check might be required for a tartan blanket than for a dress-weight fabric, but as long as the proportional difference between each colour is adhered to, the sett can then be multiplied or diminished until the desired scale is achieved. In cases where the original tartan sett incorporates relatively narrow bands or lines of certain colours, it is necessary to give these an increased emphasis to prevent them disappearing altogether once the pattern is scaled down.

The comparative simplicity of dressing, or warping, the loom with the tartan sequence and its repetitions and reversals, is in striking contrast to the complexity that occurs once that same formula is repeated across the weft of the tartan. When this stage in the process is reached, the subtleties of shading and tone produced by identical or different colours woven across each other comes into play, making the tartan simultaneously straightforward in construction yet immensely subtle in colouring. The mathematical equation governing the number of finished shades of any given tartan is surprising in its acceleration and aggrandisement. A simple two-colour tartan such as Rob Roy produces just three shades overall: red, black and the mixture of the two where they are woven together. However, this easily understood ratio very quickly becomes less logical (optically at least), so that a tartan with only six different colours produces fifteen mixtures equalling twenty-one shades overall. This increasing multiplicity also produces another paradox: generally speaking, the greater the number of colours, the more muted the overall tartan becomes, as shades very close to each other in tonal strength are mixed, and the individual vibrancy of certain colours is only revealed when closely scrutinized. The majority of tartans consist of broader bands of colour known as the under-check, which then sometimes (not necessarily always) are augmented by narrower lines of colour known as the over-check. Further complexities produced by the optical recession and dominance of certain colours results in a visual ambiguity that can produce an oscillation between what the viewer registers as under-check and over-check of a particular tartan.[1]

The sett is the primary means of differentiating one tartan from another, and the identification, establishment and accurate recording of the sett has preoccupied all serious studies of tartan since James Logan's *The Scottish Gaël* of 1831, which was the first significant attempt to record different tartan patterns.[2] In Logan's work, some fifty-four patterns were set down according to his own tabular system, and although contemporary tartan experts have identified many inaccuracies in this scheme, the book must be credited as the catalyst for all subsequent attempts to accurately notate tartan setts. Throughout the history of tartan literature, attempts to find a successful and practical method to record different setts produced a variety of approaches. Following Logan's early attempt, patterns can be found reproduced in a number of books by an array of techniques including hand-coloured lithographs, woven silk specimens, printed illustrations passed through embossing machines to give a more 'lifelike' woven appearance and, most interestingly, a form of so-called 'machine painting'. This was a technique developed by William and Andrew Smith of Mauchline, who also produced what could be considered the first true tartan souvenirs: boxes and other small wooden items covered in tartan-patterned paper known as tartan ware or Mauchline Ware.[3]

Another suggestion as to how tartan patterns might have been notated, certainly before the advent of books on the subject, is via the use of pattern sticks. Supposedly these were wooden sticks

8 Ogilvie of Airlie, a highly complex tartan with over 180 colour changes

on which were wound different coloured threads following the correct sequence of the particular sett to be woven; however, the evidence for pattern sticks is purely literary and doubtful as no actual examples survive, and as Scarlett suggests: 'Even with such modern aids as quick-drying glue and double-sided sticky tape, pattern sticks are difficult to make and soon come unravelled. They tell the weaver less than would a strip of the cloth that they are supposed to define and give no indication of the final pattern.'[4] If they existed at all, pattern sticks were probably the back sticks of looms that still bore the remains of the original dressing and were mistaken for weaving guides rather than the remains of dismantled looms.[5] It is not until the publication of J. C. Stewart's *The Setts of the Scottish Tartans* that any general consensus and standardization as to the notation of setts was reached. In the book, Stewart provided accurate patterns for some 266 tartans, and also introduced a new method of visualizing the sequences by using colour strips as a key to how the warp would appear once the loom was dressed. Today a combination of patterns and colour strips, often accompanied by an image of the completed tartan, allows the contemporary weaver to accurately reproduce any tartan sett.

Setts are generally notated by using initials as abbreviations for the different colours, which are listed in sequence as they appear, with the number of threads in each colour underneath the initial to provide the width of each different colour stripe. With the exception of asymmetrical tartans, the first and last letters in the sett are conventionally given in bold type to indicate the pivotal stripes around which the pattern reverses and about which it is symmetrical, and so the pattern sequence for Wallace tartan would look like this:

Bk	R	Bk	**Y**
2	16	16	2

(Bk = black, R = red or scarlet and Y = yellow, the pivot points being the two narrow stripes of black and yellow.)

9 Wallace

Today the popularity and growth of the modern tartan industry, whilst unregulated, can at least rely on the accurate description of the sett of individual tartans as a means of individuating new patterns, and with varying degrees of success attempt to register and patent these new tartan variations. The Scottish Tartans Authority will, for example, undertake to research any new sett, and if it is sufficiently different from others will, for a fee, enter it in their records. This process has no official standing, but it has become a convenient means by which to identify at least a proportion of the rapidly proliferating mass of modern tartans.[6]

WEAVE

The weave most commonly used in the production of tartan is the twill weave or, more specifically, 2/2 twill. In 2/2 twill, the points between warp and weft where the yarns interlace are alternated, so each time the warp threads pass first over two, and then under two, of the weft threads. The warp threads pass over the weft via a progression of one interlacing either to the left or right, producing the characteristic diagonal parallel lines or ribbed effect (technically known as a wale) on the surface of the cloth where two different colours are woven together. This technique adds to the lustrousness to be found in traditionally woven tartans, as Scarlett points out:

In plain weave the mixture of colours is of the 'pepper and salt' variety but in traditional twill weave the two colours appear alongside each other as alternate diagonal lines of shading and these present a different appearance according to whether one is looking along or across them. Because of this, even a draped piece of tartan shows 'life'; in motion, it has a vitality of its own.[7]

Much of the appeal of traditionally woven tartan cloth stems from this play of light and the optical fusion and interchange of the different colours along its diagonal ribs. Unlike plain weaves, where the front and back of the cloth are the same, twill weaves are differentiated, the side with the most pronounced wale being generally considered as the front of the cloth. Many of the characteristics of twill-weave cloth are also those that spring to mind when considering traditionally woven tartan cloth: it is durable, when tightly woven it is wind- and water-repellent, marks and stains are less noticeable on its uneven surface, it is relatively crease-resistant, and next to plain weaves the twill weave is the most basic weave that can be constructed on a simple loom.

The twill weave is the same used in the so-called Falkirk Tartan, a fragment of cloth discovered when the Falkirk hoard of silver coins was excavated in 1934. The scrap of fabric was apparently used as a stopper for an earthenware vessel containing the coins, which range in date from 83 BC to AD 230, and this has led textile historians to suggest that the fragment dates from the third century AD. The Falkirk Tartan is a twill weave using two shades of natural wool for the warp and weft yarns, one a dark brown, the other a much lighter brown with a greenish hue (the green

10 The so-called Falkirk Tartan. Cloth fragment found with a hoard of Roman coins buried around the middle of the third century AD

tint no doubt attributable to its long contact with the silver coins), which produces a two-colour check with a third transitional shade. It is a small-scale, simple check of the type that has been traditionally woven in the Highlands and Lowlands of Scotland for centuries, made from yarn spun and (if not used in its natural shade) dyed locally using indigenously occurring animal and plant stuffs for its colours. This type of woollen check was traditionally woven into a wrap known as a plaid, and commonly worn by shepherds on hills in the winter, and therefore more recently known as a Shepherd's Plaid[8] (illus. 11). These plaids (characterized by their simplicity, the use of natural dyes and typical small-scale checks) have been regarded as the textile production that links ancient Scottish Highland traditional dress and the much more contemporary phenomenon of tartan. Plaids continued to be produced alongside tartan patterns well into the nineteenth century and are directly related to the simple two-colour tartan patterns still available today.

Naming this fragment the Falkirk Tartan perhaps indicates the desire to establish Gaelic textile antecedence for tartan, rather than any serious attempt to link our contemporary understanding of the structure of tartan with that of earlier checked textiles. As early as 1948, Grace M. Crowfoot, in her article 'Two Textiles from the National Museum, Edinburgh', is at pains to point out that whilst the Falkirk fragment is possibly 'the earliest tartan too if we may claim it as such on the strength of the stripes and the checks', it is also 'no legendary or rare piece . . . but a "poor man's plaid" with two colours only, dark and light brown. It is a true folk weave . . .'[9] She also suggests that the Falkirk fragment bears a direct relationship – in the construction of the weave and simple checked pattern – to other early textiles produced in Scandinavia, such as the celebrated Gerumsberget Cloak found in 1920 and thought to be Sweden's oldest preserved garment, dating to the Bronze Age. More recently, the discovery in the Taklamakan desert in the Xianjiang province of China of a group of remarkably well-preserved mummies, some found wearing textiles that bear a similarity to twill-woven tartan, has produced a maelstrom of controversy at the centre of which is the utilization of textile research to forge a possible link between ancient Chinese and Celtic cultures. Amongst the textiles found with the mummies are some made from dyed green, blue and brown yarns woven together to produce a checked or 'tartan' pattern, and these are the most easterly examples of this type of weaving found to date. As Elizabeth Wayland Barber has suggested, they also bear a similarity to woven twill specimens, dating from around 1000 BC, found most notably at the Hallstatt mines in Austria but also in Germany and Scandinavia.[10] The 'proof' provided by the 3,000-year-old 'tartan' items in conjunction with the appearance of the mummies (some unusually tall and with light brown or red hair), has led to the belief in some quarters that the original inhabitants of Xianjiang province were in fact Indo-European.

Disregarding the rather unsavoury Eurocentrism that seems to underpin these racial speculations, what can be gleaned from the various attempts to establish an ancient antecedence for tartan is the undeniable truth that the simplest way to make decorative woven cloth is by weaving two or more differently coloured yarns together to produce a checked pattern. The universality of this technique makes it possible to find visual connections between tartan and almost all indigenous early woven textiles from all parts of the globe, and that no single culture can claim to be the first producers of such a pattern. What makes a tartan a tartan is very much more than its possible links to other ancient woven textiles.

Early tartan and its predecessors, such as the ancient examples mentioned above, would of course have been hand-woven. The earliest looms were upright, the warp threads being fixed along a wooden frame and held taut by weights at the base (instead of a beam), as Isabel Grant has

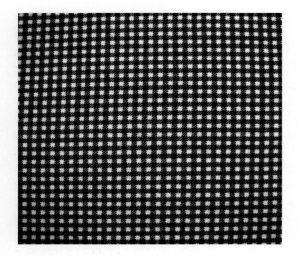

11 Contemporary example of the simple checks traditionally woven in the Highlands and Lowlands of Scotland for centuries, known as a Shepherd's Plaid

observed: 'The weights for these upright looms, flat stones with holes through them, are found on old sites all over the Highlands.'[11] Everyday items such as blankets, wraps and shawls were mostly produced at home by the women of the household, although there were professional weavers in some communities who would have travelled from village to village setting up their looms and undertaking weaving commissions. People requiring cloth would provide their own wool, dyed by themselves, and pay the weaver in kind. The large upright looms would have taken up about half the space of a weaver's cottage and were already warped to save time when setting up, and so variation in pattern would have been unlikely. Minor adjustments would have been catered for and obviously colour changes were dependent on the wool yarn provided by the customer. The width of the cloth produced on old hand-looms was governed by the distance the shuttle could be 'thrown' from one hand to the other, generally producing a length of cloth (after all the subsequent finishing processes had been carried out) of roughly three feet in width, and so for example to make a traditional belted plaid, two such pieces would have had to be sewn together.[12]

Professional weavers would sometimes use broader looms that would have been too wide for one person to pass the shuttle through the shed (the spaces between the warp threads through which the shuttle passes), and so an assistant or apprentice weaver would be required to help produce the cloth. Although the flying shuttle was invented in England in 1733 (this allowed the shuttle to be thrown across the web; wider cloth could be produced single-handedly), this took some time to be generally adopted, especially in the Highlands of Scotland.

The production of hand-woven tartan required a variety of specialist skills. Gathering the wool, dyeing, combing and spinning, followed by weaving, fulling or 'waulking', and in some instances blessings, all went into producing a finished length of tartan cloth. (Having looked briefly at the actual weaving process, these other stages will now be considered; however a discussion of dyeing will be reserved for a final section at the end of this chapter, entitled Colour, as this is not only one of the most hotly contested areas of tartan studies, but is also the vital element that distinguishes tartan from many other similar checked fabrics.)

Prior to the eighteenth century, wool was obtained from now-extinct varieties of Highland sheep. These breeds produced wool that was shed or moulted, and so could be gathered or pulled from the sheep's coat rather than having to be shorn. An analysis of the Falkirk Tartan fragment has revealed that it is made from relatively fine wool with an absence of coarse hairs, which conforms to what is known about these very early breeds. Lighter-coloured white sheep were obviously the most useful, as this wool could be dyed more easily and a greater range of colours achieved. In the eighteenth century, double-coated breeds were introduced, such as the Scottish Blackface and the Cheviot, which had a fine wool under-coat and coarse outer coat.

According to which part of the fleece was used, a weaver could produce either a soft cloth or so-called 'hard' tartan. Short, fine wool would eventually result in a soft cloth; coarser fibres produced hard tartan. The finer wool was prepared for spinning by using flat wooden paddles known as cards, which were covered with small metal hooks. The wool was passed backwards and forwards from one card to the other until it had been straightened and fluffed out into a loose roll of wool with the fibres only partially aligned. This produced a thick, soft cloth used for cheaper plaids and blankets. The production of hard tartan involved a different process, where the coarser longer hairs were gathered and then pulled through metal combs, forcing all the fibres to lie in the same direction and removing any shorter ones; this could then be spun into a worsted yarn to produce very fine finished fabrics. As Grant suggests: 'Because of their fineness, their colouring and the complexity of weaving them, the old checked plaids were articles of value. In the sixteenth century there are instances where rents were partly paid in such plaids.'[13]

Hard tartan continued to be made professionally for the Highland regiments until the reign of Queen Victoria, who thought that it was too harsh for soldiers' legs and ordered that Saxony wool be used instead. This shift to foreign imported wool can be understood as both sympathetic to the well-being of the kilted regimental soldier, and symptomatic of Victoria's promotion of all things German, an economic constituent of the Anglo-German fantasy world she and Albert constructed in the Highlands of Scotland. Today's fine-quality tartan is most probably produced using other imported breeds of sheep from New Zealand and Australia.

Once carded or combed, the fibre was spun. This was originally done by hand using a distaff and spindle: wool from the distaff was fed to the spindle and this was 'spun', twisting the fibres into yarn. The distaff carrying the un-spun fleece was often tucked into the spinner's belt, making it possible for the spinner to move about whilst spinning wool and therefore able to carry out other tasks. In the early eighteenth century, the advent of the spinning wheel in the Scottish Highlands accelerated the process further. The early spinning wheel, or 'muckle wheel' as it was known, consisted of a large wheel linked to a spindle by means of a drive belt. The spinner turned the wheel with one hand and twisted the wool with the other, causing the spindle to draw off more wool, and at a much faster rate, than with a distaff and spindle. This method could also be used to wind wool directly on to a weaver's bobbin. The Saxony wheel eventually replaced the muckle wheel, and because it was operated by means of a foot pedal, the spinner was able to sit whilst spinning. If a local weaver was employed to weave the finished cloth, the women measured out the correct proportions of the different coloured yarns required for the finished pattern. This was done by winding threads of each colour backwards and forwards between a series of pegs fixed on the walls of the barn, or alternatively on a simple wooden frame. These assorted skeins were then carried to the weaver.

The final and much mythologized stage in the production of hand-woven tartan consisted of the fulling or 'waulking' of the cloth. After the cloth had been woven, it was cut from the loom, soaked in an alkaline solution and then beaten and worked by the hands, and sometimes the feet, of about ten women to thicken and 'close' the fibres. The women sang special songs as they worked, and the cloth was pummelled and rubbed in time to their singing. There were different songs for different stages of the process – slow ones to start, gradually working up to faster and faster tunes, with the beating of the cloth providing a form of textile counterpoint to the songs. As with pattern sticks, the appeal of this somewhat mysterious process has become part of the mythology of tartan, and much time has been devoted to locating and recording the waulking songs. Most probably, they consisted of traditional folk songs augmented by newer tunes that would have covered topical subjects of the time and, it has been suggested, were often of a scurrilous or prurient nature.[14]

Obviously, the processes outlined above are for the production of hand-woven tartan, an industry that virtually disappeared with the proscription of tartan that formed part of the Disarming Act of 1746, which was passed following the defeat of the Jacobite forces at Culloden on 16 April, 1746. The Act was part of a systematic attempt to eradicate any remaining opposition to English rule and lingering Jacobite sympathies after Charles Edward Stuart's unsuccessful attempt to overthrow the reigning house of Hanover and seize the Scottish throne. The Act outlawed the wearing of Highland dress, including tartan, which was considered to be a sign of rebellion and an expression of anti-government sympathies. The Act and its ramifications will be discussed in detail throughout *Tartan* as this, more than any other single event, has shaped the subsequent history of tartan and cannot be underestimated in its importance.[15]

The ban paradoxically transformed tartan from a craft into the mass-produced commodity we recognize today. The contradiction inherent in all aspects of tartan is underscored by events immediately following its proscription, for while tartan was effectively banned as a textile in the Highlands from 1746 until the Act's repeal in 1782, it was being globally disseminated and changing its status from a lowly cloth worn by indigenous Highlanders to a fashionable, aristocratic and adaptable textile. After 1746, tartan production effectively changed into a professional industry under the control of a few key manufacturers, who benefited from supplying the newly formed Highland regiments with the so-called 'government tartans'. Simultaneously, the production of, and demand for, hand-woven tartan for ordinary Highland domestic consumption virtually vanished overnight.

Eighteenth-century commentators started to record the effect that the Act of Proscription had on Scottish indigenous weaving skills, one observing that: 'Prior to that period, the Highland women were remarked for their skill and success in spinning and dyeing wool, and clothing themselves and their households, each according to her fancy, in tartans, fine, beautiful and durable.' Whilst the industrialization of the production of tartan enabled the patterns to proliferate and reach markets way beyond their original Highland location, an encounter with examples of early hand-woven tartan in museums and private collections today helps us understand James D. Scarlett's heartfelt eulogy to what was in effect an outlawed textile:

> The cloth that came from Highland looms was hard and harsh, of great durability and often extremely finely woven. The colours were clear, bright and soft, altogether unlike the eye-searing brilliance or washed-out dullness of modern tartans and the patterns too, tended to be bolder and more clearly defined. The result was a harmonious blend of colour and pattern worthy to be looked upon as an art form in its own right.[17]

12 Variant of the Culloden tartan, which was reputed to have first been worn by a member of the Young Pretender's staff at the fateful Battle of Culloden in 1746. It is typical of the so-called Jacobite tartans, characterized by bright colours and complexity

By the beginning of the nineteenth century, the basic vertical loom had largely been replaced by the horizontal loom. In these looms the warp threads were placed horizontally and controlled with treadle and foot pedals, leaving the weaver's hands free to throw the shuttle across from side to side. Tartan production had become a cottage industry centred on villages such as Kilbarchan near Glasgow and Comrie in Perthshire, which produced cloth for customers throughout Scotland. The decline of hand-woven tartan, and the shift from what was in effect a small-scale, labour-intensive craft activity to fully mechanized mass production, had begun by the mid-nineteenth century. This shift was brought about by the invention of power looms and the establishment of textile factories, which revolutionized not just tartan production, but the textile industry as a whole. The inevitable effect these industrial and technical advances wrought on tartan production coincided with pivotal moments in its history, such as the visit of George IV to Edinburgh in 1822, and the raising of the Highland regiments, which greatly increased the demand for tartan.[18] This demand continued to accelerate throughout the nineteenth century, spurred on by Queen Victoria's championing of the textile, and could only have been satisfied by mass production, which led directly to the rise and dominance of tartan-manufacturing firms such as William Wilson & Son of Bannockburn.

COLOUR

The processes detailed above are common to much traditional hand-woven textile production, and as we have seen, comparative examples of traditional indigenous checked cloth can be found across the globe and include some of the earliest examples of patterned woven textiles known. However, apart from the specific regulations governing the formation of a tartan sett, the most distinguishing characteristic differentiating tartan from many other checked textiles is its particular colour combinations. The significance of colour in the history of textiles is a vast and fascinating subject, and the relationship between colour and tartan equally so. As with so many areas of tartan research, this aspect has generated much controversy. The subject of colour has provided convincing arguments against the notion of tartan's primary function as an indicator of clanship; similarly it has generated controversy and confusion concerning the dating and classification of early tartan. Tartan colours have also been the inspiration for painstaking botanical and chemical research into dyeing methods. Contemporary advances in the testing of textile fragments for trace elements to ascertain the composition of their dyestuffs has already led to a greater understanding of the origin and dating of early tartan, and further essential and valuable work needs to be undertaken in this particular field of tartan studies.

In a broader, cultural sense, tartan's vibrant and striking colour combinations have engendered literary and artistic tributes, and even today many of the newly invented modern tartans justify their eventual appearance via a contemporary symbolic colour system, where colour choices are typically equated to topographical features. Endless descriptions fill tartan dictionaries with chromatic justifications for what are sometimes arguably garish colour combinations such as this description for the Essex County tartan from the Province of Ontario, where, according to Mrs Edyth Baker, the designer: 'Golden Yellow represents various cereal crops and sunshine, Green for spring fields, peas and produce, Red for tomatoes, fruits and flag, Blue for skies and waterways, Black for the automotive industry and White for salt mines and fish'.[19] Leaving aside contemporary chromatic taxonomy, the issue of tartan's colourways is indicative of historical developments within the textile and chemical industries, and is responsible for the continuing debate concerning which are the more 'accurate' shades for particular tartans.

Returning to pre-industrialized tartan production, however, we find that early Highland weavers and dyers experimented with organic, locally found minerals, vegetable materials and plants. Bark, moss heathers, brackens, roots of various kinds, onion skins, bog myrtle and ragwort were all typically used to produce dyes. Once these plant materials had been boiled to release the dye, often for many days, a fixative (or mordant, as it is called) was added to the dye to permanently fix it to the fibre. The mordants were typically metal salts such as iron, alum or copper. A native British plant, woad, used as a body and face paint by the ancient Scots (as famously interpreted by Mel Gibson in the film *Braveheart*) was particularly useful as it produced a strong blue without the need for a mordant. These natural dyes would have varied immensely in terms of intensity, colour saturation and fastness, owing to a number of factors such as the mineral content of the water used to make the dye and the temperatures and times at which the wool was exposed to the dyestuff. Another crucial factor in the dyeing of early tartan was the variation in the hardness of the wool used; wool from some of the varieties of early Highland sheep was particularly resistant to dye and often required weeks to get the dye to take. All of these variables, combined with the lack of recorded recipes for dyes and dyeing, and the processes of ageing and fading on the few fragments of early tartan that have survived, have increased the speculation as to exactly what early tartans would have looked like. Similarly, they have also helped in generating the subsequent confusion surrounding the different contemporary colour variations of today's tartans.

Following the prohibition of tartan in 1746, many of the ancient recipes for dyes (which would have been passed down through succeeding generations) were lost, but in recent times, due to the interest in ancient textile traditions and the rise in popularity of natural dyeing processes, much research has been undertaken to try and ascertain the composition and appearance of some of the early dyes. Dunbar, in his *Highland Costume*, recounts experiments he carried out that underscore the highly variable nature of early Highland dyeing processes; he also furnishes us with a list of natural ingredients and the colours that they yield: lichens for yellow and shades of brown, water lilies for black and grey, ladies' bedstraw for red, roots of the yellow iris for blue/grey. He also suggests that crimson and purple could be obtained from corcur: powdered lichens combined with urine.[20]

The interest in natural dyeing processes has meant that until recently, the majority of research into the dyeing of early tartan has tended to concentrate on the composition of these very early indigenous dyestuffs. This emphasis has reinforced research into what are known as district tartans, which have topographical associations rather than clan or familial ones. The debate concerning district versus clan tartans will be discussed in more detail later, but the arguments suggesting that if early tartan was dyed using locally available dyestuffs, this would also result in tartans coming from similar geographical regions sharing a similar colour palette, are persuasive. The image of the early Highlander dressed in tartans dyed using the plants from the local area and blending harmoniously with the landscape is persistent. Reports by travellers to the Highlands as far back as the sixteenth century commented on this unity of dress and landscape, with writers such as George Buchanan, in his *Rerum Scoticarum Historia* of 1581, emphasizing its tactical advantages: 'The majority now in their dress prefer a dark brown, imitating very nearly the leaves of heather, that when lying upon the heath in the day, they may not be discovered by the appearance of their clothes.'[21]

Although many early tartans have muted colour palettes that are evocative of the Highland landscape, it also becomes immediately apparent, when looking at any textile collection or painted representations of early tartan, that there is a preponderance of reds and blues, colours notoriously difficult to produce easily from indigenous Highland flora. Even amongst the literature investigating and supporting the use of local dyes, such as the appendix 'Early Scottish Dyes' by Annette Kok, included in Dunbar's earlier *History of Highland Dress*, there are intimations that some imported foreign dyestuffs must also have been used.[22] Kok states: 'The most difficult colours to obtain with dye-plants native to the British Isles are blue and red. It seems that imported foreign dyestuffs must have been used to a certain extent in the Highlands from quite an early date, especially for blue', and goes on to suggest that whilst woad or leaves of the Devil's-bit scabious might have provided a suitable blue, imported indigo was much more likely to have been used.[23] Indigo is known to have been imported (via Holland) to St Kilda by the 1700s and would have been used to produce not only a strong blue, but also greens and purples when mixed with the naturally occurring dyestuffs. Elsewhere, Kok states: 'Of all British dye-plants the greatest number give yellow', a fact that although interesting would seem to belie the district tartan/local dyestuffs theories, in that comparatively few early tartans use great quantities of yellow in their setts.[24]

Recent research into the use of the colour red in early tartan, such as that carried out on fabric samples at the National Museum of Scotland, for example, has begun to dispel the belief that early tartan was chiefly dyed using indigenous materials. Although red is the most strikingly present colour in the majority of early tartans, its presence has been largely attributed to the use of plants such as ladies' bedstraw, or the somewhat enigmatic concoction corcur, both producing shades that are relatively unreliable and difficult to obtain. Other than these, there has been a grudging admittance that imported madder must have been used, given the preponderance of the colour, but that this would have been reserved for wealthy clients, Kok suggesting: 'It is possible that the ladies of more well-to-do families used to supplement their native dyes with madder or other red dye from abroad.'[25] The association of the colour red with wealth, due to its cost and rarity, has led to a nebulous belief that its use in early tartans, whether as a result of foreign dyestuffs or from locally produced material, distinguishes these tartans from other tartans. The assumption made is that 'red' tartans would have been worn for ceremonial or social occasions, rather than as practical everyday wear, where inconspicuousness and camouflage were paramount in the choice of colour scheme. This cannot really be supported, given that a significant proportion of surviving early tartan samples all include red as part of their sett, too many for them to have been reserved for special occasions only.

Important research has recently revealed that much more costly imported dyes from India and the Americas were used extensively in early eighteenth-century tartan production, suggesting that the trade in dyestuffs from abroad was much more sophisticated in Scotland at that time than thought previously. Tests carried out in 2004 on a number of eighteenth-century tartan samples obtained from the Highland Society of London's *Book of Certified Tartans*, kept at the National Museum of Scotland in Edinburgh, reveal a range of foreign imported dyes. The red colour in all of the samples was derived from cochineal obtained from crushed scale insects from South and Central America. Many of the blues were produced using indigo imported from India, and the flowering plant old fustic and quercitron bark, both from North America, are present in several of the vibrant yellows. Anita Quye, the chemist who conducted the tests, stated: 'It is now clear that Scotland was importing good-quality dyes, probably from well before the start of the eighteenth century, and these were all very bright.'[26]

Research of this kind will perhaps begin to dispel some of the mythology surrounding early tartan. This mythological status is partly constructed from early writing on the subject, which has an indeterminacy and subjective significance that is replicated in the actual confusion surrounding the terminology applied to contemporary tartan colour variations. Further chemical analysis of early tartan could eventually lead to a much needed revision of the current taxonomic complexity of tartan colours, of which there are three main classifications: Ancient, Modern and Reproduction.

'Ancient Colours' refer generally to a more muted, softer colour palette that attempts to emulate the early hand-woven tartans. They have no connection to the actual date in which a tartan is first thought to have been produced and were 'reinvented' around the time of the First World War. These softer tones, achieved originally by using vegetable matter, are rarely obtained from natural dyes today; instead modern synthetic dyes are used to replicate the more sombre, less vivid historical palette.

'Modern Colours' again displays a chronological imprecision, as the 'modern' attached to this description does not mean contemporary. In this instance, it refers to the proliferation of mid-nineteenth-century colours that blossomed with the adoption by commercial textile companies

13 Two variants of MacPherson that demonstrate the complexity of contemporary tartan colour terminology. Ancient MacPherson attempts to emulate the softer, muted colours of early hand-woven tartan, whilst Modern MacPherson reflects the brighter nineteenth-century palette produced as a result of the adoption of synthetic dyes

(tartan producers amongst them) of the new synthetic dyes, starting with Sir William Henry Perkin's accidental discovery of the first artificial colour, known as aniline violet or 'mauveine', in 1856. Just as the mechanization of the textile industry in the late eighteenth century hastened the demise of the old thin or hard tartans in favour of heavier and softer cloth, so too the colour palette of these new tartans changed from natural muted colours to more vibrant (or, some might suggest, cruder) tones. The brightness of these nineteenth-century tartans rendered them impracticable for camouflage and hunting purposes, and so 'hunting' tartan variations, in more muted colours, were produced. As the nineteenth century and the fashion manufacturing industries progressed, the custom of dressing for dinner, necessitating a complete change of clothes, was widely adopted. An enterprising tartan industry was keen to exploit their newly fashion-conscious customers and so literally 'dressier' tartans, often with a lighter ground colour, were invented – giving rise to today's 'dress' tartan variations.

Demand for more and more variation typified tartan production in the nineteenth century, partly as a result of the acceleration in technical and mechanical developments, but also from the desire for novelty that typified consumer society of the period. Tartans were developed to commemorate increasingly diverse events and social situations, giving rise to phenomena such as so-called 'funeral' tartans or 'mourning setts' (illus. 14). These are black and white variations of existing setts such as the variations of Macleod, Menzies, Grey Douglas, and two Stewart mourning setts, which are among the very few that are still recognized today. These mourning tartans were marketed as suitable for wearing at sombre occasions and morbidity became yet another commercial opportunity seized upon by enterprising nineteenth-century tartan manufacturers. Queen Victoria's seclusion in a perpetual state of mourning as the 'Widow of Balmoral', following the death of the Prince Consort in 1861, was a major inspiration for this particular aspect of the booming tartan industry. The classificatory confusion surrounding tartan colour variations was compounded by

14 Black and white variation of Menzies

these adaptations designed to satisfy newly invented social rituals, and it is also in the nineteenth century that tartans were further defined by notions of 'correct', 'official' and 'authentic', a practice many manufacturers maintain today.

'Reproduction Colours' were developed by a commercial company, D. C. Dalgleish Ltd., in 1946. Their intention was to reproduce the colours of a fragment of old tartan unearthed at the site of the Battle of Culloden, which had naturally faded and altered due to the peat content of the earth in which it had been buried. Other weavers followed suit after the success of this new muted colour range and further terminological descriptions were employed to describe these colours, as the term 'Reproduction' had been commercially registered as a trade name. Descriptions such as 'worn', 'soft', 'faded', or 'muted' started to be used, and as Scarlett states:

> The number of possible combinations of all these is bewildering but it helps sales. If you want one, you can have an 'ancient' tartan that was designed yesterday or one in 'modern' colours that are older than 'old' colours; if you do not like any of these you can have a 'reproduction' tartan that is not a reproduction of any tartan.[27]

The taxonomic confusion surrounding colour variants and their classification is a condition that characterizes much tartan research and is not confined merely to chromatics. Linguistic variants, etymological dissension and slippage between classifications based on location, genealogy, function and chronology punctuate tartan's many histories, and it is tempting to see the peculiarly reflexive, contradictory and mythical discourses that define tartan as being dyed into its very fabric.

15 Advertisement from 1958 for Finlay's Towels, a typical example of mid-twentieth-century commercial exploitation of the clan system

2.
EARLY APPEARANCES

LINGUISTIC ORIGINS, CRITICAL IMPRUDENCE

> …history is not the prerogative of the historian, nor even, as postmodernism contends, a historian's 'invention'. It is, rather, a social form of knowledge; the work, in any given instance of a thousand different hands.[1]

The difficulty, when writing about tartan, is avoiding the trap of trying to establish its first recorded appearances, as this pursuit has generated as much confusion as it has shed light on tartan's possible origins. What Highland dress consisted of before the dominance of the modern shorter kilt, and the development of that garment from its origins in the belted plaid, becomes part of that same search for origins. The search for accounts of early tartan, whether as cloth or as part of a particular garment such as the kilt, becomes easily misdirected amongst the checks, plaids and other patterns of diverse colours recorded in verifiable accounts as well as those of a more dubious antecedence.

Even though there is considerable debate as to when the word 'tartan' was first used to denote the checked material we are familiar with today, there is a consensus that the word is probably derived from the French *tiretaine* or *tertaine*, and its comparative Spanish word *tiritana*, meaning a blend of linen and wool also known as linsey-woolsey.[2] Linsey-woolsey was a coarse, loosely woven cloth traditionally constructed with a linen warp and a woollen weft, its name derived from the village of Lindsey in Suffolk, England. The binary composition of this cloth, made of two different fibres, and its linguistic link to tartan, suggests a model of duality that is one of the chief characteristics of tartan's history. Just as linsey-woolsey suggests a binary structure, the French derivation of the name for a cloth inextricably associated with the identity of Scotland proposes a fluidity for tartan borne out by its ability to transcend national boundaries. The combination of linen and wool successfully produced a cloth that capitalized upon the properties of both fibres, its resistant and adaptable hybridity metaphorically responsible for tartan's unique position as a cloth utilized globally for an extensive range of products.

Tempting though it is to play linguistic parlour games and suggest connections between the 'Tartan' mentioned in the Bible as the name for the Assyrian king's commander in chief, the name for a small, one-masted Mediterranean sailing vessel, and the checked fabric we recognize today, this is unlikely to significantly increase our understanding of tartan's origins.[3] But by broadening the linguistic field, we find the Gaelic word most commonly associated with tartan is *breacan*. This strictly means a plaid or length of cloth that would have been worn wrapped around the body, gathered in at the waist and finally secured at the shoulder with a brooch; the word itself is based on the Gaelic root *breac*, meaning 'speckled'. This linguistic connection returns us once again to one of the central challenges of tartan research, namely the recurrent indivisibility of tartan the textile from tartan as an item of dress. The *Oxford English Dictionary* suggests, in its definition of tartan, that the word has come to mean the cloth, the pattern, and it is even a verb: 'to tartan' means 'to clothe or array in'.[4]

The confusion that eddies around the word 'tartan' acts as a kind of linguistic contagion spreading its indeterminacy to other words related to tartan, such as 'plaid'. What does this indicate to contemporary readers? A check, a length of cloth, a blanket or the forerunner of the kilt? The particular slippage (linguistic, taxonomic and otherwise) that is repeatedly encountered when undertaking any study of tartan swiftly delivers the researcher into similar territory to that which Michel Foucault's often quoted 'certain Chinese encyclopaedia' inhabits, and to which the 'possibility of being checked' could, with little stretch of the imagination, be a possible addition to the other fabulous categories he cites.[5] This indeterminacy is one of the most challenging aspects confronting the tartan researcher, but which also makes tartan a truly unique and adaptable cloth full of contradiction and multivalence.

Leaving aside the actual derivation of the word, it is not until the early seventeenth century that 'tartan' as a term begins to be used to denote a checked or striped woollen cloth, and not until the late seventeenth and early eighteenth centuries is it used to indicate the actual pattern as separate from the garment it was made into. This last point is due in no small part to the increased industrialization of textile production at this time and its symbiotic relationship with the clan system, which demanded a more precise terminology in order to be able to successfully market tartan cloth as a specific consumer desirable.

The veracity of material relating to the possible appearance of early tartans, from those writers who first encountered them has become a primary area of debate for tartan historians. Much of the historical material relating to tartan, prior to the mid-eighteenth century at least, is perhaps best treated with some degree of circumspection. This material often survives as second- or third-hand accounts and has then been reinterpreted by subsequent historians. As with the cloth itself, its historical accounts have always been subject to a variety of national, economic and biographical interests. According to the particular proclivities of the writer, the tartan researcher is very often presented with a small roll call of supposedly early witnesses whose opinion, as to what may or may not have been the appearance of early Highland tartan, is repeatedly summoned. Virgil is possibly the earliest writer often quoted as having a probable 'close encounter' with tartan, as recorded, amongst others, by Frank Adam in his exhaustive *The Clans, Septs and Regiments of the Scottish Highlands* of 1908. In this work, we find the poet writing of the Highlanders' appearance as: '*Virgatis lucent sagalis*', most commonly translated as 'Their cloaks are striped and shining', which Scarlett suggests should be more correctly translated as 'Their cloaks are striped with bright colours'.[6] Disregarding the finer points of Latin translation, what we are left with are indications that Roman invaders seem to have had contact with Highlanders, and that they sported some form of brightly coloured cloth as part of their dress. Very early, equivocal accounts such as Virgil's seem of little value to the contemporary textile historian, but these and many subsequent writers have only had to mention terms such as 'striped', 'speckled', 'mottled' or 'chequered', when describing the dress of Scottish Highlanders, to generate elaborate tartan antecedents.

After Virgil, other often quoted and more contemporary writers include George Buchanan, who in 1582 noted that Highlanders 'delight in variegated garments, especially stripes, and their favourite colours are purple and blue'.[7] Similarly, John Taylor's description of Highland dress in 1618, containing a description of stockings or short hose as 'made of a warm stuffe of divers colours they call tartane', and Martin Martin of Skye's very detailed and much discussed description, written in the 1690s, including the famous passage: 'The plaid wore only by the men is made of fine wool, the threads as fine as can be made of that kind. It consists of divers colours: and there is a great deal of ingenuity required in sorting colours so as to be agreeable to the nicest fancy', are often called upon to provide evidence of early tartan-wearing.[8] These early literary descriptions of the colourful dress of Highlanders have an indeterminacy and subjective significance that echoes the linguistic and taxonomic confusion noted above. The passing references made in these early accounts to colourful or patterned clothing has been continuously debated, becoming, by virtue of being so often cited, a form of primary source material as to the appearance of early tartans, which they patently are not.

The mention of striped clothing in these accounts has generated a small tributary of tartan research all of its own. Historians, textile and costume experts have suggested that the Celts used a system of stripes on their clothing to denote rank or hierarchy, therefore the more numerous the stripes, the higher the rank of the wearer; thus seven stripes would denote a king, six a druid, and so on. Similarly, the colour of the cloth was reputed to hold symbolic significance for the ancient Celt. These textile 'fantasies' have then been chronologically and geographically condensed in order to suggest that tartan's clan and topographical associations might have developed from this dubious early symbolic patterning system. However, there is an obvious economic dimension to this supposition, in that producing a cloth with more stripes and colour changes required more labour and resulted in a costly cloth only affordable by those in a privileged position. Likewise, concerning the significance of colour, it is common for all ancient societies, and indeed contemporary ones, to attach significance to certain colours if only as a reflection of the properties of the natural world around them. As so much of tartan's history is constructed from what Raphael Samuel termed 'unofficial knowledge', and has often been the subject of deliberate fabrication, it is understandable that any early written account of the possible appearance and method of wearing tartan has been leapt upon and afforded the status of 'proof'.[9] However, rather than trying to locate a definitive verification of early tartan that conforms to the traditional academic notion of historical evidence, it might be more profitable to acknowledge that all traditional textiles and the garments made from them were, and still are, evolving in terms of their continued reception and utilization. The search for points of origin, indisputable proof and definitive accounts of early textile production, alongside other indigenous cultural products such as music and cooking, for example, is redundant. Instead a more heterogeneous approach is needed, which includes all information regardless of its perceived 'worth'. Therefore this study will draw on a necessarily diverse range of material in an attempt to understand more clearly the complexity that characterizes tartan, an attempt, as Samuel advocates: 'to follow the imaginative dislocations which take place when historical knowledge is transferred from one learning circuit to another'.[10]

AFORE THE KILT

Speculation as to the appearance of early Highland dress has been a contentious issue historically, and continues today to be as controversial as tartan's relationship to the clan system. Much early research is based on dubious 'eyewitness' accounts and somewhat fanciful illustrations, and as Dunbar wittily suggested:

> The emergence of Scottish Highland dress as a recognizable entity took place several centuries ago in that happy hunting ground for antiquarians known as the 'Mists of Antiquity'. Any attempt to fix its obscure origins precisely is undoubtedly foolish; nevertheless many students of the subject have attempted to do so. Their resulting arguments have usually generated more heat than light.[11]

The controversy around what constitutes its 'correct' form continues today, and is driven partly by the growth of Highland societies both within Britain and abroad, many of which are committed to undoing the influence of English imperialism by discrediting nineteenth-century conceptions of tartan and Highland dress. Similarly, the popularity of films such as *Braveheart* and *Rob Roy*, which feature 'reconstructions' of early Highland dress, has done much to generate a cinematic and often fanciful image of what the early Highlander might have worn.[12] However, rather than become enmeshed in this controversy, the discussion of tartans and early Highland dress will be necessarily brief. Those wishing for more detail are well served by established studies such as those by Dunbar and Cheape, as well the many websites serving the growing demand for information on early Highland culture.[13]

Ancient Scottish dress consisted of a shirt or tunic known as a *léine*, and a semicircular cloak known as the brat; this costume was worn by men and (in a slighter longer version) by women. Alongside the *léine* and the brat, tightly fitting trews were also worn. Trews were an element of male Highland dress, originally resembling tight-fitting hose, which later developed into straight, narrow trousers (especially after they were incorporated into military uniform) that resembled today's close-fitting styles. It has been suggested that the looser style of dress was worn by those of a higher status within the community, whilst the tighter-fitting trews and jacket were reserved for the commoner. Whether or not this was the case, the congruity of both loose and fitted garments being worn within the one Gaelic culture is interesting. One of the most familiar assertions concerning ancient forms of dress is that they can be divided between two opposing systems: loose and draped, or fitted and tailored.[14] Fitted clothing is understandably characteristic of northern cultures such as the Mongols or Gauls, whilst drapery suited people from warmer climes living along the Mediterranean and further afield. It is accepted that in Europe, fitted 'barbarian' clothing prevailed and looser draped garments survived only as ceremonial or religious costume. In the development of Highland dress, however, the typical historical ascendancy of the fitted garment is interrogated, and the simultaneity of loose and fitted garments demonstrated by the *léine*, brat and

16 Couple attending the 2005 Inverness Highland Games. His contemporary interpretation of the *fhéliidh-Mor*, or belted plaid, contrasts strongly with her version of the more familiar short, tailored kilt

trews is preserved and subsequently developed in the typical costume of belted plaid and trews. The reconciliation of opposing systems of dress in Highland costume is further evidence of the peculiar multivalency of tartan and the garments that it is used to make, this inclusiveness facilitating its perception as a textile both traditional and innovative.

By the seventeenth century, the *léine* had been replaced in the Scottish Highlands by the belted plaid or (in Gaelic) *fhéilidh-Mor*, and consisted of a rectangle of cloth roughly six yards long and two yards wide. In Gaelic, *plaide* means a blanket and can refer to any large piece of cloth, checked or otherwise; this has resulted in the contemporary terminological confusion where 'plaid' can refer to a check, a shawl or the belted plaid described above. The *fhéilidh-Mor* proper however, was worn in a specific way. A belt was placed upon the ground and the plaid laid on top of it; it was then pleated lengthways at right angles to the belt. The wearer would lie down on top of the material, wrap the two edges of the plaid around himself, belt it, and on standing up he was left with a loosely pleated skirt below the belt and swags of drapery above. This excess material could then be arranged in a number of ways: either left to simply hang down in folds at the back of the pleated 'skirt', gathered up and wrapped around the shoulders like a shawl to protect the wearer from the elements, or drawn up over one shoulder and fastened with a pin or similar device, allowing the other arm free to carry a sword or firearm. This last arrangement survives as a vestimentary relic in today's 'Highland' outfits, which consist of the shorter modern kilt and a separate plaid that is fastened to the shoulder and most commonly seen in Highland dancing costumes. The *fhéilidh-Mor*

17 Christina Young's *arisaid*. This women's plaid is reputed to be the oldest surviving example, dated and initialled 1726

was a versatile garment: the Highlander merely needed to unfasten the belt and he was left with a blanket in which to wrap himself and go to sleep. The trews worn as an alternative to the *léine* often had feet attached and were more like modern-day tights, more than likely in the same pattern as the plaid; these survived until the seventeenth century, and were eventually superseded by the regimental trews or trouser, looser fitting and much closer to contemporary practical trousers.

Early Highland dress for women consisted of a plaid or blanket, which developed into the *arisaid*, a length of material that reached from shoulders to the feet, and would have been worn simply wrapped, or belted and fastened with a brooch, and like the man's belted plaid could be gathered up over the head providing complete protection outdoors. Originating as plain lengths of cloth with striped borders, these developed into the so-called *arisaid* setts, which were characterized by open checks with fewer stripes, colour changes, and on a lighter ground than early tartans. No idea of clanship is associated with the old *arisaid* setts (clanship being passed down through the male line of a family; hence 'Mac', as in MacDonald, meaning 'son of'), and thus there is a lack of scholarship concerning their origins and variations. These lighter plaids remained the costume of lower-class women, (fashionable women usually adopted their husband's tartans for their own garments), and it was not until the development of 'dress' tartans in the nineteenth century that lighter-coloured setts became acceptable for the well-to-do. Tradition suggests that a Highland bride would wear a new plaid as part of her wedding outfit; whether this would have been part of the trousseau or a gift from the groom is unclear. Again this was most likely a custom amongst poorer people, as there are surviving examples of early wedding dresses in costly materials such as silk, and these, rather than the *arisaid*, are more likely to have been the preferred costume for more affluent brides.

DYNASTY OR DISTRICT? CLAN OR LOCATION?

> Workers in the field of tartan have too often sought to assert the great antiquity or relative modernity of tartan, and especially 'clan' tartans, rather than seek diligently for the truth and, since the available evidence is quite inadequate to prove anything, the deficiency has been made good by a strange kind of 'wishful proving'.[15]

The advent of the nineteenth century saw an increased desire to document, and in many cases invent, historical traditions for peoples and places that for varied sociopolitical reasons had become detached from any direct link to indigenous customs. It is as a product of this desire that we can also understand the rapid proliferation of information concerning the history and development of tartan and Highland dress within this same period. The urgency with which 'lost' or 'forgotten' historical voices were salvaged to construct a Romanticized version of the past for a public keen to establish national identities, resulted in a boom in tartan literature. This was augmented, and indeed complicated, by instances of intentional fabrication by figures such as the Sobieski Stuarts, who are discussed at length in Chapter 3, *Fragments and Fabrication*. For these nineteenth-century champions of tartan, their primary concern was to confirm a direct link between tartan patterns and specific families or clans. This swiftly became the most persistently held belief concerning tartan and then, as now, received the most critical and scholarly attention.

Tartan's function as a 'badge' of specific clans, and the desire to attribute specific patterns to particular families, has exerted a seductive influence over the popular perception and understanding of tartan since at least the early nineteenth century, and for some historians much further back than that. From its infancy, tartan research has been at pains to make dynastic links between clan and pattern, and as Scarlett suggests in the quote given at the beginning of this section, 'wishful proving' has been the hallmark of much of this research. Whilst there is nothing intrinsically wrong with interpretation, and indeed much of this study relies on processes of re-contextualization and interpretation, it becomes problematic when this operation becomes solidified. Scraps of possible evidence are transformed into proof of the link between tartan and the clan system; this material then becomes fixed within the confines of dynastic romance and commercial opportunity. A lucrative industry including books, exhibitions, websites, tartan days and clan associations has grown out of the ever popular exercise of assigning certain patterns to particular clans.

There is much more convincing evidence that tartans have a direct association with the area in which they were first woven, rather than with any particular family that chose to wear them. When one considers that the appearance of early tartans bears a direct relationship to the dyestuffs used to produce their colours, location rather than lineage seems a more convincing rationale as to the persistence, concentration and survival of particular patterns. It is logical that tartans exhibiting similar colour ranges are found in the same location, creating a synthesis between clan and district. Certain weavers, with their own preferences and local dyes, would provide tartans for clients coming from a similar geographical locale so the majority of older clan tartans from the west of Scotland are in blue, black and green: MacLeod, MacNeil, MacDonald, Campbell and the Mull tartan. Similarly, a number of tartans from the north-east use blue or black and green stripes on a red ground: Macintosh, Robertson, MacGillivary, Grant, and Murray. District tartans were included in the lists of patterns of the earliest tartan manufacturers such as William Wilson & Son of Bannockburn, who included setts such as Argyll, indicating both place and clan. David Stewart of Garth, in his *Sketches of the Highlanders of Scotland vol. 1*, wrote in 1822: 'Thus a MacDonald, a Campbell, a MacKenzie, etc. was known by his plaid; and in like manner the Athole, Glenorchy and other colours of different districts were easily distinguishable', which seems a fairly rational account of tartan's ability to indicate both district and clan, neither one being pre-eminent and in fact more often than not worn as an amalgam of both, personal preference also being a determining factor.[16]

One of the earliest recorded tartans, probably mid-sixteenth century in origin, is Lennox, reputed to be the tartan of the Countess of Lennox, a name associated with an area not far from modern Glasgow, suggesting that the earliest tartans were neither strictly clan-associated nor restricted to Highland areas of Scotland. The eradication, or at least synthesis, of what initially appears to be opposing theories is characteristic of tartan's history, and the merger between dynasty and district is a primary example of this. Of course this is not to say that family groups and clan members would not have worn similar patterns, if only out of necessity and the lack of variety offered by the few local or itinerant weavers producing cloth in the Highlands before the advent of commercial production in the late eighteenth and nineteenth centuries. A combination of limited pattern, the preponderance of certain colours and the concentration of affiliated groups – whether actual clan members, their associated septs or families in specific areas – all give rise to similar tartan patterns being worn by related groups of people.[17] These economically driven and geographically limited reasons, more than any purposely designed and exclusively worn idea of tartan as a visual indicator of clanship, are the foundations from which any amount of 'wishful proving' has been launched.

The clan system, whilst indisputably a major socio-economic factor of Scottish Highland history, is often romantically portrayed as a series of dynasties, each tracing their lineage directly back to

18 Lennox

a misty ancient Celtic past. The original Celtic clan system was patriarchal, with its own laws of succession and land rights, and each clan had its own branches and septs who were united as a group against a common enemy. Up until the thirteenth century, the central and eastern Highlands of Scotland were controlled by a number of native Celtic earls, but with the failure of the bloodlines of these original families, their titles were bestowed on members of the Scottish royal family or on Anglo-Norman newcomers to the Highlands. With the extinction of the old genealogical clans tracing their antecedence directly back to the original chiefs, there emerged, by the fourteenth century, new hybrid forms of the clan. These were situated in the same geographical location but now composed of a mixture of some original clan members, new blood and a host of others in some way or other affiliated to the clan by means of being tenants or in the direct employ of clan members. The clan system shifted from closely related dynasties to a modern, specifically economic institution consisting of powerful families exerting considerable influence and control. This was achieved by a combination of extensive holdings in the form of land, livestock and tenants, alliances achieved through marriage to other influential families, and a particularly aggressive approach to territorial expansion.

As Teallach and Smith suggest: 'Tartan for many was undoubtedly associated with service rather than with blood', and for as many as there are instances of tartan being worn as a sign of familial membership, opposing evidence that argues that clanship was ignored over servitude can also be brought forward.[18] For example, there is evidence that in 1704, members of the MacDonald family were ordered to wear the tartan of the Laird of Grant, rather than their own tartan, as they were his tenants. What this and similar instances suggests is that tartan was used to denote ownership, as in a livery or uniform, alongside its more palatable function as a textile declaration of increasingly attenuated bloodlines. The custom of clan chiefs dressing their armed forces in tartan uniforms meant that once the raising of the Highland regiments commenced in the eighteenth century, it was a relatively minor shift from wearing tartan as a sign of economic and feudal servitude to wearing the tartan of one's military commander.

Wearing tartan as a declaration of ancestral or topographical allegiance becomes especially salient for the increasing numbers of Highlanders who were forcibly transported from Britain from the eighteenth century onwards, and indeed for those who left voluntarily to escape economic hardship. The passion that tartan generates today outside Scotland itself is a direct legacy of its history as the textile souvenir of a lost homeland, and the global spread of that passion, a result of it being the messenger of colonial expansion. Both of these factors proved to be of paramount significance in its development from local cloth of clanship to global 'super brand'.

The blurring of ancient lineage and modern sociopolitical expediency is what gives the tartan clanship connection its peculiar potency and popular persistence. Worn as the sign of exclusive membership of a particular family, tartan can also be expressive of a much more nebulous notion of communal belonging. As a result of its voluntary adoption or, in some cases, compulsory wearing by people associated with (but not directly linked by blood to) specific clans, the wearing of tartan today connotes far more than specific familial belonging. Tartan's grids have become a network of concepts concerning nationalism, tradition, the tribal and the fashionable. Those same grids have, it could be argued, enshrined and solidified specific cultural values, restraining any possible interrogation of those same values.

The recent establishment of the independent Scottish parliament and the debate concerning deregulation have made tartan once again a contentious issue, with tartan cited by cultural commentators as a prime example of the embarrassment induced, in some quarters, by aspects of Scotland's heritage.[19] Tartan's centrality to an emergent, twenty-first century, independent Scotland invokes equal amounts of intolerance and optimism: some see it as an unwanted reminder of English colonialism, whilst others prefer to reclaim tartan as a pattern that endured subjugation by the English, making it indicative of an indomitable spirit of Scottish resistance. This ambivalence is one of tartan's most enduring characteristics, far outweighing any assumed political connotations, but it is also the reason for its disownment within some Scottish circles. However, as also happened in the eighteenth and early nineteenth centuries, tartan's contentious sociopolitical status is currently being reflected in its efflorescence within contemporary fashion.

Deeper investigation into the concept of clan-associated tartans inevitably leads to one of the few more reliable sources of information on the subject: the early portraits of tartan-clad clan leaders and other prominent figures. These, whilst allowing for artistic licence and the desire to flatter, can still be considered more useful than the mountain of so-called written evidence that has been produced in an attempt to secure the clan significance of tartan. However, the concept of 'wishful proving' again becomes evident when looking at this visual documentation of early tartans. It quickly becomes apparent that the tartans worn by the figures in the many portraits that occupy central positions in public and private collections throughout Scotland and beyond bear little or no relationship to so-called modern clan tartans. Furthermore, the majority of the earliest portraits depict the sitter invariably wearing more than one tartan in the same outfit (illus. 40). This multiplicity of tartan indicates a rather more laissez-faire approach to the wearing of clan-associated tartans than is generally believed, and which contrasts strongly with the stringent dress codes demanded by today's modern manufacturers, where every item worn must be of a uniform tartan pattern. Many of these portraits depict the sitter wearing a plaid or kilt of one check, with stockings or trews of another and perhaps a doublet or jerkin of still another variant.

One of the earliest known portraits of a Highland chief wearing a belted plaid is that of *Lord Mungo Murray*, a younger son of the Marquis of Atholl, painted by John Michael Wright in 1683.

19 The Tullibardine Room at Blair Castle, seat of the Dukes of Atholl, a tartan interior that functions as both a display of religious and political sympathies as well as a memorial. The room is dedicated to the Jacobite members of the Atholl family and is named after William, Marquis of Tullibardine, the first duke's son, who died as a prisoner in the Tower of London following the defeat of the Jacobite uprising in 1746. The tartan on the tent bed is supposed to have come from an older circular bed where the seventeen sons of Sir David Murray of Tullibardine slept

This portrait is one of the most regularly utilized images in studies that attempt to establish the links between clanship and tartan, and indeed what early Highland dress might have looked like. The sitter's plaid is in an unrecognizable and highly complex check of a predominantly brown, yellow and red palette unlike any clan tartan known today; this is contrasted with stockings of a completely different red and black check. Apart from the variant checks on display, what is most striking is the theatricality of the portrait, which had previously led Dunbar to attribute the sitter's identity to that of one 'Lacy the Actor' an 'excellent low comedian' beloved of Charles II, whose triple portrait had also been painted by Wright.[20] Dunbar discerns a similarity between the likenesses, and whilst his original theory as to the identity of the sitter is now largely discounted, his observations do reinforce a commonality between many early portraits of Highlanders in 'traditional' costume. Apart from the wearing of multiple tartans appearing to be the norm, the most salient feature of this and other Highland portraits is a sense of 'showing out', a theme which will be examined in further detail in Chapter 7, *Tartan Toffs*. It can be argued, of course, that all portraiture – certainly from the period under discussion – fulfils the purpose of aggrandizing the sitter and conveying a sense of bravado. Tartan in particular seems to encourage this demeanour; one only has to consider many of the famous examples regularly cited as evidence of early representations of clan tartan to see this thread of bluster and swagger running through them.

From the late seventeenth-century portrait of *Andrew Macpherson of Cluny*, whose plaid, trews and jacket are all made of different tartans, to the celebrated double portrait of *Sir James MacDonald of Sleat and Sir Alexander MacDonald* (known as 'the MacDonald Boys'), painted by Jeremiah Davison in 1766, where four different tartan setts can be made out on their garments, the relative unimportance of wearing the 'correct' clan tartan is emphasized time and again. What can be ascertained from the representation of tartan (clan or otherwise) in portraiture is that certainly in the period before the commodification of clan tartans that occurred in the early part of the nineteenth century, multiple tartan-wearing seems almost de rigueur, and that many of them, on closer examination, are asymmetrical. As Robin Nicholson succinctly expresses in his essay 'From Ramsay's *Flora MacDonald* to Raeburn's *MacNab*: The Use of Tartan as a Symbol of Identity':

> Tartan was at this period not a symbol of clan or local associations, but a varietal garb of loud colours and distinctive checks that were mixed and matched to suit the taste of the wearer and which, in certain instances, could be used to symbolize political allegiance.[21]

These portraits create a surfeit of tartan, using a visual rhetoric that glories in excess and approaches the textile bricolage characteristic of contemporary fashion's deployment of the textile.

The Act of Union of 1707, which attempted to unite Scotland and England and ensure that the British throne would pass to the Hanoverian George I rather than any Stuart claimant, transformed tartan into a truly political textile. From this moment, the wearing of tartan becomes a vestimentary demonstration of Scottish nationalism, Jacobite sympathy and opposition to the Union. Each unsuccessful Jacobite uprising in 1715, 1719 and finally 1745 meant that painted tartans were far more likely to be understood as components of a Stuart allegory that used the textile as a means of declaring the sitter's Scottish (as opposed to British) allegiances, rather than as a record of any specific clan tartan. After Culloden and the Act of 1746 banning the wearing of tartan as a component of Highland dress, there is an upsurge in paintings of the gentry wearing tartan costumes of various kinds. Once banned, it is as if those in positions of power and influence felt compelled to represent themselves as above this new law, and to display their continuing allegiance to the Jacobite cause, if only in private or as painted images seen by family and friends.

Many fine portraits date from this period, such as that of the young *James Moray of Abercairney* in the collection of Blair Castle which, like many portraits, remains anonymous and unsigned, the painter thus avoiding any possible reprisals for representing the banned costume. Works from this period combine the aforementioned sense of bravado with an added air of defiance in the wearing of the tartan in its time of proscription. They also serve as visual acknowledgments of the demise of the Jacobite claim, and it is tempting to speculate whether the sitters in these portraits were conscious that they were creating the artistic legacy of a cause that was in effect lost, and

20 (Facing Page) *James Moray of Abercairney*. This picture was most probably painted during the time of tartan's proscription and left unsigned by the artist in order to avoid incrimination

would exist thereafter only in representation. What these early painted tartans present is the fabric's unparalleled ability to function as a form of vestimentary defiance, a testament to the broader national and religious sympathies of the wearer rather than any particular clan loyalty.

It is from the battlefield of Culloden itself that we have the most celebrated example of the redundancy and indeed potential danger of wearing tartan as a sign of specific clan allegiance. The painting by David Morier known as *An Incident in the Scottish Rebellion, 1745* depicts Barrell's Regiment or the 4th Kings Own (Royal Lancaster Regiment) engaged in battle with men of the Jacobite army. It is believed that Morier used Highland prisoners captured at the battle as his models, and so the accuracy of their costumes seems likely. Dunbar, amongst others, has carried out painstaking studies of the painting, and counts at least twenty-three different tartans being worn by eight Highlanders, and furthermore none of them can be conclusively identified as clan tartans recognized today. When many Highlanders whose Protestant clan chiefs sided with the government forces rather than the Catholic Jacobite cause found themselves fighting against fellow Highlanders, the idea of wearing an easily identifiable clan tartan seems foolhardy if not suicidal. The custom of wearing multiple tartans, no single particular pattern having ascendancy, seems expedient; and if a reliable form of identification is to be looked for, it was far more likely to have been the custom of government troops wearing black cockades and the Jacobites wearing white ones.

Whatever the pre-Culloden alliance between clan and tartan, after 1746 the old clan system had in effect vanished, and a period of indeterminacy followed, during which some clan allegiances were maintained, others destroyed and a growing number expanded, augmented and newly historicized as part of the growing tide of late eighteenth- and early nineteenth-century European Romanticism. Nicholson's painstaking work on tartan portraits of this period leads him to conclude that tartan provided:

> ...for portraits produced in the post-1746 era, a fabric with an amorphous and indistinct definition, but a singular and highly distinct character. Increasingly it becomes apparent that for the portraitist or the satirist the details of the garb or colours of the tartan were of little consequence; it was the presence of the garb that was critical.[22]

The amorphous quality that Nicholson discerns in tartan's representations at this period is a result of its divergent utilization as an expression of the fading embers of the Jacobite cause, a newly emerging sense of Scottish nationalism and the acknowledgement of Scotland's centrality to the financial and military expansion of the British Empire. The proscription of 1746 was a pivotal moment in tartan's transformation from a material worn out of expediency by a largely poor Highland people, into a fashionable commodity. It was now worn by the privileged as an expression of exclusivity, newly forged nationalism and a fictional notion of Scottish history. The coincidence of Culloden with the industrialization of textile manufacturing was a felicitous concurrence hastening tartan's commercial growth. At the same time, the success of the recently formed Scottish regiments' defence of British interests abroad ensured tartan's lasting fashionableness. These factors helped to promote its peculiarly compliant behaviour and its ability to express any sociocultural and historical significance placed upon it, the last of these being the newly fabricated notion of it as a definitive sign of clan affiliation.

The development of tartan as a clan 'brand' played a vital role in Scotland's reinvention. In the years leading up to Culloden and those immediately following it, tartan was a convenient visual shorthand in the English vilification of the Scots, and the Highlander in particular. Caricatured as

21 William Mosman, *John Campbell of Ardmaddie*, also known as 'Campbell of the Bank'. Oil on canvas, 1749

the sign of the barbaric, primitive and licentious Highlander, tartan's ignominy was cemented by the Act of Proscription. However, this period of disrepute was both ambiguous, as we have seen, and short-lived. As Nicholson suggests, even as early as 1749 the perception of tartan, and by extension those depicted wearing it, was uniquely ambivalent. In that year, William Mosman painted a portrait of *John Campbell* (illus. 21), and Nicholson's research suggests that Campbell's appearance in the painting, dressed in tartan plaid and jacket, gives rise to a number of possible interpretations.[23] As Chief Cashier of the Royal Bank of Scotland, widely recognized as the 'Hanoverian' bank, it could be supposed that Campbell's sympathies lay with the government forces. His appearance in tartan, therefore, is a vestimentary expression of the proud Highlander, exempt from the ban as a loyal and trusted servant of the British crown, wearing his tartan with a new-found sense of Scottish – and by extension British – pride. Nicholson's research also reveals that Campbell's loyalty might well be compromised. He cites evidence suggesting that, whilst Campbell was a loyal Hanoverian purse-keeper, he also facilitated a considerable sum of money passing from the bank to Jacobite sympathizers to help the rebel army on their push south towards London, before the debacle of Culloden. Nicholson's suggestion that Campbell's portrayal was possibly meant 'to offer conflicting readings to different spectators' is extremely important, not only to an understanding of tartan's equivocal position immediately following Culloden, but also to our present-day understanding of its uniquely adaptable qualities and its ability to mean all (or at least many) things to all people.[24] Tartan's overriding contemporary symbolism may be a notion of 'Scottishness', but any further attempt to 'fix' its meaning is soon confounded by its unique historical development. The peculiar series of transformations that tartan underwent post-Culloden, including proscription, fashionability, global dissemination, and industrialization, happened over a relatively short period. Less than eighty years separate its year of proscription in 1746 and its triumphant reinvention for George IV's state visit to Edinburgh in 1822. This remarkably concentrated period of evolution is characteristic of much of tartan's history, which is marked by intense periods of proliferation and fashionability across a number of sociocultural arenas. These tartan 'concentrates' function almost homoeopathically: the more dispersed and ubiquitous tartan as a pattern becomes, the more powerful and lasting is its effect.

> So we come to the last stage in the creation of the Highland myth: the reconstruction
> and extension, in ghostly and sartorial form, of that clan system whose reality had been
> destroyed after 1745.[25]

The necessity to name tartans after a particular family, as Trevor-Roper amongst others has observed, was as a direct result of one particular historical event: the visit of George IV to Edinburgh in 1822. When the Highland chiefs were summoned by Sir Walter Scott and Colonel Stewart of Garth (the 'stage managers' of the monarch's spectacular visit) to attend the event in full Highland dress, they created an immediate upsurge in the demand for tartan. In reality, the clan leaders summoned to Edinburgh would probably have been wearing a variety of tartan patterns, which although in some cases had been worn for many generations, had none of the strictures that modern nomenclature places on the relationship between pattern and clan. Manufacturers under extreme pressure to provide 'official' clan tartans for this event found that it was more expedient and commercially viable to designate existing tartan patterns as 'clan' tartans. Customers for whom

22 (Facing Page) Sir David Wilkie, *George IV*. Oil on canvas, c.1830

no specifically recognized family or clan tartan existed would, rather than having new setts designed and woven, have been supplied with existing designs on the manufacturers' pattern books, newly reclassified as official clan tartans. George's visit necessitated that tartans fulfil a role as the textile signs of clanship, and fed the growing desire for a visual representation of Scottish dynastic lineage. This myth was successfully condoned by the king himself, who was bedecked in what subsequently became known as Royal Stewart tartan, its name an Anglicized variation of the older Jacobite Scottish Royal House of Stuart.

The early, more cavalier and, it could be argued, celebratory approach to wearing a variety of tartan, questions the frankly political and partisan nature of clan members reserving the right to wear specifically designated tartans. The evidence gathered from early paintings and other sources of multiple tartan-wearing, expresses a freedom that predates the nineteenth century's pathological desire to document, classify, and divide. Tartan underwent the same peculiarly Victorian combination of taxonomic rigour and economic improvement that transformed a host of other institutions and productions, whose often appealingly indeterminate and osmotic foundations were redefined and, in some cases, entirely reinvented in this period. The notion of clanship as a by-product or property of the rapidly advancing tartan industry proved an invaluable and lasting selling point that remains as important today as when first capitalized upon by nineteenth-century manufacturers.

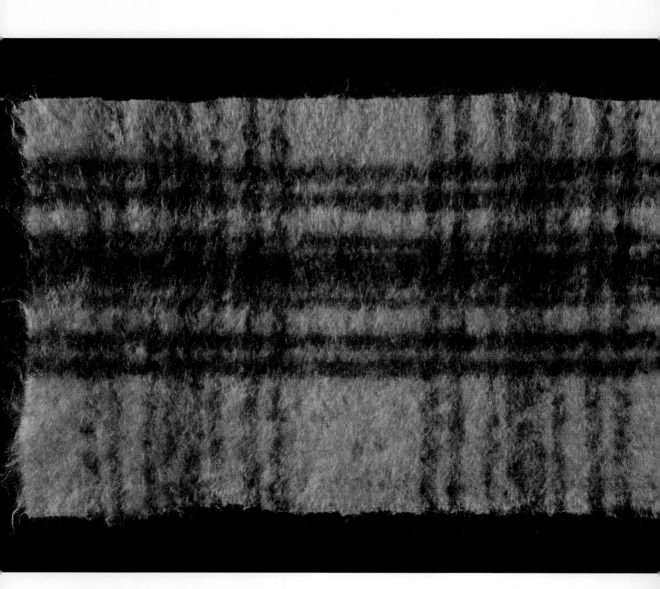

23 Textile sample, Ascher Ltd., Great Britain. Woven mohair, wool and nylon. 1957

3.
FRAGMENTS AND FABRICATION

FRAGMENTS

The terminological confusion set in motion by naming a checked, third-century textile fragment, 'the Falkirk Tartan', is illustrative of the quagmire of scholarship, popular myth and collective historical desire that surrounds the pattern. Much of tartan's history is based on fragments, and the Falkirk Tartan is by no means the only significant textile fragment that has contributed towards the history of both the cloth itself, and the particular tartan sett suggested by these often very insignificant remnants. By considering the Falkirk or any other similar tartan fragment, it is possible to initiate a series of inquiries concerning age, place of origin, historical and biographical significance, its technical construction, and so on. However, rather than load one small fragment with such a weight of significance, it might be more profitable and rewarding to consider its fragmentary status as a way of understanding and acknowledging tartan's varied and complex sociocultural and historical contexts. Negative correlations – such as incompleteness and imperfection – typically attached to the fragment, can also be viewed as a means of facilitating a more heterogeneous and discursive methodology. Raymond Bellour, the film theorist, suggests in his essay 'System of a Fragment':

> Thus, although our excerpt has its justification, it also has its arbitrariness. Neither the beginning nor the end can properly be said to constitute this segment of film as a closed and strictly definable unit. The analysis might go beyond them, even to the extent of rediscovering the whole film, by a series of extensions. But,

inversely, it is the analysis that determines the autonomy of this segment of film, precisely in the distance it covers and its possibility.[1]

Whilst this passage obviously relates to Bellour's detailed systematic analysis of film sequences, or 'segments' as he prefers to call them, much of what he suggests can be usefully transferred to our conception of tartan fragments. Any researcher is swiftly made aware of the existence of a partial tartan world constituted from the various scraps that fill museum cabinets, are kept as treasured mementos in private collections or are mounted, framed and transformed into tartan 'talismans', and that these same fragments are complete neither physically nor metaphorically. Textile fragments, like cinematic sequences, can function as indicators of the complete cloth that they were originally a part of, and lead the researcher on the path of 'rediscovering the whole'.[2] Simultaneously, they can operate independently as fragments that have an intrinsic significance of their own; Bellour's 'autonomy of the segment', once acknowledged, allows the 'possibility' of situating tartan in locations that are more extensive than the original cloth or garment from which it came.[3] Visually, the tartan fragment indicates the limits of its original sett, but due to its contingency with other fragments and other setts, it can also suggest limitlessness and a potential to exceed its woven grids.

The anonymity that is so often a condition of these fragments is also antithetical to much tartan research that attempts to 'fix' dates and provenance to tartan. The 'possibility' of a fragment, such as the example from the Seafield Collection of militaria based at Fort George near Inverness, far outweighs the little that is actually known about it.[4] The fragment was found tucked away in one of the knapsacks originally issued to the short-lived 97th Inverness-shire Regiment (raised in 1794 and disbanded in 1795), and little is known of its history, why it was kept or by whom. The fact that the fragment survives at all is remarkable given that much of the regiment's clothing and equipment was sold off in 1810, except for the knapsacks, which subsequently became part of the Seafield Collection. The remnant was discovered when the collection was being prepared for permanent display, and in itself is unremarkable, being of the typical dark blue, black and green palette of government tartans of the time.

Whenever the partial is encountered it is almost inevitable that a process of reconstruction is initiated. A fragment such as that in the Seafield Collection has the potential to usher in a number of prospective topics that could help restore its 'missing' history. These can range from the specific – such as the development of regimental setts and their often obscure and problematic relationship to district or family tartans – to the speculative – why was this scrap preserved, did it have a special significance for the soldier who carried it, and what garment did it originally come from? Of course, the charge of overstatement could justifiably be levied against interpretations of this sort; it is after all a scrap of fairly ordinary cloth, but the combination of empirical and speculative data that tends to cluster around this and many other similar fragments forms an often contradictory socio-historical network around our understanding of tartan that deserves closer examination.

Of course the fragment has always been a vital component of textile research, from Ancient Egyptian excavations to contemporary forensic science. The remnant, scrap or even fibre has contributed greatly to our understanding of past civilizations' social conventions, industry and appearance, and can also provide evidence of the movements, origin and identity of persons unknown. Remnants of any sort, textile or otherwise, automatically encourage us to provide the missing parts. Museums and other similar institutions have taught us to complete the vase from its shard, the building from rubble and the language from a few letters. But the process does not stop at this imaginary restoration of the whole, and further contextual restitutions develop as a result of the seductive communication between the remnant and its viewer. Therefore our narratives become extended and we are encouraged to imagine the dietary habits of the creators of the vessel, the function of the building and the migratory patterns of the speakers of dead languages.

Historical artefacts, especially when part of a collection and deprived of their original function, are capable of operating linguistically. That is, like words they can be understood autonomously, or reordered and combined with other words or artefacts to create a number of different 'paragraphs' with multiple meanings. As Hayden White suggests in the essay 'The Fictions of Factual Representation':

> These fragments have to be put together to make a whole of a particular, not a general, kind. And they are put together in the same ways that novelists use to put together figments of their imagination...[5]

Likewise, tartan fragments can be considered individually for particular historical or other significance, but they can also be grouped and reordered with other fragments (the actual physical appearance of the fragment, with its indeterminate frayed edges encourages this conception) to form larger theoretical and sociocultural 'lengths'. The many remnants of tartan in public museums, or preserved in private collections, act as narrative catalysts reconstructing salient moments in Scottish history, or resurrecting celebrated figures from the past, with a power that transcends their significance as sources for textile research.

The pivotal biographical narrative which a majority of tartan fragments assist in constructing is, of course, that of the Young Pretender, Charles Edward Stuart, and the events leading up to the Battle of Culloden. Like iron filings accumulating on a magnet, tartan fragments assemble and clothe the romantic figure of Bonnie Prince Charlie. So numerous are the fragments of textile reputed to have come from outfits either worn by, given to or otherwise associated with the Young Pretender, that Erasmus' famous comment concerning the surprising number of relics of Christ's Cross is called to mind: 'that if the fragments were joined together they'd seem a full load for a freighter'[6] (illus. 26). Similarly if the plethora of 'Jacobite' tartan fragments were all sewn together, there would probably be enough cloth to make Bonnie Prince Charlie an extensive wardrobe with some left over to kit out his supporters. At the visitor centre at Culloden today, it is possible to see a display entitled 'Lady Borodale's Gift', which relates the story of Bonnie Prince Charlie's escape from the battlefield of Culloden, his journey to Arisaig on the west coast of Scotland, and eventual arrival at the house of Angus and Catriona MacDonald. Catriona, or Lady Borodale as she was known, gave the Prince food, shelter and clothing, the same 'sute of cloaths' that has become one of the vital components in both the Young Pretender's biography and the history of tartan in general. This phantom suit was then worn by the prince on his further travels to the islands of Benbecula and Scalpay, during which it became the worse for wear from being continually drenched in salt water, and the prince eventually left it with Donald Campbell of Scalpay. The 'sute of cloaths' has since passed into history in the form of a number of fragments, some of which, according to the information panel at Culloden, 'have been fully researched and authenticated'.[7]

Some miles further east from Culloden, other fragments can be found in a display at the Scottish Tartans Museum in Keith. These are reputed to be from 'the outside and inside of that identical waistcoat, which MacDonald of Kingsburgh gave to the Prince, when he laid aside the Women's

24 A copy of *The Lyon in Mourning*, containing fragments of tartan reputed to come from a waistcoat given to Bonnie Prince Charlie.

Cloathes at the Edge of the Wood', and were discovered secreted in the end boards of a copy of *The Lyon in Mourning*, the collection of speeches, letters, journals and relics gathered together by Bishop Robert Forbes as a tribute to Charles Edward Stuart.[8] These scraps were then reconstituted by D. W. Stewart and included in his *Old and Rare Scottish Tartans* of 1893 as a tartan named 'MacDonald of Kingsburgh'.[9] It would be tempting to gather together all the fragments reputed to have come from various items of dress associated with Bonnie Prince Charlie, to see what some of these fabulous costumes would have actually looked like. From only a cursory examination of a few of the scraps purporting to be from the same original garments, the variation in both pattern and weight of cloth is remarkable.

Returning to the display at Culloden, it is particularly striking how the restitution of these fragments has been augmented, for alongside the explanatory text concerning the provenance of the original gift, is a reconstruction of the actual suit 'made in a style that might well have been worn by Prince Charles Edward Stuart'.[10] This costume is made from the reconstituted tartan that we are informed is: 'now available in kilts, skirts, scarves and travelling rugs from James Pringle Weavers of Inverness'.[11] So a hypothetical tartan design based on fragments is woven, and from this cloth a costume is fabricated, the whole enterprise becoming both historical reconstruction and advertisement for a contemporary tartan whose origin is steeped in Romantic wish fulfilment. This amalgamation of scholarly research, idealistic nationalism and contemporary commercialism so succinctly contained in the contemporary displays at Culloden, is the same combination of forces that characterized tartan's development from the mid-eighteenth century, when apparently contradictory elements merged to make tartan a uniquely resilient textile.

With fragments functioning as relics, the almost religious reverence accorded to these dubious leftovers of the Jacobite rebellion is understandable, but the sacred nature of the fragment reaches its apogee when they are given a status both memorial and talismanic. Many fragments of tartan found in collections of militaria, such as in the Regimental Museum of the Queen's Own Highlanders (Seaforth and Camerons), suggest a proximity to violence and death derived partly from their status as relics of specific conflicts, but also because of their actual condition as parts torn from a whole.[12]

25 Fragment of Cameron tartan taken from a kilt and sewn to the battalion flag of the 7th Camerons, carried during the Battle of Loos in 1915

Included in this remarkable collection is the piece of tartan taken from a kilt worn by a soldier of the 78th Highlanders at the first relief of Lucknow in 1857, tartan that was supposed to have been kissed by grateful British women at the garrison. A similar narrative of talismanic protection can be constructed around the faded, tattered, and stained battle flag of the 7th Camerons, reminiscent of religious relics such as the ubiquitous Turin Shroud, on which has been sewn a piece of Cameron tartan again taken from a kilt, and which was carried during the Battle of Loos on the 25 and 26 September, 1915 (illus. 25). Elsewhere in the collection is a framed fragment of what appears to be old 'hard' tartan, perhaps originally a typical government sett, but now faded, lending the fragment an uncharacteristic paler blue tone. This relic bears the legend 'Piece Tartan – Worn 1745', but whether it was picked up from the actual battlefield of Culloden Moor or some other site, was worn by someone who perished there or preserved by a survivor, is now unverifiable, but this perhaps matters less than its ability to resonate back through history.[13] These fragments forge a communion between the viewer and the past, and act as conduits to tartan's many and varied histories. These histories include the struggle for national independence, the mythology of the Young Pretender, the Highland Regiments' role in maintaining the frontiers of the British Empire, and military tailoring and its influence on eighteenth- and nineteenth-century fashion, amongst many others.

If the sett or sequence of stripes is what makes individual tartans identifiable, it is ironic that so much research is based on fragments or details seen in paintings, where the sett is often partial or obscured, and processes of speculative reconstruction become necessary. As Scarlett records:

> Painstaking reconstruction of a sett by extracting and collating fragments from different parts of a painting of a plaid or shawl will in most cases yield a plausible result for which some corroboration may then be sought.[14]

It is perhaps in the seeking of this 'corroboration' that the more imaginative and subtle constructions are made however, and as Scarlett elsewhere observes:

> Guesswork, intuition or general knowledge of patterns must be brought to bear on the problem and, although the importance of these must not be under-rated, a reconstruction based on all or any of them must remain in doubt.[15]

Whilst 'guesswork' and 'intuition' are problematic and can be a cause for concern to the textile historian whose project is to definitively date, place and classify a tartan, these same procedures can be advantageous when considering the fragments as source material with which to explore tartan's broader cultural significance. The fractional condition of the fragment, unrestricted by definite borders and with the perfect geometry of its sett eroded, assists these partial patterns to form new narrative clusters, beyond the limits of rigid tartan taxonomy.

Although the often fragmentary condition of early tartan may present problems to the traditional historian, no such difficulty confronts the contemporary fashion and textile theorist or designer when working with tartan. Fragments, absence and incompletion characterize much work in the field during the late twentieth and twenty-first centuries. Many important studies have adopted a similarly fragmented approach to chronology, effectively employing Walter Benjamin's notion of the 'tiger's leap', or *Tigersprung*, to discuss the fashion industry's continuous recycling of the past in order to create an ever-changing fashionable present. Indeed, studies that explore fashion's relationship to, and participation in, the construction of modernity (Benjaminian or otherwise) have – from Elizabeth Wilson's *Adorned in Dreams*, through Mark Wigley's *White Walls, Designer Dresses* and Ulrich Lehmann's *Tigersprung* to Caroline Evans's *Fashion at the Edge* – specifically avoided any formal idea of chronological progression.[16] Rather, they have addressed specific aspects of modernity: architecture with Wigley, and trauma and alienation as a trope of modernity with Evans, for example. The methodology of picking and choosing from the sweep of textile and dress history has become a common practice, and fragmented histories have been fundamental to a variety of sociocultural readings of fashion and, to a lesser degree, textiles, their central arguments clothed in suitably postmodern vestimentary bricolage. Again Benjamin (who seems to haunt fashion and textile theory with a ferocious persistence) has been usefully employed: his figure of the rag-picker, which provided him with a model for literary montage, continues to inspire much contemporary fashion and textile design with its assemblages of styles and references from different eras and cultures. Early tartan's often fragmented form, surviving in many cases as little more than scraps, is therefore especially appropriate as a catalyst for thinking about textiles with the same disregard for chronology and cultural division as John Galliano, Jean-Paul Gaultier and Vivienne Westwood have done with fashion. The fragment of early tartan furnishes a ready-made resource for textile studies as a form of cultural 'rag-picking'.

The process of deconstruction implicated in the tartan fragment, not only of the original garment or length of cloth but also of its actual sett, has also been a particularly fruitful methodology

26 Fragment of Bonnie Prince Charlie's plaid, sold at auction in 1999 by Philips, the Edinburgh-based auctioneers. The six-inch fragment of cloth fetched £1,650

for the contemporary designer. Whilst 'deconstructed clothing' is fast becoming an overused term within contemporary fashion theory, the benefits espoused by its advocates should not be diminished. The revelation of construction, the concept of the 'unfinished', and the implied contract between garment and wearer that literary deconstruction had previously identified between text and reader, have suggested new itineraries for fashion which bypass the well-worn paths of endless historical recycling. Jurgi Persoon's skirt, from his Autumn/Winter 2000–1 collection, consists of fragments of tartan mounted on an underskirt of black voile, and offers a similar range of inter-pretations as has been seen to exist for the museum fragment. The skirt encompasses references to other garments, other lengths of cloth that its frayed edges might once have belonged to, and like viewers of museum fragments who embark on numerous acts of restitution, so too Persoon's skirt invokes the potential of completeness. Constructed from what could be taken as swatches for future garments, the skirt acts as a set of possibilities for other clothes, a form of vestimentary working drawing or sketchbook.

If Persoon's garment resonates with the anonymity of the many unattributed and unidentifiable tartan fragments encountered in museums and other collections, then a garment such as Vivienne Westwood's deconstructed tartan kilt-skirt, from her Autumn/Winter 2004–5 collection, 'Exhibi-tion' (illus. 28), seems to reference as many known and identifiable sources. On the eve of her retrospective exhibition at the Victoria and Albert Museum, London, the 'Exhibition' collection adopted an archival approach, not only to historical dress in general but specifically to her own 'back catalogue'. Using Dress Stewart tartan, Queen Victoria's favourite for evening wear at Balmoral, many of her trademark looks were revisited, the skirt in question evoking punk with its bondage straps and matching trousers. But apart from its obvious personal retrospection, Westwood's kilt is evocative in its 'shredded deluge', as it was described, of the deconstruction both literally – in terms of its sewing – and metaphorically – as a garment that has been 'pulled apart' and reconstructed throughout history.[17] Shifting from traditional garment of the Highlander to patrician fancy dress, from uniform of the Highland regiments to the formal wear of the modern Scottish bridegroom, the kilt has undergone a series of fragmentations, which Westwood's unravelling version simultaneously evokes and reconstructs.[18] Just as museum displays provide educational narratives for the fragments they enshrine, Westwood's deconstructed kilt is situated in sartorial and historical narratives on the runway, its edges cut from a cloth that is, for her, historical and contemporary, personal and universal.

FABRICATION

The concept of fabrication, a production of something from nothing, or at least from elements markedly different from the end product, permeates any consideration of tartan. The cloth is literally fabricated from yarn producing something very different in appearance once it is woven, and yet we also recognize it as indissoluble from its original component elements. The actual process of weaving different coloured threads to produce a tartan pattern seems at once logical and straightforward, yet the complexity, depth and variation that can be achieved by the simple process of repeating a sequence of stripes in both warp and weft seems also somehow impossible. An air

27 (Facing Page) Skirt by Jurgi Persoons, Autumn/Winter 2000–1

of deception or illusion pervades the weaving process, the very act of passing the shuttle of a loom back and forth akin to the illusionist's sleight of hand, at once distracting and mesmerizing the audience, until magically the finished cloth is suddenly revealed. This analogy is introduced not so much to sing the praises of the weaving process, but is utilized to try and convey how a similar idea of almost incomprehensible and obscure manufacture results in the exceptional status that tartan holds amongst textile production.

Speculation, embroidering of the facts and the intentional manipulation of data engulf tartan's early history, particularly concerning its relation to the concept of clanship, and similar processes are echoed in the transformation of yarn into finished tartan cloth. Certain components are recognizable, but what is finally produced is so complex and far-reaching in terms of national identity and similar sociopolitical constructions that the process appears almost impossible to comprehend and, indeed, unravel. Whilst these general observations can be discerned within the histories of certain other textile productions (paisley, for example – as a pattern as well as its specific use in items of dress such as the Kashmir shawl – has perhaps a similar trajectory and as troubled a history as tartan), there are very specific instances of what could be termed 'fakery' attached to tartan itself. These specific fabrications of origin and significance, formulated in the eighteenth and nineteenth centuries, endure as factors contributing to tartan's popular contemporary perception, and set in motion a process of accretion and mythologizing that continues to adhere to tartan today.

Tartan's significance and its global recognition as a textile that can signify nationalism, tradition, rebellion, romance and many other such constructions, is in no small part due to its association with specific historical figures. The cloth has been inextricably linked to personalities who have both helped increase the pattern's status, and in turn benefited symbiotically from its existing popular perception. Bonnie Prince Charlie, George IV, Sir Walter Scott, Queen Victoria and Prince Albert have all figured prominently in many of tartan's narratives. Earlier figures such as William Wallace have been posthumously allied to tartan via Hollywood's fabrication of Scottish history, and contemporary popular culture has seen tartan colonize football terraces and concert venues alike (illus. 29). All public personae are of course constructions, which in the best tradition of illusion emphasize certain qualities and achievements whilst distracting our gaze from that which might 'give the game away' and be less flattering. Modern media manipulation has made this process commonplace and acceptable for contemporary personalities, but earlier figures have been similarly fabricated, their lives and achievements manipulated by historians, artists and other commentators.

Popular historical memory is constructed from less formal sources of knowledge, and delights in the less typical, as Samuel suggests: 'So far as historical particulars are concerned, it prefers the eccentric to the typical; the sensational to the routine. Wonders and marvels are grist to its mill; so are the comic and the grotesque.'[19] The perception, appeal and longevity of certain historical periods, events and characters are equally conditioned by the unofficial territories of oral history, song, cartoons, television, cinema, novels and, significantly, dress and textile history. Details of dress, the habitual wearing of certain colours, eccentric or unacceptable costume, and grotesque appearance punctuate and augment the more conventional accounts of prominent historical

28 (Facing Page) Vivienne Westwood, 'Exhibition', Autumn/Winter 2004–5

29 Rod Stewart, 1983

figures. Elizabeth I appearing in armour to deliver her Armada speech, J. Edgar Hoover's penchant for women's underclothes, Isadora Duncan's status as an early 'fashion victim' due to her liking for flowing scarves, and so on, are typical of the legendary vestimentary 'gossip' that becomes crystallized as popular knowledge. Likewise, anecdotes concerning tartan and garments such as the kilt figure prominently in the accounts of those with a Scottish connection.

But tartan is not just an interesting footnote in the biographies of the figures it is associated with: it is often an intrinsic component of the fabrication of those biographies, and indeed indicative of tartan's centrality to fabrication, illusion and the diverting power of spectacle. The cult of personality that sprang up around the Jacobite Pretender, Charles Edward Stuart, generated its own universe of tartans and tartan-related objects, which, if not intentional forgeries, are certainly of a dubious origin. A veritable industry sprang up to alter, or 'tartanize' existing portraits of the Young Pretender for propaganda purposes: around the period when the rebellion of 1745 was being planned, many portraits, miniatures and engravings of the prince were sent over to Scotland from the Continent (particularly Rome, the home of the exiled Stuart court), to be given a Scottish gloss by adding such items of Highland dress as a bonnet or plaid. Artefacts from this period of tartan 'makeover' join the various tartan suits, remnants and other objects littering public and private collections, and which cluster together under a classificatory field of 'believed to be', 'attributed to', or 'almost identical to'. The speculation, controversy and continuing preoccupation with aligning fragments of cloth and items of clothing to the fabulous history of the ill-fated Prince continue to exert a powerful attraction, one which has endured from the time of his departure from Scotland's shores up to the present day. Tartan and the Young Pretender's failed enterprise therefore remain inextricably linked in popular imagination and scholarly research alike.

Tartan's proscription in 1746 brought about a transformation in its status, which in turn modified its former practical function as a cloth that was hard-wearing, economical, offered effective protection against the elements and provided a certain amount of camouflage. Its original function, or at least its customary usage, shifted to being a cloth that was worn by those considered exempt

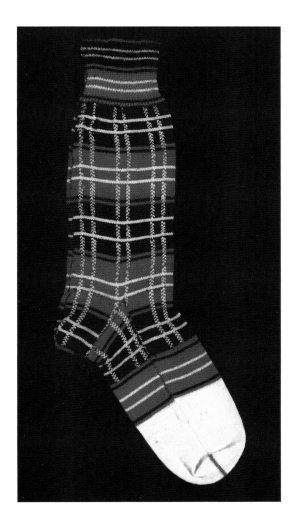

30 Child's tartan sock, by I. & R. Morley Ltd., London. Machine-knitted wool, c.1851

from the ban: the military, Lowland gentry and indeed the English. With this reallocation in both wearer and function, tartan was now ready to become the cloth of complex signification that we recognize it as today. The process that happens to the collected object, recorded by Jean Baudrillard, can also be detected during this particular stage in tartan's history, whereby the cloth 'divested of its function, abstracted from any practical context, takes on a strictly subjective status'.[20] This is not to suggest, of course, that tartan ceased to be made into wearable clothing, but rather that the form and function of that clothing is radically altered. Its adoption by the military and those who, according to status or location, continued to wear tartan meant that after 1746, tartan dress took on new and specific sets of meanings. The cloth becomes much more widely fashionable and is incorporated into military-influenced civilian clothing, the 'spectacular' mode as Dunbar characterizes it; tartan's previous habitat of the rugged Highland landscape was now replaced by the levée, the assembly and the ballroom.[21] In these situations, the cloth was worn conspicuously as a sartorial confection of patriotism for a united Britain expanding its frontiers with the help of the tartan-clad regiments, and as the freshly Romanticized expression of 'ancient' Highland culture.

Following its proscription and utilization as a regimental textile, the next, and most effective catalyst for tartan's reconstruction was royal patronage. Sir Walter Scott (the literary pioneer of historical fabrication), as stage manager of George IV's visit to Edinburgh, consciously used tartan as a primary visual component of a series of spectacular tableaux that succeeded in expressing, via clothing, a counterfeit connection between the Celtic Royal Houses of Scotland and the English Hanoverian line. George's actual appearance was apparently somewhat less than 'bonnie', as will be discussed later, but in terms of crowd-pleasing and the subsequent commercial benefit to the tartan-manufacturing industry, the spectacle was a success and united (fictitiously at least) opposing political, national and clan divisions in a dazzling tartan euphoria. This sartorial sleight of hand, whilst derided by some as a mockery, proved enormously influential in tartan's reinvention as royal-endorsed visual symbol of the union between Scotland and England, where any dissent or history of bloody resistance had been expunged and Britain lived happily ever after. The fictional nature of this contemporary drama of united royal houses was underscored in 1822, when George IV rounded off his triumphant appearance by attending a theatrical performance of another of Scott's historical illusions, *Rob Roy*. The tartanization of Edinburgh for the royal visit, carried out by Scott and his technical adviser Colonel David Stewart of Garth, is a supreme nineteenth-century example of the operation of spectacle as put forward by Guy Debord, functioning:

> simultaneously as all of society, as part of society, and as instrument of unification. As a part of society it is specifically the sector which concentrates all gazing and all consciousness. Due to the very fact that this sector is separate, it is the common ground of the deceived gaze and of false consciousness, and the unification it achieves is nothing but an official language of generalized separation.[22]

Tartan was the key visual element of George IV's spectacular visit, its pivotal role as a cloth of dissent and resistance forgotten as it took centre stage as the textile expression of a mythical national unification.

The widespread remaking or fabrication of history that occurred throughout the late eighteenth century and on into the nineteenth century was a response, it has been suggested, to growing feelings of instability following the American and French revolutions, coupled with the decline of religious faith due to the advancement of rational and scientific philosophies. The upsurge of interest in supposedly indigenous cultures that these anxieties produced is perfectly modelled in the reinvention of Scottish Highland traditions, a subject first successfully interrogated in Hugh Trevor-Roper's seminal essay. The ancient history of Scotland, specifically Highland Scotland, as opposed to Lowland English-affiliated Scotland, underwent a sustained period of reinvention marked at its beginning by the post-1745 period of proscription and culminating in the tartan extravaganza celebrating George IV's visit. During this period, Scottish history was reconstructed so that Highlanders were no longer understood to be descendants of Irish-speaking invaders of the fifth century, but were reconstituted as the Caledonians, an indigenous group already occupying the region and who, it was claimed, successfully resisted the invading Roman armies. To consolidate this new version of Highland history, ancient literary traditions were 'discovered' that claimed an antecedence and stylistic superiority over the previously established Irish literary tradition.

31 St Patrick

The leading light in this flowering of ancient Highland literature was Ossian, celebrated throughout Europe in the 1760s and 1770s as the 'Celtic Homer'. Ossian's literary refinement and prowess helped supplant the previously held notion of the Scottish as poor barbarians eclipsed by the comparatively sophisticated Irish and English traditions. By 'rediscovering' an indigenous Scottish poet who supposedly hailed from the Dark Ages when the Irish and English were still relatively uncivilized, Ossian set in motion a full-blown 'public relations exercise' that established a forgotten culture for the Scottish Highlander and which included an ancient form of Highland dress. Ossian was in fact a construct produced by two people bearing the same name: James Macpherson. One man collected Irish ballads throughout Scotland and then incorporated them into a new epic work, with the setting changed from Ireland to Scotland, and the original Irish pieces now demoted to versions of this 'original' work by Ossian. The deception was subsequently aided by the other James Macpherson, a minister of Sleat, who provided a critical context and appraisal of the poem, confirming the work as the product of Irish-speaking Celtic Scots inhabiting the area a full four centuries before the historical Irish arrived there in the fifth century. The rediscovery of Ossian captured the imagination of a Europe entranced by the idea of a forgotten culture that could produce such sophisticated literature and caused the intelligentsia of the time to regard the newly established Highlanders as *Kulturvolk*.[23]

The Ossian deception was instrumental in the 'restoration' of a set of indigenous Highland traditions and can also be linked directly to the re-emergence of tartan and Highland dress in general. In 1778, the Highland Society of London was founded; their primary objective was the preservation and propagation of Highland customs and the Highland way of life. One of the original members of the society was James Macpherson, the alias of Ossian, and to some extent the society operated as a conduit for various Highland literary productions turned out by Macpherson. However, another chief objective of the society was the lifting of the 1746 proscription on the wearing of Highland dress. To this end, the society met regularly in London, dressed in full Highland costume (this was legal in London) and recited poetry, sang songs, instituted poetry and bagpipe competitions and generally celebrated Scottish Celtic culture. Their enterprise was eventually rewarded when in 1782 the Marquis of Graham, at the request of the society, had the ban repealed in the House of Commons. In effect the ban had only been enforced (with many exceptions), for less than forty years, but during that period Highland dress and tartan had undergone a concentrated process of sociocultural and historical transformation that altered its popular perception irrevocably.

By the time of George IV's visit to Edinburgh, and with the help of Scott and Stewart of Garth, tartan had reached the spectacular semi-historical, mythological status it still enjoys today. Scott was president of the Celtic Society of Edinburgh, an association founded by Stewart in 1820 to promote the wearing of ancient Highland dress. Members of the society regularly held meetings 'kilted and bonneted in the old fashion, and armed to the teeth'.[24] Tartan and Highland dress became sartorial propaganda and in much the same manner as illusionists and conjurors have traditionally 'dressed to impress' to emphasize their showmanship, Scott and his companions no doubt cut a dash on the streets of Edinburgh in tartan confections whose intention was to promote a Romantic ideal of ancient Highland culture. Scott, a circle of Celtic aficionados, and the prosperous mercantile class that administered the economic expansion of Britain's colonial interests, seized upon tartan as the sartorial expression of a mythic Scotland that had all but become extinct during the consolidation of the same cultural, economic and industrial revolutions they helped maintain.

THE SOBIESKI STUARTS

> Not a day passed that he did not go through a searching examination of several of his illusions, touching up one moment, subduing another, and always refining that subtle technique of misdirecting the attention of his audience, which is the beginning and end of the conjuror's art.[25]

Swiftly following Scott's successful tartanization of Edinburgh, there emerged an even more concerted instance of tartan fakery that aimed to redress the propaganda of Scott's Romantic Highland production. This episode in tartan history was the work of two brothers called John and Charles Allen who came, as far as we can tell, from a well-connected naval family that probably originated in Europe. It is not known when the Allens first came to Scotland, but research has suggested that they were present in Edinburgh for George's state visit in 1822. There is also the suggestion that they may well have had contact with Wilson & Son of Bannockburn, the tartan manufacturers, and would have been aware of the Highland Society of London's activities, one of whose projects

32 *The Tartan Album*, Rel Records, 1979. Features a disc made from Buchanan tartan vinyl

was to produce a prestigious book on clan tartans. The brothers were by all accounts accomplished and charming men, multi-lingual and adept in a number of crafts including woodworking and drawing.[26] Not long after the state visit, the brothers began to make their mark on the Scottish social scene, appearing at functions in extravagant fancy-dress Highland costumes, and commencing the construction of increasingly Scottish, and well-connected personae for themselves. Courting aristocratic and influential patrons, they changed their name to the more Scottish-sounding 'Allan' and (whether it was started by the brothers themselves or not) did little to disillusion society about the rumour that they were descended from the Earl of Errol. In 1829 they revealed that they had in their possession a manuscript that was supposed to have been owned by John Leslie, the Bishop of Ross and supporter of Mary Queen of Scots, and the final flourish of this particular chapter of their elaborate deception was to claim that this manuscript had been entrusted to their father by none other than Bonnie Prince Charlie.

The manuscript was called *Vestiarium Scoticum* or *The Garde-robe of Scotland*, and purported to be a description of the specific tartans affiliated to the clan families of Scotland, dating from at least 1571 (a date they suggested was a later addition by Leslie) and possibly even earlier. The importance of the document was immediately recognized as it claimed to be the earliest 'proof' of the existence of clan tartans, and that these same tartans were also worn by Lowlanders as well as Highlanders. The Allens had only a rough copy, the original residing with their father (the first of many original documents they cited but which conveniently resided elsewhere, were mislaid or destroyed), and therefore could only be consulted as versions or copies. This in turn facilitated the climate of interpretation, discrepancy and supposition that many of their claims relied on. A transcript was made of their manuscript and was impressively illustrated by their younger brother, Charles, using William and Andrew Smith's previously mentioned 'machine painting' process. The written descriptions of the different tartans contained in the *Vestiarium* are difficult to decipher, for example: 'Mackfarlan of ye Arroquhar hath thre stryppis quhite vpon a blak fyeld', and would have been virtually impossible to use as a weaving guide; therefore it is Charles's original artwork that serves as the more reliable notation of the fifty-four tartans the work details.[27] The production was sent with an accompanying introduction by the brothers' patron, Sir Thomas Dick Lauder, to Walter Scott as the expert on all things connected to Highland culture following the success of his 'gathering of the Clans' for George IV in 1822. He did not, however, endorse it and, more tellingly, voiced his suspicions of the brothers themselves: 'Now, a word to your own private ear, my dear Sir Thomas. I have understood that the Messrs. Hay Allan are young men of talent, great accomplishments, enthusiasm for Scottish manners, and an exaggerating imagination, which possibly deceives even themselves.'[28] As a way of settling the matter, Scott suggested experts at the British Museum should take a look at the manuscript, which the brothers agreed to, but then a timely letter arrived from their father forbidding further investigation of the manuscript and casting aspersions on Scott's judgement.

Following this setback, the brothers continued to perfect their increasingly grand identities. They converted to Roman Catholicism and assumed the royal name of Stuart, the elder brother calling himself John Sobieski Stuart after the Polish royal family related to the Young Pretender. The younger brother favoured Charles Edward Stuart after the Young Pretender, and it is from this point that the brothers are generally referred to as the Sobieski Stuarts. Through the generosity of Lord Lovat, the Catholic head of the Fraser family, they were able to establish a kind of neo-Jacobite mini-court in a lodge on an islet in the Beauly River in Inverness. Here the 'princes', as they started to become known, constructed a fairy tale court around themselves, receiving visitors ensconced on thrones, decorating the lodge with coats of arms, taking part in deer hunting expeditions, and treating favoured guests to a display of Stuart relics (an early example of the re-materialization of Bonnie Prince Charlie through collections of objects of doubtful antecedence) with the intention of strengthening their claim to Stuart ancestry. They eventually published a deluxe, fifty-copy limited edition of *Vestiarium Scoticum* in 1842 accompanied by various testimonials and endorsements that, as previously mentioned, could not be verified. Sir Walter Scott (who might, on seeing the finished product have been more inclined to endorse the work) was by this time dead, and due to the limited amount of copies produced, it failed to make much impact.

33 Musical ceramic figurine of a Scottish dancer that plays 'Auld Lang Syne'

Two years later, an even more lavish edition appeared, weighing in at some twenty-two pounds, and dedicated to Ludwig I of Bavaria (recognition, perhaps, by a pair of fairy tale 'princes' of the supreme nineteenth-century royal fantasist). This second edition was entitled *Costume of the Clans* and is an impressive mix of scholarly research, fantasy and unsubstantiated references including, amongst others, reference to Ossian the bogus bard. In the preamble to the book, entitled 'To the Highlanders', the brothers construct a lament for a long-vanished Celtic Highland tradition and their own early experiences amidst the Napoleonic wars. They go on to suggest that their return to their native Scotland and current research were the fulfilment of what up till then had been a kind of waking dream: 'We lived again with the aged and the recluse, the bards of the glens, the hunters of the hill, among the deer of the desert, and the eagles of the cairn – our conversation was of the ages in which we ought to have been born.'[29]

Whilst many of the claims made in the work concerning tartan's specific clan allegiances have long since been discredited, the work is still impressive and contains enough information to maintain its central position as a primary source for the modern conception of Highland dress and of tartan in particular. The work's major proposition was that Highland dress and their recently re-presented 'ancient' clan tartan setts, with their dazzling colours, allowed direct access for the nineteenth-century reader into the true Catholic Celtic culture. The book suggests that this had been forgotten over the years and, further, that it had little or no connection to the recent tartan revival engineered by Scott and his followers, which the Sobieski Stuarts regarded as mere fancy dress. However, the brothers' delusions of grandeur ultimately ensured that *Costume of the Clans* never received the acclaim and audience it deserved, for in 1846 they produced a collection of short stories which purported to tell the story of the hundred years since the Jacobite uprising of 1745. Central to the tales were two characters claiming to be the long-lost grandsons of the Young Pretender himself, who had fought for and been decorated by Napoleon, and who were now poised to re-establish the Royal House of Stuart in Scotland. Whilst not directly stated, it was obvious to anyone who knew of their reputation that the Sobieski Stuarts were in fact one and the same as these two fictional protagonists. Their claims to royalty were publicly attacked in an article, ostensibly a belated review of the *Vestiarium Scoticum*. The older brother attempted a defence but was not convincing. As a result, their reputation, and with it their research, was brought into disrepute and they left Scotland. They maintained their fledgling neo-Jacobite court abroad and still attracted supporters, but unfortunately their reputation as scholars was irreparably compromised and the *Vestiarium* remained what it still is today: an indisputable catalyst for the revival of tartan's fortunes, containing much valuable research but always overshadowed by an atmosphere of forgery and self-aggrandisement.

As an accurate guide to tartan setts, the *Vestiarium* is now disregarded, Scarlett's comments being typical of the expert weaver's opinion: 'Whatever its value in other respects, as a source-book for tartans it is almost worthless', and citing D. W. Stewart who: '. . . checked many of the illustrations against the portraits from which it was claimed they had been copied, and found them not only inaccurate but quite misleading. The remainder seem to have been evolved out of the inner consciousness of the Sobieski brothers.'[30]

However, as a text that sought to awaken interest in a forgotten or obscured Highland culture, it was effective and retained its supporters. Dunbar, one of its chief advocates, devotes four chapters to *Vestiarium* and *Costume of the Clans* in his *History of Highland Dress*, and concludes that:

> The *Costume of the Clans* is, without doubt, one of the foundation-stones on which any history of Highland Dress is built. It cannot be ignored, and it is surprising how little it has been consulted by writers on the subject. We can think what we like about the ancestral claims of the Stuart brothers, but this does not reduce the value of their monumental book.[31]

Whatever the benefits or not of their work, the Sobieski Stuarts are prime examples of the circuits of illusion and deception that typify so many aspects of tartan history. On one side we have a genuine passion for the subject and an admirable capacity for research; on the other the brothers displayed a deluded and ultimately unsuccessful desire to consolidate their research with dubious 'proof' coupled with an increasingly megalomaniac capacity for fabricating their own lineage. Like illusionists who purposely invent, or are vague about their origins in order to increase the allure and sense of wonder at their performances, the brothers were unable to 'pull off' their last and greatest trick. The conscientiousness of their tartan research and the eventual appearance of the *Vestiarium* were ultimately not diverting enough to distract nineteenth-century audiences from seeing the sleight of hand supporting their Stuart pretensions. The year the brothers departed Scotland was 1847, a date that provides the final irony of their story, as Trevor-Roper reveals: 'In the same year Queen Victoria bought Balmoral, and the real Hanoverian court replaced the vanished, illusory Jacobite court in the Highlands of Scotland.'[32] Ultimately it was Victoria and Albert who proved to be the more adept at conjuring, creating a complete Highland Anglo-Germanic fantasy in the illusory never-never land of Balmoral, where the Royal couple retreated into a land of myth complete with its own 'house' tartan.[33]

So it could be argued that the history of tartan has as some of its primary components qualities of fragmentation and fabrication, alongside an ability to shift its function and significance according to whatever prevailing economic or cultural enterprise makes use of it. If not

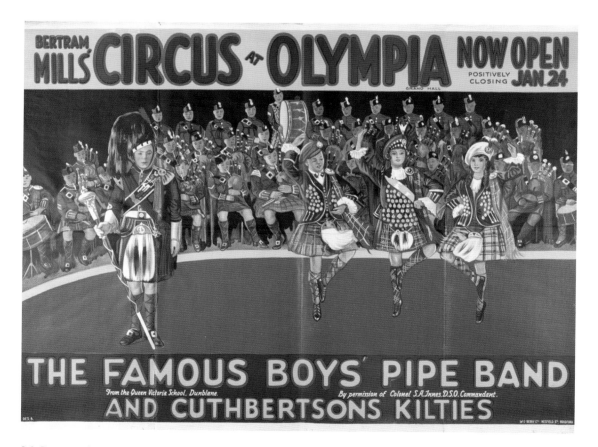

34 Poster advertising Bertram Mills' Circus, Olympia, 1930s. Featuring the 'Famous Boys' Pipe Band' and 'Cuthbertsons Kilties'

intentionally deceptive, much tartan history has a quality of excess, an excess in terms of symbolic meaning and perception. This has enabled it to be manipulated by a number of its most passionate promoters, Scott, the Sobieskis, Jacobite sympathizers, Hanoverian monarchs and many others have recognized its possibilities for adaptation, and assimilation. This chimerical quality, far from reducing its popularity, has in fact ensured its longevity, and allowed it to maintain a prominent position in both popular and 'high' culture. Tartan, whether as a fragment in a museum display, fictionalized in ceremonial ritual and historical romance, or as the inspiration for contemporary designers, functions as a cultural lodestone, universally recognized and with a constantly evolving legendary status.

Part II

TARTAN AND DRESS

35 Vivienne Westwood, 'Dressing Up', Autumn/Winter 1991–2

4.
TRANSFORMING TARTAN

BECOMING FASHION?

Before undertaking any account of the relationship between tartan and fashion, a distinction has to be made between tartan as a fashionable fabric, and tartan as the fabric from which kilts and other items of Highland dress are traditionally made. Tartan's unique position as an instantly recognizable pattern that can be applied to any number of objects, and simultaneously indivisible from specific items of historical dress, such as the kilt, marks it out from any other traditional textile appropriated by the fashion industry. Tartan has influenced fashionable dress as patterned textile and as component of traditional costume, and oscillated between these two functions since its emergence on to the world's fashion stage. As patterned textile its primary signification is of course as a visual reference for Scotland, but beyond its initially nationalistic implications it can act as the textile messenger of a bewildering variety of secondary connotations.

The formulation, by Roland Barthes and others, of fashion as a system of signifiers attached to the actual garment via written and visual representations of the actual piece of clothing, is especially relevant to tartan: relevant inasmuch as the questions Barthes poses – 'Why does fashion utter clothing so abundantly? Why does it interpose, between the object and its user, such a luxury of words (not to mention images), such a network of meaning?' – are to a large degree inapplicable when considering tartan.[1] Unlike other fabrics and garments, tartan is so full of visual connotation that the 'veil of images, of reasons, of meanings' that Barthes observes defines fashion is unnecessary with tartan fashion.[2] The popular understanding of tartan – as a signifier of clanship, allegiance and geographical location – becomes, once adopted by fashion designers, richer and more complex. If we accept, for the moment, tartan's much debated, often spurious, connection to specific clans or districts, what does it mean when such a tartan, with accredited associations, is used to fashion a garment that has none of the traditional, familial, or geographical functions? Is there any residue of traditional significance left in a tartan tuxedo worn by Bill Haley, a tea gown by Poiret from the 1920s (illus. 113), or a pair of tartan boxer shorts? Given the complexity of tartan's relationship to fashion, perhaps these questions remain impossible to answer. What is of more interest is to examine how its use throughout fashion history has drawn upon, or rejected, these

36 Bill Haley and the Comets, 1957

traditional associations, and the way that fashion designers, consumers and mediators incorporate and understand tartan's multivalency: it is this that constitutes the history of tartan and fashion.

In order to address tartan's emergence as fashion, a probable point of origin could be, as with so many other aspects of tartan's historical development, its proscription following the Jacobite defeat at Culloden. From this point, traditional Highland dress (and tartan) lost its true function as the everyday dress of a topographically proximate group of people (its debatable secondary purpose as an indicator of clan allegiance was momentarily halted, awaiting its reinvention at the very end of the eighteenth century). Almost immediately following tartan's proscription, Scottish leaders instructed to raise Highland regiments were able to demonstrate their immunity from the ban by outfitting themselves and their men in the newly designated regimental sets. Similarly, the ban was not enforced outside Scotland and so tartan could be worn in England, and there is evidence suggesting other prominent Scottish figures resident in Lowland towns were also exempt.

The proscription facilitated one of the most vital functions of a successful fashion: that of separating one section of society from another by the outward display of clothing. This is normally achieved economically, the cost of the clothing making it inaccessible to certain groups, but in the case of tartan the division was a result of legislation, making it similar to the various sumptuary laws of Medieval and Renaissance Europe. When the ban was lifted, the average Highlander could no longer afford the extra expense of returning to the kilt, and so fashion's typical economic stratification reinforced tartan's earlier legal divisions. Of course, it can be argued that all forms of traditional dress, when appropriated by the fashion industry, lose their original function as protective and ritual garments, indeed the stripping of this original function is a necessary stage of the garment's transition from clothing to fashion. But what makes fashion's appropriation of tartan and items of Highland dress unique, is that no matter how abstracted or distorted the references may become, tartan's sociocultural, political and literary histories can never be entirely subsumed by the spectacle of fashion.

In mapping tartan's relationship to fashionable dress, many sociocultural territories need to be surveyed, including the historical, philosophical, aesthetic, biographical and economic. Tartan as masquerade, as protest, as conqueror, as disruption, as erotic, demarcate these terrains, providing a backdrop for a cast of characters including Sir Walter Scott, Bonnie Prince Charlie, and Queen Victoria. The different manifestations of tartan listed above inform both historical and more contemporary alliances between fashion and tartan. The links between often apparently divergent uses of tartan result in an open-ended and infinitely reinterpretable map, following the rhizomatic form described by Gilles Deleuze and Félix Guattari where:

> The map is open and connectable in all of its dimensions; it is detachable, reversible, susceptible to constant modification. It can be torn, reversed, adapted to any kind of mounting, reworked by an individual, group or social formation.[3]

Therefore punks, Idi Amin and 'loud' gents may enter into dialogues with Jacobites, Highland officers and dandies; similarly Royal Stewart tartan could cover the Windsors, a runway muse of Jun Takahashi or a member of the Tartan Army football supporters' club. However, before continuing the exploration of fashion and tartan, it is necessary to look in further detail at the development of the kilt, as this garment, more than any other, has been the form (often as a mere approximation of

the traditional hand-made kilt) most frequently used by the fashion industry to usher tartan on to its runways, and simultaneously bring the past hurtling into its fashionable present.

THE ECONOMY OF THE KILT

Much to the continuing chagrin (and in some quarters disbelief) of certain scholars, the 'little kilt' as we now know it is generally accepted to be the invention of an Englishman, one Thomas Rawlinson, a Quaker industrialist from Lancashire. Needing a plentiful supply of charcoal for his iron-smelting furnaces, and with material becoming scarcer locally, he looked to the newly exploitable forests of the North, and in 1727 entered into an agreement with Ian MacDonell of the Glengarry MacDonells to rent woodland near Invergarry and set up a furnace there. Whilst in Scotland, Rawlinson became interested in the Highland way of life, particularly the traditional dress worn by the local workforce he employed to fell the trees and work the furnace. Observing that the traditional *fhéilidh-Mor* was uncomfortably hot and dangerously impractical, Rawlinson hit upon the idea of shortening and separating the pleated lower half from the cumbersome top half. Enlisting the help of the local regimental tailor stationed at Inverness, he developed the *fhéilidh beag*, or little kilt. This had the pleats stitched in at the back, and those at the front replaced by flat sections called aprons. Worn by Rawlinson, his employees and most significantly MacDonell, the *fhéilidh beag* was swiftly adopted by MacDonell's loyal clansmen, and as Trevor-Roper observes, it helped the Highlander: 'out of the heather and into the factory'.[4]

The *fhéilidh beag* gradually replaced the longer *fhéilidh-Mor*, although the Act of Proscription of 1746 on Highland dress made this a somewhat erratic process. Ordinary Highlanders, who had begun to accept the shorter kilt, were suddenly prohibited from wearing it and forced to adopt the Lowland suit. The *fhéilidh beag* then became a garment worn by the Highland regiments, Lowlanders, Englishmen with Scottish connections, and others exempt from the ban. Once the ban was lifted in 1782, ordinary Highlanders could not afford to revert to the costly kilt, and so during this period it became chiefly a ceremonial or military garment which, apart from the fashion industry's many variations, to a large degree it remains today. Returning once more to the kilt's actual development, its next major modification occurred in the 1790s, once again by a regimental tailor. He sewed box pleats into the recently modified little kilt in order to make the garment look neater and make it more practical as workwear and uniform. In this initial development of the tailored kilt, each pleat showed a particular coloured stripe or group of stripes, whilst obscuring others within the internal part of the pleat hidden by its outer edges. By emphasizing a particular colour or colours, the full sett is only revealed when the kilt is worn and the pleats open up with movement. In order to achieve this 'hidden' effect, box pleating is the preferred type of pleating, as it enables whole sections of the tartan's sett to be effectively 'lost' behind the outer uppermost pleat.

Box-pleated kilts were adopted by the military and remained fashionable in both civilian and military dress up to the 1860s. This method of pleating was both practical and economical, the earliest sewn kilts requiring only three and a half yards of material. As the nineteenth century progressed, the boxes became narrower and the pleats deeper, so that by the middle of the century as much as six yards of material was required. Whilst this process of fashion dictating greater material consumption can be seen to typify clothing production in general throughout the nineteenth

37 (Facing Page) Dress by Jacques Fath. Wool, lined with net and silk, 1949

38 Highland dancing competitors at the 2005 Inverness Highland Games

century, as long as the kilt remained box-pleated it still retained some of its original economic and practical functions. Due to the particular construction of the box pleat it was possible to unpick and reverse the kilt, concealing the worn-out original outer part of the pleat, and exposing the relatively fresh-looking, unfaded part of the pleat previously hidden within the internal folds. This practice of reversing and doubling the life of a kilt was common, particularly amongst the military and kilt-wearing families, where a father's kilt would typically be remade and handed down to his sons. Also, second-generation kilts could be cut down to form kilts for infants, or kilts for girls performing Scottish country dancing, a practice common until the mid-twentieth century and the rise of specialized manufacturers who recognized the commercial advantage in catering for the growing demand for children's dancing costumes.

Whilst the economic advantage of the box-pleated kilt continued to be enjoyed within sectors of the community immune to the dictates of fashion, such as the military or the poor, this was a state of affairs that could not be tolerated by the emergent nineteenth-century fashion industry. The economy that characterized the old box-pleated kilt was at odds with fashion's projection of the necessity to produce and consume more and more articles of clothing. Therefore, by the 1860s, tailors began making kilts with flat or knife pleats rather than box pleats, which were easier to make, required more material and were incapable of being reversed and renewed. As Barthes suggests:

> Calculating, industrial society is obliged to form consumers who don't calculate; if clothing's producers and consumers had the same consciousness, clothing would be bought (and produced) only at the very slow rate of its dilapidation; Fashion, like all fashions, depends on a disparity of two consciousnesses, each foreign to the other.[5]

39 Kilts pleated to stripe

A further fashionable development occurred in the 1890s, when tailors started making knife-pleated kilts that were pleated to sett rather than stripe. In this development, each pleat was pleated to a different part of the pattern, but when sewn together reproduced perfectly the complete sett, mirroring the pattern on the flat front apron. Pleating to sett swept away pleating to stripe and was highly beneficial to kilt-makers and tartan manufacturers alike, as this development required up to nine yards of material and increased production costs. Pleating to stripe was still customary in military dress, but the dictates of fashion manufacturing ensured that pleating to sett became the norm and remains so today. Unless specifically requested, a kilt-maker will invariably make a kilt pleated in this fashion rather than to stripe, and so the economic box-pleated kilt gave way to the costly knife-pleated, special-occasion garment that we recognize today.

OPPOSITIONAL TARTAN

Evidence of tartan's alliance with fashionable dress in the early eighteenth century, before Culloden, is relatively scant apart from representations of prominent clan leaders wearing variations of the traditional garments previously discussed. It is not until after the failure of the Jacobite uprisings and the years immediately following 1745 that we begin to see tartan incorporated into the changing styles of the period, accompanied by a subsequent increase in portraiture of those wearing tartan as a sign of protest against the Union and Hanoverian authority. By the mid-eighteenth century, men's fashionable clothing more or less conformed to variations on the now ubiquitous three-piece suit consisting of a coat, waistcoat and breeches. The cut of the coat had developed from seventeenth-century styles and remained relatively consistent throughout the following century. Coat patterns would typically consist of two front sections and two at the back, with no waist seam. Variations to this basic pattern were minimal, and amounted to little more than minor alterations in length, width, the flaring of the 'skirt' and sleeve, and details of collar and cuffs. The dictates of fashion were more noticeably expressed by variations in fabric and the popularity of certain colours. In the latter half of the eighteenth century, the traditionally full, flared or pleated 'skirt' of the coat was cut away to develop into what we would today recognize as a tail coat. The long-line waistcoat was the focal point of the ensemble, often highly decorated with embroidery or other surface textile embellishment; as with the coat, the waistcoat developed in the latter part of the eighteenth century, becoming shorter and generally more restrained in decoration.

The appearance of tartan in men's dress of the eighteenth century, however, is remarkable not only for whatever political, religious or dynastic signification it might have conveyed, but in terms of often running counter to the prevailing trends of European men's dress. Looking at the representation of men's clothing in Scottish portraiture of the period, there is a natural disparity between what we understand to be modish attire from the surviving articles of dress from this period, and the clothes the sitters chose to be painted in. Formal portraiture naturally demands formal costume, which can be considered as more or less immune to the vagaries of fashion. Indeed, formal attire is often fashion that has become fossilized or 'unfashion'. For example, contemporary male evening dress has remained relatively unaltered since the demise of the tail coat in the mid-twentieth century. Clothing in portraiture functions as a visual signifier of the subject's social position, wealth and in the case of tartan, sociopolitical allegiances. So, if the minor details of men's European fashion in this period are either nonexistent or negligible in these portraits, can tartan be understood or, to paraphrase Barthes, can it 'utter' anything significant concerning fashion at all?[6]

From the mid-eighteenth century onwards, it is possible to conceive of tartan as fashion's revisionist voice, its regular sartorial outbreaks providing a brief hiatus in the relentless cycles of fashion. It reminds consumers, commentators and creators alike that as well as necessarily opposing, or adapting what has previously been regarded as fashionable:

> Clothing oneself is an act of differentiation, it is essentially an act of signification. It manifests itself through symbols or convention, together or separately, essence, seniority, tradition, prerogative, heritage, caste, lineage, ethnic group, generation, religion, geographical origin, marital status, social position, economic role, political belief, and ideological affiliation. Sign or symbol, clothing affirms and reveals cleavages, hierarchies, and solidarities according to a code guaranteed and perpetuated by society and its institutions.[7]

Whilst this might seem to be overstating the case for tartan's influence, it can clarify the textile's continuous presence throughout the history of fashion, and which accelerated in terms of output and consumption throughout the nineteenth and twentieth centuries. It also helps explain the situation where, since the 1900s, no decade has been 'tartanless', and furthermore that its appearances have often been synchronous with radical shifts in style.

40 *Lord George Murray*, unknown artist, eighteenth century. Murray was the celebrated lieutenant general of the Jacobite forces, who eventually died in exile in Holland. He is depicted in a belted plaid, coat and hose, all in different tartan setts, and with the white cockade of the Jacobite cause in his bonnet

But to return to eighteenth-century portraits, the viewer is struck by a number of divergences from conventional fashions of the age. The most obvious, of course, being that in many portraits from this period men are wearing either the newly invented little kilt (*fhéilidh beag*) or a tailored version of the belted plaid (*fhéilidh-Mor*) as the third component of the three-piece suit instead of the customary breeches. As has already been discussed, the motive for this was primarily as an expression of these subjects' political and religious sympathies. By being depicted in a gentrified form of traditional Highland dress, they were able to express an allegiance to the Jacobite cause and opposition to the English government's proscription of tartan. But leaving aside the obvious political statement of wearing the plaid or little kilt, what does the wearing of these tartan garments communicate to researchers of conventional fashionable men's dress of the period, and can it initiate historical lines of enquiry that have ramifications to more contemporary tartan-wearing?

In conventional eighteenth-century men's dress, at least until the development of the cut-away coat, very little emphasis was placed on the lower body. Breeches followed conventional formats, and were modest and undecorated when compared to the sophistication and elaboration of the coat and waistcoat. Looking at tartan portraits from this period, the sitters' coats and waistcoats (often rather outmoded in terms of cut and detail) are teamed with kilts or plaids, shifting the emphasis to an entirely different body zone. A curious dichotomy occurs between the relative extravagance of pleating and draping of the *fhéilidh-Mor* and *fhéilidh beag* and the fitted restraint of the tailored upper garments. The conventional silhouette of the time, consisting of a long coat flaring outwards in structured lines, showcasing the waistcoat underneath, with the bottom line of the coat and breeches finishing at a similar level, becomes, in tartan portraits, a fitted upper half with a shorter waistcoat that seems unable to restrain the profusion of cloth forming the kilt and plaid. The implied swagger and sexual emphasis of this attire initiates a vast terrain of referents clustering around the synchronicity of ambivalent yet over-defined sexuality implied by the wearing of the kilt (a key issue discussed in further detail in Chapter 6, *Erogenous Zones*).

Just as the silhouette runs against conventional fashions of the time, so too do the areas of the body differentiated and abstracted by the ratio of plain and decorated material. For the majority of the eighteenth century, the most elaborate decoration for men's dress was reserved for the waistcoat, which was at various times richly embroidered, appliquéd or made of figured silk and other luxurious fabrics. The breeches remained plain and the coat variously trimmed, edged or in plain material often matching the ground of the waistcoat. Turning to eighteenth-century tartan men's dress, however, this ratio of patterned upper half, plain lower half is inverted, for in Scottish portraits the emphasis is either on the tartan bottom half, with a plain jacket and waistcoat, or the whole suit is made out of tartan, often of varying setts. Tartan portraiture runs counter to men's fashion in the eighteenth century, in its shift of emphasis as to which areas of the body are patterned and which plain, and also in terms of the prevailing colour scheme. The dominance and unchanging nature of the typical tartan palette of bright reds, deep greens, blues and blacks is resistant to the whims of eighteenth-century fashion, where certain colours were more or less de rigueur. For example, the predilection in the earlier part of the century for yellow in men's fashion gave way to more sombre colours mid-century, only to lighten again in the latter half of the century, with pastel shades being fashionable for coats and waistcoats.

Similarly, the embroidery and other applied decorations and trimmings on coat and waistcoat emphasized the cut and lines of both garment and wearer; whereas in all-over tartan suits, the boldness and dominance of the check tended to abstract, flatten and 'morph' the body in ways that other fabrics and patterns did not. These effects are just as noticeable when tartan outfits followed the more conventional Highland men's costume of the time, comprising of a hip-length coat buttoned down the front with a turned-over flat collar, and close-fitting trews, similar to breeches, that fastened just below the knee with bands over the stockings in a matching or variant tartan. This costume would then be completed by the plaid itself, which was variously draped and fastened, typically over one shoulder. Such bold patterning on the legs disguises, rather than emphasizes, the shape of calf and lower leg, resulting in a two-dimensional, 'cut-out', 'harlequin' effect; the antithesis of the desired look sought by conventional eighteenth-century light-coloured breeches and stockings for men, which were designed to show off a well-proportioned leg.

The abstraction of the body's form that occurs when tartan is used extensively is not confined to eighteenth-century men's clothing, however, and is noticeable in various manifestations throughout fashion history. The synthesis of particular colour combinations, boldness and rhythm of sett, historical, contemporary, national and international significance has made tartan simultaneously the height of fashion and yet able to remain outside of the system. It could be argued that other patterns have a recurrent significance in fashion: spots have a similar disruptive optical effect, especially when scaled up, paisley a correspondingly complex colonial narrative, stripes a historical tradition of oppression and sporadic prohibition, and so on. Tartan can chronicle all of these narratives and more whilst effecting a myriad of visual disruptions, which returns us again to its possible usefulness as a kind of textile 'lodestone'. Whenever tartan is incorporated into a garment as accent or main component, it can variously remind us of fashion's economic, sexual, topographical, historical, political and deforming operations; in short, tartan acts as fashion's 'reagent'.

41 Jacobite

Ye Caledonian beauties, who have long
Been both the muse and subject of my song,
Assist your bard, who, in harmonious lays,
Designs the glory of your Plaid to raise.[8]

The evidence of the use of tartan in women's dress in the eighteenth century is scarcer than that for men. The few portraits that survive show tartan used as the material for conventional fashionable styles of the period, for example Helen Murray of Ochtertyre is depicted wearing a separate bodice and skirt in red and black tartan. The bodice is close-fitting to the waist, with a basque over the skirt in a shape achieved by the dome-shaped hoops popular in the early part of the century. Significantly, she holds a white rose in her left hand, signifying her Jacobite sympathies. Another striking representation is the beautiful portrait of an unknown Jacobite sympathizer from around the time of the 1715 rebellion, who, it has been suggested but not corroborated, may have been the Young Pretender's mistress. The portrait is attributed to Cosmo Alexander but, given that Alexander was not active until the 1740s, the image was either painted in retrospect or by another hand. The woman wears a riding habit in one of the Jacobite setts, which were particular tartan setts adopted by sympathizers, though they bore no special connection to any particular clan or family. There is considerable doubt as to the validity of these tartans, and many were probably created with hindsight in the general tartan revival of the early nineteenth century, when, with the rebellions a distant memory, the idea of Jacobite tartans seemed attractively nostalgic. However, the tartan worn by the unknown woman does conform to the characteristics of the few definitely attributable Jacobite setts, which display a complexity, vividness of colour and difference between warp and weft (see illus. 41), and she once again holds a white rose.

This portrait is one of the few from this period that portray women adopting tartan as part of their fashionable costume, and joins the other more familiar images centred on the Romanticized representations of Flora MacDonald, the Young Pretender's ally. Allan Ramsay painted one of the most familiar images of MacDonald in 1747, depicting her dressed in a tartan plaid (or possibly *arisaid*) pinned to her right shoulder, with white roses in her hair and at her breast to show her

allegiance to the cause. Another familiar portrait is by Richard Wilson and shows her in a typical gown of the period, made from tartan and bedecked down the bodice and at the sleeves with the white rosettes of the Jacobites. All these portraits act as allegories of the sitters' political allegiance rather than as any accurate depiction of the women's attire. Little can be seen of their actual dress and the emphasis is placed on their countenance and the Jacobite emblems, constructing a persona of the bold and beautiful heroine ready to wear her political heart on her sleeve. Their allegorical content harks back to an earlier period of Elizabethan and Jacobean portraiture, when the sitters' associations, achievements and status were signalled by objects, as well as the dress they wore.

Apart from these and a very few other portraits depicting women wearing tartan at this period (which also act more as ciphers than accurate documentation), other accounts of tartan-wearing women are necessarily literary. The poem *Tartana*, the first verse of which is quoted earlier, was written in 1721 by Allan Ramsay, father of the painter of the same name, and is the most well known of these literary tartan tributes. These texts provide an indication of the effect produced by the wearing of the plaid and *arisaid* by Highland women. The more well-to-do the wearer, the more costly and fine the weave of the plaid would be, sometimes woven entirely from (or with certain stripes of the sett picked out in) silk:

> The Ladies dress as in England, with this difference, that when they go abroad, from the highest to the lowest, they wear a Plaid, which covers Half of the Face, and all their Body. In Spain, Flanders, and Holland, you know the Women go all to Church, and Market, with a black Mantle over their Heads and Body: But these in Scotland are all strip'd with Green, Scarlet, and other Colours, and most of them lin'd with Silk; which in the Middle of a Church, on a Sunday, looks like a Parterre de Fleurs.[9]

This beautiful account from 1723 conjures up an image of tartan, as with men's dress, being used to disguise and transform the body, the women's plaids and *arisaids* depicted as a form of polychromatic burqa. The account notes that modesty was maintained as was customary for women of the time, but their appearance was anything but discreet and retiring; instead they are described metaphorically as flower gardens formed from en masse tartan-wearing. The plaid and *arisaid* continued to be worn by women of all stations in the Highlands, but by the latter half of the century, the urban well-to-do have replaced it with silk versions or velvet cloaks lined with tartan, the original woollen plaids now regarded as outmoded.

The visually disruptive and obscuring effect of tartan is given full reign with women's costume, which takes on elements of disguise and the masquerade. The body is literally cloaked by tartan's distracting geometry, which assumes the form of a political mask signifying resistance to the dominant hierarchy. Boldness of political statement is the motivation for these fashions, rather than the subtleties of cut and detail, and fashion becomes a text that can inspire resistance in its observers. Nicholson notes of Ramsay's portrait of *Flora MacDonald* that: 'the tartan rebuffs the superficial femininity and emphasizes the strength, stoicism and patriotism of the sitter: a Scotia ready to unseat Britannia'.[10] Jacobite ladies evidently did not stop at tartan dresses; as we have seen, riding habits were fashioned from tartan, as well as domestic furnishings such as bed hangings, curtains, shoes and various other items (illus. 19). James Laver has suggested: 'It is clothes that make it possible for governments to obtain obedience, religions reverence, judiciaries a respect for

42 (Facing Page) Richard Wilson, *Portrait of Flora Macdonald*. Oil on canvas, 1747

the law, and armies discipline.'[11] But clothing can also express resistance to those same mechanisms of power, and so a woman dressed in men's riding clothes made from a cloth of insurrection, or a group of women optically fragmenting the sobriety of a church tells us of fashion's ability to subvert the status quo whilst being the product of that same regime. There is an argument to suggest that tartan is to a certain degree a gendered textile, and so its incorporation in women's dress is already an act of textile subversion regardless of its political signification. Tartan's association with the kilt, with clanship descending through the male blood line, the existence of paler, more 'feminine' *arisaid* tartans (illus. 17) and the angularity and strict geometry of tartan's grids, all go towards its perception as a 'male' textile. Nicholson, when discussing the portrait of *Flora MacDonald*, utilizes this formation of gendered tartan: 'The gentle femininity of the sitter is offset by the angular lines of the tartan check which contrast vividly with her drooping hand and the soft outlines of the flowers.'[12]

Of course it could be argued that by concentrating on the optical effects tartan produced on the silhouettes of the period, or on its manifestation as a textile of insurgent masquerade, little is added to our actual knowledge of its position within conventional fashion history. However, in a period when fashion was relatively slow-moving, and the evidence both visual and literary for tartan's appearance in fashionable dress meagre, it is necessary to seek common causalities between these early, often conventional depictions of prominent Highlanders, and subsequent fashionable tartan images. In a study that attempts to escape the conventional chronological narratives beloved of fashion history, gaps and absences are unavoidable when extracting a particular aspect (in this case tartan) from the meta-narrative of fashion history. But these spaces in the tartan/fashion axis, rather than limiting the study, should be considered as liberating, providing room for other constructions, not necessarily tied to sartorial development. Already, by looking at the eighteenth century, two dominant themes emerge: that of tartan as agent of the body's optical disruption, and tartan as cloth of rebellion, themes which when joined by others (shortly to be investigated) will be seen to form new histories, narratives and impulses that can only be interrogated once the archive of tartan in fashion is 'thawed' out from its temporal stasis.

MASQUERADE

> **1.** A masked ball. **2.** Masquerade dress. **3.** Acting or living under false pretences; false outward show; pretence. A travesty.[13]

With the disintegration of the Jacobite cause and the subsequent reinvention of Highland traditions that occurred during the Romantic period, the conception of tartan as a cloth of rebellion, expressive of the possibility of resistance, is rapidly translated into its function as a cloth of nostalgia, evoking the figure of the tragic, heroic Highlander. As it became subsumed within narratives of British imperialism, particularly after its adoption by the Highland regiments, tartan's potential as a catalyst for Scottish independence becomes purely symbolic. Its metaphorical shift from source of sedition to site of Romantic myth, when coupled with its aforementioned visual qualities of disguise and distortion, make it possible to consider tartan increasingly as a textile of masquerade. In the latter half of the eighteenth century, the craze for masquerades and other similar functions grew rapidly, particularly in London, and meant that the fashionable elite who attended such functions were constantly seeking fresh inspiration for their disguises. Encounters with other cultures as a result of the expanding British Empire meant that 'foreign' costumes featured regularly alongside historical and literary outfits. It took a period of only twenty years or so, following Culloden, for Highland dress and tartan to become suitably exotic and depoliticized enough to also be included as masquerade costume. The conception of tartan as a form of disguise or fancy dress can be seen to inform many of its subsequent encounters with fashionable and indeed other forms of popular or subcultural dress. If the radicalism of the tartan-clad clan leaders and other Jacobite sympathizers evaporated post-Culloden, then the visual swagger of many of their eighteenth-century depictions survived in tartan outfits that have a discernibly theatrical quality. This sense of drama can be traced from the designs for the Regency stage to the emergence of punk in the late twentieth century, continuing with the work of Vivienne Westwood and Alexander McQueen into the twenty-first century.

43 Hand-coloured etching of William Macready as Rob Roy, 1818

The etching of William Macready as Rob Roy, from 1818, is typical of the nascent tide of Romanticism with which the Highlands and Scottish history would be engulfed due, primarily, to the enormous popularity of Walter Scott's novels and poems. Scott's works, many of which were swiftly turned into theatrical presentations, satisfied the desire for escapist entertainments demanded by the new urban audiences, which had swelled with the Industrial Revolution. The theatres of the Regency period, such as the expanded Drury Lane and Covent Garden in London, were so vast that the emphasis was on visual spectacle rather than lengthy speeches, which in many cases would have been inaudible. Scott's novels, with their dramatic settings and plots, joined the ranks of other theatrical spectacles typified by exotic locations and historical remoteness. Tartan, as the visual signifier of the Romantic Scottish Highlander, was the perfect costume for audiences hungry for colour and richness as an antidote to the drabness and harsh realities of the new industrialized centres. *Rob Roy*, *Guy Mannering*, *A Legend of Montrose*, *The Abbot* and *Mary Queen of Scots* were all works of Scott adapted for the theatre, with music and songs interspersing the action, utilizing tartan as the immediately recognizable, scene-setting cloth of choice for the principal characters.

It is interesting to note that in the etchings depicting Macready as Rob Roy and Macbeth, tartan is combined in his costumes with decorative armour, so that tartan plaids swagged over metal breastplates seem to have been the convention used to portray Highland warriors. This combination of defence and display is most clearly seen in etchings depicting characters for theatrical interpretations of Ossian (the fictional literary catalyst for the reinvention of Celtic romance), where heroic armour is combined with Scottish trappings such as plaids and feathered bonnets to 'conjure up the Scotch-epic world of Ossian'.[14] If not employed to clothe the heroes of Scott and Ossian, then tartan could also be relied upon to provide a magical livery for the protagonists in other spectacles such as the rapidly developing Romantic operas and ballets of the period; for example, the enormously popular and revolutionary ballet *La Sylphide* premiered in Paris in 1832 with a supernatural Highland setting.[15] A similar theatrical swagger and 'larger than life' quality has been noted in Sir Henry Raeburn's celebrated series of portraits of Scottish figures from the turn of the century. Works such as *Sinclair of Ulbster* of 1795, *The MacNab* of 1810 and *Colonel Alastair Macdonell of Glengarry* of 1812 have an enduring appeal due in no small degree to their use of theatrical tartan fancy dress which, as Nicholson points out, is 'a sort of mix-and-match of styles and periods with no proper historical precedent'.[16]

Tartan's popularity increased steadily amongst the upper classes throughout the nineteenth century. This was initially induced by the tartan extravaganza staged for George IV's visit to Edinburgh in 1822, and then by Victoria and Albert's promotion of the cloth at Balmoral. Tartan began to function increasingly as ceremonial fancy dress for the aristocracy, its original political, subversive significance now traduced and made into a costume that could be put on and off in a whimsical inversion of its former power. That George IV should have recognized tartan's theatrical possibilities is unsurprising, given his acute awareness of the power of a spectacular, well-staged ceremonial (unlike his Hanoverian predecessors and, indeed, Victoria), his coronation not only being 'done well, but turned into something poised between theatrical event and historical reconstruction'.[17] So when it came to his triumphant appearance in Edinburgh, one year after his coronation, he was fully aware of the impact that his tartan masquerade would produce.

The craze for aristocratic masquerade gathered strength throughout the nineteenth century, the Eglinton Tournament of 1839 being a noteworthy example. The tournament took place on Lord

Eglinton's Scottish estate, with pageants, lavish costumes, authentic props and banqueting tents recreating what he understood to be the 'golden age' of English medievalism. By all accounts, the event was a great success, attracting around 100,000 visitors, and the tourist souvenirs sold to commemorate the spectacle were a particular favourite. The double photographic portrait of Lords Tullibardine and Murray, from 1897, is typical of the journey made by tartan towards the close of the century, i.e. transformed from cloth of nationalistic and dynastic significance (albeit largely

44 Photograph of Lord Tullibardine and Lord George Murray. Lafayette Portrait Studios, 1897

mythical by this time) to the stuff of *fin de siècle* charade. The two lords pose for the camera in tartan kilts, powdered wigs, lace cuffs and jabots, and military jackets festooned with decorations in a pastiche of eighteenth-century dress, part Bonnie Prince Charlie, part regimental Highlander; a costume all the more ironic given their family's seminal role in the Jacobite rebellion and closeness to the Young Pretender.

TARTAN DIVERSIONS

The remnants of rebellion struggling for survival in late Victorian and Edwardian manifestations of tartan are, by the twentieth century, either completely submerged within tartan's role in Scottish ceremonial traditions, or transposed to a new arena of subversive social commentary. Tartan, at the turn of century, was increasingly used in the stage costumes of a number of Scottish entertainers who became stars of early twentieth-century music hall.[18] However, with the advent of cinema and then television sounding the death knell for vaudeville, even this last vestige of tartan's rebellious power disappears, becoming the commercialized and sentimentalized view of Scotland enshrined in long-running television programmes such as *The White Heather Club* and *The Kilt is My Delight*, and worn by Scottish TV stars such as Andy Stewart, Kenneth McKellar and Moira Andersen.[19] In these 1950s and 1960s television productions, tartan is reduced to a vestimentary cipher of the Scotland of Hogmanay, Burns Night, *The Skye Boat Song*, *Charlie Is My Darling* and other 'traditional' folk tunes. But even this most commercialized aspect of the Scottish tradition has a further layer of the masquerade, given that the supposedly authentic portrait of Scottish folk tradition in these programmes is undermined by the knowledge that many of the kilted and tartan-wearing 'folk' singers were in fact professional, in some cases opera singers, rather than the indigenous amateur singers they were often billed as. These light entertainment programmes aside, the only other popular and regularly transmitted representation of tartan was in the annual

45 Group of Scottish album covers including compilations of the long-running BBC Scotland shows *The White Heather Club* and *The Kilt is My Delight*

televising of the Edinburgh Military Tattoo, the quintessential ceremonial expression of tartan's transition from indigenous cloth of insurrection to textile of British military imperialism.

British and American cinema has dealt with tartan somewhat differently, utilizing it in a variety of film genres and to different ends, from the sophisticated comedic potential of Scottish/American translation in Rene Clair's *The Ghost Goes West* (1936), to the tartan mysticism of Powell and Pressburger's Scottish-set films such as *I Know Where I'm Going!* (1945), and more recent full-blown costume dramas such as *Kidnapped* (Delbert Mann, 1971), which has Michael Caine as Alan Breck the Jacobite rebel, resplendent in tartan suit, part eighteenth-century dandy, part Kings Road peacock. However, the success of contemporary offerings such as *Rob Roy* (Michael Caton-Jones, 1994) and *Braveheart* (Mel Gibson, 1995) seem ostensibly to reinvest tartan with some of its original rebellious connotations. Whether the films' crudely drawn depictions of the Scottish–English conflict were intentionally targeted at audiences who could trace a Scottish antecedence, and who (particularly in America) were tired of being fed vehicles where England was depicted as the cultural 'well-spring' from which they should drink, is debatable. But the success of *Braveheart* obviously satisfied a desire for a representation of pre-Union Scotland and has done much to increase the already popular transatlantic genealogical research into early Highland customs and dress, and its clan associations in particular. Of course all costume film is influenced by, and in some cases influences, the Zeitgeist in which the films are produced, and so in a socio-historical context *Braveheart,* and other films that depicted early examples of civil unrest, reflected the perceived social and economic fragmentation of contemporary America.[20]

The polarization that characterized many societies, not just America, in the late twentieth century, has been construed as contributing to certain dominant characteristics within the rarefied world of contemporary fashion. It is interesting to speculate whether the thirteenth-century wrapped plaids and other glamorously 'crude' Hollywood versions of Highland dress in productions such as *Braveheart* were a cinematic equivalent of Japanese postmodern anti-fashion, which eschewed formal tailoring and favoured 'unsophisticated' wrapping and tying. Closer to home, for American audiences at least, *Braveheart*'s tartans could be seen as a response to the so-called 'grunge' look of the early 1990s made infamous by Marc Jacobs's collection for Perry Ellis, with its 'blue collar' tartans and 'slacker' approach to dressing down. Whatever the influence may, or may not, have been on the costuming of these films, it is now increasingly common to see varieties of plaids (belted or otherwise) being worn at Scottish gatherings, as opposed to the 'British' shorter kilts, as expressions of disassociation with the English domination of the Highlands. But these sartorial rebellions, whatever their origin, are fleeting, and as Mikhail Bakhtin reminds us, are temporary suspensions of the status quo, a licensed inversion where, momentarily, via the adoption of a costume, the prevailing cultural patrimony is discredited. However, this opposition is limited, and like Cinderellas these pre-Union 'Highlanders' must give up their masquerade.

The recognition of tartan as a form of masquerade, and further still the impossibility of it functioning as anything other than an 'empty' vestimentary sign ready to be filled with whatever significance the wearer chooses, has provided inspiration for designers and artists. The work of the art collective Szuper Gallery, whose videos and associated projects interrogate the shared corporate strategies of both the culture industry and the financial sector, regularly occupy the workspaces of institutions that act as self-regulating mediators of society. These have ranged from police offices to the London Stock Exchange and the headquarters of the financial news agency Bloomberg. Their practice consists of members and associates of the group inhabiting these spaces and adopting the

46 Szuper Gallery, still from *Good Morning Mr Bloomberg*, video, 9 mins, 1999

gestures, procedures, discourse and costumes that they perceive to be typical and expressive of the philosophies of the organization concerned. Ruth Maclennan, one of the members of Szuper Gallery, appeared in a specially made suit in the Maclennan tartan, giving her costume a personal as well as conceptual significance. Her tartan suit managed to convey a certain hard-nosed corporate appearance, referencing the concept of 'power dressing' that emerged in the 1980s as a marketing strategy for women's business clothing, alongside the obvious tartan connotations of tradition, stability and reliability. The ability of tartan to function as corporate masquerade is evidence yet again of the constantly shifting popular perception of the pattern. Szuper Gallery's use of the fabric plays with this knowledge and uses methods derived from the world of marketing to 'brand' one of its members with the perceived values of tartan, acknowledging the relationship between the clan system and corporate 'team building'.

INTERRUPTION

It is perhaps in the late 1970s, with the emergence of punk, that tartan recaptures some of its former rebellious associations. Tartan, along with other specific vestimentary codes, swiftly became an essential component of punk clothing, particularly after its initial 'do-it-yourself' phase characterized by bin-liner skirts, second-hand clothes, and white shirts variously embellished and

47 Punks, 1979

48 (This Page and Facing Page) Tracy and Little Debs, shop assistants in Seditionaries

pinned. It is with Vivienne Westwood and Malcolm McLaren's launch of Seditionaries, the last of their retail incarnations at 430 Kings Road in late 1976, that tartan becomes indelibly associated with punk. Having been the emerging punk movement's 'outfitters' from the mid-1970s, Westwood and McLaren had produced a series of seminal garments that drew on, and were in turn inspired by, a 'polysemy of elements drawn from the history of youth culture, sexual fetish wear, urban decay and extremist politics', as Jon Savage expresses it, in *England's Dreaming*.[21] By 1977, with punk firmly established as the favourite fodder of the tabloid press, and the success of McLaren's music project, the *Sex Pistols*, Westwood had expressed a desire to undermine previous assumptions made about her as a designer, and to unsettle her established clientele. Jordan, the archetypal muse of punk recalled: 'Vivienne wanted to go high fashion; she made these proper outfits that locked together. She wanted to create a total image',[22] and it is in this context that tartan re-emerges as the cloth of dissent (illus. 48 and 49).

Seditionaries, the shop that showcased Westwood's emergence as a major force in late twentieth-century fashion design was – from its name to its impenetrable milky glass windows, and interior photo-panels of the fire bombing of Dresden by British forces in the Second World War – an expression of mercantile anti-Establishmentarianism. The history of tartan as a fabric expressive of revolt and opposition, its remarkable status as a cloth outlawed by the English and its association with royalty made it the perfect textile for a range of clothing that aimed to make anarchy, alienation and indeed sedition wearable, and for dressing the voice of this challenging position: the Sex Pistols. The Pistols' paraphrasing of the national anthem in their 1977 hit 'God Save the Queen' is made doubly ironic when considered in the context of the original anthem's history. First reputed to have been performed in 1745 and sung in support of George II after the defeat of his army at Prestonpans by Bonnie Prince Charlie's troops, a rarely sung sixth verse was added (quoted below) which includes a prayer for the success of General Wade's army, assembling at Newcastle, and whose victory would lead to the suppression of tartan amongst the other cultural dissembling of the Highlands.

> Lord grant that Marshal Wade
> May by Thy mighty aid
> Victory bring.
> May he sedition hush,
> And like a torrent rush,
> Rebellious Scots to crush.
> God save the King![23]

The marketing of England's history of colonial atrocities, something Hollywood blockbusters such as *Braveheart* and *Rob Roy* have capitalized upon, was given perfect sartorial expression in Westwood's use of tartan, which ironically transcended its political inspiration and quickly became the subject of innumerable fashion spreads, shorn of any political overtones, from 1977 onwards. Simultaneously tartan became the key component in the clothing ranges sold in the proliferation of more commercial and affordable punk clothing outlets, starting with the establishment of BOY, also in the Kings Road. Whilst Westwood's creations were well beyond the reach of the average member of the 'blank generation', tartan, along with safety pins and bin liners, was relatively easy to find as second-hand garments that could, if not worn in their original state, be cut up and made into home-made punk items such as 'nappies' or 'apron' kilts (illus. 47).[24] This economical aspect recasts the early 1970s 'do-it-yourself', tartan-wearing punk as a possible model for the 'calculating' consumer of Barthes, previously discussed in the section on *The Economy of the Kilt*.[25] The popularity of tartan and its endurance as a staple of the punk wardrobe is of course on one level due to the influence of Westwood and her imitators, but it also managed to deliver to significantly large numbers of alienated and disaffected youth an iconic membership of a clan that had nothing to do with Scottish dynastic claims but:

> spoke of many things: urban primitivism; the breakdown of confidence in a common language; the availability of cheap, second-hand clothes; the fractured nature of perception in an accelerating, media-saturated society; the wish to offer up the body as a jumble of meanings.[26]

Whether the irony of an English punk wearing the cloth of a Highland culture that English imperialism had helped to dismantle would have registered in the majority of its wearers is debatable. But the more recent use of tartan as a form of Scottish masquerade typified by the previously discussed entertainments of the *White Heather Club* and others like it did have a popular cultural resonance that the average punk fan would have been conscious of.

Given punk's chief legacy as a musical phenomenon that delivered a cathartic shock to what was widely perceived as the moribund state of white popular music of the 1970s, it is ironic that tartan was so insolubly linked with certain Scottish artists who represented some of punk's *bête noires*: middle of the road rock 'dinosaurs' and manufactured pop. Both the Bay City Rollers (illus. 63) and Rod Stewart (illus. 29) used tartan extensively in the construction of their nationalistic, and arguably musically conservative images, whilst English punks adopted tartan as a vestimentary sign of musical rebellion. Interestingly, the Sex Pistols' 'God Save the Queen' throws up another oblique reference to the popular history of tartan, in that the hit is reputed to have sold more copies in Jubilee week than the number one record at that time: tartan-wearing Rod Stewart's cover version of 'The First Cut is the Deepest'.

FANCY DRESS

From her influence on early punk's subversion of, and homage to, tartan's revolutionary and prohibited past, to her apotheosis today as grande dame of fashion, Vivienne Westwood's career is metonymic of tartan's previously stated trajectory from rebellion to authoritarianism. Tartan's history bears an uncanny resemblance to her own progression: a series of inversions, changes of fortune and eventual institutionalization justifying tartan's constant presence within her work. Westwood's early tartan punk clothing, due to its exclusivity, was never the 'cloth of the people' that it was to the Highlander and Jacobite. But as a textile of dissent and resistance once it had 'gone downmarket' it fulfilled, for less label-conscious punks, an evocative function as a textile that unified its wearers in a common rejection of established cultural hegemony. Just as Highland culture post-Culloden underwent a process of Romanticization and fabrication, so too (after the media-driven hostile reaction to punks had become yesterday's news) there started a similar process of sentimental mythologizing, so that the heady, tartan-clad days of 1977 are remembered as a mythical golden age by contemporary pillars of the cultural establishment.

Meanwhile, Westwood was establishing herself as a significant influence in the world of design, eventually securing a place in the firmament of fashion royalty, and producing couture clothes that would not look out of place on the backs of the nineteenth-century aristocrats who had elevated tartan's status. Just as tartan's new-found popularity amongst the elite and the military influenced the growth of the commercial production of tartan in the nineteenth century, so too did her promotion of the cloth (even more noticeably with the Harris Tweed industry) help revive a flagging tartan manufacturing industry at the close of the twentieth century. The paradox of this one-time subversive designer's transformation into doyenne of the runway is not lost on Westwood, who has employed irony and parody as a constant methodology in her work, and she confessed that:

> I got tired of looking at clothes from this point of view of rebellion – I found it exhausting, and after a while I wasn't sure if I was right. I'm sure that if there is such a thing as the 'Anti-Establishment' – it feeds the Establishment.[27]

And, with an expanding illustrious clientele, her position as sartorial provider to a global cultural meritocracy is now firmly established.

Looking at Westwood's use of tartan, a bewildering array of references can be discerned. Many of her designs are contextualized by the collision of elements from French and English historical costume of the eighteenth and nineteenth centuries, underscored by her deployment of French haute couture techniques and English tailoring. This Anglo-French axis naturally invokes the 'Auld Alliance' between France and Scotland (see section in Chapter 5, *Regulation Tartan*), with which the history of tartan resonates: a resonance residing in the support for the Catholic Scottish Royal House of Stuart, as well as the subsequent fascination for tartan and the kilt that occurred with the presence of the Highland regiments in Paris during and after the Napoleonic wars. In a series of swaggering collections that pillaged historical costume, Westwood uses tartan to reference its own history as well as provide ironic comment on other conventions of dress, and in a variety of materials from traditional wool to silk taffeta. In 'Dressing Up', Autumn/Winter 1991–2, the masquerade of Lords Tullibardine and Murray (illus. 44) is evoked with pastiches of tartan eighteenth-century dress; in the same collection, tartan duster coats were teamed with busbies reminiscent of early Highland regimental uniform (illus. 35). 'On Liberty', Autumn/Winter 1994–5, used tartan to evoke the colonial venture, with Naomi Campbell appearing in full-skirted tartan dress replete with pie-crust frills and oversized head-wrap, a comment on Scotland's exploitation of the Caribbean, perhaps. 'Anglomania', Autumn/Winter 1993–4, used a similar silk tartan but this time for outfits that explored a 'chocolate box' approach to historical costume, reminiscent of the productions of the English Gainsborough Film company of the 1940s, which bordered on the sartorial 'style' of Moira Anderson (illus. 51).

Elsewhere, tartan *fhéilidh-Mor, fhéilidh beags* and jackets and trews swap gender and become evocations of Highland fantasy for Westwood's runway muses. Blanket skirts, spencer jackets, fitted bodices with leg o' mutton sleeves, smocks, miniskirts and pantaloons derived from the costumes of Victorian acrobats have all been presented in tartan (illus. 49). Dress Stewart and Royal Stewart are generally the favoured setts for Westwood's early collections, but increasingly she has used a diverse range of traditional and contemporary tartans, as well as setts she has designed herself in conjunction with the specialist tartan manufacturers, Lochcarron, such as the McBrick (using a colour palette inspired by the London urban landscape) and the tartan that she named

49 Vivienne Westwood, 'Portrait', Autumn/Winter 1990–1

50 Bodice detail. Woven trimmed tartan with silk fringe and velvet. English, c.1860

MacAndreas in honour of her husband, Andreas Kronthaler. Westwood's delight in subverting traditional chronologies, gender divisions and national stereotypes in her collections evokes the characteristic function of the carnival where for a brief period, hierarchies are inverted and disorder and chaos rule. Mikhail Bakhtin's formulation of the carnivalesque seems especially appropriate as a description of a Westwood collection from the 1990s:

> There is so much turnabout, so many opposite faces and intentionally upset proportion. We see this first of all in the participants' apparel. Men are transvested as women and vice versa, costumes are turned inside out, and outer garments replace underwear.[28]

The collision of different tartans in the same outfit, and the use of bias-cut tartan, are reminiscent of the earliest paintings of clan leaders who similarly wear a multitude of tartan and are often depicted wearing tartan trews or stockings cut on the cross. The historical custom of mixing different tartan setts and using checks both vertically and diagonally is recreated by Westwood in her love of argyle (originally based on the Argyle tartan, but adapted for knitwear), which she uses for knitted trews, ties, stockings and sweaters, in combination with tartan patterns to achieve a chequerboard overload. This quality of carnivalesque excess in much of her work incorporating tartan not only relates to the early portraits mentioned above, but to a particular series of images of the Young Pretender, which Dunbar describes as:

> the extraordinary series known as the 'Harlequin' type. In these, Charles is shown in a small, round, flat bonnet precariously balanced on top of his head, a tartan jacket and breeches, white gaiters to below the knee, large leather gauntlets and a most comic sword.[29]

With a change of gender, this could easily be the description of a Westwood ensemble rather than the description of mid-eighteenth century portraiture. The figure of Harlequin, central to the carnivalesque tradition, has an interesting relationship to tartan (which will be explored in Chapter 7, *Tartan Toffs*). But it is perhaps worth noting that the Harlequin costume with which we are most familiar today – that of an elegant, tight-fitting 'suit' covered with diamond-shaped lozenges and which Westwood's work often invokes (most directly in her collection 'Voyage to Cythera', Autumn/Winter 1989–90) – occurs in British pantomime from the same period of Regency theatre that saw Scott's works turned into dramatic productions, and tartan used as theatrical spectacle.

A virtuoso ability to 'stitch' together styles and techniques from the historical 'dressing-up box' into a seamless vestimentary collage has become the hallmark of a Westwood collection, an ability she has honed since her earliest forays into the archive of fashion, and which some commentators have suggested has become less fertile and increasingly formulaic. As with the similarity between certain of Westwood's creations and the paintings of Bonnie Prince Charlie's costume described above, an assessment of early nineteenth-century women's dress could be equally applicable to her more elaborate collections:

> Art evolved new shapes for women, or revived those which had been forgotten … and gradually from having been a picture frame, the dress developed into a picture itself of which the human body was merely the invisible support. The dress and the wearer had, in a sense, exchanged functions.[30]

Most criticism of her designs appears to condense around the collections from the mid-1990s, which interestingly are the ones in which tartan was used most extensively. This adverse reaction can in part be attributed to the perceived betrayal of tartan's original subversive power in these presentations, the significance of tartan as a cloth of resistance lost underneath a welter of historical masquerade. However, whatever the critical opinion of her continuing relevance to contemporary fashion, her utilization of tartan cannot be underestimated and a testament to this can be found in the collections of designers worldwide (particularly Japan) who reference her work, often using tartan as the instantly recognizable textile homage to her influence.

51 (This Page and Facing Page) Vivienne Westwood, 'Anglomania', Autumn/Winter 1993–4

The dissemination of tartan abroad, via the Highland regiments, coincides with eighteenth-century fashion's increasingly symbiotic relationship to military dress, the regiments' incorporation of tartan into their uniforms adding a further layer of exchange between the two hierarchies of the military and the fashion industry. When specifically considering martial tartan rather than the overall effect military styles of dress had on civilian fashion at this period, the relationship is extremely intricate. Firstly, the success of the Highland regiments in the Napoleonic and other campaigns resulted in a rash of tartan-wearing in Britain as sartorial support for the brave Highlanders defending the borders of the empire, and this was to continue apace into the early nineteenth century. Tartan then started to migrate into the fashionable drawing rooms and other spaces of polite society in major Scottish cities such as Edinburgh, and as the success of the Scottish regiments increased, so too did tartan's influence, transformed into a patriotic cloth for fashionable dress amongst English society also. Fashionable women wore female versions of military uniform, continuing the element of masquerade and gender swapping that we have already seen in some of the female Jacobite sympathizers' costumes.

AULD ALLIANCE

Congruent with tartan's popularity within British society was the French fascination for the kilted Highlander, whose appearance in Paris and other cities after the Battle of Waterloo caused an immediate sensation accompanied by a frisson of sexual excitement. The French fascination with things English, and by extension Scottish, was part of a series of sartorially centred obsessions that the French have had periodically with British forms of dress and gentleman's tailoring in particular. Relatively simple, restrained, yet impeccably tailored men's coats and sporting costumes had begun to influence French fashions in the latter part of the eighteenth century. The admiration for sober good taste found its perfect *métier* in pre-Revolutionary France, when the excess and opulence of French fashion as worn by the aristocracy was already falling from favour, soon becoming unacceptable garb for the new 'model citizen'. A contemporary account from the period comments on what would certainly not be the last in a series of French Anglomanias:

> Just now English clothing is all the wear. Rich man's son, sprig of nobility, counter-jumper – you see them dressed all alike in the long coat, cut close, thick stockings, puffed stock; with hats on their heads and a riding-switch in their hands. Not one of the gentlemen thus attired, however, has ever crossed the Channel or can speak one word of English.[6]

So noticeable have these Anglomanias been that in our own period it has inspired designers such as Vivienne Westwood to create whole collections based on the phenomenon, and the Metropolitan Museum of Art in New York recently paid homage to them in its Anglomania show of 2006, which suggested that appreciation of English style was more than just a Gallic preference. To return to the beginning of the nineteenth century, however, the presence of the Scottish regiments in Paris and the attraction they held for the fashionable Parisian can be gauged by the risqué drawings recording the encounter, which can be seen either as a logical extension of the pre-Revolutionary Anglomania, or perhaps even as a reaction to them (illus. 67). In this context, the French adoption of tartan as fashion can be understood as a rejection of the English as conquerors of Napoleon, and functions as a sartorial expression of the auld Catholic alliance, before Scotland was subsumed within the construct of Britain.

Whatever the underlying impetus might have been, during the early nineteenth century tartan was increasingly worn in France, ironically commodifying the badge of the potential oppressor and ushering in the first in a long series of 'tartanmanias'. These seem to punctuate French couture with increasing regularity and with even more lasting effect, it could be argued, than the aforementioned Anglomanias. The fascination the Romantic reconstruction of Scotland held for French designers

54 John Galliano, menswear, Autumn/Winter 2005–6

can be gauged from early twentieth-century fashion plates featuring outfits finished off with *garniture écossaise* or skirts in *laine d'Ecosse*. More recently, tartan as a component part of global fancy dress has been continuously appropriated by French designers from Yves Saint Laurent to Jean-Paul Gaultier, and sees no sign of abating, judging by the highly influential tartan Autumn/Winter 2006 collections of designers such as Balenciaga and Alexander McQueen (showing in Paris), proof that the French tartanmania is alive and well. A perfect summation of this sartorial 'auld alliance' can be gained from an outfit taken from the Autumn/Winter 2005–6 menswear collection of John Galliano (the English-trained deserter who 'ran away' to Paris), which teams a Royal Stewart combed wool tartan greatcoat with a modified sheepskin tricorne reminiscent of that worn by the Emperor Napoleon. It is an ensemble that returns us to the point of origin of tartan's Gallic transformation into fashionable dress, and which can be understood as a vestimentary triumph for the Jacobite cause some 250 years after its defeat, expressing an enduring support for Scotland that undermines England's somewhat uneasy alliance.

TOY SOLDIERS

Since the late eighteenth century, military styles had left an indelible mark on fashion, with decorations such as frogging, braiding, military buttons and other adaptable elements commonly incorporated into women's dress throughout the nineteenth century. During the twentieth century, specific items of military dress, rather than just details, were adopted as fashionable dress, such as greatcoats, reefer and flying jackets, boiler suits, and with the continuing contemporary ubiquity of camouflage and army fatigues, military styles have proved perennially popular. Military dress is constantly referenced, reinvented and collaged with other garments, year in and year out, on runways and on the High Street, with army surplus stores providing rich pickings for the fashionable and economic dresser alike.

Much has been written about the phenomenon of fashion's relationship with military dress. For example, it has been suggested that this relationship is at its most noticeable in the West during periods of intense military activity, and therefore military fashions are worn as a form of sartorial support, as in the case of the Napoleonic Wars. More recently, a similar sartorial support for the military was achieved by the incorporation of the battledress jacket into women's fashion during the Second World War. Conversely, it has also been proposed that fashion's appropriation of the military coincides with periods of relative stability, when society feels secure enough to invoke potential discord as a sartorial fantasy; fashionable military dress in this case functioning more as a presentiment of strife to come. Today, unfortunately, with the acceleration of global warfare, it is likely to be a reflection of both, given that there is always a surfeit of conflicts, great or small, from which a designer can choose to be inspired by. Perhaps the most obvious conclusion to be drawn is that military styles remain one of fashion's most enduring sartorial referents, whether expressive of patriotism or, conversely, anti-Establishment positions, as happened with the adoption of army fatigues and camouflage by youthful American pacifists during the height of the Vietnam War.

Similarly, arguments have been raised that it is only when certain garments have become outmoded or superseded, as is the case with industrial wear or workwear, as well as military forms of dress, that they can then be transformed into fashion. Walter Benjamin's conception of fashion as a

55 Figurine of an officer of the 42nd Royal
Highlanders (Black Watch). Porcelain. Dresden, c. 1815

series of annihilations, where the novel or latest fashion must inevitably lead to the death of the one preceding it, seems relevant to fashion's regular confrontations with obsolete occupations, industry and institutions, including aspects of the military. From these confrontations fashion carries off sartorial spoils of war, which it transforms into vestimentary trophies. Therefore woollen greatcoats and leather trench coats, along with other archaic pieces of kit, which have long been abandoned by contemporary armies and replaced by more practical and technologically advanced garments, are the items that crop up with most regularity within the collections of military-inspired designers. The necessity of the extinction of one form of industry for fashionable evolution to be maintained

56 Vivienne Westwood, 'Dressing Up', Autumn/ Winter 1991–2. The model's hat can be seen as an example of the continuing influence of military styles on fashionable dress

is echoed by Philippe Perrot's reference to George Darwin's (the son of Charles Darwin) suggestion concerning obsolete fashionable details:

> living beings and clothing develop in the same way: clothing, like men, evolves in terms of genetic inheritance, natural selection, and the imperceptible degradation of organic forms. This analogy illuminates the transition from the pure function-sign, the signifying 'useful', to the ornamental 'useless': the necktie, the notch on coat collars, the buttons along the sleeve, or the rivets on blue jeans seem to be the homologues in clothes of the appendix or tonsils in people, and equally devoid of use-value.[7]

Tartan's relationship to uniform and its subsequent incorporation into fashionable dress is of a different capacity, however. It is the very pattern itself that has been adapted to construct uniforms, real and fashionable, rather than any one specific garment. Tartan, particularly with the standardization of the government setts, gave the Highland regiments a necessary homogeneity whether they chose to adopt kilts or trews as part of their uniform, the tartan itself (with the minor additions of over-stripes) providing the unifying badge of Scottishness. Khaki and air force blue can register as 'military' colours, but not exclusively, whilst camouflage resonates too strongly of combat to ever escape its bellicose associations. Only tartan, presumably because of its established dynastic and nationalistic associations that pre-date its adoption by the military, can inhabit the many and varied territories of uniform, military or otherwise. As has been stated, tartan was adopted as a fashionable acknowledgement of the Highland regiments' success in the early nineteenth century, but rather than imitating slavishly any particular items of Highland regimental uniform, tartan was utilized by fashion as a fabric that was easily understood as having regimental connotations, amongst many others. Due to the fact that the major tartan components of the Highland uniform – either kilt or trews – had already existed as the 'traditional' dress of the Highlander, tartan's status within the various historical confrontations between the military and fashion has always remained amorphous, at once referencing the military when suitably underscored by other elements, but also signifying meaning beyond the purely martial.

FROM PARADE GROUND TO PLAYGROUND

Tartan, from its earliest commercial production, was immediately used as a textile for a variety of other sorts of uniforms apart from its adoption by the newly formed regiments. The Act of Proscription of 1746 is once again seen to be pivotal in this process, as once the cloth's original anti-Establishment functions had been eradicated, its residual qualities of collective identity could be tapped and adapted to make uniforms that signalled obedience rather than dissent. In the records and order books of early commercial tartan manufacturers such as Wilson & Son of Bannockburn, aside from their supplies of regimental and civilian tartan, there is evidence of it being used to clothe the workforces of Scottish-owned plantations (which will be dealt with in detail in Chapter 11, *Colonization*), and put to a variety of other uses. For example, in 1818 the company responded to a request from His Royal Highness Maximilian, Archduke of Austria by sending samples of Mackintosh, Stuart, Macfarlane and Macgregor tartans that might be suitable for clothing orphaned children. The sett that was eventually selected is unknown, but in terms of durability, economy and regulatory associations, tartan would have been an ideal choice for Maximilian's philanthropic initiative. Maximilian's tartan orphans presumably shared the same ambiguous feelings towards the wearing of uniform that Robert Walser feels as one of the members of the Benjementa Institute:

> Now, the wearing of uniforms simultaneously humiliates and exalts us. We look like unfree
> people, and that is possibly a disgrace, but we also look nice in our uniforms, and that sets
> us apart from the deep disgrace of those people who walk in their very own clothes but
> in torn and dirty ones. To me, for instance, wearing a uniform is very pleasant because I
> never did know, before, what clothes to put on.[8]

The use of tartan to make uniforms for children is one that has survived from the nineteenth century until the present day: schoolgirls wearing an approximation of a kilt in the form of a pleated tartan skirt are a ubiquitous sight. Tartan's adoption as school uniform most probably stems from the widespread popularity of what became known in the nineteenth century as the 'Scotch Suit'. The photograph, taken in 1862, of Master H. G. E. Gladstone by Camille Silvy is typical of these outfits. The little boy wears tartan kilt, dress jacket and, judging from its size, what must have been an adult sporran. Variations of this outfit became enormously popular as formal dress for boys from the mid-nineteenth century onwards, and were rivalled only by the sailor suit for less formal occasions. These outfits originated with the Victorian obsession for adult, fancy-dress versions of uniform; these had maintained their popularity from the beginning of the nineteenth century, a residue of the eighteenth-century masquerade discussed previously, and which was extended to provide uniforms for children.

57 Photograph of Master H. G. E. Gladstone by Camille Silvy, 1862

Scottish children had obviously been wearing kilts and other tartan garments for many years, as had other prominent scions such as the future George III, who is depicted in a portrait of the Prince of Wales's children from 1746, dressed in a tartan and lace-trimmed coat. But it is to Victoria and Albert's acquisition of Balmoral and the development of their Highland fantasies that the Scotch Suit owes its nineteenth-century popularity. When Victoria's sons, including her eldest, Bertie, appeared in full Highland dress at the opening of the Great Exhibition in 1851 (illus. 58), Scottish outfits for boys became fashionable, and further appearances by the royal children in Highland outfits, such as at the wedding of the Princess Royal in 1858, consolidated

58 Henry Courtney Selous, *The Opening of the Great Exhibition by Queen Victoria on 1st May, 1851*. Oil on canvas, 1851–2. Detail showing Victoria's eldest son, Bertie, the future Edward VII, in Highland dress

this popularity. An infantile version of the 'auld alliance' and revival of tartanmania was created when, during Victoria's state visit to Paris in 1855, the Prince of Wales appeared in full Highland dress and caused an immediate sensation. The fashion also spread to America where, amongst other prominent figures, the future President Roosevelt was photographed in a Scotch Suit. As the popularity of these Scottish children's uniforms increased, hybrid versions of the more usual kilt and jacket emerged, often somewhat bizarre, as Elizabeth Ewing suggests in her *History of Children's*

Costume: 'There were also many grotesque variations of the traditional attire. Kilt-like contraptions were worn as variations of the knee-length tunics of small boys. White lace-trimmed pantaloons often hung below youthful kilts…'[9]

As the fashion for boys to be dressed in fancy-dress uniforms, whether Scotch Suits, sailor suits or other costumes, dwindled with the progression of the twentieth century, elements of Highland dress migrated to school uniforms, swapping gender in the process. It is the legacy of this Victorian children's fashion that accounts for the preponderance of girls' kilts in contemporary school uniforms. The associations between school community and clan system make tartan an appealing choice for school uniform. As was the case with the Highland regiments, tartan encourages communal support and a sense of belonging, and when incorporated into school uniform identifies

59 The Russian pop duo, Tatu, filming a video in 2003 where they are accompanied by tartan-clad schoolgirls

the wearer as belonging to that institution, making its presence within the local community more prominent. The simultaneous loss of autonomy and promotion of pride in a collective identity activated by the wearing of uniform is, in the case of tartan uniforms, both reinforced and to a certain extent undermined. The visual uniformity presented by a group dressed in identical tartan, be that military, scholastic or otherwise, is undeniable, the very nature of a tartan pattern transforming separate individuals into a homogeneous gridded block. But, due to tartan's troubled history the sight of any group wearing tartan also inevitably signifies rebellion and non-conformity, an irony apparently lost during its widespread adoption as school uniform.

Tartan's Celtic heritage accounts for the high proportion of Catholic schools that have adopted it as part of their uniform, especially within Europe and America, whilst tartan's other geographical and biographical associations has meant that schools have a wealth of appropriate setts from which to choose. Alternatively, many schools have chosen to design new tartans with their own concomitant colour symbolism. In terms of the actual kilt as a component of girls' school uniform, the economy afforded by a garment whose fit can be easily altered (with traditional kilts at least), the ease of movement provided by the pleats and, not least, the pedagogical ideology expressed by the adoption of a traditional male garment by girls, who historically have been denied the educational advantages open to boys, all go towards making tartan and the kilt eminently suitable for school uniform.

The wholesale adoption of Western military uniform that took place during the Meiji period in Japan (1868–1912) also influenced Japanese school uniform. European naval uniforms in particular, compounded by the influence of the Russo–Japanese War (1904–1905), led to versions of the sailor suit being developed as school uniform for both Japanese girls and boys, although today sailor uniform is primarily used for girls. Similarly, a version of Prussian army uniform was widely adopted for boys, its chief element consisting of a military-style jacket with a standing collar. Joining these two infantile versions of military uniform, a further girls' uniform was developed during the early part of the twentieth century, consisting of blazer, white blouse and pleated tartan skirt. The particular fascination for European nineteenth-century cultural institutions that still pervades Japanese society today, particularly those aspects that are expressive of nostalgia, innocence and tradition, can partly explain the enduring allure that the contemporary uniformed schoolchild exerts.

Historically inspired school uniforms that simultaneously speak of conformity, tradition and British history have become contemporary iconic referents for Japan and populate the pages of *manga*, the storyboards of *animé*, the fantasies of the Japanese sex industry and the narratives of horror films with increasing regularity. The image of the schoolgirl in a pleated tartan skirt, in particular, generates a number of erotic and sadistic fantasies willingly served by the film industry and other more febrile cultural enterprises. *Kogal* (the term given to ordinary schoolgirls influenced by the sexualization of their uniform) have become a Japanese phenomenon, a typical *kogal* rolling up the waistband of her kilt or pleated skirt to form a mini-kilt and wearing her socks purposely loose and crumpled in a dishevelled manner. Whilst the particular sexual cathexsis associated with the kilt will be dealt with elsewhere, it is interesting to note that the eroticism that so often contextualizes the Japanese kilted schoolgirl runs counter to the traditional 'asexuality' promoted by European and North American uniforms, where the kilt suggests a less eroticized uniform than traditional skirt or figure-revealing trousers. Brian McVeigh, in his *Wearing Ideology*, suggests that in contemporary Japanese culture: 'Rather than pieces of garments associated with being dependent, childlike and asexual, uniforms are transformed into attire laden with messages about being independent, adult and sexual.'[10]

Whilst the sexual objectification of the tartan-skirted schoolgirl is firmly embedded in Japanese culture, and is a central trope of the cult of cuteness or *kawai*, tartan's ability to 'unfix' itself from any entrenched position seems to be surfacing, cinematically at least. In films such as *Battle Royale II*, the tartan-clad students of Shikanotoride Junior High, seconded into becoming a marauding hit squad, and *Kill Bill's* deadly tartan-skirted assassin Go-Go Yubari, seem at last to provide an antidote to the unremitting eroticization that typically characterizes tartan school uniform.[11] Of course, the extremely violent tendencies displayed by the children in these films might, it could be argued, only increase the sado-erotic fantasies of the tartan-loving school uniform fan. But, could it not also suggest that, just as tartan was worn as a sign of rebellion against the English in eighteenth-century Scotland, so too are these fictional depictions of tartan school uniform a rejection of the misogynistic cultural patrimony of twenty-first-century Japanese popular culture?

Tartan, it seems, has become indelibly associated with childhood since its wholesale adoption by the Victorians and this regressive connotation has joined the ranks of tartan's other sociocultural functions. Not only has tartan been used for school uniforms, but it has also become a staple element in other forms of children's clothing – the tartan party dress or at least tartan-sashed and otherwise trimmed frock, a reliable garment signalling tradition, nostalgia and a retreat to a lost age

60 Chiyaki Kuriyama as Go-Go Yubari, the kilted schoolgirl assassin in *Kill Bill*

of innocence. Again the Victorians were the instigators of this fashion, led by Victoria and Albert, who dressed their female offspring in tartan dresses that were widely copied, the trend becoming abbreviated to the tartan sash as an essential component for girl's dresses. This aspect of tartan as infantile uniform has also periodically inspired mainstream fashion, where the use of tartan has often been a textile indicator of certain trends towards the 'childish' in fashionable clothing. The reaction against the sophisticated and elaborate fashions of the previous decade that revolutionized fashion in the 1960s naturally referenced the easier simplicity of childhood garments. Alongside hats reminiscent of babies' bonnets and balaclavas, Mary Jane shoes and short, empire-line shift dresses, tartan, bold checks and short kilt skirts became characteristic of mid-1960s women's fashions. And this trend towards clothing reminiscent of childhood has been subsequently revived and adapted throughout the latter half of the twentieth century and into the twenty-first. Tartan – used as an indicator of childhood fantasies and as the uniform of childhood – has been capitalized upon by designers as much as for its nationalistic, tribal and other socio-historical associations, and according to the particular formations of childhood being referenced at any given fashion moment, tartan is a reliable point of entry into those constructions. So, a Zandra Rhodes white chiffon party dress replete with petticoats and silk tartan sash from 1982 bears an uncanny resemblance to the Victorian girl's party dress of almost exactly 100 years earlier, whilst the American 'preppy' look (beloved and popularized by designers such as Ralph Lauren) with its inherent Anglophilia, regularly appropriated the tartan kilt. A typical outfit by Bill Blass (another exponent of this look) from 1991, features not only a schoolgirl kilt, but also teams it with beret, pea coat, knee socks and loafers in a perfect amalgam of patrician Anglo-American uniformity.

Tartan's association with dressing up has also meant that the pattern can serve as a reliable stalwart for any number of anxious Christmas party-goers, who, unsure of current trends, will adopt recreations of children's tartan taffeta dresses or, if male, tartan accessories such as bow ties and cummerbunds in the steadfast belief that these tartan 'uniforms' will create the appropriate air of festive sophistication. The persistence of tartan's childhood associations thereby remains unchallenged and continues to function as an instant transmitter of concepts such as 'playfulness' or a 'relaxed attitude' to dressing for any number of editorials and fashion spreads.

UNIFORMITY

At Balmoral, Victoria and Albert insisted that their staff wore Highland dress, and in the tradition of a clan leader's retinue wearing their chief's tartan, members of the royal household wore the Balmoral tartan, specifically designed by Prince Albert, alongside other setts. Elsewhere on Highland estates in the Victorian period, tartan was also being worn less as a sign of clan allegiance or geographical origin and increasingly as the uniform of servitude. Victoria's faithful gillie, John Brown, and her piper servants can be seen as the forerunners of today's corporate tartan-clad employees who wear tartan uniforms as a combination of public relations exercise and sign of company loyalty, and just as Albert had designed a specific Balmoral sett, so too many companies today register new designs for the specific purpose of creating a livery in which to clothe and identify their workers.

A cursory glance at any archive or register of contemporary tartan designs will reveal an astonishing variety of occupations and businesses that have registered a company tartan, and whilst it makes perfect commercial sense for Caledonian Airways or the Scottish whisky distilleries, for example, to clothe their employees in tartan, increasingly firms that have little or no Scottish connection adopt tartan as the perfect cloth for their uniforms. The tartans of the FBI Pipe Band, Salvation Army, MacMedic and American Express give some idea of the scope of contemporary corporate, commemorative and commercial tartans registered with increasing regularity by established and new organizations. Tartan, it would seem, offers uniformity without soullessness, brand identity without blandness, recognition without crassness. It manages to avoid the inhumanity of the typical corporate livery, and convey an identity characterized by a certain sense of bonhomie rarely found in the contemporary commercial world. Following the nineteenth-century creation of tartans inspired by fiction, most notably those named after Walter Scott's characters, the contemporary fictional tartan uniforms found in various cinematic and TV productions are also suggestive of a similar relaxed, progressive or even subversive attitude to workwear. So, for example, fictional tartan liveries are often donned for comedic effect such as the tartan uniform worn by Eddie Murphy and his fellow workers at McDowell's fast-food franchise in the film *Coming to America*, surely a side-swipe at the lack of a tartan uniform at McDonald's, equating to their corporate 'facelessness'.[12]

61 Eddie Murphy in his McDowell's tartan uniform in *Coming to America*

So far tartan has been considered as a uniform that its wearers are constrained to adopt, whether by parent, head teacher, estate owner or corporation. Arriving at fictional transatlantic tartan uniforms, however, introduces the concept of tartan as the cloth of unofficial, self-imposed and distinctly American workwear. The tartan (or, to give it its American terminology, plaid shirt) has become a vestimentary sign of the American working man, not so much blue collar, rather tartan collar. Economical, practical and bold without being too individual, the typical cotton shirt, most often in an approximation of Royal Stewart tartan, has become the staple item of workwear available in any number of discount clothing stores. The original popularity of the tartan shirt is to a large degree the result of Pendleton's, the American manufacturing company. Originally founded by an English weaver in the early twentieth century, the company swiftly filled a gap in the market for durable shirts for working men, which subsequently became a cultural icon of 1950s and 1960s America. Immortalized in pop songs, and worn over white T-shirts, tartan and plaid shirts became the uniform of a generation, sported by young and old alike, the shirts even providing the inspiration for the original name of that most quintessentially American of groups, the Beach Boys, who started their career as the Pendletones. As the uniform of the American working man (no matter what his job, as long as it involves manual labour of some kind), the tartan shirt is almost as ubiquitous as jeans or overalls and has come to symbolize a basic, unpretentious sensibility. Obviously, partly derived from the plaid shirts of cowboys, the tartan shirt is also the badge of the urban pioneer, the construction worker and engineer who helped build the great American cities.

Any number of American TV sitcoms call upon the tartan shirt to symbolize a character's integrity, from *Roseanne's* husband Dan to *Frasier's* father Martin, the tartan shirt retains its working-class origins even if worn in an elegant Seattle apartment.[13] Whilst epitomizing traditional working-class American male attitudes, it is so evocative of the pioneering spirit – historically referring back to the original Scottish immigrant settlers in North America – that it is often worn ironically in these productions. So the aforementioned Dan, sometime dry wall constructor, failed bike shop owner and frequently unemployed paterfamilias of *Roseanne*, and parcel delivery man Doug, the 'King of Queens', are characterized by a free-thinking individualism and portrayed as tartan-wearing, reluctant 'new men' married to fiercely independent partners.[13]

The tartan shirt has become so synonymous with hard-working masculinity in American popular culture that it has, like all successful vestimentary signs, been able to be subverted; and so the tartan or plaid shirt teamed with jeans, hard hat and Timberland-style boots becomes a component in the subcultural costume of the 'clone'. In this context, tartan's association with the traditional 'straight' American male is pushed to the limits of caricature and becomes a masquerade for gay culture. As an antidote to the prevailing strait-laced, clean-cut images that dominated American men's fashion with the rise of the yuppie in the 1980s and through to the 1990s, the working man's uniform – including the checked shirt – was appropriated by members of the emerging 'grunge' movement. Whilst primarily a music-led phenomenon and adopted by the disaffected offspring of wealthy middle-class parents, rather than the genuinely dispossessed, its anti-authoritarian stance included a typical disregard of fashion. 'Dressing down', second-hand and oversized clothing worn in multiple layers, and cheap American workwear became the typical components of the grunge look. The use of baggy thrift shop tartan or checked shirts by certain American subcultural groups that were linked ideologically, if not necessarily economically, to followers of grunge, such as skateboarders,

62 (Facing Page) The tartan or plaid working man's shirt as a component of gay style

brings us full circle to the surfing culture of the late 1940s and 1950s. Early surfers, through economic necessity and as a rejection of the aspirational conservatism of the period, rather than as fashion statements, wore second-hand and cheap workwear shirts over surfing shorts as cover-ups. In the space of half a century, the tartan shirt has earned a unique position within American subcultural and mainstream dress, developing into a use-all vestimentary statement that, as with all tartan, offers its wearers a multitude of ideological orientations.

Within the American social spectrum there exists another form of self-imposed tartan uniform: that of the aforementioned 'preppy' look enshrined within the work of Ralph Lauren and emulated by subsequent successful American designers such as Tommy Hilfiger. The promotion of an attitude to dressing derived from the British aristocracy at play, the 'weekend in the country' look, combined with American cowboy and Ivy League sporting references, has resulted in Lauren and his imitators producing clothes that naturally rely heavily on traditional fabrics and uniform styles. Tartan, along with tweed, regularly punctuates his collections for both men and women, and is used for garments such as women's kilts, men's accessories and children's wear, and interior furnishing fabrics in direct emulation of the Victorian use of the fabric initiated by the tartan interior schemes of Balmoral. As Antony Shugaar has stated:

> The whole landed aristocracy look once identified the British male, but it took an American Jew of Russian descent – Ralph Lauren – to commodify that look into something that could be worn by men, women, Brits, Yanks, and every other variation on gender, nationality and persuasion.[15]

This aspirational function of American tartan has been widely influential, particularly in the world of interior design, with figures such as lifestyle entrepreneur Martha Stewart doing much to promote a nineteenth-century British–American interior fantasy world replete with tartan ribbons, soft furnishings and well-fed, tartan-bedecked children. Ironically this can coexist side by side with a more plebeian love of tartan, and again it is American sitcoms that can provide evidence of this simultaneity. Both *Roseanne* and *The King of Queens* feature tartan soft furnishings (albeit neither Ralph Lauren nor Martha Stewart), and more tellingly still, the aspirational Deborah, wife of the sports writer Raymond, in *Everybody Loves Raymond*, has a tartan-accented bedroom signalling her desire to shake off her husband's working-class Italian roots.[16]

TARTAN TROOPERS

Leaving further consideration of the Balmoral effect on interior design for Chapter 8, *Balmoralization*, and to return to tartan as uniform clothing rather than domestic interior livery, we arrive back at a point not too distant from the regimental origin of uniform tartan. The organization, strategies and objectives of fan culture bear many similarities to military systems and hierarchies, but this present study is not the forum to consider this complex sociological mimesis. Nevertheless, before leaving tartan uniform it would be remiss not to acknowledge, however cursorily, the notable instances where tartan has provided the uniform for specific fan bases. Amongst many tartan-clad entertainers, perhaps none has capitalized quite so effectively on the power that tartan can

63 (Facing Page) The Bay City Rollers

demonstrate as a visual sign of collective adoration as the Bay City Rollers in the 1970s. Performing in a variety of tartan setts, the Rollers inspired a generation of fans to join sartorial forces in a collective 'tartanmania', easily achieved by the acquisition of widely available and affordable tartan scarves and a tartan augmentation of the fashion for high-waisted, wide-legged trousers in the early 1970s. Originally the garment of devotees of Northern Soul, who wore similar loose trousers in which to perform their acrobatic dance moves, the fashion for 'baggies' was seized upon by the Rollers' image-makers. With a typical Scottish economy and ingenuity, the trousers of the Rollers and their fans refer directly back to the legacy of the kilt and its traditional ability to be reworked and have its wearable life extended. The Rollers fan was able to convert an old pair of baggies by adding a 'gusset' or appliquéd strip of tartan to the side seams and to the bottom of the trousers, instantly extending the life of the trousers and creating the identifying garment of the Roller 'tribe'. The trousers were worn at half-mast: the short length perhaps functioned as a vestimentary sign of the tribe's working-class Scottish origins where trousers are still wearable even if too short, and garments can have their life extended by the addition of extra fabric, in this case, tartan.

Sporting tartans, as well as the previously mentioned corporate and other modern designs, have become a customary means of identifying a team with Scottish connections. Often produced to commemorate participation in specific events such as the Olympics and Commonwealth Games, tartans are also regularly produced to 'brand' specific golfing tournaments. But it is Scottish football that has understandably and most effectively utilized the clan associations of tartan to unify both fans and players. Scottish club tartans tend to be based on team colours, but an exception to this is the tartan designed in 1997 for the Scottish national team: the Tartan Army sett. This was based on Royal Stewart and Black Watch setts as an amalgam of the two most popular 'use-all' tartans. Unlike the distinctly sectarian nature of Scottish club football, which resurrects and maintains Scotland's history of religious division and violence, typified by the clash between Rangers and Celtic fans, the national team and particularly its fans, the Tartan Army, attempt to mask the partisan nature of Scottish football under a welter of tartan parody. Whether in the Tartan Army sett, or more likely the ubiquitous Royal Stewart, the foot soldiers of the Tartan Army can choose from any number of uniform elements, including a kilt, either traditionally made or tourist approximation: a 'See you Jimmy' hat complete with attached orange acrylic wig; or an oversized bonnet, or 'big bunnet', an exaggeration of a Tam o' Shanter decorated with pheasant's feathers. As global emissaries of Scottish football, it is tempting to see this vestimentary parody as a subversion of the Highland regiments' (the original tartan army) tartan colonizations. The tartanization that blankets towns (in Europe and further afield) during the team's away fixtures is reminiscent of the tartan invasion of Paris in the aftermath of the Napoleonic Wars. Tartan, as worn by the Tartan Army, acts as a signifier of a unified Scotland. However, just as the imperial expansion carried out by the tartan-clad regiments in the late eighteenth century and on into the nineteenth century belied the internal socio-economic divisions besetting the newly 'unified' Britain, so too does the tartan-clad national football fan mask what Jack McConnell (then first Minister of Scotland) referred to as 'Scotland's secret shame': the religious bigotry engendered by Scottish football's sectarian fan base.

Whether providing the uniform of the Tartan Army, children's fancy dress, the schoolgirl's kilt, the adult's return to childhood, the contemporary corporate uniform, or the sign of the American working man, tartan is eminently adaptable to a variety of contexts and wearers. Its historic, dynastic, military and geographical symbolism ensures that it remains as popular today as when it was first incorporated into uniform in the eighteenth century.

64 Scotland vs. Germany football match at Hampden Park, Glasgow, 2003. Tartan Army fans display ensembles including elements of 'traditional' Highland and regimental dress, First Nation American Indian accessories and 'cyberpunk' biker boots

6.
EROGENOUS ZONES

As previously discussed, military clothing of all sorts had a great impact on civilian dress throughout the eighteenth and nineteenth centuries. One of the major shifts in menswear, namely the abandonment of breeches for trousers, whilst typically credited to Beau Brummel, was also presaged by Sir John Sinclair of Ulbster's uniform for his new regiment, the Rothesay and Caithness Fencibles, which he devised in 1795, a good few years before Brummel's sartorial trend-setting. Sir John was a president of the Highland Society of London and a committed promoter of Highland culture, publishing numerous works on the subject including, in 1804, a pamphlet entitled *Observations on the Propriety of Preserving the Dress, the Language, the Poetry, their Music and the Customs of the Inhabitants of Scotland*. He maintained that the traditional Highlander wore trews rather than the kilt, particularly the recently established shorter kilt or *fhéilidh beag*, which he regarded as a recent travesty of true Highland dress. Sinclair's incorporation of the trews as part of the uniform of the Fencibles reasserts his belief that they were the preferred form of attire for the noble Highlander, as Nicholson points out:

> Trews had invariably been the dress of the Highland chieftains and tacksmen, not least because it made horse riding easier. Prince Charles Edward certainly never wore a kilt (until obliged by circumstances) and the kilted plaid was very much perceived as the practical, unglamorous, garment of the rough Highlander.[1]

No doubt influenced by the tide of Romantic reinvention permeating Scottish culture at this period, Sinclair constructed a uniform that was a perfect amalgam of bravado, elegance and historical influences, the sartorial Zeitgeist of men's attire in the late

65 (Facing Page) Giselle Bundchen modelling Highland-inspired underwear at the Victoria's Secret fashion show, 2006

eighteenth century. The magnificent portrait of him by Henry Raeburn, in the National Gallery of Scotland, shows him in his full dress uniform, including silk tartan trews of a typical dark blue and green government sett with an added yellow over-stripe and buff insets at the inner side seam and hem (an eighteenth-century military forerunner of the adaptations made to the Bay City Rollers' 'baggies' perhaps?). In addition to the trews, he is wearing checked red and white stockings, a plaid of the same tartan as the trews, a red jacket with yellow facings, a plumed bonnet and a sporran of an extravagant size. So passionate was Sinclair about the trews that he composed a rather sanguinary regimental marching song with the lines:

> Let others boast of philibeg,
> Of kilt and belted plaid,
> Whilst we the ancient trews will wear,
> In which our fathers bled.[2]

Once again, the auld alliance is invoked by the juxtaposition of the trouser and blood-letting, for at the time of the French Revolution the pantaloon – a long, tight-fitting, ankle-length trouser (not dissimilar to Sinclair's trews) – became fashionable.

The emergence of the pantaloon at the close of the eighteenth century, and its eventual abandonment in favour of the looser-fitting trouser by the 1830s, coincides with widespread changes in men's clothing. A concurrent shifting of concentration on regions of the male physique commenced with changes to the shape of men's coats, which were increasingly cut away at the front and narrower at the sides, revealing the upper leg and concentrating attention on the crotch area. Simultaneously waistcoats were shortened, jackets and coats were subtly padded, collars enlarged and neckwear became more elaborate, emphasizing the chest and upper torso, confirming Anne Hollander's assertion that: any change in a style of dress 'has a basically subversive purpose: fashion keeps present to the public eye the fact that normative human arrangements are always under unexpected threat from unstable human impulses, sexual expression being the main one…'[3]

By the turn of the century, this new sexual emphasis was accompanied by a decline in elaborately embroidered and decorated coats and waistcoats in favour of plain fabrics, with the tight-fitting pantaloons made of light coloured nankeen (a form of closely woven cotton), close-fitting stockinette, or from fine doeskin, which created a 'nude' effect and emphasized the shape of the leg and the genitals. Beau Brummel is credited with heightening this effect by inventing a kind of strap or stirrup that fastened the bottom of the trousers under the foot, producing a wrinkle-free line, but also stretching these garments so tightly that even further emphasis was placed on the genital area, which was already demarcated by 'the sharp break and bunch of woollen fabric or doeskin at elbow, waist, or crotch'.[4]

The simplified silhouette that typified the end of the eighteenth century was most noticeable in women's dress which, influenced by the 'rediscovery' of the classical world, altered radically both in cut and fabric. Simple shift dresses based on Ancient Greek forms were introduced, made of light cottons and muslins newly arrived from India. Many of these dresses were diaphanous and women wore a minimum of underwear and no corsetry; some even wore flesh-coloured tights underneath, giving an illusion of nudity. Given the lightness of these garments and the fashionable dictates that made it necessary to show off the long, clinging lines of the dress, warmth and protection from the elements became an issue for the fashionable dresser, and once again the craze for military dress provided a practical solution. The spencer was a short tailored jacket that was based on military uniform and which, when shortened even further and suitably embellished, often with military-style decoration such as frogging and metal buttons, became the perfect upper layer to go over the new shift dress. The spencer was adopted by both women and men and remained popular until well into the nineteenth century. It had the general effect of accentuating the top half of the body and revealing the body's outline below the waist; the female lower half encased in diaphanous folds, and the male in the newly adopted close-fitting trousers. Tartan aficionados of the time would have had fashionable garments such as the spencer made up in the cloth, as in the man's jacket in the collection of the Regimental Museum of the Queen's Own Highlanders.

Similarly useful as an extra layer to wear over the new lightweight dresses was the Kashmir shawl, yet another Indian import, which remained a staple element in women's dress during the early to mid-nineteenth century, with silk tartan once again replacing paisley for those with a Scottish allegiance. The traditional Highland plaid re-emerged on the shoulders of fashionable women, but

66 Civilian coat, 1820s. Made from what is probably the oldest surviving piece of 79th Cameron Highlander hard tartan

was now reduced to a tartan accessory emphasizing the classically revealing clothing of the period. One such fashionable figure of the time – Jane, Duchess of Gordon, the celebrated beauty known as 'The Tartan Belle' and favourite of George III – is said to have introduced tartan into court fashion, and on moving to London in 1787 she famously hosted Scottish-themed parties where she dressed in tartan and her guests danced to Scottish music. Tartan played a significant part in perhaps the most celebrated story associated with the Duchess of Gordon, concerning her role in recruiting men for the new regiment her husband was raising to fight in the French Revolutionary wars and which would become the Gordon Highlanders. It is said that she rode to fairs and other meeting places dressed in regimental bonnet, jacket and plaid, promising a kiss to every man that enlisted; a further addition to some accounts being that between her lips was a guinea, an erotic synthesis between tartan masquerade and money. Further proof of tartan's emerging fashionable status in the eighteenth century is provided by Nicholson, who cites Aileen Ribeiro's early research on eighteenth-century masquerades in which she notes that in 1789 the Prince of Wales ordered 'A Belted Kilt, Plaid Coat, Waistcoat' in which to go to a masquerade.[5]

'A MAN IN A KILT IS A MAN AND A HALF'

An emphasis on freedom of movement and sexually emphatic clothing characterized the first two decades of the nineteenth century, but it is the kilt that has permanently eroticized tartan. Even before the adoption of the little kilt or *fhéilidh beag*, its predecessor, the belted plaid (*fhéilidh-Mor*) was considered a garment that signified an indolent – even licentious – lifestyle, given its adaptability as both clothing and blanket. The perceived inherent lewdness of its wearers was put forward as one of the justifications for the proscription of Highland dress, a view upheld by John Pinkerton, an antiquarian who endorsed Sinclair's adoption of the trews, and who suggested, as Trevor-Roper notes, that the kilt was 'grossly indecent' and that for a kilt-wearer 'the parts concealed by all other nations are but loosely covered'.[6] As has been noted earlier, the presence of the kilted regimental soldier in Paris following the Napoleonic Wars sparked an obsession with tartan and the kilt, which has remained undimmed ever since, but accompanying this enthusiasm was a fascination with what these tartan occupiers wore under their kilts. In an unusual reversal to the typical eroticization of the colonial 'other', the defeated French set about the construction of a sexual mythology centred on the Scotsman and his kilt that is as enduring and commercially productive to the tartan industry as its clan associations. The libidinous speculation as to what is worn under the kilt, and the associated ruggedness and sexual bravado required to wear such a potentially exposing garment that has become such an enduring cliché, is already firmly established in contemporary illustrations of this early Parisian encounter. A number of elegantly risqué representations documenting this fascination were produced, such as the etching dating from 1815 in the collection of the British Museum entitled *La Prétexte*, in which a pair of kilted soldiers are bending down to choose some fruit, whilst two women who are sitting behind them adopt the pretexts of tying a shoe lace and retrieving a child's ball in order to look up their kilts. Similarly the print in the National War Museum of Scotland (formerly the Scottish United Services Museum) has another fruit-seller, this time the recipient of the view as a gust of wind lifts the kilt of the regimental soldier standing in front of her, whilst in the background more soldiers carrying out a drilling exercise show a united 'rear' to three astonished women at the edge of the parade ground.

LE PRÉTEXTE.

Se vend chez Martinet Rue du coq

67 *Le Prétexte*. Hand-coloured etching published by Aaron Martinet, 1815

Whilst the question as to what a Scotsman might wear or not wear under his kilt has provided an endless source of innuendo and titillation that has continued unabated from the Regency period onwards, it is the stars of the late Victorian and Edwardian music hall, succeeded by their cinematic counterparts, who realized the full comedic value of this eternal question. The interrogation of gender that the kilt suggests – put crudely, 'a man in a skirt' – makes the insistence on the affirmation of masculinity afforded by the chance glimpse of male genitalia all the more urgent. The perceived 'threat' to dominant sexual hierarchy (a threat, it should be noted, perceived only by the non-kilt-wearer) accounts for the continual comedic reaffirmation demanded by society when presented by this transgressive garment. The endless jokes, sketches and other re-enactments serve to undermine the possible threat to the socio-sexual equilibrium and proximity to effeteness offered by the kilted 'other'. The assumed danger of sexual subversion implied by the kilt is not the only target for the litany of ridicule that has been directed at its wearers, but the decorative nature of tartan itself has also played a part in its mockery. At a period when men's clothing began the increasingly sombre transformation that would result in the monochromatic severity of respectable Victorian men's dress, the appearance of visually striking tartan seemed at odds with a time 'when men gave up their

68 John Brown's underpants

right to all the brighter, gayer, more elaborate, and more varied forms of ornamentation, leaving these entirely to the use of women, and thereby making their own tailoring the most austere and ascetic of the arts'[7]. If tartan-wearing strayed outside strictly confined institutional or geographical boundaries such as the army, liveried service or the Highlands themselves, then it was fair game to be lampooned as either effeminate or hopelessly anachronistic.

The sexual exoticization of the kilted male initiated by nineteenth-century Parisian commentators has continued to flourish, generating fantasies as to the virility of its wearer summed up in Sir Colin Campbell's familiar 'man and a half' adage used for the title of this section.[8] Whilst Regency attitudes to the sexual frisson engendered by the kilt were typically forthright, tartan, and along with it the kilt, had undergone by the Victorian era an intense period of reinvention and Romanticization that allowed no room for the lascivious speculations of the previous age. In a typical process of Victorian sublimation, tartan's erotic associations via the kilt were repressed, re-emerging in Balmoral, the fantasy world where kilted servants were ordered to 'cover up' and John Brown's underpants survive as the supreme tartan fetish. The full extent of Balmoral's unreality will be considered later, but John Brown's tartan underwear initiates another series of questions concerning the erotic charge of tartan. If the answer to what a Scotsman wears under his kilt is nothing, then the concept of tartan underwear seems to suggest a number of contradictory positions to this assumed explicit display.

John Brown's underpants can be seen as the antecedent of the ubiquitous tartan boxer shorts, a staple element of the wardrobe of the American 'jock' as well as the seasonal Christmas gift idea for a boyfriend, dad or brother. But it is possible to find alternative tartan undergarments such as the 'kilt thong', a mini-underkilt produced by the underwear company Gregg Homme. This 'fun men's thong' allows its wearer to 'own your own mini-kilt without having to play those annoying bagpipes', a somewhat contradictory garment that simultaneously undermines the received wisdom that a true Scot is hardy enough to wear nothing under his kilt, and yet by its miniaturization

69 Kilt thong by Gregg Homme

suggests superhuman virility.[9] Perhaps the ultimate tartan underwear is the so-called 'cheeky breeks' available from the website of the Tartan Army as the perfect answer to the perennial question of what to wear under a kilt. The 'breeks' consist of a pair of tartan boxer shorts adorned with external plastic buttocks, so that if an inadvertent glimpse, or more probable, intentional 'flash' of what is under the wearer's kilt is given, the owner of these particular 'novelty shorts' can be both exhibitionist and modest.

The sexual cathexsis emitted by this taxonomy of men's tartan underwear is testament to popular culture's profoundly ambivalent relationship to Highland dress, tartan and the kilt in particular. The notion of protection and durability historically attached to the wearing of tartan is paraphrased

70 *Dildoll* project, Matthias Herrmann, 2003

by the use of tartan in underwear, often made of the lightest materials and therefore affording little or no actual protection, its function instead is to act as a titillating textile that subverts its traditional role as a visible sign of clanship and geographical origin. Tartan used in underwear is visible only to the wearer and chosen intimates, unlike the traditional kilt-wearer whose tartan, and perhaps genitals, are visible to all. The limits of tartan's equivalence to male sexuality, however, are possibly reached in the work of the Austrian artist Matthias Herrmann, who in his *Dilldoll* project of 2003 indulges in an act of tartan auto-eroticism that reduces his identity to an oversized tartan fetish.

X-CERTIFICATE TARTAN?

Tartan in the form of the kilt has had a long and successful, if not exactly illustrious, career in the movies. As with its earlier mediated appearances, whether in literature, satirical imagery (illus. 71), or as costume for popular entertainments from traditional theatre to vaudeville, its appearances on film invariably assist in the affirmation of constructs of Scottish masculinity. Whilst these constructs generally conform to standard nineteenth-century conventions of the ideal male image (strength, courageousness, potency, comradeship and so on) they are achieved, broadly speaking, in one of two ways. In a comedic situation, the tartan kilt is initially regarded by other non-kilt-wearing protagonists in the film as a barrier to the recognition of those same masculine qualities. The wearer must then necessarily undergo a trial by ridicule in order to establish these qualities, an example of Baudrillard's 'operational negativity' where 'Everything is metamorphosed into its inverse in order to be perpetuated in its purged form'.[10] So, typically, the kilt-wearer's masculinity, seriousness, propriety etc. will be in question until the various lampooning and slapstick rituals associated with the kilt have been completed. For these particular scenarios to be most effective, the kilt-wearer must be literally displaced and become the 'other' both in terms of appearance and topography.

Within the history of cinema there are numerous examples of the kilted 'stranger in a strange land', which substitute tartan's original eighteenth-century political and economic proscription with a parody of sexual censorship. *Putting Pants on Philip* (Clyde Bruckman, 1927) is an early Laurel and Hardy short which casts Laurel as Philip, the Scottish nephew of Piedmont Mumblethunder, who is played by Hardy. Philip arrives fresh from Scotland in the USA, kitted out in kilt and beret, with a twisted walking stick of the Harry Lauder type, much to the amusement of the crowd and the embarrassment of his uncle. Equally embarrassing are Philip's sexual proclivities, which include jumping in the air – causing his kilt to fly up – every time he spots an attractive woman. The kilt-lifting puns escalate and we see that unusually, Philip wears American-style boxer shorts under his kilt. However to maximize the comedic potential these are literally dropped after he sneezes violently. A sequence pre-dating Marilyn Monroe's famous appearance in *The Seven-Year Itch* (Billy Wilder, 1955) follows, where the now underwear-less kilted Laurel stands over a subway vent causing his kilt to blow up and female observers of this event to swoon. This prompts a policeman to comment, 'This dame ain't got no lingerie on', and his uncle decides to have him 'properly' attired in respectable American clothing – pants.[11] Scenes in the outfitters afford further sexual slapstick with attempts by the tailor and Hardy to measure Laurel's inside leg, which they finally manage to do but not until physically tackling him to the ground resulting in a 'violated' Philip declaring that the 'Bide-a-Wee club will hear of this!'[12] The overt characterization of Laurel's oversexed Scot is unusual for the time, and its repetitious 'flashing' scenarios escalate to a point where the usual light-hearted tartan parodies are transcended, and an unsettling predatory dimension is added to the more familiar 'what's under the kilt' routines.

No such sinister overtones, however, disturb the hearty cheer of what is one of the classic British films that feature the Scotsman abroad – *Geordie* (Frank Launder, 1955). As we watch Bill Travers as the eponymous Geordie progress from 'seven-stone weakling' to Olympic-standard hammer thrower, we also understand his increased prowess as the necessary endowment that will enable him to wear his father's altered, hand-me-down Black Watch tartan kilt with pride, first at the Highland Games and then at the Melbourne Olympics. On arriving in Australia, his mettle is tested as he must endure ridicule and even possible disqualification from the games because of his insistence on wearing his tartan. Tellingly, the pompous British team manager's exhortation to wear the Olympic uniform of blazer and flannels, and abandon his kilt (which he refers to as a 'rig out') prompts Geordie to reply that his kilt is not a 'rig out' but 'the Scottish National dress', an example of the pride and courage that will eventually lead 'the gentle giant from Scotland' to triumph in the Games.[13]

The staple cinematic device of using tartan and the kilt as an overture to a number of comedic narratives concerning the Scotsman and sexuality entails a succession of inversions and visual puns, or 'carnivalesque' imagery, and this has long been the dominant mode of its representation. The kilt and all the previously discussed libidinous speculation that has contextualized its popular reception invoke the Rabelaisian excess Bakhtin examined:

> This logic of the 'wrong side out' and of 'bottoms up' is also expressed in gestures and other movements: to walk backward, to ride a horse facing its tail, to stand on one's head, to show one's backside.[14]

The question of the stability or otherwise of male sexuality when wearing a kilt is central to the film *The Battle of the Sexes* (Charles Crichton, 1959), a comedy based on the upheaval caused by a female American efficiency expert's attempts to revolutionize the old-fashioned patriarchy of the House of Macpherson, a textile firm based in Edinburgh. As a prologue to the film and against visual backdrops of kilted pipers, old Edinburgh characters in Highland dress and men dancing a Scottish reel, a voiceover suggests that Scotland is 'one of the last bastions of man's supremacy' but is also 'a world in which the shortest skirts are worn by … man' and where 'even the cancan is danced by men'.[15] This visual prologue acts as a distillation of the comedic mileage derived from the apparent contradiction between traditional 'manly' qualities and the wearing of the kilt, explored in this film and many others like it.

In more recent and highly successful Hollywood narratives of Scottish independence, such as *Rob Roy* and *Braveheart*, there would appear to be no room for the sexual innuendo and inversion that characterizes so many other less 'serious' cinematic depictions of the kilted Highlander. Much has been written about the popularity of these films, especially in America, and the particular socio-historical narratives that they construct, concerning pre-Union Scotland, national identity, the Jacobite cause and the demonizing of the English. These films have found a role within the proliferating transatlantic heritage industry, often cited as a form of cinematic vindication for those Scots dispossessed during the Highland clearances and who came to America as immigrants.[16] They have also left their mark on popular culture generally, influencing the revival of interest

71 Two typical Scottish-themed comic postcards

in pre-Victorian, so-called 'traditional' Highland culture, and enhancing the careers of firmly established Scottish Hollywood stars such as Sean Connery. Similarly, the reputation of newer stars such as Ewan McGregor has benefited from the 'Braveheart effect': in 1998 he was photographed for *Vanity Fair* by Annie Leibovitz as a kind of Highland fantasy, mud-stained and dirty in *fhéilidh-Mor*, holding a rooster – the 'cock o' the north', perhaps? However, if these Scottish 'historical' films are looked at in more detail, the sexual horseplay and innuendo that permeates more light-hearted offerings is also discernible, but serves a different function. The otherness created out of the kilted Scotsman is of a positive order, established to emphasize a difference from the effete, often overdressed English. Invariably the English in these films are depicted as sadistic, heartless and remorseless in their reprisals against the recalcitrant Scots. The usual comedic references to the sexual prowess of the tartan-wearing Highlander function to emphasize 'healthy' sexual appetites as opposed to the sexual sadism of the misogynistic English, who are often portrayed as rapists. The underlying message of Scot equals 'good sex' is part of the use to which 'accurate' tartan dress is put before the adoption of the English little kilt, the *fhéilidh beag*, in these films.

Early in the film *Braveheart*, Mel Gibson, as William Wallace, tries to impress his future wife by speaking to her in French. She suggests she would be more impressed if he could do the same standing on his head, to which he replies: 'My kilt'll fly up, but I'll try!' This reduces her to shocked and excited amusement; later we see Wallace being lovingly 'dressed' in his plaid the

72 Wedding of Corinne Hussey and Alexander Ross. Newport, Rhode Island, 13 November 2004

morning after their wedding night, a visual equation of successful consummation and the wearing of the tartan, that finds an echo in the contemporary bridegroom's outfit.[17] The equation between possible fecundity and the 'healthy' freedom afforded to the male kilt-wearer perhaps explains its continuing popularity as acceptable modern wedding attire, one of the few instances when the kilt is still worn by the contemporary male. To return to *Braveheart*, the light-hearted and tender moments with his new wife are abruptly terminated as we see her violated and killed, and his own increasing torment leads to his eventual martyrdom. Similar sexual satisfaction before the eruption of English violence is acted out in *Rob Roy*, in a scene of remarkable visual crassness. Sitting amongst some ancient standing stones, Mary MacGregor proceeds to recount what the 'old wives say' about the stones as she runs her hands up Rob Roy's belted plaid as a form of Highland foreplay. When Rob Roy enquires what they say, Mary replies: 'The stones make men hard and the women fertile', to which Rob responds: 'We've no need of them, you and me' and in the heavy-handed visual analogy between standing stone and MacGregor's potency that follows, the film relies on the tried and trusted tradition of kilt-wearing as indicative of virility and wholesome consensual sex – a sharp contrast to Mary's violent rape, perpetrated by the Englishman Cunningham, that follows.[18]

Cinematic tartan, it would seem, remains firmly embedded in a carnivalesque tradition that licenses, for a period, what appears to be an inversion of established vestimentary sexual signals. The apparent destabilization suggested by the sight of a man in a 'skirt' and the proximity of genital exposure is lampooned and paraded only to ultimately reinvest the wearer with an increased masculinity and sense of propriety, outstripping the 'normal' non-kilt-wearer's (often English) sexual values. The initial 'otherness' presented by the kilted Scotsman is familiarized and rendered safe by a process of ridicule that must be undergone in order for its true orthodoxy to be revealed.

TARTAN MAKETH WOMAN

In *Casino Royale* (John Huston et al., 1967), Ursula Andress plays Vesper Lynd, the richest spy in the world and, as British *Vogue* of April 1966 also suggested, 'a killer in a kilt' – referring to a scene in which she appears in a Dress Stewart kilt leading a massed band of pipers.[19] Amidst the swirling mists and precision drilling of the pipers, Peter Sellers emerges, also fully kilted, and encounters Peter O'Toole, who gives his sporran a suggestive tug. They both then narrowly miss annihilation by the deadly Miss Lynd when she despatches the entire regiment with her bagpipe/machine gun. The spoof gender-swapping implied by the killer Andress, in a traditional male garment and occupying a position at the head of a pipe band normally reserved for a man, although part of the film's satirical chaos, is indicative of the ironic fact that kilts are now far more likely to be items of female, rather than male, dress. Despite recent attempts to make kilts more popular as menswear, aided by the emergence of non-tartan versions in a variety of materials, they have remained resolutely reserved for special occasions such as weddings and other formal ceremonies, as part of a military uniform or confined to the pages of fashion magazines and runways. Women in tartan, whether kilt or some other garment, are a much more customary sight, however. From the previously discussed school uniforms to street wear, high fashion and traditional older women's wear, the opportunities for women to wear tartan would appear to transcend age and location. This is primarily due to the rise in fashionability of tartan itself, which commenced at the beginning of the nineteenth century, and

73 Marie Lloyd. Sepia-toned photograph, Great Britain, c.1890. The sexually ambiguous tartan costume she wears in this image befits her notoriously suggestive stage act

the simultaneous decline in the wearing of the kilt by men, the shorter version of which had already replaced the belted plaid and other forms of male tartan such as jacket and trews.

An etching by George Cruikshank entitled *Anticipated Effects of the Tailors' 'Strike' – or Gentlemen's Fashions for – 1834* shows, amongst the tattered, patched and threadbare clothing worn by the fashionable gents during this imaginary 'strike', a man wearing a kilt under his riding coat and boots (a form of Regency 'flasher'). The image suggests that by this time tartan and the kilt was deemed not only unfashionable and improper, but also somehow impoverished, certainly unsuitable for the southern fashion-conscious male. Tartan had started a return journey to the position it had held before the time of its proscription, as a cloth suitable only for the uncivilized Scotsman. This situation persisted throughout the century, with some modifications, for as Scarlett suggests:

> With the near-demise of the kilt for daily wear, tartan became more usually worn by women than by men, who are not generally able to display anything larger than a tie, so the popularization of tartan leaned heavily in the female direction. A catalogue of 1908 lists, among other more usual feminine accessories, blouses, petticoats, underskirts and

stockings in a wide variety of tartans – ninety-seven in the case of petticoats, though only eight in stockings. Men had to be content with braces, ties, cummerbunds and socks.[20]

It is interesting to note in Scarlett's list that with the exception of socks, tartan is used for explicitly male accessories that bear a heavily gendered socio-sexual significance. Braces hold up, and cummerbunds 'bind' the tops of trousers, sealing off access to the lower half of the body and emphasizing instead the upper torso rather than the genital area, which it is left to the tartan tie to substitute as a vestimentary phallus, all of which inverts the traditional access afforded by the tartan kilt.

The sanitization of tartan that was necessary for it to be transformed into the favoured textile of Queen Victoria and become a regular part of women's fashionable dress throughout the nineteenth century meant that the kilt, with all of its sexual connotations, was reserved for children and servants,

74 Portrait of Prince Albert. Lithograph, England, nineteenth century

or the well-to-do during periods of unregulated leisure time, such as when Albert indulged his Highland fantasies at Balmoral (illus. 74). It was not until the twentieth century and the revolution in women's dress, which included the raising of hemlines as part of the wholesale liberation from the literal and moral restrictions of the previous century's attitudes to clothing, that the kilt re-emerges as a popular style for women. In the hands of radical designers such as Chanel, traditional male items of dress such as the short kilt, with its promise of unrestricted freedom of movement, was ripe for appropriation, and from the 1920s onwards women's fashion has regularly produced variations on this traditional male garment. Again in *Casino Royale* (a rich deposit of subversive tartan-wearing), we can see the newly eroticized female version of the kilt given free expression at the banquet given by Deborah Kerr (as the secret agent Mimi, posing as the Scottish Lady Fiona). As the banquet continues, Lady Fiona's Highland 'virgins' (or spies) gradually become more and more uninhibited as they consume their drugged refreshments, ending up performing a frenzied reel which displays their off-the-shoulder plaids and short kilts to perfection. The camerawork provides the viewer with ample evidence that when transposed to the female body, no such suggestion of nakedness under the kilt is entertained.

Divorcing tartan from its symbiotic relationship to the kilt, and unlike fictional uses, fashion's use of tartan retains – and indeed often capitalizes on – its Victorian residue of primness. Repeatedly used as the perfect textile for smartly tailored suits or sensible overcoats, it took punk's championing of the textile to liberate it from its vestimentary treadmill of country convention, preppy decorum or party dress playacting. Following punk and Westwood's designer-led historicism, it was left to the wave of Japanese designers who emerged in the late twentieth century to imagine a whole new set of possibilities for the textile, based not only on its obvious socio-historical references, but also its potential for bodily disruption, which will be discussed in further detail later. Before leaving the consideration of tartan's relationship to a notion of repressed sexuality inherited from the Victorians, it is interesting to note that like the Japanese designers' radical view of tartan, it has fallen to an American (rather than British) designer – Marc Jacobs – to produce what is perhaps the quintessential collection of recent years that fully exploits tartan as a sign of sublimated sexuality. His Autumn/Winter 2004–5 collection for Louis Vuitton acts as a form of tartan sartorial retrospective, described by Jacobs himself as: 'some good old punk, some good old Goth and some good old glamour'. The collection displayed a truly postmodern sensibility by showing outfits that trawled tartan's back catalogue, and yet retained a coherent eroticism that is often lacking in tartan fashion that is more strictly historicist or referenced from popular culture.[21] Sensible coats and suits in tartan, prim blouses, capes and stoles were worn provocatively and accompanied by sexually charged tartan accessories that resulted in a collection that conveyed the opposing characteristics of the textile. Simultaneously repressive and liberal, reserved and exhibitionist, these were clothes one could imagine Miss Jean Brodie wearing if she gave up teaching to work in a Berlin brothel, resulting in a kind of 'erotic frumpery'. The collection – being relatively free of kilts – relied on tailoring and garments reminiscent of the late 1930s and 1940s, a period that saw the rise of a particularly insular form of British Surrealism. Jacob's collection evoked this look, at once instantly familiar and yet also somehow strange and unsettling, or, as he put it himself using an American referent, 'a Tim Burton view of the Highlands'.[22]

75 (Facing Page) Marc Jacobs for Louis Vuitton, Autumn/Winter 2004–5

What Jacobs's collection manages to excavate is tartan's inherent sexual allure, which is so often buried under a welter of crass innuendo or mock historicism. Tartan is, after all, composed from variations on grid patterns and many architects, design historians and cultural theorists have observed the intersection of horizontals and verticals that are the basic components of any grid system, as also suggestive of physical union. In Piet Mondrian's early writing, he characterized the horizontal line as representative of the horizon and the earth, whilst the vertical suggested human impact on that space; simultaneously the horizontal also signified female and nature, whilst the vertical signified male and culture, the two vectors' intersection expressive of both mystical and secular union. It is this underlying universality that can perhaps explain the recent explosion of interest in tartan as both textile and pattern, and many of the most inventive contemporary designers have produced collections in recent years that include tartan in some form or another. It appears that tartan finally, in the twenty-first century, has managed to extricate itself from previous socio-historical constructions and become expressive of the fecundity inherent in its woven structure.

7.
TARTAN TOFFS

ROYAL SWAGGER

> A pair of fine gold shoe rosettes, studded all over with variegated gems ... a goatskin Highland purse with a massive gold spring top ... three black Morocco belts, a fine gold head ornament for his bonnet consisting of the Royal Scots crown in miniature, set with diamonds, pearls, rubies and emeralds; a large gold brooch pin with variegated Scotch gems; a powder horn finely mounted in fine gold; a fine basket; a Highland sword of polished steel; a pair of fine polished steel Highland pistols; 61 yards of royal satin plaid; 31 yards of royal plaid velvet.[1]

This is part of a bill submitted to George IV by the Edinburgh outfitters George Hunter of Token House Yard, on the occasion of his state visit to the town in 1822, for various fabrics and accoutrements used in the construction of his costume. Apart from being a testament to his profligacy, the bill gives an indication of the theatricality of his appearance. This is perhaps fitting, given that the whole visit was stage-managed by Walter Scott to function as a kind of *tableau vivant* representing the concept of a Britain unified under a Hanoverian king. Edinburgh, the town that was reinvented as a British city rather than Scottish capital at the end of the eighteenth century, complete with Hanoverian street names, was soon to be engulfed in a tidal wave of tartan thanks to the labours of Scott. Ignoring the fact that the last Hanoverian prince to enter the Scottish capital was Cumberland the Butcher, on his way to crush the Jacobite rebellion at Culloden and afterwards to decimate the Highland way of life, George's visit seventy-five years later managed, primarily through presenting himself clothed in sartorial signifiers, to promote a fictional alloy of Catholic Jacobite and Protestant Hanoverian

76 (Facing Page) Pompeo Batoni, *Colonel William Gordon of Fyvie.* Oil on canvas, 1766

77 Satirical print, *The First Laird in Aw Scotia or A View at Edinburgh, August 1822*. Coloured print on paper, 1822

dynasties.[2] The result was a new British royal 'super brand', whose trademark was the Royal Stewart (rather than the Jacobite Stuart) tartan. The king – making his appearance accompanied by the drunken lord mayor of London, Sir William Curtis, also in a kilt – was a boon to caricaturists of the day. A cartoon subtitled *A View at Edinburgh in August 1822* depicts a kilted George on a stage, below which a row of Edinburgh ladies positioned to receive a perfect view shield their eyes from the horrors revealed beneath his kilt. In another cartoon entitled *Equipt for a Northern Visit*, George and Curtis exchange views on each other's kilts, George suggesting that he, being 'every inch a Scot', cuts a more dashing figure than Curtis, who seems primarily worried that his kilt will frighten the 'lasses' as it affords him little more protection than 'Achilles' fig leaf'.[3] Whilst providing the wits of the day with material familiar to us now from countless variations on the previously discussed question of what a Scotsman wears under his kilt, it is a testament to Scott's skill as a master of ceremonies, that he was able to transform George IV into a symbol of British, rather than Hanoverian English, royalty. This was achieved with the help of copious amounts of Highland symbolism, tartan being the chief element. The feat was even more remarkable, given the bloated and debilitated appearance of the king, who by this time would have had great difficulty moving about unaided, and wore flesh-coloured leggings under his kilt (more out of the necessity to cover his ulcerous legs rather than from any sense of propriety, one imagines).

George's physical condition aside, the visit was a great success and Scott, aided and abetted by Colonel Stewart of Garth in matters of Highland tradition, created a twenty-day-long fiction that can be regarded as tartan's defining moment of transition from Highland habit into fashionable fabric. George's appearances at banquets, balls, church services, troop reviews, processions and theatre visits were met with cheering, tartan-clad crowds, and one of the final events was a recently

78 Ceramic figurine of William Macready as Rob Roy. Moulded earthenware with painted decoration. Staffordshire, c.1840

dramatized version of Scott's *Rob Roy* at the Theatre Royal – a form of early tartan theatre in the round – with audiences treated to fictional history on stage as well as in the making in the royal box. Selected members of the Celtic Society were chosen as guards of honour to protect the king and the Scottish regalia newly rediscovered by Scott, and they no doubt cut a spectacular, if somewhat bizarre picture, outfitted in their own conceptions of ancient Highland dress. As previously noted, Scott summoned the clan leaders to attend the extravaganza, dressed in appropriate tartan, precipitating the demand for 'clan tartans' and giving an enormous boost to the tartan manufacturers.

The previously produced 'tailor's tartans' (tartans that did not have specific clan associations) were rapidly redesignated as 'official' tartans for the clan leaders and their attendants clamouring to dress as spectacularly as they could for the royal visit. Manufacturers such as William Wilson had, during the period of the proscription, only been able to supply the new Highland regiments with tartan but, since the lifting of the ban in 1782, tartan manufacture had increased, the growing fashionability of tartan at the close of the eighteenth century playing a significant role in this. But this was nothing to the demand created by George's imminent arrival, an indication of which can be assessed from the estimate that tartan manufacture at the time of the royal visit increased tenfold in as little as three weeks. Clan leaders competed to see who could turn themselves out in the most finery, and there are accounts of the time noting that some families bankrupted themselves for the occasion. Not everybody was impressed with Edinburgh's 'tartanization' in 1822, and Walter Scott's own son-in-law, J. G. Lockhart, commented upon Edinburgh's collective 'Celtic

79 Red Stewart tartan suit made for Alexander Stewart some time before 1817, when he emigrated from Perthshire to Canada

hallucination', whilst another observer suggested that a 'tartan fit had come upon the city'.[4] The tartan obsession continued, however, and the dramatic rise in commercial weavers' output played no small part in its continued popularity. Firms like that of William Wilson were keen to fuel the lucrative desire for tartan, and with Victoria and Albert's imminent creation of a fantasy Highland kingdom at Balmoral, the collective 'hallucination' and 'fit' witnessed in Edinburgh soon took on the characteristics of a full-blown national psychological disorder.

Returning to the early nineteenth century, an indication of the kind of tartan dress that became de rigueur at this period can be gauged from an outfit in the collection of the Scottish Tartans Museum in Keith, dating from a period just prior to George's visit to Edinburgh, most probably from around 1817. Alexander Stewart's red 'Stewart' tartan suit is the perfect marriage between Highland trappings as fancy dress and the fashionable tailoring of the day. Outfits such as these provided an antidote for successful Scottish businessmen who, during the day, kept the mercantile wheels of empire turning from the increasingly powerful and influential centre of Edinburgh. After business hours, these plutocrats would dress up and retreat into a fantasy of Highland life remote from the hum of urban commerce. Stewart's suit comprises of box-pleated kilt, a waistcoat and tail coat cut fashionably short, on the bias and with a typical collar shape and detail of the period. The theatrical sporran is bound with red tape, and the rosettes decorating the garters and shoes are made from loops of the same stuff. His plaid is fastened with a jewelled brooch and sports a powder horn set with gems, a dirk and a pair of steel pistols. This kind of 'stage costume' was tailored and constructed with the drawing room and levée in mind rather than the Highland landscape, and epitomizes the growing tide of historicism sweeping fashionable dress of the period. Robert Louis Stevenson's later comment concerning Sir Henry Raeburn's celebrated series of portraits (referred to in Chapter 4, *Transforming Tartan*), about dashing military men of the period in their tartan finery 'compared with the sort of living people one sees about the streets … are as bright as new sovereigns to fishy and obliterated sixpences', employs a suitably mercantile discourse that one can imagine would just as appropriately have described fashionable Edinburgh's tartan-clad tycoons.[5]

The royal patronage of tartan continued apace with Victoria and Albert's championing of the textile, but the Victorian use of the material is of a different order to that of George's tartan exhibitionism. Albert wore his tartan with suitable decorum and a belief in the accuracy of his re-creation of Highland dress. Similarly, Victoria's love of the material is strictly confined within the parameters of respectable Victorian fashion. George's appearance, however, is less concerned with conformity and propriety and more with separation or rather distinction. George's fascination with sartorial matters is well known; his love of dressing up (1822 was not the first occasion he had worn tartan 'fancy dress') and his association with Beau Brummel is legendary. The example that they set provided a model for fashionable men of the period, the dandies who cultivated a style of dress that whilst conforming to the new sobriety in men's clothing that emerged at the beginning of the nineteenth century, still managed to signal, sartorially, a separation from the rising middle classes. Tartan's role in this operation of distinction will be discussed shortly, but to return to George IV, his separation from the masses was self-evident, so his sartorial excesses were designed to emphasize wealth and power, to be visible by a crowd, to be memorable – all functions, in fact, that were an anathema to the true dandy, whose costume was never allowed to become *outré*.

From George's excess it is not until the twentieth century and the figure of Edward VIII that we find a comparable instance of royal tartan swagger. Edward VIII, like George IV and Edward VII before him, all had lengthy periods as the Prince of Wales during which they could devote time, energy and considerable income to sartorial concerns whilst unburdened by the matters of state that would occupy them once they had ascended the throne (albeit for Edward VIII this was exceptionally brief). Like George and Edward VII, Edward VIII swiftly established himself as a leader of fashion, and in his own opinion suggested that one of his chief functions as Prince of Wales was to be seen as well dressed: 'more of a clothes-peg than the heir apparent'.[6] His enormously influential style was based on the relaxation of what he considered to be the strict dress codes of the aristocracy, and one of his first acts on accession was to abolish the frock coat as court dress. Amongst his sartorial signatures was his love of tartan, often wearing a kilt in one of his favourite setts, which included Royal Stewart, Hunting Stewart, Balmoral, Lord of the Isles and Rothesay; these would often be teamed and indeed clashed with other traditional fabrics such as dog's-tooth and other checked tweeds, argyle and Fair Isle knits and socks, and contrasting ties. Edward suggested that he did much to popularize tartan in the 1950s, when all sorts of men's garments in tartan became fashionable, particularly in America, including dinner jackets, cummerbunds and even beach shorts. This American vogue can perhaps be partly explained by Edward's enduring transatlantic popularity as the English king who had given up his throne for the love of an American woman. Whether this is the primary cause or not, tartan certainly became increasingly popular in America from the mid-century onwards. It is ironic that whilst in the powerful position of heir apparent, Edward had espoused a more relaxed and democratic attitude to men's fashion. However, once he had abdicated and taken up residence in France as the Duke of Windsor, he rediscovered a fondness for pomp and ceremonial forms of attire, as Winston Churchill remembered from a dinner party:

> The little man himself dressed up to the nines in the Balmoral tartan with dagger and jabot etc. When you think that you could hardly get him to put on a black coat and tie when he was Prince of Wales.[7]

KINGS OF TARTAN

> As if in divine confirmation of my train of thought, when Idi stood up for the vows, he was wearing a kilt. The sea-green jacket was just part of the Highland get-up, spats and sporran, skean-dhu and brogans … the full, romantic, nonsensical lot, the same as I had seen in the mountains.[8]

George and Edward's apparent love of swaggering fancy-dress Highland uniform had a clear, if contestable, monarchic function: to signify its wearer as the ruler of a United Kingdom that included Scotland. However, the context and desired effect of the outfits adopted by other autocratic tartan-lovers can often be somewhat puzzling, if not bizarre. Worn with no less gravitas than by the members of the British royal family, these 'kings of tartan' wear the textile with a self-importance bordering on megalomania. Idi Amin felt (amongst many other similar beliefs) that both Scotland and Uganda had suffered under centuries of British imperialism and identified with the Scots, even suggesting that he would join them in their fight for independence and be more than willing to become their king if asked. Giles Foden, in his novel *The Last King of Scotland*, from which the quote above is taken, describes how Amin's love of fancy-dress uniforms extended to Highland dress, and as Abler notes:

The 4th King's African Rifles was recruited in Uganda, and after staging a coup in 1971, Idi Amin, the rather erratic dictator of that newly independent nation, briefly put his army in kilts of the Royal Stewart tartan.[9]

The power of tartan to inspire ideals of independence and justified resistance, however delusional, makes it a fitting textile to join the collection of Napoleonic uniforms and nineteenth-century regimental finery that feature so often in a despot's wardrobe. Tartan, as a result of its regular historical reconstructions, has not only been freed from its original signification but has amassed a host of secondary ones, allowing it to act as an indeterminate textile sign, which when adopted by a particular wearer or incorporated into a specific garment, can bring to that context all of its accrued symbolic references as well as adapt itself to new meanings. Thus Amin wears it as a symbol of Scottish independence, a textile that refers to English imperialism and symbolizes courage and strength, allowing him to become, as Foden puts it:

> Idi Amin at Hollyrood ... Idi as Prince Charlie ... Idi Amin as Cumberland the persecutor ... Idi running on the track at Meadowbank ... Idi spitting on the cobbled Heart of Midlothian...[10]

Interestingly, this list can be enlarged to include Idi as Macbeth, following the stage production presented by the Out of Joint Company in 2004, which featured an African 'dictator' as *Macbeth*. His characterization referred directly to Amin and he appeared complete with kilt and other tartan trappings.

Whilst Amin's symbolic use of tartan was complex and transcended the customary tyrannical fondness for uniform, the actual garments he favoured were of the strictly regimental variety, as befitting a military dictator. There are examples of tartan aggrandisement worn with no less martial hauteur, but which have looked to an earlier era for their sartorial inspiration. As with the early appearance of trousers as part of Scottish regimental costume discussed previously in the consideration of Sir John Sinclair, so too the influence of classical antiquity, which characterized fashion at the end of the eighteenth and beginning of the nineteenth centuries, makes a premature entrance in the remarkable portrait of *Colonel William Gordon of Fyvie* painted by Pompeo Batoni in 1766 (illus. 76). Posing against a backdrop of classical ruins and flanked by a statue of Roma, he wears an extravagantly draped and kilted plaid, his hose, as Nicholson suggests, resembling the buskins of a Roman soldier. As an example of portraiture being put to the service of the prototype souvenir industry, supplying cultured gentlemen with a record of their experiences on the Grand Tour, Batoni's image is particularly striking, but when coupled with the bizarre conjunction of the plaid being worn in the style of a Roman toga it is truly remarkable. The collision between Scottish regimental dress foregrounded against the ruins of classical Rome sets up a host of possible readings for the picture, not least that of a presentiment of the newly constructed Britain post-Culloden as eventually doomed to failure, the ruins of what appear to be the Colosseum providing an architectural memento mori for this representative of the emergent nation. His use of the plaid as a kind of Caledonian classical drapery is testament not only to his self-image (Roman emperors being a favourite source of identification, alongside Napoleon, for the emerging megalomaniac), but once again to tartan's unique ability to assume any number of associations – political, historical and otherwise – and to the process of its historical reaffirmation that these same associations encourage. This early outburst of vestimentary historicism oscillates between the fascination with the classical

80 (This Page and Facing Page) Scenes from Out of Joint's tenth-anniversary production of *Macbeth* by William Shakespeare, 2004. Danny Sapani's portrayal of Macbeth drew upon Idi Amin's well-known fascination for all things Caledonian

past initiated by the discovery of the ruins of Herculaneum in 1709, the classically inspired costume of the latter part of the century, and the characteristic use of tartan in the next century – as a kind of fancy dress that expressed the desire for a fictional sense of the past represented in romanticized, condensed and disguised forms.

Contemporary evidence of tartan bravado, outside the sphere of entertainment (which will be considered shortly) is rarer. Alexander McQueen, if not literally a tartan king, is certainly fashion 'royalty' and has adopted a ceremonial McQueen tartan uniform that easily rivals those of Gordon and Amin. On being made a Commander of the British Empire in 2003, McQueen arrived at Buckingham Palace to receive his award from the Queen in full McQueen tartan *fhéilidh-Mor* and pheasant feather bonnet and, reportedly, expressed disapproval at the lack of formality shown by other recipients. No such relaxation of dress by guests was evident, however, at another occasion at which McQueen sported his tartan finery. For the Metropolitan Museum's gala benefit dinner to celebrate the opening of its show 'Anglomania: Tradition and Transgression in British Fashion' in

81 Alexander McQueen and Sarah Jessica Parker at the Metropolitan Museum's Costume Institute gala benefit to celebrate the opening of 'Anglomania: Tradition and Transgression in British Fashion', 2006

2006, McQueen once again donned tartan *fhéilidh-Mor*. This was teamed with tail coat, footwear that was a hybrid of Lonsdale-type boxing boots and Scottish dancing shoes, enlarged 'badger' sporran or *sporran molach*, and a silk satin tie reminiscent of the one worn by Lorne Green in *Bonanza*. This characteristic McQueen vestimentary bricolage was accessorized by the appearance of Sarah Jessica Parker, in an evening gown also of McQueen tartan, as transatlantic tartan 'arm candy'.

THE DANDY, THE SWELL AND THE GENT

> They were dressed in full suits of flaming large-checked red-and-yellow tartans, the tartan of that noble clan the 'Stunners,' with black-and-white Shetland hose and red slippers.[11]

George's triumphant appearance in Edinburgh in 1822 marks a sartorial transition in fashionable men's dress of the period. From this point and increasingly throughout the nineteenth century, as men's fashions became ever more proscriptive, reserved and discreet, there emerged a particular sector of male society, a 'subculture' in contemporary terminology, that favoured a distinctly showy (and for many contemporary critics, vulgar) dress sense. The 'swell' or 'fast' gent's personal style was characterized by a fondness for exaggerated versions of the prevailing fashions in men's tailoring, and as the century progressed, showed a particular preference for bold or 'loud' textiles, tartans and vivid checks being especial favourites. The rise of the swell is in complete contrast to that earlier sartorial expert, the dandy, with whom it might reasonably be supposed he had much in common. The dandy was born from the general shift towards egalitarianism that occurred in men's clothing after the French Revolution. From that moment, men's clothing became less and less about outward displays of wealth and power, and increasingly concerned with equality; and during the nineteenth century appeared progressively practical, dignified and thus suitable for most types of professional employment (although manual labour and other working-class occupations retained their strictly demarcated clothing). The possibility of a true democracy of clothing was, of course, untenable in reality, and the bourgeoisie needed a way to differentiate themselves from the rising middle classes who, ostensibly at least, were indistinguishable from their social and economic superiors.

Enter the dandy, whose sartorial aim was not to signal his superiority by obvious sartorial difference, but to register his separateness by a number of discreet vestimentary signs that should perform the simultaneous task of alerting those small sections of society who could perceive these subtleties of dress, whilst also remaining generally unnoticed. As Barthes puts it:

> Since it was no longer possible to change the basic type of clothing for men without affecting the democratic and work ethos, it was the detail (the 'next-to-nothing', the 'je ne sais quoi', the 'manner', etc.) which started to play the distinguishing role in clothing: the knot on a cravat, the material of a shirt, the buttons on a waistcoat, the buckle on a shoe, were from then on enough to highlight the narrowest of social differences.[12]

The rise of the fashion industry, where concepts such as exclusivity and *le dernier cri* became commodified and easily available, if at a price, signalled the demise of the true dandy who had championed modes of dress that couldn't be 'sold'. The swell, however, who can perhaps be thought of as typically British as opposed to the archetypal Gallicism of the dandy, became the exceptional sartorial model for the nineteenth century's increasing commercialization.

82 Waistcoat of woven silk velvet tartan. Back made from black ribbed silk; lined with brown sateen. Scottish, c.1850

The swell was active, swaggering and conspicuous where the dandy was passive, reserved and subtle; the swell or 'Corinthian' who emerged in London in the early nineteenth century was fond of so-called gentlemanly pursuits such as dog and cock fighting, excessive drinking and forays into the seedier parts of town in pursuit of pleasure. To a certain degree the swell accepted the sartorial mantle of the dandy, but with a heightened conspicuousness aided and abetted by the many distractions and entertainments that the nineteenth century's increased mechanization and commercialization offered these young men about town – a way of life that would have seemed alien to the true dandy of old. By the mid-century, when Robert Surtees wrote his *Mr. Sponge's*

83 The sculptor Andrew Logan in Logan tartan suit

Sporting Tour, from which the earlier quote concerning the 'stunner' tartan is taken, the swell had become somewhat of an anachronism, as Soapey Sponge and his friends suggest:

> At length we crossed over Oxford Street, and taking the shady side of Bond Street, were quickly among the real swells of the world – men who crawled along as if life was a perfect burden to them – men with eye-glasses fixed and tasselled canes in their hands, scarcely less ponderous than those borne by the footmen. Great Heavens! but they were tight, and smart, and shiny as any of them.[13]

Soapey Sponge considers himself a 'gent', the next stage on the nineteenth-century man's sartorial ladder. From the 1850s onwards, the swell – who although adopting the pleasures and pursuits of the lower classes could still be considered to be a gentleman – had been replaced in the sartorial stakes by the 'gent'. The gent, who more than likely was not a gentleman, was characterized by his love of 'loud' clothing, a typical outfit consisting of an exaggerated version of the short, wide men's topcoat teamed with narrow-legged, bold plaid or tartan trousers. Even fonder of sporting pursuits, carousing and pursuing the opposite sex than his swell predecessor, the figure of the gent was an amalgam of urban swagger and bucolic heartiness. The checks, tartans and tweeds beloved of the gent were perfect textile messengers of his sporting proclivities, particularly when worn out of context on the fashionable streets of London and other metropolitan European centres. The gents' versions of country clothing, unrestrained behaviour, and often garish appearance meant that the well-to-do were constantly warned against emulating their appearance, advice reminiscent of John Pinkerton's tirade some years earlier, where he suggested: 'Nothing can reconcile the tasteless regularity and vulgar glow of tartan to the eye of fashion.'[14] It is tempting to see an analogy between the reaction to the loud gent's love of country checks and tartans and the contemporary popularity of the Burberry check (which is considered in detail in Chapter 9, *Tartan, the Grid and Modernity*), with its bucolic, patrician origins becoming the favoured textile of a new urban class: the 'chav'.

The 'loudness' of the clothing of a typical gent can be understood as an antidote to the sombre black and grey garb that respectable gentlemen had voluntarily condemned themselves to wearing as a mark of sobriety, morality and professionalism. Tartan and other bold checks provided the perfect visual counterpoint to the universal restraint which men's clothing conformed to for most of the nineteenth century. Simultaneously signifying the countryside and made fashionable by Queen Victoria's endorsement of the pattern, it appealed to the gent's sense of British traditions aligned with a certain exhibitionist tendency, hence the 'flashy gent'. Aileen Ribeiro, in her *Dress and Morality*, quotes from the *Natural History of the Gent* (written in 1847) for this account:

> They like dancing though they do it badly, performing 'fandango atrocities' in the polka, they like to ogle actresses in the theatre, they stare at women bathers at Ramsgate, and they accost respectable women in the street ... their costume ... [is] 'a short odd coat', 'large check trowsers of the true light comedian pattern', loud cravats and tie-pins and bright yellow kid gloves over which are worn lots of rings.[15]

With the close of the nineteenth century, male clothing had to a certain extent relaxed some of its formality, and the concept of more casual, 'off-duty' clothing for men became acceptable. Lighter suits were favoured particularly for summer and holiday wear, and for sporting activities such as boating. Checked lounge suits, consisting of a high-buttoned, close-fitting jacket and narrow trousers also became popular, and whilst still not suitable for professional wear, this was

84 Steve Linnard, early 1980s. Bonnie Prince Charlie meets the New Romantics

widely adopted by middle-class men as informal daywear. Ribeiro, in her quote, also evokes the character of the comedian and it is in the entertainment industries that the tartan and the check find their true and lasting position in men's (and occasionally women's) dress, and where the migratory journey of dandy to swell to gent comes to rest.

PERFORMING TARTAN

> Whether these men are nicknamed exquisites, incroyables, beaux, lions or dandies, they all spring from the same womb; they all partake of the same characteristic quality of opposition and revolt; they are all representatives of what is finest in human pride...[16]

Baudelaire's formulation of the dandy and his close relations couldn't be further – sartorially – from the swell and the gent, but ideologically the quality of 'opposition and revolt' that he identifies is closely related to the figures who inherited the late nineteenth-century love of loud dressing.[17] Tartan and closely related plaid patterns distinguish a succession of popular entertainers from the late Victorian period up to the present day. Oversized and garish tartans have come to signify a stage persona that is invariably brash, vulgar, cajoling and also essentially of the people. The great 'turns' of the nineteenth- and twentieth-century music hall, entertainers noted for their tartan costumes – for example Harry Lauder, Dan Leno, Marie Lloyd (illus. 73), or clowns such as Coco – donned their tartans as a masquerade that would allow them to become the transgressive characters beloved by their audiences. Their swaggering tartan costumes invested their performances with the spirit of rebellious and subversive clowning that can be traced back to the figure of Harlequin, British nineteenth-century pantomime's translation of Arlecchino from the original *commedia dell'arte*.

85 Harry Lauder, the tartan comic famous for his twisted walking sticks and songs such as 'I Love a Lassie' and 'Roamin' in the Gloamin' '. From a sketchbook of caricatures by George Cooke, 1903–1905

As is well known, Harlequin, the all-knowing and cunning servant, is a complex character, simultaneously an amorous figure also endowed with magical powers. Reinvented as a popular figure in the Regency theatre, Harlequin's costume underwent a series of changes worthy of the theatrical transformations his own magic sword was able to trigger. The original baggy *commedia* outfit covered in patches was replaced by the now familiar tight-fitting and elegant costume, where the patches have become multicoloured diamond shapes outlined with spangles. The colours of these shapes symbolized different emotions, and by pointing to a particular diamond, Harlequin could convey to the audience what he was feeling at any given point. Yellow indicated jealousy, red anger, blue constancy and black rendered Harlequin 'invisible' to the other performers on stage. By the late Victorian period, the popularity of the traditional Harlequinade had begun to wane and was subsequently reinvented as the pantomime form still recognizable today. However, in its migration to today's popular Christmas entertainment, the figure of the Harlequin was dropped, resurfacing in the checked costumes of the subversive, clowning stars of the music hall, where their love of tartan can be regarded as echoes of Harlequin's emotionally loaded multicoloured diamonds.

As has already been noted (in the section discussing Vivienne Westwood's influences), there is a more direct association between tartan and Harlequin. A series of portraits (and copies of portraits) of Charles Edward Stuart, known as the 'Harlequin-type' portraits, depict the Young Pretender in a suit with tight-fitting breeches in a multicoloured chequerboard pattern (illus. 86). The typical background is a castle, and thistles are often included as an emblematic representation of Scottish resistance. These images are most probably based on a famous suit of clothes sent to the Pretender by James, the 3rd Duke of Perth, whilst he was in exile with his Stuart court in Rome; also included in the gift was a sword and targe (or shield), and these accessories increase the posthumous readings of these images of the prince as a Harlequin figure. The understandable conflation between the painted misrepresentation of tartan, a certain Italianate influence, and the persona of Bonnie Prince Charlie as a dashing, romantic figure has produced a fascinating, if somewhat anomalous subset within the representation of early tartan. What is relevant to the present discussion, however, is the use of tartan, or an approximation of tartan, in these images to construct Stuart as an elegant figure of 'opposition and revolt'.[18] Nicholson's 'varietal garb of loud colours and distinctive checks' results in the slightly comic appearance of these Harlequin portraits to contemporary eyes, but they are akin to the music hall entertainers and their checked costumes, whose performances cloaked a subversive and anarchic programme under a comedic disguise, similar to early tartan's ability to 'symbolize political allegiance'.[19]

The sexual innuendo, topical satire, bawdy singing, audience participation and tartan anarchy that were performed in the music hall and by circus entertainers are direct descendants of Harlequin's clowning. A legacy of this resurfaces today on the golf course, where certain players have taken the love of argyle sweaters, socks and caps to a multicoloured excess, their crowd-pleasing exhibitionism a sartorial distant cousin of Harlequin's diamond-patterned antics. The golf course – that most Scottish of arenas – is, like the pantomime stage and the Edwardian music hall, transformed by extrovert players who take full advantage of the short cut to popular appeal and empathy that boldly checked textiles appear to induce. The argyle check beloved of golfers is, in effect, an original tartan rotated by 45°, becoming the perfect vestimentary distillation of tartan's unifying checks and Harlequin's magical diamonds.

Harlequin's key role in the comic–grotesque world of medieval and Renaissance carnival has been widely discussed, most notably by Bakhtin. He relates how, by the second half of the eighteenth

86 (Facing Page) 'Harlequin' portrait of Charles Edward Stuart. Coloured line engraving based on a painting by an unknown artist, signed 'Wassdail'

87 (Above) Noddy Holder, lead singer of Slade, 1973

century, there was a critical and dramatic backlash against Harlequin as a grotesque figure, which prompted various commentators of the time to come to the Harlequin's defence. Part of this defence consisted in suggesting that Harlequin and other associated comic–grotesque characters belonged to a world that had 'its own legitimate order, its own criterion of perfection'; that this world was capable of 'combining heterogeneous elements'; and that 'it violates natural proportions, thus presenting elements of caricature and parody'.[20] Whilst this assessment of the world of Harlequin was produced to reconcile its position within the broader context of eighteenth-century enlightenment philosophy, the notion it puts forward, of a heterogeneous system that allows for hyperbole and parody, is directly related to the world of the tartan-clad entertainer, whether from the nineteenth century or today. Tartan's subversive signification is arrived at out of a complex mixture of its historical rebellious associations and its unique ability to function as a vestimentary indicator of sartorial exhibitionism, as well as its specific theatrical antecedence via the figure of Harlequin. A tartan suit allows a performer to be a satirist, be risqué or act the fool; to break with convention and yet still engender popular appeal and recognition.

In more recent times, a performer who recognized the full potential of tartan excess was Noddy Holder, during his time as front man for the successful British pop group, Slade. In the 1970s, Slade released a remarkably successful series of hit singles and albums, regularly topping the British charts. A large part of this success was due to the persona of Holder himself, who, in his immaculately tailored tartan suits and mutton chop side whiskers, suggested a direct sartorial link from the late nineteenth-century gent to 1970s glam rock (illus. 87). With his guttural voice, platform boots, purposely misspelt song titles – *Mama Weer All Crazee Now* (1972), *Cum On Feel the Noize* (1973), for example – and above all his extensive wardrobe of tartan, Holder carved a particular niche in the decadent and at times manufactured world of 1970s British pop. More accessible and democratic in appeal than some of his glam rock contemporaries such as David Bowie or Roxy Music, for example, whose stage personae often suggested difference and detachment, Holder's performances forged direct visual links with the unifying popular experience of the music hall tradition.

As has been suggested, tartan can be conceived of as a textile of excess, and it is this excessive tendency that is most often capitalized upon when donned by the entertainer. This excess can be of a sexual, comedic, or transgressive order, the tartan suit often a sign of those who are outside conventional societal norms, its ostentation and vulgarity an indication of an inherent decadence or weakness. The flashy or loud dresser, in popular culture, wears his tartan and plaids as a disguise, lending him an affability and attractiveness that masks a proclivity to corruption, even degeneracy. Sporting Life, the drug dealer in George Gershwin's *Porgy and Bess*, the assorted petty criminals in the film adaptation of Graham Greene's *Brighton Rock* (John Boulting, 1947), Archie Rice in John Osborne's *The Entertainer*, the boorish two-bit tycoon Harry Brock in *Born Yesterday* (George Cukor, 1950), Daniel Day-Lewis's swaggering Bill 'The Butcher' Cutting in *Gangs of New York* (Martin Scorsese, 2002) or Fredo the weak and treacherous member of the Corleone family in *Godfather II* (Francis Ford Coppola, 1974) all wear their 'loud' checks as a mark of deviance, dissipation and sometimes sadism. The bonhomie and affability suggested by the check, a legacy of the hearty, sportsmanlike origins of the swell's loud checks, is often used in fictional representations as a lure. The innocent or naive is literally mesmerized by the boldness of these characters' textiles, and it is only when it is too late that their protective disguises fall away to reveal their truly flawed and corrupt dispositions.

> …and all of them, every ace, every dude, out there just getting over in the baddest possible way, come to play and dressed to slay … so that somehow the sons of the slums have become the Brummels and Gentlemen of Leisure…[21]

Henry Louis Gates, Jr., in his *Figures in Black*, traces the connections between the figures of Harlequin and the American minstrel, calling upon eighteenth-century writers such as Marmontel and Florian to suggest that Harlequin's black face, or black and white mask and shaved head, are derived from his origins as an African slave. Similarly, his multicoloured costume is a result of his being clothed 'by three sons of a cloth merchant, who pieced together "three half-ells" to clothe the stranger'. Gates then goes on to cite a Harlequinade dating from 1836 entitled *Cowardy, Cowardy, Custard; or Harlequin Jim Crow and the Magic Mustard Pot*, as an example of how characters from American minstrelsy such as Jim Crow became conflated with the figure of Harlequin.[22] Leaving aside the contention invoked by the suggestion that Harlequin's origins might be anything other than Italian, Gates continues his study with an exploration of the concept of 'signifying' in black discourse, which although bearing some relationship to conventional notions of signifying has an especial resonance within black culture. Using Roger D. Abrahams for a definition, signifying

> refers to the trickster's ability to talk with great innuendo, to carp, cajole, needle, and lie. It can mean in other instances the propensity to talk around a subject, never quite coming to the point. It can mean making fun of a person or situation. Also it can denote speaking with the hands and eyes and in this respect encompasses a whole complex of expressions and gestures.[23]

The discursive links between the idiomatic elements listed above, the dialogues and exchanges that were an essential part of the minstrel show, Harlequin's transforming powers and the popular subversion of Edwardian music hall entertainers, are forged within the spaces of performance. The essential element of all of these popular forms of entertainment is that the performer should be seen as well as heard.[24] Looking specifically to the history of popular music, from the earliest jazz artists onwards, dressing to be noticed, or 'showing out', was an essential component of the performance, and 'loud' checked suits in fashionable tailoring and cuts of the moment (and sometimes exaggerations of it) were staple elements in most performers' wardrobes. The tartan and other checks worn especially by black artists signified and indeed were 'signifying' a knowingness, an urbanity and wit. This called upon tartan's long history of sartorial exhibitionism and pride, along with the specifically culturally situated tradition of the Trickster in African mythology, who 'is also a spirit of creativity, a refuser of rigid systems, and thus is both credited with founding culture and accused of violating the norms of culture'.[25]

The act of distinguishing oneself from everyday society was essential for the performer: it meant that he was visible, memorable and also able to convey instantly, by vestimentary signs such as tartan and bold checks, a certain lifestyle resonating with a history of sartorial trendsetting – the black diamond of Harlequin's costume no longer meant invisibility. However, it could be argued that popular culture demonstrates that this freedom of sartorial expression is comparatively recent and indeed available only to male performers. In the 1951 film version of *Showboat* (George Sidney, 1951) Ava Gardner plays Julie LaVerne, the entertainer who, unbeknown to those on board, is of

88 Harlequin figurine, Johann Joachim Kändler. Porcelain, German, *c.*1738

mixed race. In a key scene, where Julie teaches the showboat owner's daughter a cakewalk, she wears a tartan-trimmed dress typical of the late nineteenth century. At the revelation of her background Julie is expelled from the boat, the strictly enforced outlawing of any notion of miscegenation in the American South making it imperative that Julie's dissembling be punished. Even the protective plaid of the entertainer fails to work its magic in this case and, like Harlequin, she effectively disappears from the plot to become an alcoholic nightclub singer.

89 Music sheet for the song 'Lucy Long'. Mass-produced monochrome lithographic print, nineteenth century. Joel Walker Sweeney, born in Virginia in 1810, claimed to have learned the banjo from African-Americans and is the first recorded white banjo player to have appeared on stage. During 1843–4 (the probable date of this music sheet), he made an extensive tour of Britain with the Virginia Minstrels, donning tartan waistcoat and Harlequin trousers along with blackface in order to complete his transformation into the minstrel character 'Mr Sweeney'

The loud checks beloved by jazz performers of the 1930s through to the 1950s remained popular throughout successive decades and musical styles from soul and funk on to rock. And so Jimi Hendrix favoured a tartan suit that in its tightness, particularly at the crotch, rivalled the skin-tight trousers promoted by Beau Brummel in the early 1800s; whilst during the 1970s, every 'superfly' guy wore what Tom Wolfe has described as: 'plaid bell-bottom baggies ... with the three-inch-deep

elephant cuffs tapering upward toward the "spray-can fit" in the seat'.[26] Naturally, tartans and loud checks were not the exclusive preserve of black musical artists: many white artists favoured a bold check also, from bluegrass performers in obligatory plaid working men's shirts, to rock 'n' roll entertainers such as Bill Haley and his Comets resplendent in tartan tuxedos with a satin shawl collar (illus. 36), and more contemporary performers who wear tartan as an ironic vestimentary collage made up of references to 1950s 'sleaze', Ivy League preppiness and post-punk rebellion. The tartan suit, however ironically it is being worn, conveys a sense of sartorial awareness that is as prevalent amongst contemporary performers who like to 'show out' as it was in the middle of the nineteenth century when Surtees noted that: 'Young men, too, dressed as if they were dressed – as if they were got up with some care and attention...'[27]

One such contemporary careful dresser is André Benjamin, better known as André 3000 of the group Outkast, who has done more in recent times to promote the renaissance of the 'loud' gent than any other figure in popular entertainment. In a succession of stage outfits as well as those worn for other public appearances, Benjamin lavishes as much care and attention to the details of his toilet as would have any nineteenth-century swell. Surfing the crests of various historical vestimentary waves, his ensembles reference sporting costumes such as golfing plus twos and plus fours, jockey's caps and breeches, and hunting outfits, and also the back catalogue of American subcultural styles from existentialist beatnik to Hendrix-inspired acid head or 1970s pimp. These looks are teamed with elements derived from more patrician American clothing as worn by the college freshman of the 1950s, or in the 1974 film version of *The Great Gatsby* (Jack Clayton, 1974) – an acknowledged influence on his own clothing label. Throughout his stylistic journeys, Benjamin (voted the world's best-dressed man by *Esquire* magazine) has kept a love of tartan and other plaids as a constant. It is perhaps fitting that as the contemporary reincarnation of the dandy (albeit more *outré* than Baudelaire's or Barthes's models), the artwork for his 2003 double album *Speakerboxxx/The Love Below* has him 'showing out' in tartan waistcoat and trousers at the foot of the Eiffel Tower in Paris, the site of tartan's original entrance on to the fashionable stage in the early nineteenth century.

It is a testament perhaps to the power of the entertainment industry's ability to construct fashionable personae for its subjects that even the kilt, a garment so long associated with tradition, and not regarded as fashionable since Edward VIII had worn it, was, when sported by a suitably influential example of a contemporary 'fast' gent, made briefly popular. 'One mean mother in a kilt' was the epithet earned by Samuel L. Jackson in the film *The 51st State* (Ronny Yu, 2001), in which he played the kilt-wearing pharmaceutical 'expert', Elmo McElroy. The blurring between reality and fiction, between the kilt, drugs and Jackson's image as a sartorial leader, made the kilt instantly irresistible to those who considered themselves daring enough to wear one, and suggests that 'mother' should perhaps be added to the vestimentary taxonomy of dandy, swell and gent.

Finally, whilst on the subject of taxonomy, the term 'fast' – as it was originally applied to mean someone who lived too fast and was therefore disregardful of restraint – has a more direct correlation with velocity when considered in the context of tartan miscellanea. Jackie Stewart, the Formula One racing driver, three times World Racing Champion and archetypal 'fast' gent, was

90 (Facing Page) André Benjamin, lead singer of Outkast, photographed during the Democratic National Convention, Boston 2004

92 MacBean. In 1969, a fragment of MacBean tartan was left on the surface of the moon by Allan Bean, crew member of Apollo 12

known for wearing a swatch of Stewart tartan on his crash helmet; and Allan Bean, crew member of the Apollo 12 space mission, laid a piece of MacBean tartan on the surface of the moon in 1969. If space travel were not fast enough, Rod Taylor, in the cinematic version of H. G. Wells's *The Time Machine* (George Pal, 1960) chooses a tartan smoking jacket in which to go time travelling to the year 802,701 – obviously the only pattern that the true 'fast' gent knows will never date and which will always cut a dash, lending an air of authority to Colley Cibber's suggestion from 1696 that: 'One had as good be out of this world as out of the fashion'.[28]

91 (Facing Page) Kilted Samuel L. Jackson and Tara Palmer-Tomkinson attend the British premiere of *The 51st State*. London, 2001

Part III
TARTAN'S EMBRACE

93 Machine-printed wallpaper depicting Highland fishing scenes with kilted anglers. English, *c.*1870

8.
BALMORALIZATION

HISTORY LESSONS

> In the idea of eternal recurrence, the historicism of the nineteenth century capsizes. As a result, every tradition, even the most recent, becomes the legacy of something that has already run its course in the immemorial night of the ages. Tradition henceforth assumes the character of a phantasmagoria in which primal history enters the scene in ultramodern get-up.[1]

Historicism in nineteenth-century fashion has long been recognized as the prevailing symptom, and indeed cause, of an ever-accelerating series of vestimentary mutations that cloaked women's bodies from approximately the third decade onwards. Once the relative stability and simplicity of twenty-five years or so of neoclassical body-conscious fashions had been cast off, women's dress underwent a series of regular convulsions, which it still endures today. At an unprecedented rate, the shapes of women's clothes reflected a mania for recreations of past historical costume, and constructed a carousel of shifting erogenous zones that switched the emphasis from waist to buttocks to shoulders and back again, discovering limitless possibilities with the aid of an accelerated manufacturing industry for the modification of body shape and the treatment of textile surfaces. Women's dress of the nineteenth century perfectly encapsulates the inherent dichotomy of the age, simultaneously reflecting incredible technical innovation, imperial expansion and a pathological desire for a romanticized past.

Tartan's signification of Highland tradition, of the doomed Jacobite enterprise and its perfect tragic hero Bonnie Prince Charlie, its centrality to Walter Scott's best-selling escapism and its recent royal endorsement by George IV, made it a favourite drawing room 'phantasmagoria' for the fashionable nineteenth-century wearer.[2] Silk

94 Detail of edging from a woman's cape. Tartan velvet ribbon, machine lace, and blue, green, red and white silk fringing. British, c.1860

and velvet tartan excrescence trimmed dresses, capes and bonnets, draped and ruched over fashionably padded, puffed and distended forms; and in dazzling displays of dressmaking, tartan made its periodic 'ultramodern' entrances throughout the nineteenth century.[3] None of this fashionable production seemed to acknowledge that less than a century before, tartan had been regarded as seditious and liable to catalyse revolt. After 1822, dressmakers and their clients could choose to have their confections made up in Caledonia, Wellington and Sir Walter Scott fancy tartans, and join a panoply of temporal and topographical signs such as *Medici* collars, *Marie* sleeves, double skirts *à la Watteau,* outfits in *le style troubadour, Yokohama* crêpe, *Kashmir* shawls and *Muscovite* velvet. With such an excess of taxonomic resonance, it is little wonder that fashions rotated so rapidly and moved dramatically away from the minimalism of the beginning of the century:

> Each generation experiences the fashions of the one immediately preceding it as the most radical anti-aphrodisiac imaginable. In this judgement it is not so far off the mark as might be supposed. Every fashion is to some extent a bitter satire on love; in every fashion perversities are suggested by the most ruthless means. Every fashion stands in opposition to the organic. Every fashion couples the living body to the inorganic world. To the living, fashion defends the rights of the corpse. The fetishism that succumbs to the sex appeal of the inorganic is its vital nerve.[4]

95 Bodice detail from a Royal Stewart silk tartan dress. The bodice is cut in the Italian fashion popular at the time. British, *c.* 1847

This kaleidoscopic sartorial spectacle is symptomatic of the nineteenth-century's obsession with obscuring technical development with historicism, and the ever restocked department store of historical moments that was nineteenth-century fashion, bedecked capitalism under a welter of ruffles and bustles. Increased manufacturing and the proliferation of commercial outlets as the century proceeded demanded that clothes had a built-in obsolescence materially, but also socially, hence the limits imposed on the fashionability of a style, and why to this day manufacturing, retailing and fashion journalism will always function symbiotically. And so, as Walter Benjamin suggested, fashion's periodic revisitation of the past is indicative of its propensity to be topical, but its leaps back into history are like a tiger's in an arena: measured, sanctioned and conforming to the nature of a spectacle. Whilst Benjamin devised the image (*Tigersprung*) to comment on the French Revolution's imitation of ancient Rome, it can also be gainfully employed to understand the fashionability of tartan in the nineteenth century. Tartan's topicality was indisputable, especially after Victoria had made the pattern her own personal badge, but the tartan tiger leapt only into a Romantic Highland landscape, its bounds providing a frisson of excitement but remaining ultimately tamed and harmless.

It is perfectly fitting then that tartan in the nineteenth century imbricates with fashion, defining the contours of stylish dress at high days and holidays, its modish outbursts fed by a number of specific transformations and elitist endorsements. Tartan's starring role as fancy dress for off-duty royalty holidaying in the Scottish outposts of a European aristocratic never-never land ensured its popularity, whilst its function as the ideal gift and 'super brand' of British royalty sent by Victoria to assorted relatives, made the kilt – and the other trappings – all that was needed to turn a Prussian prince into a reconstituted Highland chieftain. Similarly, tartan was the perfect pattern to demonstrate the technicoloured vividness and strength of the new aniline dyes that became the rage in the 1850s and 1860s. As a textile for fashionable dress, tartan underwent periods of greater or lesser popularity throughout the nineteenth century, although a certain level of fashionability was constant as a result of Victoria's Scottish sojourns and the Balmoral effect. It is the kilt, the article of clothing most associated with tartan's repressed and oppressive past, that undergoes the most convulsive transformation, however – a transformation that is manifested in specific arenas and by select sections of society.

Outside its primarily ceremonial use by clan, family leaders and Highlanders who still wore kilts that had been handed down through the family, and the previously discussed adoption of the kilt as children's uniform, kilt-wearing in the nineteenth century became typically constrained. During this period, the kilt underwent a sort of chrysalid state away from the public gaze, ready to emerge and re-clothe the fashionable form throughout the following century. If the primary function of the kilt in the nineteenth century was as the costume of a fictional construct, a sartorial expression of a Scotland that never was, referencing a past demarcated by a privileged society, could it then recall any of its other histories? What of its supposedly prurient reputation? Was the Victorian voyage into the past so assured that whilst dredging up a motley assortment of connotations for tartan and the kilt, it managed to avoid other potentially embarrassing encounters? Encounters such as the Emperor of Russia who, during the occupation of Paris, became particularly interested in Highland Regimental uniform and after scrutinizing one Sergeant Thomas Campbell's hose, gaiters and legs, pinched his skin, 'thinking I wore something under my kilt', upon which Campbell lifted his kilt 'so that he might not be deceived'.[5] Or, if leaping even further back to avoid such an erotic confrontation, the Victorians would have perhaps come across the English opinion of

96 Photograph of Mary Emma Roper by William Edward Kilburn. English, 1857

97 Tartan silk bag with thistle embroidery. English, c.1850

the *fhéilidh-Mor* as recounted in the letters of Edward Burt, an English officer who comments on the kilted lower half of the plaid being worn 'so very short that in a windy day, going up a hill, or stooping, the indecency of it is plainly discovered'.[6] So, whilst the rest of fashionable Victorian society was busily disguising, deforming and obscuring the body in increasingly elaborate carapaces – the 'fetishism that succumbs to the sex appeal of the inorganic', as Benjamin terms it – it would appear that, ironically, Albert and his companions at Balmoral and at certain state occasions were enjoying the 'freedom' of the kilt both sexually and (if one regards it as a garment that had largely resisted the vagaries of fashion) economically as well.[7]

98 Prince Charles, 1978

But perhaps if we look more closely at the manifestations of tartan at Balmoral we can detect a somewhat fettered freedom, so abstracted and fetishized that it does in fact accord perfectly with prevailing Victorian sensibilities. As Mansel suggests: 'Many Scottish neighbours remarked, like the future Edward VIII, on the unnatural length of the royal kilts, almost covering the knee: "so very German"',[8] which would seem to suggest that Victoria and Albert's adoption of tartan and Highland dress was inflected by a somewhat prudish sensibility; whether the result of a particularly Teutonic response or not, it did suggest a detachment from reality and retreat into fantasy that any overt sign of sexuality might shatter.

Victoria herself wore a long silk tartan scarf almost every evening whilst staying in Balmoral, a schematic version of the original *arisaid* now reduced to a luxury fabric accessory to be worn over conventional Victorian evening dress. Similarly, Albert sported a kilt when hunting and at other occasions whilst in Scotland (illus. 74). Indeed, representations of his costume (kilt, sporran, hose and either hunting jacket or formal black for evening) are familiar to us today from innumerable wedding photos and celebration dinners. These men's and women's outfits, although merely the fashionable styles of the period, with tartan accessories (and bearing little or no relationship to actual Highland dress), have nevertheless become the mediated and commodified image of Scottish formal attire and, as has been suggested, whilst some 'felt patronized by Victoria's easy subscription

99 Photograph of the wedding of Lord Ninian Stuart. Lafayette Portriat Studios, 1906

to a Scottish ethnicity through her choice of dress … such activities helped make the Crown more inclusive, more "British", and less "English".[9]

As previously discussed, from 1848 onwards the royal princes wore Scotch Suits and Victoria's delight in dressing her offspring in tartan outfits can be seen as a legacy of her obsessive childhood interest in fashionable dress. The strength of this can be gauged by the collection of dolls, which were dressed by Victoria and Baroness Louise Lehzen in a series of remarkably detailed outfits. Victoria's hobby appears to have been transferred, in her adult life, to her fixation with national

100 Doll dressed as a Scotsman. By Alt, Beck & Gottschalck. Bisque with moulded hair. Germany, *c.*1880

costumes and the appearance of the 'foreigners' who wore them, but now instead of dressing dolls she preferred to represent the various costumes she encountered in meticulous drawings. Having ensconced herself in her private fantasy realm of Balmoral, the chance to dress up real live dolls – her children – in a newly invented national costume obviously proved irresistible to Victoria. Both she and Albert could indulge their fantasies of creating a hybrid Scottish-German theme park, peopled with assorted 'natives' in national dress. The Highland fantasy of the court at Balmoral has all the hallmarks of the self-contained, idealized world of the doll's house or toy theatre, where time has stopped and nothing can shatter its ordered perfection:

> The miniature world remains perfect and uncontaminated by the grotesque so long as its absolute boundaries are maintained. Consider, for example, the Victorian taste for art (normally transformed relics of nature) under glass... The glass eliminates the possibility of contagion, indeed of lived experience, at the same time it maximizes the possibilities of transcendent vision.[10]

SATURATION POINTS

It has been suggested that Victoria and Albert indulged themselves in a form of amateur ethnography at Balmoral, creating tableaux in stage settings designed and decorated by the royal couple, and where Albert's theories on the merits of a mountain upbringing on physical and psychological development could be observed. The exterior walls of the newly extended Balmoral were emblazoned by the royal crests of England and Scotland, a bas-relief of St Hubert, the patron saint of hunting, Albert's personal coat of arms, gilded crests of Saxe-Coburg-Gotha, and the Scottish thistle intertwined with the letters 'V' and 'A'. The whole architectural confection resembled Schloss Reinhardsbrunn near Gotha, a castle restored by Albert's father, Ernst I. The interiors were completely 'tartanized', including carpets in Royal Stewart tartan, chairs and sofas in Dress Stewart poplin; even the draperies in the estate carriages were of tartan, a decorative effect that has led to the term 'Balmoralization' being coined to denote a scheme whereby tartan of all setts and in a variety of materials reaches saturation point. The ballroom was decorated with stags' heads and suspended stuffed eagles, and sporrans were hung on the walls in the manner of sporting trophies – an extreme example of interior decoration as tableau, due no doubt to its creator James Grieve being a theatre designer. In such an environment, dressed in tartan themselves, it is tempting to imagine the royal party camouflaged to the point of disappearance, sucked into a tartan limbo that satisfied their desire for escapism and where, as Victoria suggested, 'All seemed to breathe freedom and peace, and to make one forget the world and its sad turmoils...'[11]

A more contemporary cinematic manifestation of this tartan terrain, where furnishings and people merge into one all-encompassing tartan topography, can be found in the film *Casino Royale* (the cinematic 'mother-lode' of tartan fantasy). In the previously discussed banqueting scene, Lady Fiona is resplendent in nineteenth-century tartan taffeta pastiche, accompanied by her 'Highland Virgins' and waited on by liveried staff, all in matching tartan. The guests sit on tartan-covered chairs in a banqueting hall carpeted and papered in the identical sett. The unreality of this tartan saturation adds to the heightened air of spoof espionage and Caledonian surrealism that are the central themes of the film. A similar unreality and atmosphere of sentimentality and longing (*sehnsucht*, the German word for 'longing', was apparently often used by Victoria when having to

101 Tartan stair carpet

leave Balmoral and return to England) pervaded Balmoral and was, it seems, all-inclusive. Guests at the Highland retreat, who were also encouraged to don appropriate costume, echoed the couple's delusions and found it 'almost unbelievable that the most powerful monarch should get rid of all state to such a degree. It is a simple family party here'.[12] Whether one can quite believe that the head of the most powerful empire in modern history could ever be a member of a 'simple family party' is debatable, but the illusion created at Balmoral is the product of a quintessentially Victorian dialectic of psychological fantasy and economic pragmatism.[13]

The aristocratic traditions and rural cosiness simultaneously suggested by tartan's use in Balmoral's interiors have meant that ever since the mid-nineteenth century, it has remained a firm favourite for decorative schemes. Tartan carpets and wallpapers in hotels, pubs and restaurants have for many years been employed to signify warmth, traditional values and seclusion from the outside world, whilst in domestic settings in Europe and particularly in America it conveys an aspirational quality derived from its royal associations. More recently, tartan has been incorporated into the schemes of a number of contemporary interior designers, the utilization of the pattern guaranteed to add that particular 'note' to a decorative scheme. Design companies such as Precious McBane referenced the inherent surrealism of the engulfing Balmoral effect, producing a remarkable series of anthropomorphized tartan furniture (illus. 104). Other companies, including Anta and Ralph

102 The entrance hall from Blair Castle, a quintessential example of the Victorian baronial style, was designed and built in 1872 by the Edinburgh architect David Bryce. Amongst the displays of weaponry are targes and muskets used at the Battle of Culloden. The Atholl Highlander is standing next to 'Tilt', a stag kept in the castle grounds until his death in 1850 aged thirteen. His antlers (from the age of three onwards) decorate other areas of the castle

Lauren Home, rely on tartan to retain their traditional values, 'worth, wit, whimsy' being the qualities that sum up Anta's design philosophy, whilst a typical exercise in journalistic tartanization comes from the April 2006 edition of *World of Interiors* magazine, which notes: 'Rich tartan fabrics are certainly suitable subjects for reverie', the stylist of the feature having woken up to her 'kilt complex'.[14] However, none of the above could perhaps match the tartan or rather plaid Fall 2000 edition of the subversive American interior design magazine, *Nest*. In this issue (which came complete with plastic-covered tartan cover and 'gridded' pages) was an article entitled 'Patterns for

103 'Tartan' wallpaper designed by Mary Storr from a John Line & Sons pattern book, 1952–3

Slatterns', which detailed an all-white minimal interior 'transformed' by a scheme composed of woven plastic tartan loose covers and floor cloths, combining fantasy with a 'wipe-clean' reality.[15]

COMMERCIAL DOMINATION

The idealized microcosm of Balmoral was of course untouched by the harsh realities of life that the majority of Victoria's subjects endured during her reign, and which supported the macrocosm of accelerated British nineteenth-century imperial expansion, technological enterprise and economic supremacy. Victoria and Albert could content themselves with a model of Highland society, tartanized and indebted to the sentimental vision of their literary hero, Walter Scott – the 'Wizard of the North' – but it is tartan that ironically reconciles the apparent dichotomy residing at the core of their Highland project. On her early visits to Scotland, before she established herself at Balmoral, Victoria had promised manufacturers that she would endeavour to make tartan more popular, especially outside the Highlands, and it is fair to say that she made good her promise. The appeal made to her by manufacturers was due in no small part to the virtual monopoly held by one tartan manufacturing firm in particular.

104 Pieces from 'Tartan Tales', Precious McBane's first furniture collection, which launched the design company of the same name in 1994. Items dressed in Lochcarron tartan included (top left) 'Lankie Lassie', an hourglass-shaped chest of drawers in its own made-to-measure outfit, (bottom left) 'Kiltie Kiltie', a bureau complete with its own sporran, and (top right) 'Perfect Peeked', a dressing table and stool hiding beneath matching kilts

105 Letters addressed to William Wilson & Son, the pre-eminent nineteenth-century tartan manufacturers of Bannockburn, on display at the Scottish Tartans Museum, Keith. The letters, many with tartan swatches, are dated 1820–28, and include correspondence from British clients as well as those in New York, Baltimore, Montreal, Barbados and Rio de Janeiro

The centre of eighteenth-century tartan production was at Bannockburn near Stirling, and William Wilson & Son dominated the industry. They transformed what was in effect a small, multi-locational cottage industry into the tartan business that we recognize today. The earliest written records of the firm date back to 1765, but it is known that they were supplying tartan to the newly raised regiments around the time of Culloden and may have been producing tartan well before that. During the period of the proscription, they not only supplied the army with tartan, but were also exporting cloth to Norway, the West Indies, North America and Brazil. The company utilized travelling salesmen who generated business, gauged the popularity of the patterns in different areas, and also actively researched and collected new patterns during their travels: these were then modified, reproduced and added to their own books. The controversy surrounding the naming of individual patterns and especially the association of specific setts with particular clans has, as has already been discussed, raged long and hard. Closer examination of the methods and business practices of firms such as William Wilson & Son has finally laid to rest many of the more extravagant claims for clan-related tartans, and John Telfer Dunbar's pioneering research into the company's business correspondence, pattern and order books has made clearer the relationship between clan tartans and the growth of tartan manufacture in the nineteenth century.[16]

A cursory examination of this material immediately reveals that the tartan taxonomy we are familiar with today, as with many classificatory systems, has been reached by a process of modification, and only becomes fixed in response to specific ideological demands; in the case of tartan these demands were to establish a textile antecedence and relationship to the Highland clan system. What the records of William Wilson and others suggest is that whilst there were existing popular tartan patterns that may, or may not have been worn extensively by one clan family and their adherents, the majority of tartans that survive today have only comparatively recently been labelled as such. Before being renamed they were more than likely to have had (if any) a name associated with the district in which they were commonly produced, or were given names that had biographical or other associations which tended to change according to prevailing trends, particular events, or for purely commercial reasons. Other than that, the vast majority of the Wilson patterns were originally known only by number; this was subsequently replaced by an actual name. As we have already seen, the major taxonomic shift occurred as a result of George IV's visit to Edinburgh in 1822, when clan leaders and other prominent Highlanders felt compelled to claim what had hitherto been anonymous tartans as their own particular clan setts. Whilst the importance of this classificatory scramble cannot be underestimated, it has also served to eclipse much other useful material that can be gleaned as to the emergence of the nascent tartan industry. This includes how prevailing trends dictated the survival of some patterns and the demise of others, and also, in particular, what other hierarchical structures the textile helped define and sustain alongside its role in supplying military and 'clan' tartan.

In one of the earliest of the surviving sample books from Wilson & Sons, dating from 1820, most tartans are identified by number only, but some are named and give an indication of the scope such names may cover: Durham, Smallest 42nd, Robin Hood, Meg Merrilees, Clarke, Eglinton, White Wellington and Large Gipsy. From this list we can see tartans named after districts, fictional characters, illustrious figures of the day, regiments, indigenous groups and family or clan names. Tartan names were just as likely to be commercial as familial in origin, and were commonly named after the particular towns or locations in which they proved to be most popular. In some cases, they were named after the representatives who sold them: Logan tartan, for example, was most probably named after a merchant called Thomas Logan, who by all accounts procured a number of new tartan patterns for Wilson. Other tartan names mask multiple signification, referring to both district and family perhaps, but also shift according to where they were manufactured, who they were supplied to, and how they were latterly referred to in subsequent tartan lists and directories. For example, the pattern known as Argyll is first recorded in Wilson's pattern book of 1819 as both 'Argyll' and 'No. 230'. Accounts dating from 1798 also refer to an 'Argyll tartan' which may have been the same sett; it is also referred to in W. and A. Smith's *Authenticated Tartans of the Clans and Families of Scotland* of 1850 as 'Cawdor Campbell'. The pattern was worn by the 91st Argyllshire Highlanders as 'Campbell' between 1865 and 1881, bringing the story full circle and connecting the pattern, via the regiment, to the county of Argyll once again. It has finally become known as 'Argyll District', and is referred to as such in W. and A. K. Johnston's *The Tartans of the Clans and Septs of Scotland*.[17] This classificatory complexity is typical and can be even further elaborated if Hunting, Dress and other variants of the same named tartan are considered.

Certain Highland traditions were also the inspiration for tartan terminology. For example, it was customary for a bride to receive a new plaid as part of her wedding outfit, and to honour this tradition, setts could be named after the newly married woman, as is the case with the pattern known as Janet Wilson, named in 1775 by William Wilson for his spouse. The naming of tartan was a vital marketing tool to firms such as Wilson's, and naming tartans after recent events, or personalities, often ensured commercial success. Unsurprisingly, two of Wilson's best-selling lines immediately after George's state visit to Edinburgh in 1822 were the patterns known as King George the Fourth and Sir Walter Scott. Conversely, external events could necessitate the changing of a tartan's name: before 1820 Wilson had successfully sold a pattern named Prince Regent, but on George IV's accession to the throne this title became redundant, yet it stayed on the books as a popular pattern and eventually ended up being renamed as one of the Maclaren tartans.

William Wilson's position as the pre-eminent tartan manufacturer of the day coincided with the beginnings of tartan research – part of the general increase in interest in Highland traditions and history – and the firm enlisted the aid of experts as a means of authenticating and endorsing their patterns, their most profitable alliance being with the Highland Society of London. In 1819, in preparation for the royal visit, Wilson prepared a Key Pattern Book and sent samples of the tartans to London for 'certification'. The pattern book included weaving instructions for over 240 tartans,

106 Swatches of Wilson & Son tartan

of which some 130 were named; others were identified by number. The patterns were divided into hard tartans (densely woven, coarse wool varieties that went out of fashion as the nineteenth century progressed), super-fine tartans, and merino or soft wool tartans, which were introduced in 1816 to capture the ladies' market, a growing trade as can be seen by the following communication from one Donald McPherson, a tailor in Inverness: 'Send me good quality fine tartan as it is intended for the wear of Ladies who are desirous to dress in the uniform plaids of their husbands.'[18] Also included in the pattern book were serges and 147 fine plaids, or fine kilts as they were known; these two types of cloth were the most popular weight and quality for cloaks, ladies' and children's dresses and scarves. So great was the demand for tartan as a result of the royal visit that Wilson opened a new weaving shed named the Royal George, which could accommodate forty looms, and as Dunbar notes, a copy of the *Stirling Journal* reported that: 'All persons formerly engaged in the weaving of muslin in this quarter have commenced the weaving of tartan in consequence of its affording a better return for the labour.'[19]

107 Installation views of *The Manhattan Tartan Project, Phases I and II* by J. Morgan Puett and Suzanne Bocanegra, 1999–2001

Alongside the hasty redesignation of numbered tartans with clan names, Wilson also increased the production of the so-called fancy tartans (these had nothing to do with clan, regiment or even district, with names such as Wellington and Caledonia, a nomenclature expressive of contemporary cults of personality and Romantic nationalism). Setts at this period of increased production and innovation would often be enlarged or reduced according to the actual weight of the cloth and its intended use, so smaller checks were typically used on children's garments or trimmings, larger checks for blankets. This pioneer example of tartan adaptation provides a connection with Burberry's contemporary experiments in scaling up the grid of its trademark Nova check.[20] Tartans from this period were also often augmented by the addition of woven silk stripes contrasting with the rest of the cloth.

The adaptation and augmentation of tartan to accommodate different markets and political climates is an area that has been explored in one of the most fascinating contemporary tartan art projects of recent times: *The Manhattan Tartan Project*. In 1998, American artists J. Morgan Puett and Suzanne Bocanegra started research on a design for a tartan to represent New York City. The setts they produced were arrived at by utilizing economic, topographical and demographic data to determine the thread counts and colour ratios of the different stripes that made up their eventual tartans. For example, Manhattan Financial tartan no. 599 takes the different income brackets of the city to determine colour (so an income of over $100,000 a year was represented by silver), and the distribution of this economic pattern across the north-south postal code system to determine its relative width. Similarly, Manhattan Ethnic tartan no. 600 used population census material to determine its eventual colour palette, so the shade 'golden sand' represented Asian Pacific people, whilst 'shell' represented Europeans. Working with a Scottish textile mill, Geoffrey Tailor Highland Crafts Ltd., to weave their tartans and have them officially registered, the artists made a variety of garments and objects from their designs. Referencing tartan's deployment by the Highland regiments, they produced a variety of 'unifoms' including a dustman's overalls, Stock Exchange worker's smock, waiter's apron, and a Wall Street broker's suit. Similarly, they acknowledged the importance of tartan to the history of Scottish tourism, producing a series of updated tartan-covered artefacts such as a CD player and headphones, household items and soft furnishings. Versions of more traditional tourist souvenirs were also produced, such as tartan-covered boxes that refer directly to Mauchline Ware, the first true Scottish souvenir, which will be discussed shortly. Their tartan products, however, act as souvenirs of Manhattan rather than Scotland, referencing the large-scale nineteenth-century migration of Scottish settlers to America.

Returning to nineteenth-century tartan manufacturing, the classification, naming and adaptation of existing patterns was a commercial necessity more pressing than any desire for authenticity or historical accuracy. It was a way of ensuring standardized production, analysing sales figures, estimating popularity and responding to fluctuating trends. In this regard, tartan can be seen as a forerunner of many marketing strategies that are common today in the commercial sector. Patterns were continually adapted, renamed and altered according to prevailing fashions and changes in taste, and probably only when a pattern had proven its commercial worth did its name become fixed. The renaming of tartans carried out by Wilson can be regarded as a nineteenth-century prototype of contemporary branding exercises, where Caledonia, Scott, Rob Roy etc. act as a 'prefix' to the actual tartan, a 'qualifier of character' in the same way as Levi's is for jeans or Hoover for vacuum cleaners.[21] A particular pattern name could generate royal, topographical, Romantic and many other associations in the consumer, particularly in the ever-expanding foreign markets, where an evocatively named tartan would prove all the more saleable. It is interesting to note that at this period of tartan's increasing commodification and transformation into a global signifier of Scotland, clanship, and tradition, Wilson's archive can also be used to demonstrate just how fragile and unstable taxonomy can be, in that as recently as 1825 his firm received an order for 'plain, green-coloured tartan without pattern', implying that the term 'tartan' could refer specifically to the type of cloth rather than any particular pattern, almost a form of 'non-branded' cloth perhaps?[22]

There were a few rivals to Wilson's dominance as tartan manufacturer: around 1800, for example, Norwich tartan-makers were evidently undercutting Wilson's prices; closer to home, John Callander & Co. of Stirling was a competitor. Callander, alongside Wilson, made Stirling probably the most important Scottish weaving area. But tartan's global proliferation in the early part of the nineteenth century must primarily be due to Wilson. They were the major suppliers of regimental tartan, which was being carried far and wide by soldiers defending and increasing the British Empire, and as Dunbar suggests: 'Practically every Highlander who fought at Waterloo and in the Crimea must have worn some item of clothing from the Bannockburn firm.'[23] Apart from regimental tartan, it can be seen from the firm's correspondence and order books that it was also supplying tartan for civilian consumption to Aberdeen, Glasgow, Kirkcaldy, Elgin and Edinburgh, where Messrs. J. Spittal & Son wrote to Wilson in 1829 complaining: 'We are like to be torn to pieces for tartan, the demand is so great we cannot supply our customers.'[24] England was obviously a major consumer (in the period immediately following the visit of 1822, one London company was ordering six dozen tartan shawls a week) and tartan was supplied to customers in New York, Baltimore, Montreal – 'Tartans are much worn in America, and seen at all seasons, tho' best in the Fall' – as well as Barbados and Rio de Janeiro.[25]

The rapidly growing tartan industry expanded dramatically with Victoria's purchase of Balmoral, where, as has already been noted, she wore tartan herself and decorated Balmoral throughout in the pattern. By making Scotland, and the Highlands in particular, fashionable as a holiday destination for the Victorian well-to-do, and as a popular tourist attraction for countless others since that time, she effectively transformed tartan from the cloth of a recently Romanticized Highland culture into the global brand of 'Scottishness' it is today. Her endorsement of tartan made it the textile prerequisite of the fashionable, who dressed themselves and their living spaces in the pattern. Similarly, the demand for tartan abroad increased as the British Empire grew ever larger and those who found themselves running it adopted tartan as a suitable textile reminder of home. Tartan emerges from Balmoral as a technicoloured butterfly nourished by a heady nineteenth-century mix of historicism, spectacle, ethnography and sublimated sexuality, as well as having growing global signification as the textile of British imperialism. Its previous resonance as a visual reminder of Scottish identity and rebellion against the English throne was now subsumed within its new status as a highly complex shifting signifier, where insurrection becomes just one colour of its sett, given more or less prominence according to its momentary utilization.

108 (Facing Page) Advertisement for Camp Coffee. Anonymous. Chromolithograph, English, late nineteenth century. Robert Patterson & Sons, the Glasgow food company, launched their coffee-based drink in 1885. It was originally intended for soldiers on campaign in India and the firm chose Major General Sir Hector Macdonald as the perfect image for their new beverage. Major Macdonald, a decorated Gordon Highlander, epitomized the rugged Scottish warrior. He was known as the scourge of Afghans, Boers and the Dervishes of Sudan and was credited with saving Lord Kitchener's imperial army at the Battle of Omdurman in 1898

After reaching a peak in the second half of the nineteenth century, tartan manufacture began a steady decline, primarily due to the vicissitudes of the fashion industry and inefficient production methods. The production of Scottish traditionally woven tartans deteriorated as the production of cheaper, mass-produced foreign and printed tartan patterns increased. By the twentieth century, Scottish tartan manufacture had come to occupy a prestige position; although preferred for its high quality and traditional manufacturing methods, it found it hard to compete with cheaper foreign alternatives. Certain companies, by becoming specialists in a particular aspect of tartan manufacture, have managed to survive in today's tough textile marketplaces. For example, firms such as Robert Noble have continued the laborious and slow process of weaving regimental tartans, which has to be carried out on old-fashioned dobcross looms. However, this has also been to their advantage, as it is only older technology such as theirs that can guarantee the accuracy and consistency of the tartan sett across the whole length of the fabric required for a traditional kilt length, thus allowing them to capitalize on this lucrative specialist market. At the time of writing, Noble's has secured the contract to supply the tartan that will be made up into kilts for the highly controversial new 'super regiment' – The Royal Regiment of Scotland – formed from the amalgamation of the Royal Highland Fusiliers, the Black Watch, the Highlanders, the Argyll and Sutherland Highlanders, the King's Own Scottish Borderers and the Royal Scots regiments due to Ministry of Defence cuts.[26] Another surviving specialist tartan manufacturer is Lochcarron, based near the border town of Galashiels, which has cornered the market in weaving contemporary tartan designs for a host of international fashion designers, Vivienne Westwood being one of their most important clients, and kilts for a list of celebrities including Sean Connery, Ewan McGregor and Samuel L. Jackson. It produces garments and accessories as well as actual cloth and has developed from a craft-based industry into a world leader of contemporary, high-quality tartan manufacture claiming to have the most comprehensive range of modern and traditional tartans on its pattern books.[27]

ÜBERTARTAN

Victoria, or the 'Countess of Balmoral' as she liked to call herself when travelling abroad incognito, popularized Dress or Victoria tartan. She often wore this variation of Royal Stewart, claiming an attachment to Stewart ancestry, joking that she was at heart a Jacobite, a further example of tartan's centrality to the role-playing that her Scottish sojourns seemed to encourage. In Dress Stewart, the broad band of red is replaced by white, producing a lighter effect that lent itself perfectly to the ultra-feminine fashions of the mid-Victorian era. Dress tartans have remained popular ever since, allowing manufacturers to increase profits by a form of tartan 'artificial acceleration', whereby an existing sett is adapted into a Dress set by the substitution of white for darker colours, in effect allowing the same tartan to be marketed again. Apart from Dress and Royal variations, Victoria and Albert also used Royal Hunting Stewart at Balmoral, and Albert (who also designed dresses and jewellery for his wife) invented a new tartan around 1850, called Balmoral. Balmoral's sett was composed of black, red and lavender stripes on a grey ground, the colours evidently inspired by

109 (Facing Page) Six variations of Stewart tartan. 1. Royal Stewart Modern. 2. Dress Stewart Modern. 3. Prince Charles Edward Stewart Modern. 4. Black Stewart Modern. 5. Hunting Stewart Ancient. 6. Hunting Stewart Weathered

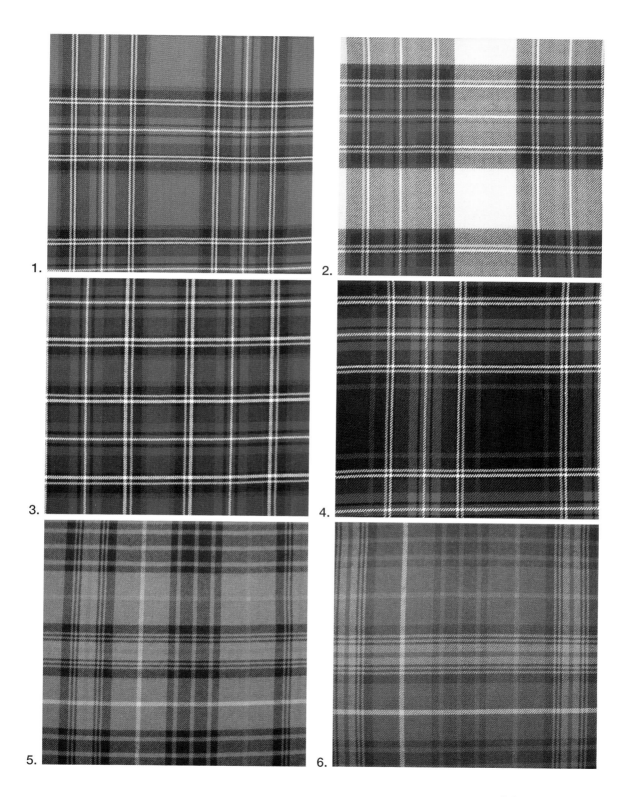

1.

2.

3.

4.

5.

6.

Deeside granite and the Grampian Hills. The sett was primarily used for estate workers and other members of the royal staff and today it is still the only tartan that the general public are prohibited to wear.

Leaving these variations aside, it is the tartan known as Royal Stewart that has come to dominate all other patterns. It seems that this tartan, above all, is the one able to carry all the various signifiers loaded upon it, which is due largely to its association with the Scottish royal House of Stewart, or Stuart, to give it its pre-Anglicized spelling. This tartan boasts at least fifty variations used by, or made in honour of, this particular Celtic family. However, it is Royal Stewart (as it has become known) that is the most commonly seen and which appears most often on the High Street and the runway. Royal Stewart dates from about 1800 and, most importantly, was the tartan chosen by George IV on his state visit to Edinburgh in 1822. It is worn by the Scots Guards and is still the personal tartan of the Queen today. In the same manner that clansmen can wear their chief's tartan, so too does any subject of the Queen have the right to wear this particular tartan. This royal antecedence coupled with its reinforcement throughout popular culture, musicians favouring it especially (one only has to think of Rod Stewart), makes it the pre-eminent tartan for fashion and other industries alike. The origin of Stewart tartan, as with most tartan patterns, is shrouded in a combination of historical myth, 'wishful proving' between other earlier equivocal tartan patterns and more contemporary scholarly research. This imprecision, combined with the numerous variations produced by a bewildering number of manufacturers and designers, has resulted in a generalized, predominantly red tartan pattern that apart from actually being reproduced as a textile, can be found covering every imaginable surface and 'branding' a vast array of products. In its ubiquity and adaptability it has become the generic tartan, standing for all tartans, in effect an *übertartan* that fulfils all the necessary requirements of showiness, royal association and instant recognition.

Traditionally the House of Stewart, according to the sixteenth-century Scottish historian Boece, can be traced back to the ancient house of Kenneth MacAlpine, or Banquo the Thane of Lochaber, an association encouraged by Shakespeare when writing *Macbeth* as he was keen to ingratiate himself with James VI, the first Stuart monarch to occupy the English throne. (James was the son of Mary Queen of Scots, who changed the spelling of 'Stewart' to 'Stuart'.) Historical research shows that in fact the Stewarts are descended from a Breton (therefore Celtic) noble, Alan, a seneschal of the towns of Dol and Dinant. Alan was a crusader who died in 1097 leaving no heirs; his nephew Fitz Flaald accompanied Henry I to England, eventually becoming Sheriff of Shropshire. His third son, Walter, was appointed High Steward of the Royal Household by David I, who claimed the Scottish throne in 1124. The office of High Steward was made hereditary to the family by King Malcolm IV, the name Stewart being derived from a corruption of 'steward'. The fifth High Steward, James, supported both Robert the Bruce and William Wallace in their struggle for Scottish independence, and Walter, the sixth High Steward in the line, married Robert Bruce's daughter Marjory, their descendants forming the Royal House of Stewart. This royal connection to the early Scottish kings has proved irresistible to tartan historians over the years, an example being that in one nineteenth-century collection, a tartan example that would be considered Royal Stewart by contemporary experts is named Royal Bruce to cement an ancient royal antecedence for the pattern. It seems however, that the pattern recognized today as Royal Stewart was not named as such before 1800, and one of its earliest recorded appearances is as a plaid or kilt variation of a tartan on Wilson's pattern books called Prince Charles Stuart's Tartan, which itself is taken from the pattern of trews supposedly worn by the Prince or one of his followers during the Jacobite rebellion of 1745.

As has been noted, George IV wore the pattern on his state visit to Edinburgh, affirming its royal association, and it continues to be worn by Queen Elizabeth II. As can be seen from the above mixture of historical fantasy, nascent tartan research, shifting commercial nomenclature and more recent tartan study, Royal Stewart is almost indivisible, as a pattern, from its mythology. The belief in its royal status and connection to some of the most cherished turning points in the Scottish national consciousness, allows it to occupy a unique position today. This brief excursion into the complexity of specific tartan history has not even taken into account its many variants, including those associated with the three main branches of the house of Stewart that settled in the Highlands during the fourteenth and fifteenth centuries: the Stewarts of Appin, of Atholl and Balquhidder.

The only other tartan pattern approaching Stewart's popularity is Black Watch and similar regimental or government setts characterized by a predominant palette of dark blues, blacks and greens (illus. 53). If Stewart is the favoured tartan of the extrovert who revels in its bright reds, yellows and greens, then Black Watch (and its variants) is the ideal pattern for the more reserved tartan dresser, its military associations signifying order, authority and courage. It is ironic, if unsurprising, that the two most popular tartans are directly linked to the sublimation of an independent Scotland within the English construct of Britain. Royal Stewart, as the tartan messenger of Hanoverian supremacy worn by George IV, and Black Watch, as the sign of British military imperialism, constituted them as quintessential British (as opposed to Scottish) tartans and paved the way for their lasting global saturation as textile messengers of the 'United Kingdom'.

SELLING SCOTLAND

Plunged into mourning following Albert's premature death in 1861, it is doubtful whether Victoria ever wore anything as colourful as tartan during her remaining years. By the 1860s, however, her endorsement of it, the privileged position it had occupied in her attire and that of her children, and its use in interior decoration, ensured that tartan was regarded as a pattern that could, with the typical ingenuity of the age, be gainfully employed across a variety of surfaces and products. Tartan's new-found applications meant that it was no longer regarded solely as a textile irrevocably linked to items of ceremonial or historical dress. Due to its fundamental grid construction, tartan as a pattern (rather than as a woven textile) lent itself perfectly to the variety of printing methods that were transforming nineteenth-century graphic reproduction. Printed tartan patterns soon started to appear on a number of different surfaces and covered an increasing variety of objects, from wallpapers to printed fabrics. Tartans appeared with increasing regularity on the pattern books of a growing number of manufacturing industries, carrying the pattern far and wide as the graphic symbol of all things 'Scottish', 'traditional', 'royal' etc. One of the earliest and, for its time, most successful examples of tartan's dissemination as a form of global Scottish 'super-branding' was 'tartan ware', a type of Mauchline Ware developed by William and Andrew Smith of Mauchline, Ayrshire, and which can justifiably be considered the first commercially produced Highland souvenir. By the 1860s, the period of its greatest production, some 400 people were employed in the manufacture of Mauchline Ware: the name given to the small wooden items, mainly boxes of various sorts, which the factory produced. These souvenir objects, apart from satisfying the domestic market, were exported as far afield as Australia, South Africa and North America as well as closer to home in Europe.

110 Examples of tartan Mauchline Ware in the collection of the Scottish Tartans Musuem, Keith

The firm of W. & A. Smith became the pre-eminent manufacturers of these items, far out-stripping other firms, but originally the company started out as one of a number of decorative snuffbox manufacturers. Due to this particular company's dominance, the objects they and others produced have subsequently been named after the town in which the Smith factory was situated: Mauchline. The origins of the industry can be traced to the beginning of the nineteenth century and the development by one James Sandy, a keen amateur inventor, of a 'hidden-hinge' snuffbox, where the actual components of the hinge are formed from alternating joints or 'knuckles' made of the same pieces of wood as the lid and the base. These were joined together by a rod passing through a small-bore hole drilled through the joints. The last stage in the process was to finish off the ends of the hinge by a plug of wood, which resulted in a virtually invisible joint and an airtight fit admirably suited to keeping snuff fresh. This invention was developed and put into production by a number of manufacturers, but the decline in snuff-taking as the century progressed made the market unsustainable and many firms went out of business, leaving W. & A. Smith as the market leaders. This position was due to their innovative approach to the industry and their ability to adapt and expand to the changing demands of the market, producing a range of other wooden items as well as snuffboxes. The objects were generally made of sycamore, which had a close grain and pale golden colour perfectly fitted for the application of a number of decorative finishes. 'Transfer ware', the most widely produced range, incorporated transfers depicting scenes of local Scottish – and eventually worldwide – interest, which were applied to the objects and then highly varnished. 'Transfer ware' items are one of the earliest and most successful examples of mass-produced souvenir objects, bought specifically to remind the purchaser of a location, or sent as a form of greeting from that same area, in effect a three-dimensional 'postcard'. Other techniques included 'photographic ware' and 'lacquer ware' (generally thought to be produced in the aftermath of Albert's death, when the country was plunged into mourning along with the queen and the demand for commemorative mourning items of all sorts escalated). W. & A. Smith's most fashionable range, however (and certainly its most desirable and sought after today), was 'tartan ware'.

'Tartan ware' consisted of ingeniously produced tartan-patterned papers, which were then skilfully applied to the wooden boxes and other items. The workers were particularly adept at disguising the paper joins on round, curved and other complicated shaped items, by applying black paint and sometimes a wavy gold line; great care was also taken to match and line up the separate sections of tartan paper. The finishing touch was to name the particular tartan patterns used on the object in gold lettering, reinforcing tartan ware as the ultimate Scottish souvenir item: attractive, reasonably priced and with the potential to become a true collectable due to the labelling of the different patterns and the variety of shapes available. Originally, the tartan pattern was painted directly on the items by hand, but this process was costly and laborious and so in the early 1840s, the enterprising Smiths developed their ingenious tartan 'machine painting' process. The 'machine' consisted of a number of ruling pens mounted on a sliding bar, so that a series of parallel lines could be drawn or 'painted' using opaque inks on black paper. According to the particular tartan pattern being reproduced, the pens would be loaded with different coloured inks and other pens that were not needed were lifted clear of the paper. The pens were mounted about a quarter of an inch apart, but by fine adjustments, broader stripes could be produced by a series of fine lines of the same colour drawn adjacent to one another. Once the 'warp' had been drawn, the paper was rotated through 90° by means of a turntable and the same operation was then repeated, producing the 'weft'. The lightest colour of the tartan was drawn first, the darkest last. The result was particularly effective and realistic, and when applied to the various objects produced a highly attractive result. Apart from the boxes, many tartan ware items were produced including vases, jewellery, buttons, cufflinks, parasol handles and eggcups. One of the most appropriate uses was the production of tartan boards for the covers of books, particularly works by Scott and Burns, and the previously mentioned work on clan tartans published by the Smiths in 1850 used their process to provide illustrations of some sixty-nine different tartans.

From this early example of tartan's deployment within the tourist industry, the pattern today can be found on a bewildering variety of products from souvenirs to foodstuffs, and used as the corporate liveries and logos for an ever-growing number of commercial enterprises. Certain products and companies have become indivisible from their chosen tartan brand identities – Walker's shortbread immediately conjures up an image of supermarket and gift shop shelves groaning under their distinctive red tartan tins and boxes; and for American consumers particularly, adhesive tape is synonymous with Scotch tape. Whatever the brand or product, the addition of tartan as a visual element guarantees an audience identification of tradition, strength, reliability and independence, and so embedded are these qualities that the name alone can 'brand' a particular product with some or all of these attributes. Similarly, tartan's rebellious, anti-authoritarian history can evoke useful associative qualities when branding a product. Hamish McAlpine, the Scottish film producer and

III Group of tartan products and souvenirs

distributor, set up Tartan Films in the 1980s to bring Independent and World cinema to a wider (particularly British) audience. By naming his company 'Tartan', he can rely on the name to signify to its customers an independent and defiant attitude perfectly suited to the extreme nature of some of its productions. McAlpine's statement concerning Tartan Films' achievements could be just as applicable to the actual textile's often subversive and challenging contemporary usage:

> For the last twenty-one years, Tartan has established a reputation for walking a line which others fear to tread. Sometimes that can take us into sexually explicit territory and other times into intellectually explicit arenas.[28]

In whatever form tartan may be used in advertising, whether as a direct signifier of Scottish tradition or for more abstract, amorphous connotations, its proven track record as a successful visual messenger makes it as desirable in the highly volatile consumer landscape of today as when Victoria made her promise to textile manufacturers in the nineteenth century.

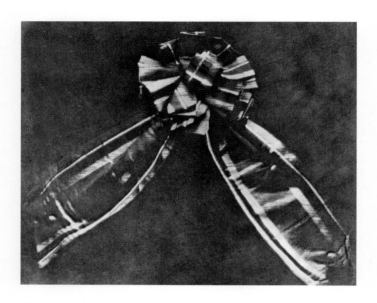

112 (Top) Tartan ribbon, considered to be the first colour photograph, produced by James Clerk Maxwell in 1861. (Bottom) Recreation of Maxwell's original demonstration; photograph taken by Peter Stubbs in 2004

9.

TARTAN, THE GRID AND MODERNITY

At the Exposition des Arts Décoratifs held in Paris in 1925, Paul Poiret, the great pre-war couturier, staged what was arguably his last sartorial spectacular. Using three barges named Amour, Délices and Orgues, he constructed a floating runway on which he staged an aquatic fashion show. Sensational as this show was, his popularity as a designer had by this time been superseded by a new generation of artists who made his pre-war orientalism, use of opulent surface decoration, and cutting and draping derived from the dress of the Far and Middle East, seem anachronistic. Given that the Exposition helped popularize many of the central tenets of modernist design, it is especially ironic that it should also have been the scene of Poiret's final triumph. Shortly after 1925 he ceased designing altogether, the cataclysmic upheaval of the First World War making his particular exotic design aesthetic seem irrelevant to the emergent modernist-influenced dress of the 1920s and 1930s. In this same year, however, Poiret produced a dress, now in the collection of the Victoria and Albert Museum, London, which demonstrates the same radical spirit that informed his revolutionary unstructured garments from the earlier part of the century. The silk tartan dress utilizes an enlarged grid as its decorative device and, whilst fairly typical of much of Poiret's oeuvre at this time (the dropped waistline, wide, square neckline and tubular underskirt, for example), its relative simplicity and reliance on the fragmentation of the check when gathered into the skirt's fullness, are unusual. His use of a modified silk tartan suggests an abandonment of his previous reliance on 'fancy dress' and a more disciplined reliance on the grid itself to demarcate the silhouette of the garment. Poiret has found for this outfit a form of

exoticism closer to home, concomitant with his interest in European folk costume. His tartan dress references the French fascination with Scottish costume that, as we have seen, was first awakened by the appearance of the Highland regiments in Paris after the defeat of Napoleon. Unlike the normal brocades and other figured fabrics that he utilized, this form of tartan exoticism produces a somewhat different effect and, one could argue, presages a move towards a more dynamic, less nostalgic form of dress, in tune with other designers from this period who (to a degree) had eclipsed Poiret and his orientalist fantasies.

Rosalind Krauss, in her essay 'Grids', suggests that the grid is 'a structure that has remained emblematic of the modernist ambition within the visual arts'.[1] If one accepts that tartan's fundamental structure is the grid, then many of the more conservative elements Krauss identifies are equally applicable to tartan's historic and national associations. The accompanying dichotomy that she also proposes as being symptomatic of modernism's deployment of the grid in art, becomes in turn a transparent and enriching process when considered in the context of tartan's grids. As has been stated previously, a tartan is composed of a sequence of stripes of varying width and colour – the sett; this same sequence is then repeated at right angles to the vertical one. Whilst the tonal qualities and rhythms set up between stripes of different widths, their frequency or repetition, and the relative complexity of the sett all contribute significantly to the overall effect of the tartan, its fundamental structure remains resolutely grid-like. In fact, all woven material conforms to a grid by the intersection of warp and weft. The addition of the simplest check, by the introduction of contrasting colours, immediately adds a further series of grids to its fundamental structural one.

As has been noted earlier, a simple two-colour tartan such as Rob Roy, with its alternate checks of red and black, demonstrates the underlying complexity inherent in tartan and the grid (illus. 7). The initial weave takes the form of a grid and then, by the introduction of two contrasting colours, further chromatic grids are formed so that where the black stripe crosses another of the same colour, a solid plain black is produced; the same effect is produced where red crosses red. However, where black and red cross, a mixture of the two in equal proportions is the result. So Rob Roy, consisting of just two colours, provides one mixture resulting in three shades in total: solid black, solid red and red-black. This ratio of colours to shades and mixtures has been analysed by Scarlett:

> The number of mixtures increases in rapid disproportion to the number of colours that we start off with, in accordance with the formula:
>
> $$M = (C^2 - C)/2$$
>
> where 'M' is the number of mixtures and 'C' the number of colours. Two colours, that is a simple check, give only one mixture (three shades in all) but six colours give fifteen mixtures, twenty-one shades: thus the more colours to begin with, the more subdued the final effect. This is not the only paradox to be found in tartan![2]

The paradox that Scarlett reveals in the colour ratios of tartan will be returned to later, but if we continue with Rob Roy as a model for our simple tartan grid, apart from the three shades now produced, a chromatic spatial relationship is established. Whilst it is possible to see the grid of Rob Roy as a simple two-dimensional pattern, it can also be 'read' three-dimensionally. Due to the resonance of the two colours and the optical effect of the black stripes appearing to be in the

113 (Facing Page) Day dress by Paul Poiret. Silk tartan. French, c. 1925

foreground, with the red receding and forming a background, a three-dimensionality is produced from its grid. The dominance of black over red means that where the two colours cross, the black registers optically as a lighter black or grey, enabling the tartan to be 'seen' as a black grid placed over, or floating above, a red ground. Obviously, the more complex and 'filled up' with different coloured stripes the tartan becomes, the less impact this effect of foregrounding and backgrounding has, but it is still possible to discern even in the most complex setts this process of recession and prominence.

Returning to the Poiret dress, it presents itself initially as a basic black and white tartan, consisting of broad stripes of white followed by two broad stripes of black interspersed with a narrow stripe of white, the pivot point being this narrow white stripe: black is foregrounded and occupies a plane above the white ground. A further complexity is introduced by the overlaying of what appear to be weft-only stripes of cerise edged with alternate narrow stripes of black and white, resulting in what could be considered as an 'obscured' tartan, the over-stripes of pink appearing optically in front of the black. A spatial interplay is thus set up, most clearly seen on the bodice, where it is possible to see the upper portion of the dress as a series of overlapping grids receding optically from pink through black to white. The clarity of the flattened-out bodice is in stark contrast to the gathered skirt where the geometrical perfection of the upper vectors is disrupted and broken. The contrasts in the Poiret gown therefore help demonstrate the inherent duality of grids, tartan or otherwise. This paradoxical, multivalent spatial dimension of grids has contributed to their persistence and accounts for much of the resonance and visual registration of tartan also.

Grids demarcate and order the surface plane of objects, rendering what was blank, unknown and unbounded as quantifiable and locatable. As with graph paper and Ordnance Survey grids, they render the abstract concrete, the unnoticed remarkable. In this respect they can be considered as ultimately conservative and oppressive, the product of rational, empirical thought, the enemy of indeterminacy and possibility. That is one conception, but grids and tartans are paradoxical structures and no more impressive demonstration of a grid's (or, in this case, a tartan's) duplicitous possibilities can be found than in the kilt. As has been stated previously, the 1890s saw the development of kilts pleated to sett rather than stripe, where each pleat is pleated to a different part of the pattern, but when sewn together reproduces perfectly the complete sett, mirroring the pattern on the flat apron of the kilt (it is tempting to see the Poiret dress as a transcription of this process, with the tight, flattened bodice leading into the as yet unstitched pleats of the skirt). What the domination of the kilt pleated to sett over the one pleated to stripe invokes is the rigidity, uniformity and ultimately conservative function of the gird that Krauss interrogates: 'No form within the whole of modern aesthetic production has sustained itself so relentlessly while at the same time being so impervious to change.'[3] And it could be argued that the maintenance of the sett in the contemporary kilt is indicative of the inflexibility within which tartan often appears to be constrained. The necessity of keeping to its exact sett, whether because of the proscription of clan accuracy or for other reasons, is what so often makes tartan resonate with a conservative, clichéd Scottishness.

However, one only has to look a little way back into the history of tartan's most iconic garment – the kilt – to see that, when pleated to stripe, the kilt displays both the fundamental structure and limitless variants inherent in grids and tartans alike. The effect most commonly achieved when pleating a tartan to stripe or colour is to transform the grid, or checks, into a series of stripes. The vertical or warp sequence of stripes is lost in the pleats of the kilt and only the horizontal weft stripes remain, which on a kilt produces a stunning oscillation, both graphically and chromatically, between

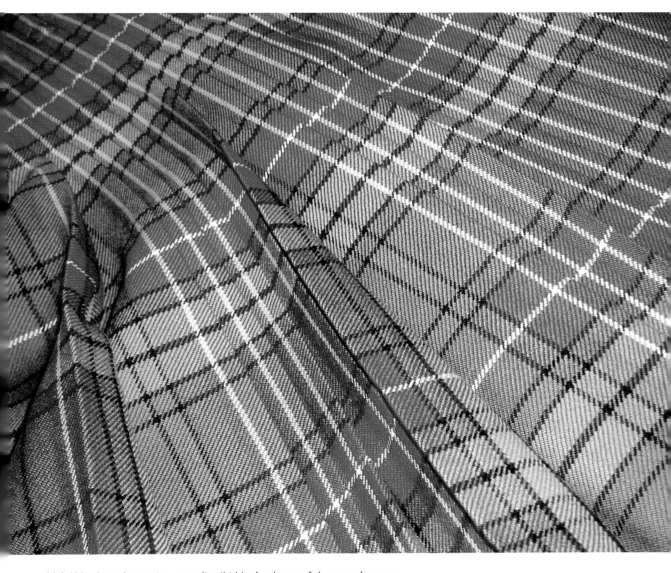

114 Kilt pleated to stripe, revealing 'hidden' colours of the complete sett

the complete sett of the apron and the transformed banding of the pleated skirt. Whilst this might appear to be a somewhat fanciful vestimentary association with what, after all, was Krauss's critique of the twentieth-century avant-garde's claims to originality, the contradiction demonstrated by the tartan 'schizophrenia' of the kilt – one moment a check, the next a stripe – perfectly encapsulates the dichotomy that Krauss explores in the grid. The front of the kilt presents the rigid perfection of the tartan's sett, which, as with all grids, is suggestive of containment, delineation and territorialization, yet, when viewing the pleated section of the kilt, the fragility of this rigidity is exposed. The sequence of coordinates, or cells created by the intersection of horizontals and verticals, disappears and we are left with a series of lines – unbounded, limitless and unfathomable. Added to this, when the pleats are animated by the movements of the wearer, the pleated section of the kilt suddenly reveals a momentary glimpse of wholeness or perfection achieved by the restoration of the complete tartan sett; however, no sooner is this revealed than it disappears again, reinforcing the transitory nature of this perfected state.

TARTAN ON CANVAS, IN STONE

Since 1997, the Shanghai-based artist Ding Yi has been producing a series of works entitled *Appearance of Croce*, in which he paints a series of crosses and Xs over a ground of tartan cloth. The crosses sometimes follow the original intersections of the tartan, sometimes occupy the spaces formed between the lines of the tartan (a kind of noughts and crosses without the noughts), and at other instances the crosses become so dense as to completely obscure the tartan ground. In his output dating from 1997–98, a margin was typically left unpainted as a remnant of the original material, but subsequent work often obscures the tartan completely. It has been suggested that with his 'discovery' of tartan, Ding Yi's 'artistic vision moved on to a higher plane', although Ding Yi's own comment on his work is somewhat more pragmatic, suggesting that, 'The cross is simply the basic element of composition of my works' and that tartan meant that he 'took advantage of what this industrial product had to offer'.[4] What tartan appears to have offered Ding Yi is what Krauss also suggests the grid offered a number of quintessentially modern artists such as Mondrian (one of Ding Yi's acknowledged influences), namely the ability to simultaneously express both the sacred and the secular.

Grids provide an articulation between scientific, rational perfection and the route to a form of spiritual meditation, whilst abrogating the artist from any need to depart from the grid's perfection once found, as Krauss suggested:

> One of the most modernist things about it is its capacity to serve as a paradigm or model for the antidevelopmental, the antinarrative, the antihistorical.[5]

However, whilst this might be true of grids, it is, it could be argued, only partly true of tartans. Tartan patterns do indeed display a dazzling mathematical possibility, their very notation often bearing a remarkable similarity to mathematical formulae, the colour changes, pivot points and repetition having a familial bond with the ordinates and abscissas of the mathematical and topographical grid. But although tartan's grids can be understood as mathematical and geometrical structures, and concurrently contained, containing and boundless, they are also, as Krauss maintains of grids in art, supremely mythic: a condition more cogent with tartans than any other form of grid. Krauss's argument that grids are essentially devices with which to mask an essential paradox at the core of modernist art practice, that allow us 'to think we are dealing with materialism (or sometimes science, or logic) while at the same time it provides us with a release into belief (or illusion, or fiction)' is certainly true of tartan's grids.[6] But when Krauss goes on to suggest that grids are 'stridently modern to look at' and leave no room for 'vestiges of the nineteenth century to hide', a further paradox occurs in that tartan not only signifies modernity in terms of its geometrical precision, but doggedly insinuates historical, social, located, literary and a myriad of other conditions, until we

115 Beat Zoderer, *TESA No. 2*. Used masking tape and paint on wood, 1996. *Bandage No. 5.* Wool on canvas, 1997

reach a condition of excess.[7] Tartan becomes the overloaded signifier so replete with signification that the only recourse perhaps is that taken by Ding Yi – to disguise (or, in his case, obliterate) the mythic tartan by equally saturated signs: crosses and Xs.

Another interrogation of the grid's autonomy, which has resulted in a form of degraded tartan, is found in the work of the artist Beat Zoderer. Zoderer uses everyday materials such as adhesive, masking tape, woollen threads and strips of colour obtained from brochures and other printed ephemera, to weave colour-saturated grid pictures. The work often bears a striking resemblance to tartan, due to his use of alternating bands of different colour and repetitive striped groupings. For example, in his *TESA No. 2* of 1996, Zoderer constructs a grid from used masking tape that bears the traces of other paintings, spaces and temporalities along its painted edges – the residue of its former location. From these relics of painted surfaces (the whereabouts and form of which we can only fictionalize), he weaves an indeterminate multivalent tartan that forms a discursive link to the equally complex, remote and fictional histories that permeate an actual tartan weave.

As the vestiges of lost paintings, imagined decorator's schemes and masked-off areas to be spray-painted cling to the edges of Zoderer's tapes, so too does the residue of political struggle, patrician ascendancy and industrial expansion thicken and tease out the threads that construct a tartan's weave. The grid of *TESA No. 2* is unending, its edges arbitrary and only limited by the dimension of the wood on to which the tapes are woven. The painted obscurity of the taped edges extends beyond *TESA's* actual dimensions into other arenas, temporal and spatial. Zoderer's statement that 'Nothing is sacred to me, but everything is blessed', and his opinion that 'It is essential to know about tradition, but I try to treat it undogmatically and thus to shift it into our own times'[8] has a specific resonance often encountered when examining the work of artists and designers who consciously or unconsciously evoke tartan patterns in their works. Tartan's ubiquity and its mystical associations accrued throughout its turbulent history as a textile of disassociation and unification are traditions constantly shifted and brought 'into our own times' by those with the ability to recognize the possibilities inherent in its complexity.[9]

The spirituality invoked by tartan's grids is perhaps most notably felt in the work of Dom Hans van der Laan, the Dutch architect, theorist and Benedictine monk. Van der Laan produced just four buildings during his long lifetime, but these buildings followed closely his meticulously formulated architectonic theories. He proposed that the essence of architecture lies in its proportions, everything else being secondary, and further that these proportions are derived from tripartite relationships between the secular and the spiritual, the figure against the ground, human production against the natural world. Whilst his practice was obviously inflected by his Catholicism, and his few buildings certainly exude a contemplative religious calm, this is derived as much from his mathematical approach to spatial and philosophical relationships as it is to any specific religious dogma.

For van der Laan, certain Scottish tartans contained, within the spatial and chromatic relationships of their setts, perfect examples of the relationship between what he termed 'figure' and 'ground' and, on a more philosophical level, of the relationship between the natural world and the artefact. In his essay 'On a Scottish Tartan' in 1969, he suggested that tartan is 'a supreme example of the integration of technique and form', and likened tartan to architecture, suggesting that just as a weaver makes flat cloth out of threads, so too does an architect create walls out of building materials.[10] He pushed this analogy further towards his customary tripartite formulae comparing the trio of block, column and wall to fibre, thread and cloth. He then went on to employ a detailed study of Grey Douglas tartan to demonstrate how the spatial relationships between the light grey and black of the sett are indicative of, and can generate, a formula with which to consider how human relationships mirror architectural structures, and in turn how those same structures might relate to landscape. His enthusiasm for relatively simple tartans (he also analysed the setts of Scott, Menzies and MacLachlan tartans amongst others) expressed a certain monastic approach to the simple, handcrafted object. Van der Laan espoused the benefit of methodical repetitive patterns, whether used in the construction of buildings, mathematical formulae, church vestments and altar ware, or indeed as models of behaviour for existence.

Van der Laan's essay opens with the promise that he is 'bringing this Scottish tartan to your attention so that you may create good buildings', an expression of his belief in the efficacy and power of tartan that it is difficult to find outside its customary promulgation as the visual expression of clanship, valour and unity (elsewhere in the same essay it is apparent that van der Laan believed strongly in the notion of clanship and its relationship to what he termed 'authentic tartans, which each belong to a particular clan').[11] He executed detailed drawings of the proportionate width

116 Grey Douglas

of the different coloured stripes, of the actual appearance of tartans, and of demonstrations of the changing relationship between figure and ground according to how the width of a stripe is varied. His studies occupy a fascinating interdisciplinary space located somewhere in the vicinity of a traditional weaver's tartan thread counts, architectural draughtsmanship and quasi-religious, mathematical treatise. For van der Laan, Grey Douglas tartan enshrined a mathematical precision and power, and from only two colours – grey and black, or 'light' and 'dark' as he termed them – an arrangement is produced that 'is exceptionally strong'.[12] He analyses the formula produced by the ratio of the number of colours used in a tartan to the eventual number of shades created in the finished woven cloth. Van der Laan then concentrates on the particular spatial relationships between the different widths of the coloured stripes and how they exchange functions, manifest first as background colour, then as foreground, or 'figure' as he terms it. The dependence on specific widths to achieve the optical effects of recession and prominence are most easily seen on the simplest of tartans, such as the example of Rob Roy (illus. 7). Van der Laan also employed this particular tartan in his analysis, noting that when of even width, 'one inevitably sees this as a red tartan with overlaid black bands'.[13] He goes on to point out that it only takes the expansion of the black bands by making them a seventh wider, and the red a seventh narrower, to make 'the contrast ambivalent; we can now see either the light or the dark equally well as background'.[14]

It is tempting to see van der Laan's fascination with the spatial interplay of the stripes of a tartan as a form of transubstantiation where the elements of the cloth; thread and colour etc. are incorporated into a mathematical liturgy of thread counts and ratios to produce, as he termed them, 'points', 'stripes' and 'plains'. These in turn apparently 'recall the trio fibre, thread and cloth', their almost mystical relationship, a form of textile 'three-in-one', eventually leading him to find in tartan an 'outstanding illustration' of the basic tenet of his earlier work, *The Plastic Number*.[15] Ultimately, for van der Laan, the ordinates of Grey Douglas tartan's grid bridge 'the gulf that exists in nature between discrete and continuous quantity, the "how-many" and the "how-much" '.[16]

Ding Yi's crosses, Zoderer's 'blessed' degraded grids and van der Laan's tartan catechism position the study of tartan as a grid firmly in the spiritual terms that Mondrian, van Doesburg and Malevich formulated, as Krauss notes: 'From their point of view, the grid is a staircase to the Universal'.[17] The utopian, spiritual awareness that members of the De Stijl movement hoped would be presaged by their formulation of a new ascetic minimalism characterized by Mondrian and van Doesburg's grids seems distant now and firmly embedded in the canon of twentieth-century modernism, its spiritual optimism surviving only in discrete pockets such as the monastic hideaway of their countryman van der Laan.

However, it is possible to trace other remnants of De Stijl's manifesto, ironically surfacing in that most secular of fields, the fashion industry. For example, if we select from fashion's back catalogue an image of a Pierre Cardin outfit from 1965 taken by the photographer John French, we find a typical coat of the period, with a hemline finishing above the knee, tall, cowl-like collar and high waistline. So much for the cut, but what is most immediately striking about the image is the garment's construction from oppositional or juxtaposed areas of tartan. The bodice and sleeves use the fabric in its conventional 'upright' form, with the lines of the tartan running vertically and horizontally; the lower half of the coat and the collar, however, rotate the same tartan pattern through 45° producing a tartan composed of diagonal lines and lozenge-shaped cells, as opposed to the conventional square or rectangular spaces. A line of tension and confrontation is formed at

117 Hiroko wearing Pierre Cardin outfit, London, 1965

the high waistline of the coat where the two pieces intersect, simultaneously disrupting the garment and emphasizing its construction.

As has been noted previously, tartan has the effect of flattening out the body, of abstracting and disguising physical irregularities, and this garment displays these characteristics in a notably urgent way. The bottom half of the coat, with its diagonal grid, seems self-contained and finite, terminated by an accentuated black hem and, along its upper edge, by its collision with the horizontals of the upper 'straight' section of tartan. The sides of the lower half of the coat appear to travel round and continue behind the model's body, wrapping and containing the form as would a net – an essential characteristic of the rotated grid. The upper bodice of the coat opposes this operation of containment, as here the horizontal (weft) stripes of the tartan travel across the upper torso and arms of the model and suggest continued extension beyond the woman's actual silhouette. The dichotomy inherent in the grid – that of containment and limitlessness – is expressed in this garment, which acts as a visual distillation of De Stijl's *Manifesto 1* of 1918, which states:

> There is an old and a new consciousness of time. The old is connected with the individual.
> The new is connected with the universal.[18]

If this is applied to the Cardin tartan coat, then the diagonal tartan can be 'read' as connected to the individual and therefore 'old', whilst the upper section extends beyond the individual to connect with the universal and is therefore 'new'.[19] But this presents a problem, in that traditionally, verticality is the accepted presentation of a tartan and, in order to be 'read' as clan, district or any other tartan classification, a sett is always represented in this upright mode, suggesting that this is the conventional and, therefore, 'old' manifestation. Conversely, the lower rotated tartan, with its net-like, lozenge-shaped cells, is an unconventional (and, one could suggest, subversive) representation of a tartan, connoting instability and impermanence and, therefore, 'new'.

So far, so contradictory, but as always with the study of tartan, further complexities emerge once an initial attempt to define its function and significance is undertaken. The equivalence of 'old' with vertical and 'new' with diagonal representations of the sett, undergoes a further interrogation if we turn to some of the earliest surviving depictions of tartan dress found in the portraits of clan leaders and other Scottish noblemen. In these, the sitter often wears a tartan jacket or waistcoat cut from vertically laid-out tartan, whilst the trews are fashioned from tartan cut on the cross, resulting in a diagonal pattern. The Cardin outfit we have been considering could, therefore, be regarded as a sartorial reminder of tartan's first emergence as fashionable civilian dress, when more than one tartan and both vertical and diagonal use of the cloth was commonly found incorporated in the one outfit.

Before leaving this outfit, it is tempting to trace one further reverberation of the grid's problematic relationship to modernity. As we have seen, its use of both diagonal and vertical tartans refers to the grid's duality as both a constraining and limitless structure, as well as specifically to the changing fortunes of tartan's utilization within the history of fashionable dress. But it also encapsulates the spiritual and secular aspects that were capitalized upon by van der Laan, and which also presaged the divergence of two of modernity's key figures: Mondrian and van Doesburg. The two founding members of De Stijl had, in their own work, wrestled with the relationship between verticals, horizontals and diagonals. Mondrian attempted to reconcile the spatial relationship by tilting his canvases so that his familiar vertical and horizontal grids occupied a diamond-shaped frame, whilst van Doesburg adopted the opposite route and produced works that consisted of diagonal grids contained by square or oblong frames. The dichotomy revealed by the analysis of the grid is pertinent also to our study of tartan, the essentially dialectical characteristics repeatedly encountered in tartan studies resurface again in the garment under discussion, and its explicit rotation of the same sett invokes tartan's potential for stability and instability, topographical specificity and globalization, temporal particularity and expansion.

COPIES, MULTIPLES AND ENLARGEMENTS

Krauss, in her essay, is at pains to make clear that the grid must always refer to other grids, former grids and underlying grids, and that the paradox of modernity's embrace of it as a unique primary structure veils its intrinsic multiplicity and reproducibility. She asks:

> What would it look like not to repress the concept of the copy? What would it look like to produce a work that acted out the discourse of reproductions without originals…[20]

To remain with our equation of De Stijl and mid-1960s fashion, we could find the answer to her question in Yves Saint Laurent's cocktail dress from his Autumn/Winter 1965 collection, which was inspired by the paintings of Mondrian. The so-called 'Mondrian' collection was an instant success, making the cover of French *Vogue* in 1965. The 'Mondrian' dress inspired many manufacturers to flood the market with cheap copies of the garment, which although perhaps not in Saint Laurent's silk crêpe, were convincing enough due to the inherent reproducibility of Mondrian's grids. Similarly, tartan is infinitely reproducible, no matter how debased or far removed it might be from an original woven tartan sett, due to the fact that its fundamental structure is a grid composed of horizontal and vertical lines.

As long as the order and proportion of the original sequence is adhered to, it can then be scaled up or reduced and still be considered a tartan, as Dunbar suggests:

> There is no such thing as a tartan of the 'correct' size; it is the proportions which must be correct. This means that a system can be devised whereby the correct 'sett' of a tartan can be recorded, and from this it can be reproduced in any size.[21]

This challenge to the limits of tartan's legibility (just how large can a tartan be scaled upwards until it no longer registers optically as a tartan?) has provided inspiration for a number of significant fashion designers of recent times. Junya Watanabe's Autumn/Winter 2001–2 collection for Comme des Garçons featured magnified tartans in electric pink, scarlet and black wool, so enlarged that the herringbone effect of the traditional twill weave of woven tartan that is only noticeable with close scrutiny, became a series of diagonal bars crossing each other to form exaggerated dog's-tooth checks. These tartan patterns were then disrupted further by his complex pleating and dissection of the fabric, often interspersing the seams of the garments with PVC sections.

More recently, Nicolas Ghesquière's critically acclaimed collection for Balenciaga, Autumn/Winter 2006–7, produced garments that skilfully referenced a number of divergent historical influences, all in the oversized grids of magnified tartans and windowpane checks. A typical tartan

118 (Facing Page) Balenciaga, Autumn/Winter 2006–7

suit consisted of short, sloping-shouldered jacket, with seven-eighths-length sleeves and small, turned-down collar reminiscent both of eighteenth-century portraits of Scottish clan leaders and the typical sculptural shapes beloved of Cristóbal Balenciaga (illus. 21). This jacket was teamed with a miniskirt resembling an extravagantly box-pleated, unstitched kilt, the whole outfit accessorized by riding-style hard hat copied from Balenciaga's archive and platform shoes, lending the ensemble an equestrian air. Interestingly, Ghesquière's outfits used oppositional diagonal and vertical tartan grids on the same outfit, forming a discursive link to the Cardin outfit from 1965 discussed above, the same era that witnessed the devoutly Catholic Balenciaga producing the last of his classic designs inspired by art history. The sense of religious devotion that clings to many of the examples of grid-inspired design discussed in this section finds a fitting context in Ghesquière's use of tartan as a homage to Cristóbal Balenciaga's legacy (Balenciaga, like van der Laan and Mondrian, led an ascetic, almost monastic, lifestyle amidst the distinctly worldly atmosphere of Parisian high fashion).

Christopher Bailey, the design force behind the Burberry brand, has perhaps been the designer who has most consistently experimented with the relationship between scale and the grid. By enlarging, or 'exploding', as it has been termed, the company's ubiquitous Nova check, he has injected new life into a fashion brand that had relied heavily on this particular pattern. Bailey, since his appointment to the company, has repeatedly magnified, disrupted and sectioned off parts of the Burberry check to simultaneously reference the strength of its brand identity, and also to liberate its products from the tyranny of the grid. Other experiments have been carried out, including changing the instantly recognizable colour combination of the check and abstracting its grid so completely as to make it all but unrecognizable. In terms of its actual structure, the Burberry check conforms to the most basic and perhaps the only true essential criterion of what constitutes a modern tartan pattern – its sett; this, in the case of Nova, is an identical warp and weft and two pivot points. Given the many points of similarity between its history and that of tartan, and its status as an instantly recognizable and memorable sett, the insistence on it being designated a check seems somewhat pedantic, and yet tradition insists that this is how it should be referred to rather than as a tartan.

The company originated in 1856, when Thomas Burberry opened a store in Basingstoke, which swiftly established itself as a successful outfitter specializing in outdoor wear. In 1880, Burberry invented gabardine: a waterproof, lightweight material, which furthered his reputation for supplying practical yet comfortable clothing. In 1901, the company was commissioned by the War Office to design officers' uniforms (a similar shift to that made by Wilson & Son, the tartan manufacturers, after the proscription on tartan and their commission to supply fabric to the newly formed Highland regiments). Responding to the demands of modern warfare, in 1914 Burberry developed what would eventually become its trademark garment: the trench coat. It is tempting to regard Burberry's deeply embedded association with one particular garment as like that of tartan's indivisibility from the kilt. The trench coat was a garment that (similar to the kilt's progression from practical garment to fancy dress) shifted its function from protective covering designed for the battlefields of France to elegant urban outerwear, which, primarily due to the influence of Hollywood, acquired a glamorous and somewhat risqué air. Just as for many people tartan means the kilt, so too does Burberry mean the trench coat, specifically one lined and faced with the distinctive red, camel, black and white check. The label became increasingly popular with an aspiring middle- and upper-class customer, who associated it with the typical outdoor country pursuits of the privileged and well-to-do. By the end of the twentieth century, Burberry's appeal was beginning to wane, even though the brand was still actively endorsed by the aristocracy. In fact, being favoured by the aristocracy is further proof of its similarity to tartan: Burberry has received two royal warrants, a demonstration of the present royal family's support for the nearest thing to a 'home-grown' English tartan, and perhaps could even be seen as a form of redress for George IV's and Victoria's previous patronage of Scottish tartan.

At the close of the twentieth century, Burberry found increasing favour with an overseas clientele, particularly the Japanese, who were attracted by the check's synonymy with British heritage, taking its place alongside other quintessentially British brands signifying quality and longevity, and having, as a bonus, royal endorsement. The Japanese attraction to the Burberry check has been generally categorized as part of a fascination with traditional British luxury goods, but it could be argued that these consumers were also able to discern the latent force of the check's ability to reawaken the concept of clanship previously associated with tartan, and that would soon erupt with the rise of the 'chav', an exact inversion of tartan's progression from cloth of the common man to off-duty aristocratic livery. At a time when the Asian economic star was at its zenith and Burberry as a company was, to a certain extent, kept afloat by this new customer base, the check began to be worn by another very specific sector of English society, the 'casual'. Casuals emerged as ardent football fans who had travelled to Europe in the 1980s to follow their team on away matches and who developed a fondness for expensive European designer clothing, which was soon augmented by British labels, Burberry becoming the most highly desirable. And so, by the late 1980s, the Burberry check was worn by three distinct groups: the remnants of British aristocracy and aspiring upper middle classes, the new East Asian clientele, and the casual, all three of which (in true subcultural fashion) wore the check not as fashion but as 'anti-fashion'; a badge of tribal unity. As Ted Polhemus makes clear:

> the fashion system functions as a symbol of change and social mobility, whereas anti-fashion styles function as indicators of social identification and symbols of social tradition.[22]

The mimesis between the histories of Burberry and tartan is most notable when one considers the transformation of the Scottish textile during its proscription years. During the period immediately following its proscription, tartan was worn by aristocratic Jacobite sympathizers, the newly formed Highland regiments (distant cousins of the so-called football 'firms' or 'armies' of which many casuals were members), and an emerging overseas tartan fan base in the form of those who came into contact with the regiments, most notably the French during the Napoleonic wars. And, just as tartan was poised to become the reinvented, imperial and fashionable cloth beloved by the elite and those with royal pretensions, so too the Burberry check at the end of the twentieth century was about to undergo a binary process of reinvention as fashion brand and badge of the chav.

Faced with the realization that Burberry had become anti-fashion, and its clientele comprised of groups for whom the necessity for constant fashionable change was unnecessary, groups who according to Polhemus 'give up the freedom of social mobility for the security of social stability, and the adventure of fashion change for the reliability of anti-fashion',[23] steps were taken to re-brand the company. This move, it was hoped, would make Burberry more fashionable, and therefore profitable, and in order to effect this change, Rose Marie Bravo was appointed as its chief executive in 1997. It is tempting to see the American efficiency expert's shaking up of the old-fashioned

119 Fake Burberry cap. Vauxhall 'Chavalier' customized by *Max Power* magazine for Welsh rappers Goldie Looking Chain to promote their 2004 single, 'Your Mother's Got a Penis'

Edinburgh textile firm in the previously discussed film *The Battle of the Sexes*, finding a real-life re-enactment in the American Bravo's appointment to the traditional firm of Burberry.

Such was the success of this rejuvenation that Burberry's distinctive check almost immediately became one of fashion's most desirable and copied patterns, and the Burberry check started its peripatetic parallel existence. It became both a vital component of high-fashion clothing under the Burberry Prorsum label and, most importantly for its continued economic viability, as the check beloved of a new breed of customer hungry for its buff, red and black grid. The economic and sociocultural tension encapsulated in Burberry's widely divergent clientele has come as a godsend to a host of cultural pundits, generating documentaries, books, and a cornucopia of journalism covering all aspects of 'chavdom' and its symbiotic relationship to the company. It is tempting to examine the media construction of chavs and their love of all things Burberry (as long as it's checked) in the same critical light as the Romantic literary construction of the tartan-wearing Highlander in the late eighteenth and early nineteenth centuries. The desire to mythologize and construct a cultural context for what, after all, amounts to no more than a checked textile, is comparable in terms of the persuasive hijacking of popular imagination (if not in the supposed historical antiquity) that occurred during tartan's reinvention. The meteoric rise of the chav 'tribe' can be understood as newly invented *Kulturvolk*, with not one Ossian, but a whole host of tabloid journalists and cultural commentators to construct their personae.

The Burberry check, during the first half of the noughties, occupied uniquely polarized positions, fêted simultaneously at polo meetings and football terraces, and the check's habitats mirrored tartan's historically divergent consumers. With the success of Burberry's reinvention, its endorsement by B-list (if not quite A-list) celebrity, and the check's seasonal modifications on European catwalks, the temptation to produce copies of its expensive checked items has been irresistible. The deluge of 'moody' Burberry goods, particularly the baseball cap (the apogee of the chav wardrobe) forced Burberry to register the Nova check as a trademark in 2000, and to stop production of the baseball cap due to the destabilizing of the brand's public image that the 'Burberry ape's' mediated exploits produced. As with tartan, but temporally greatly condensed, the Burberry check's influence and global recognition have grown exogenously, a host of primary and secondary signification attaching to its distinctive sett, making it the uniquely ambiguous brand it is today. Burberry's democratic odyssey from the preferred protective patterning of the privileged to its global proliferation as moody check beloved of the chav, is an inversion of tartan's odyssey 200 years earlier. The trajectory of the Burberry check seems to be a microcosm of tartan's all-inclusiveness, managing to absorb any clichéd attack on its elitist heritage and yet still signifying tradition, quality and a certain bucolic chic. Burberry's recent ironic manipulation of the scale of its check has been considered as an attempt to shake off its chav associations. The check's ability to remain faithful to its sett no matter how magnified the scale, however, seems an appropriate metaphor for both Nova and tartan, in that no matter how extended, transformed and diluted the pattern may become, it retains its power to act as a signifier of both tradition and change.

An indication of the universality and significance of the Burberry check as a sociocultural sign can be gauged by its centrality to the work of the Chinese video artist, Cao Fei. In her work *Rabid Dogs* of 2002, a cast of office workers adopts the characteristics and pack mentality of dogs. Wearing dog make-up, the actors crawl on all fours, lick each other, carry objects in their mouths, and cock their legs. To emphasize 'breeding' and competitive behaviour of the 'dogs', Cao Fei dresses her actors in a bewildering variety of fake Burberry garments. The 'top dog' wears a complete 'Burberry'

120 Cao Fei, stills from the video *Rabid Dogs*, 2002

suit, the other 'pups' and 'bitches' wear skirts, shirts, ties and even shoes in variations of the Nova check. The 'dogs' carry Burberry bags and briefcases, read from folders with Burberry covers, smoke Burberry cigarettes, make drinks with milk from Burberry cartons and even use Burberry toilet paper to clean up after the office juniors who are not yet 'house trained'. The equation between branding and breeding is explicit, the fake Burberry items symptomatic of the globalization of Western consumer desirables. This is the chav's slavish obsession with the Burberry check made explicit, the hierarchies of canine interaction and the economies of office politics are plotted as coordinates on the grids of the Burberry check. Cao Fei explains:

> We don't dare bark. We work docilely, faithfully, patiently, like dogs. We want to behave like animals and be locked into the cages of modernization.[24]

Reproducibility is the true mark of modernity, as Walter Benjamin famously suggested in his *Work of Art in the Age of Mechanical Reproduction,* and which Krauss utilizes in her answer to the question concerning the non-repression of the copy, suggesting that:

> The answer to this, or at least one answer, is that it would look like a certain kind of play with the notions of photographic reproduction.[25]

Having considered Cao Fei's video exploration of the copy and the multiple, it is fitting to end this consideration of tartan's relationship to modernity and the grid with two final examples of its manifestation in photographic media.

In 1861, James Clerk Maxwell, the Scottish mathematical physicist and pioneer in the study of physiological optics, produced what is widely considered to be the first colour photograph. The subject for this pioneering demonstration of the three-colour photographic process was a length of tartan ribbon formed into a central rosette (illus. 112). His demonstration to members of the Royal Institute entailed a photographer making three black and white collodion negatives of the multicoloured tartan ribbon, the separate exposures taken through red, blue and green liquid filters. Positive transparencies were then made from the negatives, and for the demonstration, each image was then projected through a similarly coloured filter and superimposed one on top of the other, forming an approximate photographic reproduction of the original colour palette of the ribbon. This effect relied on the research by Maxwell and others into the mechanisms by which the human eye perceives colour; the full colour spectrum can be 'seen' by the eye by the appropriate mixture of just three colours: red, blue and green. It seems especially fitting that tartan was chosen as the object of this pioneering experiment. Tartan was redolent of a culture and a way of life that by the time of the demonstration had been reinvented via a Romantic nostalgia for a past that never was. Simultaneously, tartan as both cloth and pattern was being disseminated and reproduced by the proliferating industrial technologies (of which Maxwell's photographic research was a part) into a global signifier of imperial Britain. Nearly 150 years after Maxwell's image was produced, the ribbon perfectly encapsulates tartan's intrinsic duality. The solitary image conveys both the memorializing process at the heart of all photography, particularly pioneer photography and its desire to 'fix' the moment, and yet due to its status as a reproducible image declares its immortality in tones as vibrant as this early colour experiment. Tartan similarly derives much of its immortality from this commingling of past and present, the relic with the prototype.

Before leaving this consideration of tartan and the grid, the 1960s will be invoked once more to consider a series of animated works that literally deconstruct tartan, reducing it to its basic components of verticals and horizontals. Norman McLaren, who was born in Stirling in 1914 and received his formal art training at the Glasgow School of Art, is regarded as one of the chief exponents of experimental film-making. McLaren's suggestion, that film-making's complexities should not impede invention, provided the key to his lifelong investigation of the possibilities presented by the manual manipulation of film by drawing, scratching or otherwise directly marking the actual film stock. Although never directly citing Scottish textile traditions as an influence on his work, certain of his investigations into purely abstract film-making, particularly a group of films he made in the 1960s consisting solely of lines, could be contextualized as a form of animated 'unravelling' of the grid structure that forms the weave of tartan. *Lines Vertical* and *Lines Horizontal*, both from 1960, consist only of lines multiplying and clustering together and moving from left to right in the case of the vertical film, and from top to bottom in the case of the horizontal film. This is reminiscent of the linear complexities and optical oscillation created when looking closely at the threads of a dressed loom and, in these two films, McLaren's distinction between the two axes can be visualized as the separation of warp from weft. However, in his later film, *Mosaic* (1965), vertical and horizontal are reunited, but not by a simple overlapping of one on top of the other to form a grid, but rather as a series of pulsating, and constantly shifting technicoloured tartan checks. In the film, 'tartans' – sometimes highly complex, at other times simple and reminiscent of early

121 Edward Bawden, design for wrapping paper (bagpipe player). Colour linocut, white gouache, pencil and collage on paper, 1960

arisaids – appear momentarily and then mutate into new 'setts', syncopated to the soundtrack. Due to the constant variation in both colour and density of foreground lines and background colour, the grids continuously 'throb' as spatial planes shift position and successive dazzling tartans illuminate the screen only to be swiftly supplanted by new variations. McLaren's insistence on the direct manipulation of film achieved by haptic means rather than via remote mechanical processes suggests an emphasis on craft, which invokes tartan's earliest history, and yet the purely formal investigation of the components of the grid and his testing of the limits of abstraction seem entirely modern. The final irony of the fact that his films occupy simultaneous positions as time-based media and handcrafted artefact, using animation to produce minimal explorations of spatial relationships, provides us with yet another model with which to assess the complexities of tartan's aesthetic, philosophical and historical articulation with modernity's grids.

10.
SUPERNATURAL TARTAN

FORCE FIELDS

> How very important it is, when chaos threatens, to draw an inflatable, portable territory on my own body, I'll territorialize my body.[1]

A model advances towards the audience: she is dressed from head to toe in tartan – tartan skirt, jacket, jumper, leggings, T-shirt, belts and gloves – all in the same blue, red and white sett, one article merging with the next and only differentiated by texture. But this is not all: the model's face and hair are also painted with the same tartan pattern: she is Jun Takahashi's muse from his 'Melting Pot' collection of Autumn/Winter 2000–1; she is tartan. She is also the spirit of seventeenth-century Scottish women criticized for wearing the plaid by William Lithgow in 1633 – 'Should women walke lyke Spirits? Should women weare Their wynding sheets alive? Wrapt up I sweare From head to foote in Plades, lyke Zembrean ghostes'[2] – now raised from the dead in twenty-first century Japan. In the same year, Jean Claude de Castelbajac fashions another tartan apparition for his Autumn/Winter 2000–1 'Bellintelligentsia' collection, consisting of cashmere tartan evening dress, shawl, gloves, collar and tartan shoes. A slightly less formidable presence than Takahashi's perhaps, but similarly saturated by tartan, her body 'territorialized' by tartan, to use Deleuze and Guattari's term expressed above. These examples are just two from a legion of tartanized spectres that haunt runway and street alike. Mere tartan accessories, accents and details are an anathema to these visions who understand the power of full tartan 'body armour', its impact undeniable, its progress unstoppable and its protection impenetrable. Outfits such as Takahashi's

122 (Facing) Matthew Barney, *Cremaster 3*, 2002. Production still © 2002 Matthew Barney

or Castelbajac's are on one level expressions of the limitlessness of the grid discussed previously, an acknowledgement of its extension beyond the frame and the body. But these particular images recall a spirituality that has little to do with modernism's perfect geometries. Rather, these spectres reach further back into the history of tartan, distant from the earthbound arena of fashion, into other spaces or territories, intermittently occupied and constructed by tartan within film, literature, art and military history.

When tartan was still woven by hand, amongst the numerous processes that went into the manufacture of a length of tartan, examined previously, was the 'waulking' or fulling of the cloth. This consisted of soaking the cloth in an alkaline solution and then beating, pummelling and generally working it to thicken and 'knit together' the threads. It is believed that the workers recounted folk tales and legends and sang songs during this process, a form of incantation intrinsic to tartan's production. Often, one further process (or, more accurately, ritual) completed the production of tartan: the blessing and consecration of the finished length of cloth. This, together with the waulking chants, reinforced tartan's sanctified – and possibly charmed – status. Every person who was to receive a section of the cloth would be mentioned in the blessing, and an indication of the form these blessings might have taken survives in some of the waulking chants, one of which Dunbar reproduces:

> This is not the cloth for priest or cleric, But it is cloth for my own little Donald of love, For my companion beloved, for John of joy, And for Muriel of loveliest hue.[3]

It is interesting to note that this list is expressly prohibitive of the clergy and, as we shall see, tartan's supernatural transformations are often manifested in a distinctly non-Christian or pagan context.

It is tempting to see the protective and talismanic properties of tartan originating in this ritualized aspect of its construction. Chanting and consecration is a recognized stage in the production of an object, magical or otherwise, and the recipes for early tartan dyestuffs, their methods of fixing, and other aspects concerned with the preparation of the wool for spinning and weaving have a distinctly alchemical nature. Stale urine (male), lichens, blood, loom blessings and chanting are by no means ingredients and procedures peculiar to tartan-weaving, and similar recipes and rituals characterize ancient weaving traditions worldwide. However, even in an age of mass-produced synthetic tartan, the special resonance attributed to the pattern and specific garments such as the kilt, form intangible yet enduring links to this ritualized space of ancient textile enchantment.

By the eighteenth century, however, especially during the years following Culloden, tartan's sanctified status was shifting to a territory closer to the satanic. Highland dress (and tartan) was subject to a sustained 'smear campaign' where it became characterized as the vestimentary expression of sedition, lewdness and resistance against the Union; this reformulation of tartan as a cloth of evil was necessary to ratify its proscription. As the visible sign of support for the Jacobites, and spur to Protestant anti-Catholicism that dubbed Charles Edward Stuart the 'Satanic Agent of the Pope', tartan incited religious bigotry with an intensity that had previously only been experienced in medieval Europe, with its multitude of textile proscriptions and sumptuary laws. As Nicholson suggests,

> The trappings and tartan of the patriotic Jacobite prince – and by inference, Scots in general – have become the uniform of a loathed and scheming cabal...[4]

123 (Facing Page) Jun Takahashi/Undercover, 'Melting Pot', Autumn/Winter 2000–1

124 Princess Anne takes advantage of the protection afforded by a floor-length tartan cape whilst attending the seventieth birthday celebrations of King Harald of Norway, in Oslo, 2007

Tartan's perceived potential, in eighteenth-century Scotland, to corrupt and undermine is reminiscent of the censure with which certain colours or patterns of cloth were regarded throughout Europe in the Middle Ages. The ferocity of the oath suspected tartan-wearers were forced to take, quoted in *Regulation Tartan*, and which included the following – 'and never use any tartan, plaid, or any part of the Highland garb; and if I do so, may I be cursed in my undertakings, family, and property' – invokes these medieval fears of vestimentary and textile ungodliness.[5]

Tartan's supernatural associations, whether blessed or cursed, have endowed it with an uncanny ability to protect its wearers, and fashion designers and tartan fans alike have exploited this potential by fabricating all-over tartan apparel. Historically, after its period of vilification, tartan soon regained its protective qualities, not only in a literal sense when widely adopted by the Highland regiments defending and expanding the limits of Empire, but ideologically also. Tartan's reinvention, at the end of the eighteenth and beginning of the nineteenth centuries, as the traditional cloth of a noble indigenous race, endowed its wearers with, as Nicholson puts it, 'a glamorous visual metaphor for an innate sort of virtue that remained impervious to the scurrilous goads of the satirist'.[6] As has been seen when considering the talismanic properties of the tartan fragment, scenes of historical conflict provide a wealth of examples with which to assess tartan's supernaturally protective qualities, and one of the most striking examples of the pattern's ability to transcend mortality occurs during the First World War. In the collection of the regimental museum of the Seaforth and Cameron Highlanders

125 *An Incident at Arras, 9 April 1917.* Oil on canvas

is a painting entitled *An Incident at Arras, 9 April 1917*, which depicts a legend concerning the 1st and 4th battalions of the Seaforth Highlanders who were attacked at Arras on the night of 8 April. Two men from the regiment, killed by a shell bursting overhead, were subsequently found in a clearing after a heavy snowfall, and it is this precise moment that the painting memorializes. One soldier kneels, New Testament in hand, the blood from his wounds visible below the hem of his kilt, whilst the other sits with outstretched arms, stigmatic wound to his chest, frozen in a moment of what could be interpreted as religious ecstasy. Their figures are illuminated in the sanctified snowy whiteness by an eerie shaft of light from the darkened skies above. Both soldiers are wearing kilts of regimental tartan and, if not for their deathly pallor and the visible wounds, could be taken to be deep in prayer rather than dead. The work seems to present the men in a state of perpetual grace bestowed on them by a combination of religious fervour and extraordinary bravery, immune to cold and even death whilst protected by the regimental tartan.

Tales of mystical and religious happenings are not uncommon in the folklore of the First World War, a reaffirmation of faith necessary in a time of crisis or 'when chaos threatens', and within the Highland regiments the significance of tartan often achieves a numinous status.[7] Whether in the form of fragments with supernatural and disproportionate significance, as an advancing barrier of tartan constructed from a line of kilted soldiers ('ladies from Hell' as they were dubbed by the Germans), or as worn in *An Incident at Arras, 9 April 1917* as a tartan force field or 'portable territory', tartan protects the wearer's body with a pattern organized around a series of historical, national and cultural nodes.[8] The two soldiers in the painting are perhaps twentieth-century inheritors of the invincibility of tartan that has recently been capitalized upon, if not caricatured, in productions such as *Braveheart*, where William Wallace's plaids endow him with such superhuman strength that one can almost believe in his survival beyond the graphic torture and disembowelment at the close of the film. As with the painted soldiers, Wallace's reputation, if not his actual body, has become immortal. Tartan's protective properties were amply demonstrated some years before the First World War when John Brown, Queen Victoria's devoted tartan-wearing gillie, wrestled to the ground a would-be assassin who had pointed a gun at the queen whilst she was travelling in an open carriage. Even though it was later found that the gun wasn't loaded, Victoria was convinced that Brown's courage had saved her life, and it is tempting to see the inclusion of a lock of John Brown's hair and his mother's ring in Victoria's own coffin as a form of residual tartan protection in the afterlife: Ancient Egyptian beliefs in reincarnation seen through the lens of Victorian Highland fantasy, perhaps?

TARTAN INVOCATION

> By the pricking of my thumbs, Something wicked this way comes. Open, locks, whoever knocks.[9]

At other times, tartan's ability to ward off evil is defeated as the protective territory it produces is permeated, not so much by the supremacy of that which it attempts to ward off, but rather because all tartans, no matter what the sett, are contiguous with other setts past and present. The painful histories and oppressive associations that tartans are often implicated in act like contagion and prove irresistible to the wearer's tartan, and so the individual's territory is re-territorialized into a larger nexus of harm. It is almost as if the appearance of a tartan has the power to call up and muster others more powerful than it. A poster by Edmund Dulac (the Edwardian master illustrator of all things magical) advertising a production of *Macbeth* at His Majesty's Theatre in 1911, depicts one of Macbeth's confrontations with the three witches. Macbeth wears what appears to be a tartan *fhéilidh-Mor*, which flutters and flaps around his body in the flickering light playing across the cave, his tartan protection here absorbing the witches' spell – 'Root of hemlock digg'd in the dark, … gall of goat, and slips of yew' – so reminiscent of the ingredients and dyeing rituals of early tartan production, and encouraging his gestating proclivity to murder, megalomania and madness.[10] His tartan is re-territorialized by the history of other tartans: 'A territory borrows from all the milieus;

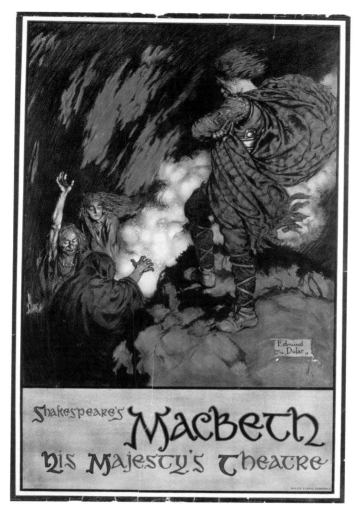

126 Edmund Dulac, poster for a production of *Macbeth* at His Majesty's Theatre, *c*.1911

it bites into them, seizes them bodily (although it remains vulnerable to intrusions). It is built from aspects or portions of milieus'. Macbeth's tartan, signifying valour and clanship, is being eaten into by the larger, more universal territories of ambition, conflict and destruction that comprise tartan's history.[11]

The consideration of tartan as a form of invocation, with the power to summon forces of evil, joins a particularly rich theatrical and literary mythology concerning the power of objects to summon harm. In *Rosemary's Baby* (Roman Polanski, 1968), Mia Farrow plays Rosemary Woodhouse, recently married, and at the opening of the film just moving into a forbidding New York apartment building, where the well-known plot concerning her unborn child possibly being the spawn of the Devil unfolds. In the scene just after the Woodhouses first encounter their eccentric neighbours the Castevets, who it is revealed later are witches and part of a metropolitan coven that meets regularly in the same building, Rosemary is seen dressed in a stylish maxi skirt made of tartan. This garment simultaneously signifies fashionability, comfort, protection (afforded by its length as well as being constructed from 'defensive' tartan) and, given tartan's Celtic associations, even Rosemary's Catholicism, which she reveals in another scene. Rosemary's tartan defence, however, proves too weak when confronted by two of the members of the coven whom she invites across her threshold, her proud display of tartan – a form of late 1960s *arisaid* perhaps – apparently summoning the forces of evil. There is another significant use of tartan that occurs prior to this scene when we see Rosemary modernizing – or rather territorializing – the apartment; this includes the lining of the shelves of a closet (which had previously been made mysteriously inaccessible by a large bureau) with tartan lining paper. As it turns out, this hidden closet is in fact an alternative entrance into the Satanists' neighbouring apartment and, until the climax of the film, the tartan shelving acts as an effective block to this harmful point of access. However, the distraught Rosemary, after having given birth, realizes the secret the closet holds, tears out the shelves and emerges from her own territory into a meeting of the coven. At the close of the film, Rosemary's reluctant acceptance of her maternal feelings towards the child is only possible after the removal of her last line of defence: the tartan shelving.

If tales such as *Rosemary's Baby* and *Macbeth* inform us as to tartan's ability to engender harm, other representations (again cinematic and theatrical) use tartan to herald the entrance to supernatural spaces or, conversely, as indicator of the earthbound. These manifestations are arguably less bloody than Shakespeare's or Polanski's visions, but nevertheless are shot through with a fatality that seems to characterize tartan's confrontation with the supernatural. As has been discussed, Highland Scotland underwent a dramatic reinvention in the nineteenth century as a fabled land replete with valiant warriors and doomed heroes. A region peopled by a noble race with an indigenous culture that had lain dormant, and by implication unsullied by harmful contact with the 'outside' world. This civilization in hibernation was ready to be awakened from its slumbers by the tide of Romanticism sweeping a Europe hungry for the kind of prime source material for fantasy and narrative invention that the Highlands seemed to promise. The appearance of the kilted regimental soldier in Europe and the dissemination of tartan imagery and depictions of Highland dress meant that, as Nicholson suggests:

> Such spectacular costume only served to enhance the fascinatingly alien qualities of the Highlander who, for many in cosmopolitan Paris or Rome was perceived as a Rousseau-esque ideal, the quintessential 'homme sauvage'.[12]

With the recasting of the Scottish Highlands and its people as an exotic land full of strange customs and beings, in a terrain seen as remote, inaccessible and often harsh, its people were viewed as a special race. Equipped with the necessary skills to survive this landscape, literally super- or extra-natural, and it was only a short step to include in its population other inhabitants of a truly supernatural nature.

> The territory is first of all the critical distance between two beings of the same species: Mark your distance. What is mine is first of all my distance; I possess only distances... It is a question of keeping at a distance the forces of chaos knocking at the door.[13]

Of course processes of mythologizing and fabrication are invariably set in motion when one culture encounters another, and according to the circumstances of this encounter, whether as the oppressor and potential colonizer or as the subjugated; the intensity and form of these myths alters according to the purpose which they are made to serve. At the time of the Jacobite rebellions, tartan myths, concerning those who wore it and their potential threat to the English colonizing forces, served as an excuse for slaughter, enforced economic deprivation and cultural annihilation. However, less than one hundred years later this threat was re-mythologized and the tartan-wearing High-lander became the Romantic tragic figure tortured by self-destructive tendencies and supernatural, rather than corporeal, foes. The notion of the Highlands and its traditions as a form of 'sleeping beauty' waiting to be roused by the 'kiss' of European cultural patrimony evokes the world of Romantic ballet. It is in one of the first of these ballets that an enduring image of a tartanized Scotland as the site for supernatural occurrences can be found, fulfilling the perfect Romantic requirements of otherworldly disruption, unrequited love, unfulfilled heroes, and a tragic climax.

The premiere of *La Sylphide*, originally choreographed by Filippo Taglioni, took place at the Paris Opera in 1832. The ballet's setting, in an exotic and otherworldly Scotland, consolidated the construction of a Celtic *kulturvolk* that had captivated Europe since the 'rediscovery' of Ossian, 'the Celtic Homer' and Walter Scott's phenomenal popularity (his historical novels providing the inspiration for numerous nineteenth-century operas, including Donizetti's *Lucia di Lammermoor* of 1835). *La Sylphide* gave Parisian audiences the opportunity to continue their fascination with the Scots (and particularly the kilt), which had begun when the kilt first caused a stir when worn by the occupying Highland regiments. In the ballet, James (a Scottish peasant who invariably dances in a stage costume version of a kilt) is preparing to marry Effie. However, the wedding plans are interrupted by the Sylphide, a supernatural creature who is half-woman and half-bird, and who is doomed to an eternity of dancing. She reveals herself to James, who promptly falls in love with her and abandons his impending marriage to Effie.

James's act of spontaneous recklessness and the rejection of his carefully mapped out future of domestic ennui to pursue true happiness, acted as a clarion call to the Romantic audiences who attended its first performances and hailed the ballet as revolutionary. *La Sylphide's* fantasy of Scotland as a tartan refuge away from the dreary pragmatism of contemporary nineteenth-century society restores the textile's rebellious signification, albeit now centred on personal and privileged dissatisfaction rather than widespread economic and physical hardship. James's intention to be united with the sylph is thwarted by her constant state of ethereal elevation and perpetual motion, his earthbound, lowly status making it literally impossible to be by her side. Tartan's role in this scenario seems to reinforce the mortality of James, who is hampered by his 'traditional' peasant costume of kilt and other Highland garb in his attempts to rise above his station, the message being that good, honest Highlanders should have no truck with supernatural beings. His striving after an unobtainable dream is a recognizable enterprise of the Romantic hero, but in this particular context can also be seen as the collapse of the Jacobite cause and the failure of the archetypal Romantic figure, Charles Edward Stuart, to recapture the Scottish throne.

In an attempt to keep the elusive Sylphide from constantly flying away from him, James enlists the help of Madge, a witch, who suggests that he should bind her with a magic scarf, perhaps a supernatural variation on the *arisaid* – the traditional garment of the mortal Highland woman.[14] Unfortunately James's plans to 'tie' her to him once and for all fail, and the scarf, rather than causing her wings to disappear, results in her death, and also that of James, who is vanquished

127 Scene from Johan Kobborg's 2005 production of *La Sylphide*

by the witch. At the opening of *La Sylphide*, James inhabits a territory defined as Scottish by the presence of tartan, but then this space is breached by the arrival of the sylph. He then abandons his habitat and attempts to territorialize the sylph but, unable to do this, he is left ultimately de-territorialized – dead. As Deleuze and Guattari suggest:

> What romanticism lacks most is a people. The territory is haunted by a solitary voice... The hero is a hero of the earth; he is mythic, rather than being a hero of the people and historical... The territory does not open on to a people, it half-opens on to the Friend, the Loved One; but the Loved One is already dead, and the Friend uncertain, disturbing.[15]

This is a perfect description of the principal relationships of *La Sylphide*: between James, his intended, Effie, her former suitor and eventual partner, Gurn, and the loved one in the shape of the elemental Sylphide.

Matthew Bourne's ballet, *Highland Fling* or 'A Romantic Wee Ballet', as it was billed, is a contemporary reworking of *La Sylphide*, which originally premiered in 1994 and was revived and expanded in 2005. *Highland Fling* supplants the nineteenth-century Romantic vision of the Highlands with an equally romanticized twenty-first-century vision of the 'mean streets and nightclubs of Glasgow'.[16] Bourne's knowing pastiche utilizes tartan sets and costumes to emphasize James's transition from routine urban existence, unfulfilling job and momentary escapes via clubbing and drug-taking, to a 'magical world beyond' – a significance that would register with contemporary audiences as much as it did with those attending *La Sylphide* in the nineteenth century. However, instead of Ossian or Walter Scott whetting their appetite for supernatural rural Scottish balletics, it is the more nihilistic, but equally altered, states of Danny Boyle's 1995 film, *Trainspotting*, or the BBC Scotland drama series *Tinsel Town*, that are the more likely informers of the audience for Bourne's production.[17]

Lez Brotherston's designs for the first act of *Highland Fling* present a form of suburban Balmoralization, with interiors decorated with tartan wallpaper, curtains, furniture, lampshades etc., and the principal dancers in kilts or tartan dresses. This invocation of Victoria and Albert's nineteenth-century, Anglo-German, tartan fantasy land emphasizes the otherworldliness of Bourne's *mise en scène*. Whilst somewhat less grand than the Victorian version, James's environment indicates that this too is an altered space, the possibility being, of course, that this alteration might be chemically

128 Scene from Matthew Bourne's 2005 revival of *Highland Fling*

induced. Its overemphasis on tartan as the textile signifier of the clichés and claustrophobia of contemporary urban existence makes James's desire to escape, and the intrusion of the sylph into this tourist territory, all the more effective. Again, as with the earlier ballet, tartan proves too earthly to allow James to achieve the heights he aspires to, but he at least reaches a form of apotheosis at the conclusion to *Highland Fling*, as we see the now winged James float past the window, heavenwards.

If tartan, in both *La Sylphide* and *Highland Fling*, represents the quotidian that must be escaped if happiness and some form of higher plane is to be reached, it can also act as the very symptom of psychologically altered states. Dumbo, in Walt Disney's feature-length animation of the same name, made in 1941, drinks what he assumes to be water to cure his hiccups, but in fact it is water accidentally laced with wine, and in his drunken state he begins hallucinating, leading to the celebrated 'Pink Elephants on Parade' sequence. Amongst a host of cavorting, psychedelic and nightmarish elephants we see two emerge, trunk first, from worm-like creatures to the lines:

> I could stand the sight of worms, and look at microscopic germs, but Technicolor pachyderms is really too much for me![18]

The two elephants, one striped horizontally in orange and purple, the other vertically in turquoise and scarlet, advance towards each other and merge into a single tartan elephant, its pattern arising from the crossing of vertical and horizontal (or warp and weft) coloured stripes. As soon as it is formed, the pachyderm pulls apart again with an explosion that sends the 'tartan' elephant hide scattering in all directions. The equation of tartan with hallucinations suggests that the pattern itself is unstable, out of the ordinary and even a little deranged perhaps, and therefore entirely fitting to be associated with beings and locations, supernatural or otherwise, that are similarly strange and bewildering.

One could speculate that similar multicoloured tartan visions occurred to James Logan, the author of the *Scottish Gaël*, which *was* published in 1831. This work is held to be the first attempt to describe different tartan patterns in layman's terms, and includes an appendix of tables describing some fifty-four tartans via a system that lists the different-width stripes in unit measurements of one eighth of an inch, as they occurred across the pattern from left to right. However, one wonders if Logan would have attempted this work if not for a near fatal and, by all accounts, character-altering accident. Intending to pursue law as a profession, his college studies were abruptly terminated by a severe blow to the head at an athletics meeting, caused either by a carelessly aimed quoit or a badly thrown hammer. Whichever was the case, and there is no clear consensus, it nearly resulted in his death. However, on recovering, he appears to have abandoned law and became a collector of historical and antiquarian material as well as an enthusiastic amateur archaeologist. *The Scottish Gaël* resulted from a tour of the Highlands he undertook in 1826 and remained his most successful enterprise, his accident leading, in later life, to unpredictable outbursts of temper and difficulties with his benefactors and supporters.

BRIGADOONIZATION

Whether as a result of a bump on the head, a surfeit of alcohol or drug-fuelled club nights, tartan regularly manifests itself as the favoured pattern of the alternative space. As Lady Lyttelton wrote to her daughter in 1849 concerning Queen Victoria's obsession with Balmoral: 'Scotch air, Scotch people, Scotch hills, Scotch rivers, Scotch woods, are all far preferable to those of any other nation in or out of this world…': a sentiment no doubt borne out by Tommy Albright, the principal character in *Brigadoon* (Vincente Minnelli, 1954), the film version of Lerner and Loewe's hit Broadway musical that premiered in 1947.[19] Tommy fulfils all the necessary requirements of the Romantic hero: he is bored, unwilling to commit to his long term fiancée and longs to leave his everyday existence, which he does by travelling to Scotland from New York, accompanied by his friend Jeff Douglas, the pragmatic semi-alcoholic. At the beginning of the film, Tommy and Jeff are lost in a misty Scottish glen, unable to find their whereabouts even with the aid of map and compass, but coincidentally they have arrived at the exact location of Brigadoon, the enchanted village, and furthermore on the one day in every hundred years that it rematerializes. As privileged viewers, we are given a glimpse of Brigadoon before the two tourists stumble upon it, and we follow an illuminating shaft of light across the bridge and into the village itself. The first inhabitant of the magical village revealed to us is a young woman sleeping under a tartan blanket, which she promptly throws off on rising from her enchanted hundred-year slumber, abandoning her protective plaid. This action, as has been previously noted, will be swiftly followed by an encounter with the 'other',

129 The town square of Brigadoon

but in this case her act of tartan disarmament reverses the usual chain of events and it is the mortal Americans who are summoned up by the supernatural Brigadoonians.

In Minnelli's film, tartan performs very specific functions, many of which accentuate its supernatural and literally timeless qualities. As we are introduced to Brigadoon's population, Irene Sharaff's distinctive costume designs utilize tartan to construct a historical vestimentary synthesis contextualized within a mid-twentieth-century aesthetic. Her designs manage to convey sartorially the chief supernatural aspect of Brigadoon: its reappearance once every hundred years (or 'blessing' as it is called by its inhabitants). The original intention of the blessing was to prevent harm befalling the village, as 'two hundred years ago the Highlands of Scotland were plagued with witches', and by materializing from hibernation for just twenty-four hours every hundred years, the villagers remain untouched and uninfluenced by successive centuries.[20] But not so their clothing it would seem, as in *Brigadoon* styles of dress can be found from each of the three centuries since its enchantment. Hollywood versions of *fhéilidh-Mor* and *fhéilidh beag*, the *arisaid*, and trews are sported by the singing and dancing inhabitants spanning the eighteenth through to the twentieth centuries. Many of these same garments are made of 'supernatural' tartan, their setts shot through with stripes of silver, adding an ethereal shimmer to their wearers. The costumes seem to echo Benjamin's thoughts concerning fashion's prognostic inclinations:

> For the philosopher, the most interesting thing about fashion is its extraordinary anticipations... Each season brings, in its newest creations, various secret signals of things to come.[21]

However, in *Brigadoon* (which has remained untouched and blissfully unaware of centuries of change), we can see in its tartan costumes not just a sartorial presentiment of things to come, but a virtual archive of past, present (whose present this is remains unclear) and future developments.

The full skirts of Christian Dior's 'New Look', the theatrical drapery of Balenciaga, the corsetry of Westwood, mid-century Capri pants, nineteenth-century military-style tunics, Romantic era full-sleeved shirts – all merge and are unified by the glittering Brigadoon district tartan. Specific details of cut, accessories and abbreviated nationalistic symbolism from across the centuries often collide on the one design, such as in the unusual dresses worn by many of the ingénues. These costumes consist of an approximation of an eighteenth-century sack dress with mid-1950s detailing in necklines and sleeve shape. The skirts are made of a fabric that could be taken for greatly enlarged, or exploded (as Burberry would term it) portions of a tartan sett, resulting in the front of the skirts being demarcated by large crosses, or magnifications of the interstices of a tartan's vertical and horizontal stripes, the most striking being those figured in blue and white and reminiscent of the Scottish saltire. These outfits are then topped off with curious headgear that refers back in time to shepherdesses of the mid-eighteenth century or *bergère* straw hats, and forwards to the rigid geometry of 1980s accessories such as those produced for Claude Montana. Similarly, at the wedding of one of the villagers, the bride wears another hybrid eighteenth- and twentieth-century garment, its shoulders and upper arms decorated with tartan rosettes that recall the cockades worn by female Jacobite supporters on their dresses and hats.

Brigadoon's tartan fantasies act as proof of fashion's continual confrontation with the past, a form of laboratory where temporal indicators intersect. This permeable territory is geographically limited (if any of the inhabitants cross its boundaries Brigadoon will disappear forever), but unfettered temporally. Ironically, whilst its territory is rigidly fixed and defined for its inhabitants, to the outsider its tartan terrain is nowhere and even nothing, as the two tourists Tommy and Jeff discover at the beginning of the film whilst trying to orientate themselves with map and compass. Jeff asks the map-reading Tommy, 'What's in the middle?', to which Tommy replies: 'Nothing!' Jeff then concludes: 'That's where we are!'[22] The insubstantiality of *Brigadoon* acts as kind of limbo, a non-place – like a transit lounge at an airport – between the mortal world and the world of myth, history and the supernatural. It is a territory in a state of flux, bounded yet able to be breached (after all Gene Kelly as Tommy only had to walk over the bridge), indeterminate yet concentrated; it is both new and yet reeks of the permanence of myth.

The first performance of *Brigadoon* the musical, rather than the film, took place at the Ziegfeld Theater in 1947 and was an instant hit, running for some 581 performances. Its blend of romance, the retreat from reality and depiction of a land of tradition and stability untouched by twentieth-century nihilism provided a tartan blanket for audiences recovering from the global traumas of the Second World War. If we take this date as Brigadoon's most recent appearance and calculate backwards, we arrive at the dates 1847 and 1747 (it is 200 years since the village first became 'blessed'). By the difference of only one year in each case, these dates are particularly significant ones in the history of tartan. The year 1848 was when Victoria first obtained the lease and took up residence at Balmoral where, according to her journal, it was possible to 'forget the world and its sad turmoils'; the year 1746 marks the date of the Act of Proscription, when the wearing of Highland dress and tartan was made illegal, and the Highlands entered what was popularly known as the 'time of grey'.[23] Given these annual coincidences, is it surprising that *Brigadoon* presents us with such a concentrated set of tartan clichés from exhibitions of country dancing, a 'gathering of the clans' at the wedding celebration, and even scenes of spinning, dyeing and weaving in the marketplace? If Balmoralization refers to a spatial operation, specifically the covering of surfaces with tartan patterns so as to demarcate a particular area, or succession of areas, and the objects and people situated within them, then perhaps 'Brigadoonization' can be thought of as a durational operation, whereby for a limited period a whole area becomes 'infected' by tartan, only to disappear again.

Brigadoon, both on stage and screen, has certainly had a significant impact, particularly in countries outside Scotland. The fantasy of a fully tartanized society and landscape magically appearing holds a particular attraction for communities that regard themselves as spiritually and genealogically, if not geographically, connected to Scotland. Before leaving *Brigadoon* (for another hundred years?), mention must be made of one of the more remote contemporary manifestations of the mythical village, that which occurs annually at the town of Bundanoon in the Southern Highlands of New South Wales, Australia. As their promotional literature suggests:

> After the mists have risen at dawn, the town of Bundanoon becomes Brigadoon for a day (even the name on the station changes to Brigadoon!)[24]

The day's attractions include displays of massed bands, country dancing, Highland games, and the 'Kilted Dash' (to participate in this, the programme suggests: 'You don't need to wear a kilt, but you must wear something tartan!'), the day's events drawing to a close as 'the mist descends, and the mythical village of Brigadoon falls under a spell, to sleep again until next year'.[25]

TRANSCENDENTAL TARTAN

If *Brigadoon's* borders are somewhat insubstantial, no such problem confronts the viewer of Michael Powell and Emeric Pressburger's 1945 film *I Know Where I'm Going!* In the film, Joan Webster makes her way northwards on the night train from London to Glasgow, the first leg of her journey to the remote Scottish island of Kiloran, where she will marry her future husband, the temporary laird of the same island. She falls into a reverie, during which she envisions becoming the future Lady Bellinger literally married to her husband's chemical industry, and as she falls deeper into sleep, the train crosses the border into Scotland. To the strains of 'You Take the High Road' we are presented with an aerial view of the train passing through a landscape consisting of tartan mountain ranges, through one of which the train passes via a tunnel. Whether this is a continuation of Joan's fantasies, or in fact a view of the actual landscape outside the train is not definite, but in either case, after this scene Joan's elaborately detailed itinerary goes awry as she enters the 'land of tartan'.

This remarkable sequence of British cinematic surrealism is one of the most direct expressions of tartan as a form of supernatural livery, territorializing Scotland as a land of myth and fantasy. The different tartan hills and mountains constitute a whole territory, each landmass a different milieu inhabited by tartan: myth, clanship, tradition, warfare and the supernatural amongst others. As the train passes through this landscape, a voice is heard intoning: 'Next station Gretna Green – you're

130 The tartan hills from *I Know Where I'm Going!*

over the border now', emphasizing both the purpose of Joan's journey (to get married) and her entrance into another realm (both geographically and, as it turns out, emotionally).[26] Although brief, this sequence is pivotal to the film as it marks a shift from the brittle and somewhat dated 1930s sophistication of the early scenes that inform the viewer of Joan's history of wilfulness, and prepares both Joan and the viewer for the more lyrical and reflective pace of the rest of the film. This takes place in a Scotland imbued with the pastoral rapture and delirious experiences characteristic of Powell and Pressburger's visual aesthetic. Joan's threshold-crossing, marked by the train's progress through the tartan landscape, is the first (or liminal) stage on her journey to fulfilment, and as with all ritual passages is transformative and 'confers or renews identity or purifies and restores order in the self or to the world through sacrifice, ordeal or enlightenment'.[27]

Once in Scotland, other examples of tartan are more conventionally encountered, such as kilts, skirts and on pipers, but its magical appearance in the night train sequence is reaffirmed by the significance of who wears it and at what point it is evoked in the film. The next encounter we have with tartan is the pleated skirt worn by Catriona Potts, with whom Joan lodges whilst waiting for better weather to cross to Kiloran. Her wild, almost feral character, out in all weathers accompanied by dogs, and with luxuriant untamed hair, is the perfect contrast to the prim and orderly Joan. Catriona is perhaps a successor to the romantic figures that populated nineteenth- century Scottish imaginings, the sylph and the dryad; she is at one with the landscape of Scotland and is marked in the film as such by her tartan costume. Similarly Torquil, the true Laird of Kiloran and Joan's ultimate love, once the weather has become worse the day following Joan's arrival, changes from his naval officer's uniform into a kilt, aligning himself with the elements of his native land and abandoning the uniform of Britain. As the film continues, we see Joan becoming increasingly concerned that she is falling under Scotland's spell and is losing her determination to become the wealthy Sassenach industrialist's wife.

Part of this 'spell' is woven when she visits one of Torquil's old friends, Rebecca Crozier (a contemporary witch, perhaps), who tells Joan of the magnificence of a Highland gathering in a manner that can only be described as incantatory:

> And at night, at night they give a ball. You can't imagine what a wonderful sight it is…
> The men, the men are more splendid than the women. With their velvet doublets, and scarlet waistcoats, their lace cuffs and jabots, their buttons of gold and silver, their cairngorms, their buckled shoes and *fhéilidh beags* of every shade and colour.[28]

Set amongst the obligatory swirling mists and Highland cattle, *I Know Where I'm Going!* also has its ceilidh scene, at which Joan is treated to the full force of a Highland clan tartan spectacle and it is in this environment of dancing tartan and bagpipers that Torquil declares his love for her. At the conclusion to the film Joan, having abandoned her future as Lady Berringer, is summoned up by the sound of bagpipes and returns to Torquil in the haunted castle of Moy to fulfil the 'curse' that he be chained to a woman (he loves) for the rest of his days. Her progress along the road is preceded by the three kilted pipers (three wizards in this instance, rather than witches) who were to play at her marriage, now sanctifying her journey into myth.

The notion of sanctification and of ritual purification returns us to the supernatural visions with which this section began. Pipers dressed in regimental tartans audibly marking, cleansing and reinforcing a territory by pacing slowly round castle battlements, parade grounds and other specialized locations and ceremonies, has become a common sight in reality as well as in fictional representations. The Edinburgh Tattoo, perhaps the most recognizable of these ceremonies, can be considered as an annual nocturnal outbreak of Brigadoonization that occurs against the theatrically lit backdrop of Edinburgh Castle. The measured tread of a tartan-clad figure, be that on runway or rampart, territorializes the space as sacred to the sett:

> For sublime deeds like the foundation of a city or the fabrication of a golem, one draws a circle, or better yet walks in a circle as in a children's dance ... a mistake in speed, rhythm, or harmony would be catastrophic because it would bring back the forces of chaos, destroying both creator and creation.[29]

At the finale to Matthew Barney's film, *Cremaster 3*, is a sequence entitled 'The Order' in which Barney, as the Entered Apprentice, must perform various tasks and overcome obstacles in order to complete his initiation (illus. 122). His Masonic induction takes place in the supernatural architecture of Frank Lloyd Wright's Guggenheim Museum, its spiral ramp and circular balconies forming the setting for Barney's five strenuous and suspenseful challenges. Like the piper patrolling the castle walls, like Takahashi's tartan avenger striding down the runway, Barney too familiarizes the peculiar architecture of the Guggenheim and makes it his own. Aside from his abseiling equipment, he too enlists the aid of a protective tartan in his task of territorializing Manhattan's architectural landmark. The Entered Apprentice knows 'how very important it is, when chaos threatens, to draw an inflatable, portable territory on my own body; I'll territorialize my body', and so wears a *fhéilidh-Mor* of buff, cerise, pale blue and white tartan, blue and white argyle socks and a military bonnet of pink ostrich feathers in which to make his ascent and overcome his obstacles.[30]

Amongst other tasks Barney undertakes in his tartan continuum is the reassembly of a large, fragmented set of bagpipes made from the flayed body of a Loughton ram. In order to do this he must toss, like a caber, each of the pipes so that it lands exactly in the correct position. His reworking of the traditional displays of expertise and tests of strength and endurance that make up the spectacle of Highland games requires an equally specialized translation of traditional Highland dress. His costume – a combination of military swagger, bucolic weaving traditions, Hollywood glitz, and contemporary practicality (he wears trainers rather than traditional brogues) – recalls the precise moment when wearing tartan shifted from the Highlands of Scotland to the barrack rooms of the newly formed regiments and fashionable drawing rooms of Edinburgh. Tartan, as worn by the Entered Apprentice, is spectacular and dazzling to the enemy; in the setting of Wright's museum, camouflage is redundant and contrast and definition are the order of the apprentice's day, his vibrant tartan endowing him with the supernatural strength and determination required to complete his initiation. Barney's belief in the power of tartan is obvious, as can be deduced from another of the *Cremaster* cycle, *Cremaster 4*, where the location is the Isle of Man, which Barney territorializes by the use of the Manx tartan, one of the many district tartans celebrating strong Celtic traditions outside the Highlands of Scotland.

The all-encompassing tartan surrealism of Powell and Pressburger's cinematic visions and Barney's tartan bravado finds a sartorial synthesis in the pastoral tartan fantasies of the Scottish designer Bill Gibb. Throughout the 1960s and 1970s, Gibb produced a remarkably sustained sartorial aesthetic, drawing on traditional Scottish crafts, most notably tartan, combined with an acute sense of global historicism. Full-length pleated tartan skirts, tartan breeches and elongated gaiters, smocks, kaftans and sweaters in a bewildering assemblage of different setts, are combined with other patterns and textures as diverse as argyle knits and silks printed with early Renaissance maps, in Gibb's sartorial

131 Suit by Bill Gibb. Brushed wool, multicoloured tartan. Mid-1970s

collage. This heady mix of bucolic romanticism, elaborate craftsmanship and a kaleidoscopic approach to tartan, predates both Galliano's and Westwood's historical bricolage, and resulted in garments that resonated with the full historical force of the Scottish textile traditions, worn by the ethereal hippie descendants of *Brigadoon* and *La Sylphide*.

Tartan, in the territory of the supernatural, acts as a catalytic and transforming textile. Whether protecting its wearers on catwalk or battlefield, marking them as supernatural eternals as in *Brigadoon*, or summoning up more harmful forces, it has the power to change both wearer and environment. Satanic or blessed, it is implicated in curses and charms, marking its territory and cloaking those who wear it with a force that can be both invigorating and destructive.

11.
COLONIZATION

> We are used to the ideas of great cultures feeding and being fed by distant civilizations along trade routes and pilgrimage roads, as well as through exploration and various forms of aggression across seas and borders throughout history. Textiles, pottery, cookery, music, works of art, elements of language, modes of war, and science, love and politics have all moved around the world, giving people a steady idea of otherness and of their own relation to it.[1]

The way cloth circulates from its original centre of production is a complex intersection of economic, migratory, religious and colonizing processes; the history of tartan's distribution is one of the most intricate and, at times, romanticized syntheses of these contributing processes. Many of its modes of dissemination, both voluntary and enforced, occurred simultaneously and produced a situation where the wearing of tartan post-Culloden, both within Britain and abroad, became increasingly ambiguous. In Scotland, for the Highlander who attempted to maintain an agrarian existence, wearing tartan was not only illegal but now signified a set of cultural values undergoing systematic dismantling and a way of life that economically was increasingly impossible to sustain. For other former tartan-wearers conscripted into the Highland regiments, the new government tartans represented a militarized reinvention of the old clan system. Fellow countrymen, who previously had lived and worked in the same Highland areas, now formed new garrison communities united by the wearing of the regimental setts, rather than old familial or district tartans. This shift from Highland to regimental dress was, as we have seen, accompanied by tartan's increasing fashionability in Lowland Scotland and England.

132 (Facing Page) Sean Phillips, cover artwork, *2000 AD*, 'Tartan Terror'. Issue date 24 May, 1996. The tartan-clad warrior brings the colonial venture to the planet Hsin

Similarly, tartan's inculcation abroad followed a number of divergent paths, and is the result of a lengthy history of enforced and voluntary Highland migration from Scotland. These migrations were either the result of imperial expansion carried out by tartan-wearing Highland regiments, Scots exiled as a result of criminal proceedings, or voluntary emigrants leaving Scotland due to economic deprivation. For those émigrés compelled to leave the 'old country', tartan evoked associations of deprivation and loss, and a way of life now permanently destroyed. Yet for those who were successful abroad, tartan was also a way of establishing a presence and colonizing a territory. A further layer of dissemination was added by tartan's enforced imposition on subjugated peoples – such as slaves who laboured on Scottish-owned plantations, or Highlanders who left Scotland as indentured workforces or as exiles bound for the British Colonies. For these groups, tartan represented oppression and bondage.

Fashion's appetite for, and commodification of, 'other' cultures, which had grown since the eighteenth century, meant that the collision between the nineteenth-century Romantic exoticization of the Highland way of life, coupled with the rise in commercial textile production, ensured tartan's regular appearance in fashionable circles, both domestic and foreign. Tartan, via this final means of fashionable distribution, eventually reached parts of the globe that had hitherto remained unaffected by the sight of tartan-clad Highland regimentals or immigrants.

Modes of dress and distinctive textiles, alongside other cultural productions such as music and cooking, function as immediate signifiers of the presence of another culture, whilst also being the products most readily appropriated, assimilated and adapted by colonizer and colonized alike. Because of their fundamentally evolving and adaptable formation, they are able in turn to reflect external influences and circumstances, be they practical (different climate, flora and fauna, langue system etc.) or in a broader sociocultural sense. Considering tartan in this context allows an understanding of how it has migrated from the original woollen cloth to become the universal pattern recognized today, covering every imaginable surface and in a variety of materials, both natural and synthetic. More pertinently, it explains how it has been able to incorporate historical associations, both negative and positive, and remain an adaptable and globally desirable textile. The way tartan was first introduced into other cultural systems is part of the complex and rich history of the pattern, and determined how it developed after this initial phase. Also, the fact that it continued to remain in circulation after its original wearers had departed – the pattern then migrating further and reaching new communities in different contexts – can provide reasons for its contemporary multivalent osmotic status. By considering key moments in its dissemination, how they imbricate and how its history has been augmented, both domestically and internationally, can assist in assessing tartan's contemporary global ascendancy.

MIGRATION AND ADAPTATION

Scottish migration had, of course, occurred long before Culloden and its aftermath, and tartan started its global journey in earnest from the seventeenth century. The most common causes for the Highland diaspora were economic hardship, religious intolerance and political dissent, the primary factors in most textile migrations. For example, the influx of Huguenot silk weavers to England is a celebrated example of textile dissemination as a result of religious and political persecution. Initially, the most common destination for Highlanders was Europe. France was an obvious choice, capitalizing on the 'auld' religious and dynastic alliance between the two countries. Other popular destinations were Poland where, according to a seventeenth-century traveller's account, some 30,000 Scottish families were residing in 1616, and also Scandinavia, which shared with Scottish Highland culture an ancient weaving tradition that produced checked cloth, such as that from Gerumsberget in Sweden.

133 Nova Scotia (left) and British Columbia (right)

The Scottish presence in the New World was boosted by James VI of Scotland's accession to the English throne as James I in 1603, which coincided with the first tidal wave of British imperial expansion that continued unabated into the nineteenth century. In 1621, Sir William Alexander, Earl of Stirling, established a colony on land he had acquired in Canada; this colonial venture was named New Scotland or Nova Scotia. The enterprise was unsuccessful and failed to attract any significant numbers of Scottish settlers, and the territory eventually passed into French control. It was not until the large-scale Highland migration to North America in the eighteenth century that Scottish settlers established themselves in any great numbers in this region. Other early Scottish colonization of the Americas proved more successful: for example, records show that in 1685 Sir Aeneas Macpherson of Inverestrie owned some 5,000 acres of land in Pennsylvania. It is hard to say how much actual tartan travelled with these early settlers, but one can surmise that the practical Highland garments made from it would have been eminently suitable for the harsh climates of the Americas.

By the eighteenth century, Highland interests abroad and migration patterns had increased substantially. Deportation to the colonies was increasingly deployed as punishment for both political dissenters and convicted criminals alike. Some sentences were for a fixed term only, but on their release many deportees preferred to remain in their new-found lands rather than return to the privations of Highland life. Others, less fortunate, were often sold on by unscrupulous sea captains as indentured servants to work in the plantations. Alongside these enforced migrations, Scottish settlers began colonizing areas of America in increasing numbers. Even though the sea crossing could often be perilous if not actually fatal, the early eighteenth century saw the colonization of New Jersey, the Upper Hudson Valley and Georgia, where General Oglethorpe, acting on a charter granted to him by George II, landed with some 114 or so Highlanders replete with plaids, to help defend the colony's southern frontier against the Spaniards. Later, a body of men from Inverness-shire, led by John 'Mohr' MacIntosh, was formed into a Highland Independent Company of Foot and, wearing the Black Watch tartan, aided Oglethorpe in his colonization of the area. Listed in *District Tartans*, the contemporary sett called Georgia commemorates this tartanization of the area, its colour scheme derived from the red and turquoise of the Royal Company of Archers' uniform and the green and black from the government sett worn by Mackintosh[2] (illus. 135). The other area most effectively colonized was North Carolina, which became the location of significant Scottish settlement.

Printed and Published by W. Davison Alnwick.

134 Coloured print of a Highland soldier taking snuff and a slave smoking a pipe. Possibly an advertisement for tobacco. Printed and published by W. Davidson of Alnwick, c.1790

The commonly held belief that the First Nation Indians who encountered early Scottish Highlanders were immediately attracted to tartan and its striking colour combinations, is one of those unverifiable, but appealing stories that litter the history of tartan. Perhaps the marriage of a Mackintosh to a member of the Creek tribe, whose descendants survive to this day as prominent members of the Creek Nation based in the Oklahoma area, is as much a testament to the similarity of clan and tribal systems as it is to a shared tradition of colourful personal adornment. The evidence that Highlanders fought side by side with First Nation Indians against the Spanish is indisputable, however, as can be seen in this extract from a letter sent by Oglethorpe to the Duke of Newcastle in 1740:

> At the request of the Creek Indians, who had frequently complained to me of the building of the Fort Saint Francis on their lands and in His Majesty's dominions, from whence the Spanish Indians could at pleasure harass them, I ordered all the boats to be ready, and with a detachment of the regiment, the Highland Rangers, a strong body of Indians, the Chickasaws commanded by the Squirrel King and Mingo Stobo, the Uchees under their king, the Creeks under the command of Hillyspilli and Wally and some small pieces of cannon, I embarked on the first instant and went up the River Saint John's or Saint Matthias, sending on the Indians before.[3]

If one were to take a less romantic, but none the less biological view of this incident, we could contextualize tartan's attraction to, and colonization of, America as similar to the action of a bacterium. Its spread and grip over the popular consciousness of large sections of North America, in particular, follows the standard physiological stages of initial infection, followed by subjugation of the host cell and ending with its colonization. In the particular case of the First Nation Indian, it is tempting to see the tartan invasion in parasitical terms, with tartan finding a new host – its original one (the Scottish Highlands) now in demise – and in turn bringing about the eventual extermination of the new one. As with so many cultural confrontations, reminders of these often violent and ultimately annihilating meetings survive as sartorial referents, and the confrontation between Highlander and American Indian is possibly enshrined in the Highland regimental feather bonnet, as Abler suggests:

> By the time Highlanders returned from active military service among North American native peoples, at the end of the eighteenth century, the foundation had been laid for the fully developed feather bonnet that has adorned the heads of Highland soldiers from the earliest years of Queen Victoria's reign.[4]

Immediately after Culloden, regiments were raised to carry out the dual function of quashing any residual Jacobite insurrection and also defending Britain in the various wars and revolutions that swept the eighteenth century. The raising of a regiment was often a method by which a former Scottish nobleman with Jacobite tendencies might prove his new-found loyalty to the British crown, and many families formerly supportive of the Young Pretender found their descendants at the head of these new regiments. Their global spread continued apace and during the years 1756 to 1763, regiments were sent to the Americas to defend New World territories against the French in the so-called Seven Years War. After the dispute had been settled with the signing of the Treaty of Paris, the presence of these regiments was no longer needed, and many of the men were given the option of returning home or remaining in the land in which they had fought, a preferable option to many who otherwise would face economic hardship back in the Highlands. Amongst these pioneering regimental settlers were members of the 78th Fraser Highlanders who remained in Canada, many marrying French women and from whom numerous contemporary Canadian families are descended. Other Scottish settlers, particularly those who remained loyal to the British crown after the War of Independence, migrated northwards and became major economic and social forces there, developing the fur trade, forming trade routes, getting involved in the setting up of the Canadian Pacific Railway and helping to establish cities such as Montreal.

Another major influx of tartan occurred soon after the Seven Years War, when Scottish regiments were sent to fight in the American War of Independence. Many of the previously enlisted soldiers who had settled in North America were called upon to fight again, and from these re-enlisted troops a new regiment was formed: the 84th Royal Highland Emigrant Regiment, which was based in Canada. At the Battle of Moore's Creek, many Highlanders were defeated and captured, but on their subsequent release, whilst some chose to return either to Scotland or Canada, many stayed in the area and became citizens of the newly formed United States, joining the already significant Scottish population in this north-eastern area. In fact, by the mid-1700s, it is estimated that up to 50,000 Scottish settlers (a mixture of those loyal to Hanoverian rule and Jacobite sympathizers) had landed in North Carolina, particularly the Cape Fear region. The most famous of these incomers were Flora MacDonald, the saviour of the Young Pretender, and her husband Allan, who landed in North Carolina in 1774 to take possession of their 475-acre plantation. Allan evidently arrived dressed in tartan plaid, large blue bonnet, tartan waistcoat with gold buttons and tartan hose.

Scottish settlers swiftly established themselves in a variety of enterprises, the most lucrative and invidious of which was the buying and selling of slaves, a trade in which North Carolina became pre-eminent. Needless to say, the contemporary American district tartan, Carolina, does not acknowledge the importance of the slave trade in its Scottish-American history; instead it

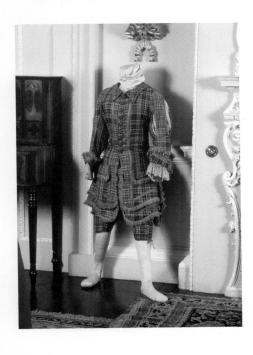

135 Uniform of the Royal Company of Archers, eighteenth century

references the complex Stuart connections via its historical association with the influx of Jacobite supporters to the area post-1745. The tartan, designed in 1981, is based upon a variation of Royal Stewart taken from a fragment of tartan from a coat in the uniform of the Royal Company of Archers of about 1730. According to Teallach and Smith's *District Tartans*, this is also supposed to be the same sett used for decorative trimming on the coat worn by Charles II at his wedding, thus establishing a Stuart lineage for the present-day American wearers of the Carolina tartan.

These early North American and Canadian settlers swiftly formed clubs that acted as mutual 'self-help' societies, assisting settlers establishing themselves in their newly adopted country and also aiding new Scottish immigrants. Popularly known as St Andrew's Societies after the patron saint of Scotland, these organizations prospered and multiplied throughout the eighteenth and nineteenth centuries; St Andrew's Day on 30 November is still celebrated by many such societies today. It is partially due to the efforts of the St Andrew's Societies and also the endeavours of Mrs Jean Watson in Canada that the contemporary phenomenon of Tartan Day was established. President Woodrow Wilson, the son of a Scots-Irish Presbyterian minister, declared that: 'Every line in America's history is a line coloured by Scottish blood', and it has been suggested that half of the signatories of the Declaration of Independence and three-quarters of all US presidents could claim Scottish ancestry. The move to have this significant sector of the American and Canadian population officially recognized and celebrated was finally achieved with the passing of The Tartan Day Resolution of 1997 by the US Congress. The resolution includes the following statement: 'Scottish Americans successfully helped shape this country in its formative years and guided the nation through its troubled times.' The 6 April was the date chosen to celebrate Tartan Day in North America and Canada, in commemoration of the anniversary of the Declaration of Arbroath of 1320, which declared Scotland's independence from England following the Battle of Bannockburn, and on which the American Declaration of Independence was modelled.

Following the American model other countries have instituted Tartan Day celebrations (events even starting to be held in Scottish and English cities), and interestingly Australia and New Zealand chose the 1 July for their Tartan Day celebrations, the date on which the Act of Proscription was repealed, allowing Highland dress and tartan to be worn once more. Tartan Day is now firmly established in America and elsewhere, and joins the list of other Celtic celebrations such as St Andrew's Day and St Patrick's Day, as well as Independence Day itself, as regular fixtures on the Scottish-Irish expatriate calendar. Tartan Day is now celebrated with an enthusiasm that confirms the suggestion that 'such expatriates have a tendency to become more Scottish than Scots living back home'.[5] A cursory examination of the variety of events and locations at which one can now celebrate Tartan Day gives some idea of the extent (and it must be said commercial advantages) that it can encompass. Parades, ceilidhs, country dancing, 'kirkin' or blessing of the tartan (a peculiarly American combination of textile and religious fervour) and Highland Games, the most celebrated being the Grandfather Mountain Highland Games, which take place against the spectacular backdrop of the Blue Ridge Mountains. These events are supplemented by less obvious 'Scottish' celebrations. For example, Tartan Day 2006 in Newport, Rhode Island included amongst its festivities a 'Catch a Scot' event sponsored by the Atlantic Technology Group, which promised a 'prize for use in your business' if the kilted Scot wandering around Newport was apprehended. Similarly in Brisbane, Australia one could enjoy The Gaelic Demon Dancers, a band called Scotch on the Rocks, Highland cattle, Scottie dogs, and a display of Scottish-built cars including Arrol Johnston, Galloway, Sunbeam Imp Sports and the Hillman Imp. Outlandish as some of these activities might appear, it seems somewhat unfortunate that in Charleston, South Carolina, site of one of the first significant Scottish colonies, the Blind Tiger Pub on Broad Street presented Scottish 'music by CD – unless some Drummers and Pipers come along!'[6]

TARTAN EXOTICIZATION

Of course America and Canada were not the only areas of the globe to undergo a systematic process of tartanization. Due to the combined factors of British imperial expansion carried out by Highland regiments, the inextricably linked commercial enterprises of the slave and tobacco trades, and an increasing number of exiled and disaffected Scots leaving the 'old country', tartan's influence was spread far and wide. The original influence of the Highland regiments' role in the expansion of the British Empire in the eighteenth and nineteenth centuries can still be felt today, especially when considering the global incidence of tartan in many contemporary uniforms. As Abler states:

> Military units in both hemispheres and on four continents beyond Europe have dressed as Highlanders. In some cases these were units composed of emigrant Scots, many veterans of service in British Highland regiments. In other cases a large population of emigrant Scots and their descendants supported the raising of kilted regiments. Enlistment in these units was not restricted to those with Highland ancestors, and it was not unknown to see kilts on soldiers of Asian or African background.[7]

Textile assimilation as a legacy of colonialism can be understood as the reason for tartan's unlikely presence today in the Caribbean, South America and India, for example. Tartan's often surprising incorporation into the indigenous cultural products and modes of dress of these countries tells a narrative of oppression, violence and rapacious commercialism.

One of the first overseas expeditions by a Highland regiment occurred just prior to Culloden in 1743, when the 43rd Regiment, the original Black Watch, was removed from its 'peace-keeping' duties in the Highlands to serve in Europe. This detail was partly due to growing fears that the 43rd might switch loyalties and side with the growing Jacobite cause. During the march south to London, word spread around the company that they were in fact bound for the West Indies. The notorious reputation of the sea crossing to the Caribbean and the ignominy with which serving in the colonies was associated, partly due to the custom of sending lawbreakers there as indentured labour on Scottish-owned plantations, caused over a hundred of the company to mutiny. Eventually the mutineers were captured, some ironically ending up being assigned to new regiments which were then sent to serve in the West Indies and Georgia. The importance, in this account, of a relatively minor case of military insurrection lies not so much in the infraction itself, but rather its cause, namely the already loathsome reputation that life in the British colonies, including the many Scottish-owned plantations, was earning at home.

The process of 'shedding' part of a regiment's complement, which occurred in America after the Seven Years War, for example, happened elsewhere and tartan 'detachments' soon proliferated. These spread the access to, and influence of, tartan far and wide and in some cases, it could be argued, materially altered the indigenous cultural productions of those countries in which they remained. For example, when looking at some of the remarkable similarities between certain tartans and the madras checked cottons produced in southern India for local use, and which were also

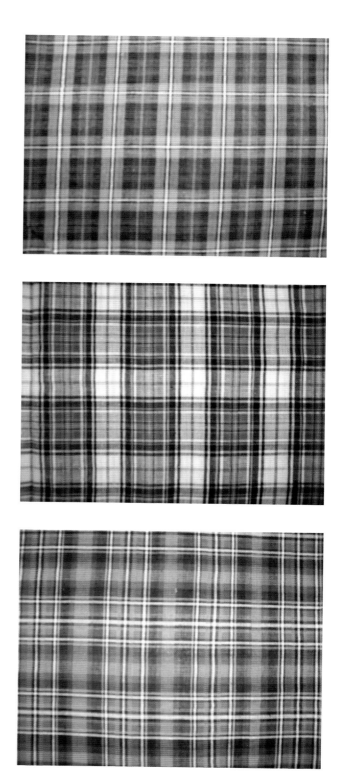

136 Three Madras checked 'handkerchiefs' woven in southern India for local use but also bought up by the East India Company and then exported. Cotton, Tamil Nadu, mid-nineteenth century

bought up by the East India Trading Company, it raises the question as to whether the presence of the 78th Highlanders in Madras in 1782 (sent there initially to quash any resistance to the East India Company's expansionist enterprise) may have had an influence on local textile production. Some of the surviving examples use a noticeably dissimilar colour palette to that normally found in madras checks, bearing a much stronger resemblance to the colour palette of government and other traditional tartan setts. This subtle process of textile colonization, whilst initially less destructive than the various campaigns the Highland regiments were engaged in against the Indians is, however, much more lasting and ultimately one could argue more permanently damaging to the colonized

137 Vivienne Westwood, 'Anglomania', Autumn/Winter 1993–4

cultural identity. The possible influence of tartan on indigenous Indian textiles is but one of the earliest manifestations of tartan as a 'textile of oppression', which joins the compulsory stripping of the plaid from the Highlander to the enforced clothing in tartan of slaves working on Scottish-owned plantations.

The colonizing threads of tartan become increasingly complex as the eighteenth century progresses, and so those same madras checks that bear a relationship to tartan patterns might well have ended up being sold on for a variety of uses including cheap, plentiful textiles in which to clothe slaves. Returning to the Caribbean, the widespread use of checked or tartan fabric for the draped skirts influenced by eighteenth-century women's fashions, scarves and head wraps that make up the 'national' costume of Jamaica is unmistakable. This checked ubiquity is obviously the result of the East India Company's mercantile monopoly on the supply of cheap textiles, but the cultural influence of Scottish plantation owners and immigrants, proud of their tartans, may also have been a contributing factor. Examining the many global instances of what could be termed 'colonial' tartans, the biological metaphor invoked previously can describe their continuing popularity and longevity, forming an intrinsic part of the cultural identity of the 'host' country they originally 'infected'. The persistence of this 'infection' can be gauged by looking at a typical example of this sartorial colonization in fashion journalism. In 1949 British *Vogue* dispatched its fashion editor, Vicomtesse d'Orthez, to Bermuda to report on 'clothes for wintering in the sun … perfect not only for Bermuda, but for the West Indies and all winter resorts' and whilst there found that: 'There is no all-over black, but some navy, and much tartan which Bermudians adore.' Further in the same article, a photograph taken at the Mid-Ocean Golf Club shows a model dutifully served by her Bermudan caddy, her clothes comprising of a 'youthful golf outfit – three-quarter-length tartan shorts (tartans are very popular for the winter months) with a classic white shirt by Jaeger'.[8]

Any colonizing body will in turn undergo colonization, and it is a fact that whilst the Scottish regiments were engaged in foreign conflicts abroad and directly influencing the textile production of countries such as India, commodities from those same countries began to flood the markets of eighteenth-century Europe. Comparatively cheap, attractive textiles such as printed cottons and muslins were indispensable to the neoclassical revolution in women's dress that occurred at the beginning of the nineteenth century. Particular garments such as the Kashmir Shawl and the *banyan*, or dressing gown, which for the first time allowed men the luxury of a less formal mode, radically altered fashionable European dress. Tartan's complex relationship to the processes of European colonization that gathered apace throughout the eighteenth and nineteenth centuries can be understood by examining an item of dress such as the tartan turban held in the collection of the Victoria and Albert Museum, London (illus. 138). The apparent orientalism expressed in a fashionable Western woman's accessory that appropriates the traditional male headgear of Far and Middle Eastern cultures, conforms to the eighteenth- and nineteenth-century fascination for various forms of dress that the West had first encountered through economic or military expansion.

This tartan silk turban seems to answer the questions posed by Richard Martin and Harold Koda in their introduction to *Orientalism: Visions of the East in Western Dress*:

> Can we, however, divorce this process of clothing assimilation and textile adaptation from the politics of hegemonic colonialism? Is dress incriminated in the long, inexorable dossier of economic plunder and the racial presumption of a white West meeting with other worlds and ways?[9]

138 Tartan turban. Silk. English, 1820–39

But perhaps the turban can also provide an approach to the complex issues of colonialism and the textile and fashion industries, which moves beyond the polarization of East and West and the binary opposition of colonizer and colonized. How are we to understand a pastiche of an Indian or Turkish accessory when made from a cloth so redolent of civil colonization? If made for a fashionable Scottish woman, what does this communicate about the relationship of one dispossessed nation, whose textile expression of identity was not long ago outlawed, with that of a nation whose textile output was rapidly being exploited and was already being seen as a source of cheap mass production? What is the relationship between an item of dress, the form of which corresponds to a Western notion of the 'exotic', and the fabric from which it is constructed, regarded as similarly exotic by the tide of Romanticism sweeping Europe at the time of the turban's manufacture? Indeed, the object is manufactured from a textile that clothed the very forces that secured for Britain the cultural proximity that the turban references, as Abler points out: 'Britain recruited its first exotic warriors from its northern frontier'[10] – Scotland.

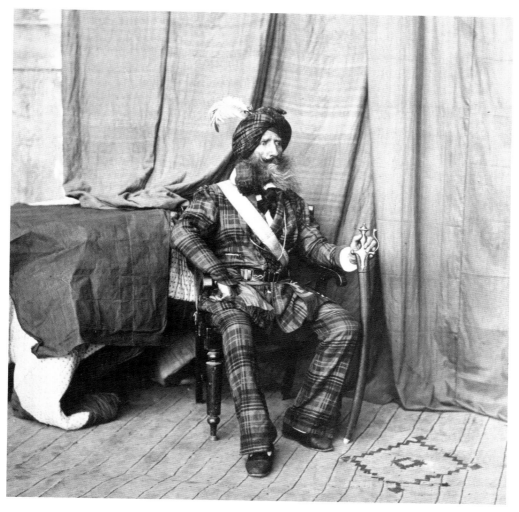

139 Photograph of Colonel Alexander H. Gardner by Samuel Bourne and Charles Shepherd. Albumen print, India, 1863–4. Colonel Gardner, the adventurer, is known to have been in Ranjit Singh's court in 1831. Gardner was an eccentric character who joined the local types and Indian landscapes that regularly appeared in front of the colonizing lens of the pioneering photographers Bourne & Shepherd, who set up studios in Simla, Calcutta and Bombay

The sociopolitical complexity that tartan so often demonstrates is central to many of the debates currently engaging textile and fashion historians. Tartan, being so redolent of its own internal history of subjugation and appropriation, when incorporated in an orientalist Western fashion accessory, functions as a reminder that indigenous items of dress or textiles are always subject to the same assimilations and caricatures that the colonized nation's dress undergoes, and that the exchange between one culture's dress and another's is never a simple process. When we consider other cultures' fascination for tartan, starting with the presence of the Highland regiments in France during the

Napoleonic Wars, and continuing today with certain Japanese designers' work with tartan, the artists Amrit and Rabindra Singh's depiction of their father in his specially commissioned Singh tartan in the style of Indian miniature painting, or Mohammed al Fayed's (owner of Harrods) recreation of himself as a Scottish laird – 'Mohammed of the Glen', as he has been dubbed – we can begin to discern the vast complexity of the subject of textiles and appropriation. The notion of tartan as an 'exotic' textile is one that recurs with increasing regularity from the late eighteenth century onwards, and once tartan had embarked on its colonial dissemination, it has simultaneously been the subject of external appropriation and modification.

OPPRESSED AND OPPRESSOR

> Like the Hapsburgs with Hungarian dress, the Hanoverians used Scottish dress as a weapon to assert their claims over, and to calm the irredentism of, a potentially rebellious kingdom.[11]

Alexander McQueen's fifth collection, entitled 'Highland Rape', presented in March 1995, generated fierce criticism primarily centred on his use of seemingly violated and distraught models wearing slashed and revealing garments, which in conjunction with the collection's title led many critics to believe that he was advocating violence to women. However, closer examination revealed a historic Anglo-Scottish contextualization of the term 'rape'. The runway was covered in heather and brackens, whilst many of the outfits that referenced nineteenth-century bodice shapes were made up in the McQueen tartan. As Caroline Evans suggests in *Fashion at the Edge*:

> Whereas Westwood's tartans evoked swaggering eighteenth-century individuality, Alexander McQueen's 'Highland Rape' collection reprised a harsher moment, the eighteenth-century Jacobite rebellion and the nineteenth-century Highland clearances that McQueen referred to as genocide.[12]

McQueen went on to state that the collection was a result of his research into that period of Scottish history and the 'rape' of the Highlands by profit-driven English landlords. In the breast-exposing, tartan-trimmed jackets, and figure-hugging tartan bodices teamed with 'second skin' synthetics topped off with 'decimated' lace, McQueen's tailoring is expressive of the barbarism meted out to the fragile Highland way of life and its ecology. Westwood's and Galliano's clothes, for all their disjunctions, display a historical seamlessness, representing historical moments as a kind of collaged collective imagining. In McQueen's work, however, the operation whereby references to the past are grafted on to contemporary garments is still fresh. The signs of these procedures (the suture lines of his much vaunted 'surgical' tailoring techniques) are still visible as awkward abutments between historical transgression and contemporary uncertainty.

The wave of barbarity that the government forces meted out to Highlanders suspected of being sympathetic to the Jacobite cause immediately following Culloden was swift and devastating. Hundreds of Highlanders were either shot or burned alive, prisoners were treated so harshly that in many cases they died in custody, whilst government troops were sent out into the countryside to round up further suspects, rape, loot, burn houses, and drive away cattle. Those who weren't killed were often deported, so for example it is estimated that some 1,150 survivors were rounded up immediately after the battle and sent to Barbados to end their days in slavery. This, combined

140 Alexander McQueen, 'Highland Rape', Autumn/
Winter 1995–6

with the effects of the ensuing Disarming Act and those who fell foul of it, and others fleeing from poverty and the threat of further violence, resulted in migration from the Highlands rising dramatically in the latter half of the eighteenth century.

Apart from the immediate wave of emigration following Culloden, a steady escalation of Highlanders from their native habitat came as a result of the determination by the Hanoverian government to shatter the strength of the clan system. This was achieved in a variety of ways, beginning with the confiscation of Jacobite clan leaders' lands and the revoking of the Heritable Jurisdiction Act. The revoking of this act meant that those who did not comply with English jurisdiction had their lands confiscated and given to government-appointed surrogates. Pro-government landowners had, even before Culloden, gravitated southwards to take up residence in the newly expanding and fashionable urban centres, becoming in effect absentee landlords. Post-Culloden, as economic conditions declined further, these landlords found their traditional roles as landowning tribal patriarchs unable to provide them with sufficient revenue to maintain their lifestyles as southern socialites. From the 1760s, rents rose dramatically and, in order to make the land more profitable, crofting communities characterized by tenants working small areas of arable land were replaced by sheep farms requiring large tracts of grazing land.

This shift towards sheep farming necessitated clearing the traditional tenants, often by force and with little or no recompense; some idea of the relentlessness of this process, if not its inhumanity, can be gauged by the following statistics: between 1760 and 1815 around 27,000 men, women and children emigrated to escape poverty, whilst between 1815 and 1914 an astonishing 1.9 million were forced from their homes. At the height of the clearances, as many as 2,000 homes were burned and their occupants removed. Typical of the prevailing attitude of the landowners is this comment made in 1821 (ironically one year before the whole of Edinburgh wallowed in a tartan fantasy of reinvented 'Highland tradition' to mark the visit of George IV) by the Marquis of Stafford, later Duke of Sutherland:

> Strathbora is now effectually Cleared of all its turbulent people. The removings were completed on Friday night and the houses demolished without a single word. Some are off for Caithness but the bulk of them seem to have a wish to go to America. We are now I think settled for a few years.[13]

As is suggested by this account, some newly dispossessed Highlanders preferred to take their chances in the south, where they joined an increasing urban underclass, rather than risk the often perilous ocean voyages on what became known aptly as 'coffin ships'.

Whilst the concept of tartan being disseminated abroad on the bodies of dispossessed and exiled Highlanders is seductive, it is more than likely that it would have only been in the form of shawls, blankets and other coverings that had survived the period of proscription, as any other form of traditional dress had been forcibly abandoned. The crippling expense incurred by having to adopt Lowland or English forms of dress after 1746 would have meant that in the further economically straitened circumstances that the exiles now found themselves in, reverting back to the traditional *fhéilidh-Mor* or *beag* once the ban was lifted, or even as a gesture of defiance on leaving Scotland prior to 1782, would have been unthinkable. Tartan's initial presence abroad was due primarily to the regiments, and to those Highlanders sent abroad by wealthy Scottish landowners to colonize newly acquired territories, who seized upon tartan as a way of stamping their ownership on their foreign enterprises. Some of the enforced settlers did find their fortunes in far-flung lands, however, and tartan, a textile so expressive of ancestry and traditional culture, obviously played a pivotal role in Scottish colonization, as for any colonizing force a necessary part of that process is the visual expression of its antecedence. But this process was dependent on a readily available and exportable supply of tartan, which was not possible until the close of the eighteenth and beginning of the nineteenth centuries, with the ascendancy of commercial textile manufacturers such as William Wilson & Son.

BRANDING

Tartan's mercantile and military dissemination can be contextualized within a discourse of oppression. As a result of imperialist expansion, many people's first contact with tartan would have been a violent one, for the ferocity and effectiveness of the tartan-wearing Highland regiments in defending and expanding colonial borders was legendary. Tartan became a textile that presaged subjugation and utilizing the records of Wilson & Son, we can find evidence of the relationship between tartan and oppression. The custom of 'rechristening' tartan patterns according to the

141 J. Wilson, cartoon depicting a Seaforth Highlander at the battle of Tel-el-Kebir, 1882

dictates of fashion and commercial expediency, whilst demonstrating clearly the relatively recent origin of many clan tartans, can also elide the other major market for tartan textiles in the late eighteenth and nineteenth centuries: that of clothing for slaves. Trevor-Roper gives such an example from the time of the clan scramble for 'authenticated' tartan:

> So Cluny Macpherson, heir to the chief of the discoverer of Ossian, was given a tartan from the peg. For him it was now labelled 'Macpherson', but previously, having been sold in bulk to a Mr Kidd to clothe his West Indian slaves, it had been labelled 'Kidd', and before that it had been simply 'No. 155'.[14]

Dunbar notes that in 1793 David Auchterlony of Dundee 'asked for some of the scarlet, black, blue, green, yellow, and white "Kidd" tartan for a customer in Norway'.[15]

Tartan's durability, its relative cheapness, its emergent associations with a particular family name and its conspicuous and immediately recognizable appearance all added up to make tartan the ideal cloth for Scottish plantation owners. Actual physical evidence of tartan slave clothing is necessarily rare, due to a number of obvious factors. Unlike ordinary dress, slave clothing is unlikely to have survived given that it would have been worn until it literally fell apart, also none of the usual visual representations that survive of historical dress such as portraiture, pioneer photography or written accounts of styles of dress, would have been employed to record the clothing of slaves. It is likely that in many cases, the tartan used for slaves consisted of little more than blankets or wraps and if it was used to fashion more elaborate garments, these would presumably be for household servants and other liveried attendants, rather than those who worked in the fields.[16] Whatever tartan slave clothing may have actually looked like, the cloth was certainly in great demand as William Wilson's records show. For example, as Dunbar notes, in 1802 a Mr Donald Fraser from Bridgetown, Barbados contacted Wilson suggesting that he could become an agent for the firm's tartan on the island, as it was harder wearing than English broadcloth, Dunbar going on to explain: 'Many of the slaves were dressed in tartans and John Sommers of Midcalder exported hundreds of yards of Wilson's tartan to Rio de Janeiro for this purpose.' Elsewhere he notes that: 'Between the years 1797 and 1830, Wilsons were exporting large quantities of tartans to North and South America, and the material was popular on the plantations of the South, being both conspicuous and cheap.'[17]

Aside from its cheapness and durability, the characteristic that is regularly cited as making tartan suitable for slave clothing is its conspicuousness. An attempt by a runaway slave to pass unnoticed dressed in a tartan such as the Kidd sett described above, would be extremely difficult, its colours more suitable for camouflage in the Highlands rather than the West Indies. The tartan would act as a form of textile branding, marking the wearer as the property of the plantation owner, less sadistic than conventional branding, but none the less effective. Tartan as a brand in the context of enforced marking of the subjugated body is closely related to the traditional notion of indelible marking which, as Jane Pavitt notes, 'signalled a loss of esteem that could not be restored and could be publicly recognized'. Whilst expatriate plantation owners were keen to preserve and promote their ancestral heritage via tartan's familial signification, for the slave or indentured servant, that same tartan stripped its wearer of any trace of autonomous identity. Just as slaves were 'rechristened' with popular English names or those derived from Ancient Greece or Rome, Scottish-owned slaves were clothed in tartans that in many cases had ironically been freshly reconstructed as signifiers of foreign clanship.[18] There is a further irony in that when the original Scottish owners sold their plantations, or when they changed ownership for other reasons, in many cases the slaves who worked on them would have been sold on alongside the land, buildings and other assets. It is unlikely that a new owner would have gone to the expense and trouble of re-outfitting the slaves, and therefore slaves wearing tartan would have been in evidence on estates no longer having any Scottish connection.

Tartan provided uniformity, a means of cloaking individual identities and making the wearer part of a larger unit, be that workforce or other abstract grouping. Tartan's grids, to use Linda Nochlin's theories on the fragmented body, provided: 'Total contingency: An equivalent of the meaningless flow of modern reality itself, a casual reality which has no narrative beginning, middle or end.'[19] The inexorable logic of the slave system, where a process of dehumanization is necessary to make people into commodities, which then become part of a larger economic system of exchange, makes the contingency and mathematical logic of tartan the perfect textile of oppression and servitude.

As has been seen, one of the original reasons given by the English government for banning tartan in the Highlands was due to its ability to camouflage the wearer, and therefore possibly avoid detection or capture when engaged in rebellious activities.[20] The colour palette of many older tartan setts reflected the locally obtained dyestuffs and William Wilson's records once again give an indication of the subtlety of some of these pre-aniline shades, with appropriately evocative names: bloom – a pale pink, shade green – a kind of pale green, officers' blue – lighter than standard military indigo, and sextian blue – closer in fact to a shade of mauve. However, translated from their natural Highland habitat to urban environments or territories overseas, these colours, rather than blending with the landscape, would register as conspicuously memorable. Tartan's ability to demarcate, identify and locate was a deciding factor in its utilization in the slave trade, but evidence of its implication in criminalizing its wearers has been found closer to home than the Americas and the Caribbean. Dunbar recounts the story of a forger who escaped from Inverness jail in 1810, the *Inverness Journal* carrying this description of the escapee's appearance on 23 March: '…a light green tartan coat of the Bannockburn manufacture, a blue waistcoat of home-made stuff, with artillery buttons; a dark green kilt with red stripes running through it…' An example of double branding perhaps, firstly by the sett of the tartan itself and also by its obviously recognizable brand 'label' – Wilson & Son.[21]

Michel Pastoureau, in his *The Devil's Cloth: A History of Stripes and Striped Fabric*, presents important research concerning the reception throughout history of striped fabric. Many of the issues he raises are also germane to tartan's conspicuous setts, but as always with tartan, further layers of complexity and signification are exposed whenever an attempt is made to contain it within particular conceptual parameters. Pastoureau discusses how the stripe and striped fabric have passed through distinct stages of censure, tolerance and eventual respectability. These same perceptions were, if not

142 Postcard extolling the attractions of the regimental kilt

exactly reconciled, coexistent from the eighteenth century onwards, and a chronological similarity exists for tartan's shift from regional textile to global dissemination. Whilst the stripe for Pastoureau is a gradual journey from – as he calls it – the 'diabolic' via the 'domestic' on to the fashionable and other constructions, tartan as we have seen has had only relative brief periods of ignominy, which were very swiftly annulled by opposing contemporaneous developments. For example, if tartan had once been considered the lowly textile of the common Highlander, with the Romanticization of the Highlands this swiftly translated to it being considered one of the cultural artefacts of an admirable indigenous tradition. Similarly, if at the time of Culloden tartan was defamed by the English as a seat of textile sedition, it was emerging as a fashionable cloth championed by Europeans who came into contact with it via the Highland regiments, and also by those in the mercantile and intellectual milieu of Edinburgh. As Nicholson states, 'Tartan had ceased to be a rough uncultured fabric; instead it was part of the uniform of British glory and British greatness.'[22]

Pastoureau's proposal that the stripe, from the end of the eighteenth century, is defined by 'the coexistence of two opposing value systems, based on one and the same surface structure', is a conception that has defined tartan at least since Culloden, being both reviled and prized, oppressive and rebellious, commonplace and fashionable.[23] Whilst Pastoureau is able to categorize particular forms of stripe as representative of social standing, e.g. broad prison stripes equalling shame, pinstripes equalling respectability, no such easy subdivision of tartan can be established. As we have seen, a slave might well have been dressed in a tartan that in a different location or context would have been worn with pride. The distance constructed between the wearer and the viewer of certain textiles, which Pastoureau illustrates by the example of the striped prisoner and the guard, is compressed when we consider tartan's use as an oppressive textile. Tartan has in its history been worn by oppressor and oppressed with no obvious intrinsic devaluation of the tartan pattern itself, unlike the broad prisoner's stripe, which is immediately recognizable as such and exclusively worn by the incarcerated; tartan's hierarchical distances are therefore maintained not by the form of the pattern but by the status of the wearer and the actual garment it is made into.

An extreme example of the dichotomy that can exist between the wearers of tartan can be found in the abhorrent history of Bance Island. Richard Oswald, a successful Glaswegian merchant working for his cousins importing and exporting tobacco, sugar and Madeira wine, went into partnership in 1748 with two other London-based entrepreneurs, Alexander Grant and Augustus Boyd. Together they purchased Bance Island in Africa on the Sierra Leone River. Once owned by the Royal African Company (pioneer slave traders in West Africa), the island's buildings had become derelict. However, the trio rectified this situation by repairing the buildings and extending the site to form a slave 'factory' where newly captured slaves could be held before being transported to the West Indies or America. The development included a 'great house' for the chief agent, a slave yard, slave houses, storerooms, dormitories, watchtowers, a jetty, and a fort with sixteen cannons. The island became one of the most profitable slave trading centres in the eighteenth century, and it is estimated that annually around 1,000 men, women and children were shipped from there across the Atlantic in horrendous conditions, and that at its peak in 1765 this figure doubled.

The island acted as a kind of labour exchange for young Scots, many of whom were related to the partners. Between 1751 and 1773, 25 per cent of the white staff were Scottish and nine out of the thirteen agents for the slave trade were also Scottish. It would seem safe to assume that given the high concentration of Scots based at the station, or working as slavers in the area, plus Scots based elsewhere who stopped off at the island to trade, that tartan of various sorts would have been much in evidence in this Scottish enclave. One traveller to the island said he knew when he was 'amongst a parcel of Slave traders, for besides their cursing and swearing, they had all on check shirts, a black hankerchief round the neck and another round the waist, all insignia of the bloody trafic in human flesh.' It is probable that the 'check shirts' were in fact tartan, a textile which had, certainly on Bance Island, if not at other predominantly Scottish centres of slave trading, become a textile directly related to slavery – the sign of the slaver in fact.[24] Apart from this possible incidence of tartan on Bance Island, there is a much more notorious example of its deployment on Bance Island's golf course, an account of this phenomenon being given by a Swedish botanist who visited the island in 1773. Bance Island's golf course, the only one in Africa, and even more exceptional given that Britain at that time had only a handful of courses, had been devised for the entertainment of visiting captains, the island's traders and other soldiers of fortune. The course, bordered by mangrove trees, was a crude version of today's greens, consisting of only two holes roughly a quarter

143 Teddy bear dressed in Black Watch kilt and khaki beret, with his own gas mask. Bear by M. Steiff. German with English clothes, 1905 and 1940 respectively

of a mile apart, the game itself being played with wooden clubs and balls the size of tennis balls. The final irony to what must have been a bizarre sight was that slaves were forced to caddy for the players wearing loincloths of woollen tartan imported from Scotland, most probably from Wilson. Unlike the ironic histories of other sports, originally brought by colonial powers to the colonized, who eventually excelled at those same games (one is immediately reminded of the success of the West Indian and Pakistan cricket teams), there appears to be no such legacy attached to Bance's introduction of golf to Africa, and it can only be considered as a sadistic sartorial amusement for bored and homesick slavers.

Tartan's association with the slave trade and other forms of economic and military oppression transform its grids into cages that imprison its wearers within a violent economic system that is as much a part of tartan's history as its romantic, royal or dynastic significance. As the vestimentary sign of mercantile and military colonizers, it could signify brutality and greed, and as the textile imposed on the colonized, it replaced individual liberty with geometrical subjugation, its weave, to paraphrase Marx's definition of capital, dripping with blood and dirt. A twenty-first-century cinematic rejoinder to the invidious history of the Bance Island golf course can be found in the film *The 51st State* (Ronny Yu, 2001). In a final post-credit sequence, Elmo McElroy, the previously considered 'mean mother in a kilt' is seen playing golf with the local laird. After sinking his shot McElroy, much to the disbelief of his opponent, steps out of his kilt declaring 'This is the tartan of my slave masters', and walks bare-bottomed from the green, finally free of his textile of oppression.[25]

144 Plate, Qing dynasty. Porcelain with overglazed enamel decoration of Scottish Highlanders. Chinese, c.1745

12.
TARTAN'S TRANSLATION

> In fact there are no 'national costumes' but rather local, regional, or international costumes. It would be fruitless to confine them within political boundaries.[1]

The dissolution of boundaries between types of dress associated with particular countries, which Perrot suggests, is both instantly appealing yet problematic. Many of our contemporary notions of 'national' dress originate from nineteenth-century literary and political constructions of nationhood, rather than the survival of ancient indigenous vestimentary forms. And yet, as is most clearly demonstrated by the development and reinvention of the kilt, these versions and reinterpretations of national dress swiftly become firmly embedded in popular consciousness. Furthermore, any subsequent debate concerning the authenticity of such costumes tends to increase the number of its defendants, and the argument swiftly becomes tautological, with attempts to interrogate the myth of nationalism represented by such costumes merely serving to reinforce its existence, as Barthes suggests:

> It thus appears that it is extremely difficult to vanquish myth from the inside: for the very effort one makes in order to escape its stranglehold becomes in turn the prey of myth: myth can always, as a last resort, signify the resistance which is brought to bear against it.[2]

Rather than struggle against the powerfully mythic histories of both the kilt and tartan itself, perhaps their inculcation in fictions of nationhood, genealogical certainty, independence, resistance and so on should be accepted. In place of attempts to dispel these myths by establishing 'truths' and 'origins', further layers of myth should be added and a host of secondary signification acknowledged, until a condition of excess is reached and the myth of tartan and the kilt begins to collapse under it own 'weight'. This condition has been the methodological intention of this book, a desire to demonstrate tartan's essentially fictive condition and its continuous reconstruction, and which this concluding section examines via its relationship to Japanese dress, as Barthes advocates: 'Truth to tell, the best weapon against myth is perhaps to mythify it in its turn.'[3]

As has been stated previously, basic two-colour checked patterns are by no means exclusive to early Scottish weaving, and checks, grids and other patterns formed by the intersection of vertical and horizontal stripes can be found in all ancient cultures, as it is the easiest and most effective way to produce strikingly patterned decorative textiles. One need only compare ancient Japanese woven cottons, African cloths and South Indian madras checks with simple tartan patterns such as Moncreiffe or the Macgregor variant Rob Roy, to comprehend the universality of the check. As has also been noted, the requirement of modern tartans to be identical warp and weft was not essential for early tartan production, and some of the oldest surviving fragments of eighteenth-century tartan differ between warp and weft, making them even more proximate to other cultures' checked textiles. Indeed, the earliest fragments of textiles that have been found and since classified as precursors of tartan could, with little stretch of the imagination, originate from many parts of the globe. As suggested in an essay by Haswell Miller quoted in Dunbar:

> The type of pattern commonly known as 'tartan', far from being peculiarly Scottish, is one of the simplest types of design to invent, and there are few quarters of the world where it is not to be found as a native production. A tartan may be found in a fifteenth-century Sienese painting; they appear frequently in Japanese prints of the eighteenth and nineteenth centuries.[4]

The desire to establish textile antecedents for every scrap of checked cloth has proved an almost irresistible procedure for many tartan historians, and examples such as the Falkirk Tartan (illus. 10) have often been excised from any broader textile taxonomies in a bid to establish a discrete nationality for tartan-like textiles, as Dunbar goes on to suggest: 'When we give such fabrics the classification of "tartan" we must include similar fabrics from all over the world'.[5] For example, the similarity between certain traditional Japanese textiles and tartan is striking, the difference lying not so much in colour or weave but in the actual fibres used and the eventual weight of the cloth. Traditional tartan was made of wool spun into yarn, whereas traditional Japanese checked cloth would have been woven from cotton or *bast* fibres such as elm bark or banana fibre. The relationship between these two traditions of checked cloth production transcend purely textile parameters, however, and the multivalency that has characterized this study of tartan is manifest most forcibly in the imbrications of Japanese and Scottish dress history and Japan's use of tartan in contemporary fashion design.

The dichotomy that resides in the popular perception of tartan and the kilt as traditional and modern, conservative and rebellious can also be detected in so-called 'traditional' Japanese dress, particularly the kimono. In a remarkable case of mimesis the development of the garment now recognized as the kimono was, as had happened with the development of the kilt in Scotland, primarily a nineteenth-century construction. Of course, as with the kilt, the kimono was based on more ancient forms of Japanese dress, but it was as a direct response to nineteenth- century socio-cultural and economic shifts brought about by the reopening of Japan to the West in 1853, that the kimono took on specific political and other functions. Like the kilt, it was effectively reformulated to symbolize 'Japaneseness', and just as the kilt became the symbol of Scotland for the literary

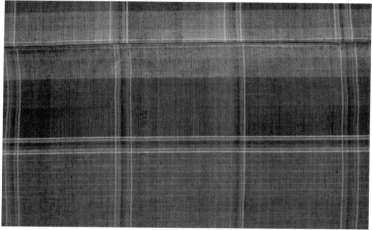

145 (Top) Textile fragment, striped plain-weave cotton. Japanese (Tamba district), nineteenth century. (Bottom) Detail of a kimono entitled 'Ise' by Shimura Fukumi. Checks, woven silk. Japanese (Kyoto), 1988

imaginations of nineteenth-century Europe and a focus of British imperial expansion, so too the kimono was highlighted amongst other traditional garments to signify the newly opened Japan. As Hollander observes in her essay 'Kimono', the garment recognized as the archetypal Japanese costume today, particularly in the West, was a nineteenth-century crystallization of a number of stylistic variations of a form of dress that had been worn for hundreds of years. The process of fossilization that occurs when items of dress pass from being worn garments to ceremonial and 'traditional' garments meant that wearing a kimono became an act of national affirmation. As happened with the kilt, the kimono became static, any major developments or modifications perceived as a threat to its function as ideological garment. Thus the kimono becomes 'elegant' and 'passive' whilst the kilt becomes 'rugged' and 'active', and these images are continuously reinforced both internally via the cultural productions of their respective countries and externally by foreign observers.

The 'solidification' of the kimono into a 'national' costume came about partly as a response to the wholesale adoption of Western modes of dress that occurred in the Meiji period, and to which the kimono was seen, if not exactly as an antidote, certainly a suitably distinct and, most importantly, exportable 'traditional' cultural garment. Hollander makes clear the similarities between the development of the kimono and the kilt's reinvention as a symbol of Scottish-British tradition and Highland Romance:

> ...seemingly unchanged in form and laden with wonderfully ancient rules of wear that have been observed for centuries... It is perhaps a little more like the present-day Scottish kilt, which has great importance in Scottish self-awareness and also dates from the nineteenth century, even though it invokes remote times.[6]

The commercial success of the nineteenth-century construction of Japanese traditions is well known, its influence permeating all aspects of European and North American culture, and the kimono as tangible garment or as artistic representation was an essential component of this tsunami of *Japonisme*. However, as some critics were at pains to point out, this construction was as illusory as was the reconstruction of the Scottish Highlands at the same period, Oscar Wilde opining: 'The Japanese people are the deliberate self-conscious creation of certain individual artists' and continuing with customary acerbity that it was probably better not to seek out this fictional country as: 'The actual people who live in Japan are not unlike the general run of English people; that is to say they are extremely commonplace, and have nothing curious or extraordinary about them. In fact the whole of Japan is a pure invention.'[7]

As artificial as some aspects of the kimono's 'history' may have been, it nevertheless did serve a purpose as a vestimentary sign of indigenous culture, an opposite to the 'other' of Western dress and customs, which increasingly saturated the country in the nineteenth century. The adoption of Western dress was seen as an essential part of Japan's modernization and vital if it was to be taken seriously as a nation that could earn the respect of the global 'superpowers' of Europe and the United States. Alongside the implementation of civilian forms of Western dress, the Emperor of Japan, in 1871, adopted and imposed on his officials European-style military uniform and it is from this period that Western styles of dress such as the tartan skirts and sailor suits, previously discussed (see Chapter 5, *Regulation Tartan*), emerge as Japanese school uniform. At this time also, Japanese weavers were sent to Europe to study contemporary textile manufacture, foreign weaving books were translated and Japanese textiles were exhibited in Europe and America. At these exhibitions, Japanese textile manufacturers (aside from exhibiting their own products) would have been exposed to examples of contemporary Western textile manufacturing as well as traditional fabrics including tartan.

The similarities between nineteenth-century Scottish and Japanese vestimentary developments can be considered as a contributing factor in the noticeable regularity with which tartan occurs in contemporary Japanese culture. Other parallels between the two nations can furnish further possible causes for the Japanese attraction to tartan, which, unlike other countries that express a similar admiration for the textile, had no significant influx of Scottish immigrants or contact with kilted regimental Highlanders. For example, there is a dynastic similitude between the system of Scottish clan leaders and their followers, and the Japanese feudal system of samurai loyal to their *daimyo*.[8] Topographically, the Scots and the Japanese are island races, and this may be another contributory factor in Japan's tartan affinity. Overriding any of these, however, is the British royal endorsement of tartan, making it particularly desirable to a nation that in the nineteenth century modelled itself on European society, and which possibly accounts for the attraction that most traditionally royal label, Burberry's, holds for Japanese clients today. However, where the intertwined histories of kilt, kimono and tartan have most dramatically been revisited is in the arena of late twentieth- and twenty-first century fashion:

> within one season, they gave French fashion an inferiority complex verging on a communal nervous breakdown; excited hopes and dreams in young British designers and students; panicked the Italians and totally bewildered the Americans.[9]

146 Comme des Garçons, Spring/Summer 2004 and Autumn/Winter 2003–4

Colin McDowell's assessment gives some idea of the impact Rei Kawakubo and Yohji Yamamoto's first Parisian collections had on the fashion world of the early 1980s.[10] Much has been written about the so-called 'Japanese revolution' in fashion, some of which is pretentious, and some trite bordering on the offensive, as in the post-atomic, Hiroshima imagery beloved of fashion commentators whose prose smacks of an indignation derived from their incomprehension of Kawakubo's work in particular. As Barbara Vinken records:

> This critical counter-attack was carried out with an aggressivity which did not baulk at a cynical and tactless use of national and sexist stereotypes. In the USA, the press of the nation that had dropped atom bombs on Japan was not above disparaging remarks about a 'post-atom-bomb-fashion,' marked by death, tattered shrouds, depression, destruction, poverty and hunger.[11]

European reaction, whilst perhaps more subtle, employed the tried and tested historical strategy to be used when confronted by the 'foreign' and non-assimilable, that is to emphasize its separation and distance from European cultural patrimony. This process then allows the product, in this case Japanese fashion, to conform to its own Western notions of Japanese culture and society as inscrutable, alien and by extension undesirable, which accounts for the recurrent reaction to Kawakubo's and Yamamoto's work as unglamorous and asexual. It is tempting to compare this sort of criticism to the caricaturing of Highlanders and their dress, particularly tartan, by eighteenth-century English commentators who, as Nicholson suggests, associated the textile 'with the Scottish people as a whole who, by this time, were subject to an almost constant barrage of criticism and ridicule from many levels of cosmopolitan English society'.[12]

However, since the early 1980s the critical opinion has shifted, although the litany of descriptive terms such as 'difficult', 'gloomy' 'religious' and 'unglamorous' persists, and many commentators have perceived the genuine challenge to Western traditions of fashionable dress that the Japanese designers represent. Western fashion's reliance on the sexual objectification and fetishization of the body, its obsession with tailoring and its self-imposed labour of constant accelerated reinvention – Benjamin's 'collective medicament for the ravages of oblivion' – have been systematically interrogated by contemporary Japanese designers.[13] The insistent presence of tartan in the collections of a group of designers, including Kawakubo, and also newer talents such as Junya Watanabe and Jun Takahashi, who otherwise eschew most traditional Western fabrics and tailoring techniques, presents an opportunity to trace specific affinities between Scottish 'traditional' dress and contemporary Japanese fashion. The proximity of many of the vestimentary tenets of Japanese design to early Highland dress, particularly the *fhéilidh-Mor* and the *arisaid*, is unmistakable. Both dress systems rely on wrapping, tying, pleating and draping to construct garments, rather than traditional Western tailoring techniques. Fastenings such as buttons, lacings and more modern methods of closure such as zips are often absent from contemporary Japanese fashion, as it was from early Highland and Japanese garments such as the belted plaid and kimono. The belted plaid's ability to function as both clothing and bedding, and the variable ways in which it can be worn (hanging loose, draped over one or both shoulders), and the *arisaid's* ability to entirely cloak the wearer from head to foot, form sartorial pathways between the pre-proscription Scottish Highlands and the conceptual clothing appearing on runways in Paris and Tokyo.

147 Comme des Garçons, Autumn/Winter 2000–1 and Spring/Summer 2006

> These avant-garde designers reconstructed the whole notion of women's clothing style; thus they do not reveal sexuality, but rather conceal it just like the kimono.[14]

The asexuality that is often evident in contemporary Japanese fashion owes, as Yuniya Kawamura suggests, its inspiration to traditional garments such as the kimono, and as she points out, 'There is little difference between men's and women's kimonos. In terms of shape and design, they are almost gender-neutral.'[15] Here again, parallels can be detected between Highland Scottish dress and that of contemporary Japanese designers; the original *fhéilidh-Mor*, whilst a garment worn only by men, is, when unbelted, a simple rectangle of cloth, as is the traditional women's *arisaid*. This historical precedent is a clear demonstration of the dismantling of gender via the deconstructive methodology of many contemporary Japanese designers. Whilst the belted plaid and its successor the shorter kilt, or *fhéilidh beag*, cannot be considered historically 'gender-neutral' like the kimono, the challenge the kilt presents to Western notions of gender-specific dress is undeniable, as has been discussed in Chapter 6, *Erogenous Zones*. Furthermore, the kilt's subsequent transformation into a unisex item, worn traditionally and fashionably by both sexes, places the kilt and, by extension tartan, in the same oppositional position to Western fashion and its emphasis on sexual distinction that Kawakubo and her colleagues occupy.

The eruptions of technicoloured tartan amidst the typical swathes of monochrome, distressed and 'defibred' textiles, or *boro* as they are referred to in Japan, can be understood as functioning on a number of levels.[16] As a means of visually disrupting and distorting the body's appearance, tartan, as has been noted from eighteenth-century Scottish portraiture onwards, is particularly effective, and when a variety of setts are used in the one outfit this optical disruption is heightened. The optical transformations played out across the bodies of clan leaders and other figures in eighteenth- and nineteenth-century Scottish portraiture form discursive links to the deforming padding and bundling favoured by Kawakubo and Watanabe. The famous Spring/Summer 1997 Comme des Garçons collection featured models swathed in padded and distended checked garments, enacting a doubled process of body-morphing, firstly by the unexpected distensions of the body produced by the padding, and secondly by the optical disruption of the clash of differently coloured, stretched and compressed checks. Since that seminal collection, both Kawakubo and Watanabe have continued to use tartan and other checked textiles in their collections in a variety of forms and to different ends, their regular deployment of tartan emphasizing its essentially amorphous qualities. Continuing the task of distorting the body, Watanabe used padded tartan and plastic in his Autumn/Winter 2004 collection to fashion capes and 'duvet' dresses that again capitalized on the clash of different tartan setts and pneumatic forms to interrogate the silhouette (illus. 148). In the previous year, Watanabe presented skirts, coats and suits in loosely woven, ragged and unhemmed simple checks highly reminiscent of the lighter setts of Highland women's *arisaids* (illus. 17) and traditional woven Japanese country textiles (illus. 45).

Tartan's ability to register tradition and notions of constancy has meant that it functioned as a form of visual anchor and contrast in two successive Spring/Summer collections for Comme des Garçons: in 2003 yellow and black tartan pieces were 'grafted' on to all-white, complex knotted and draped ensembles, whilst in 2005 vibrant tartan 'horned' hats were the only chromatic relief in a show that consisted of variations on just one skirt and sheer, gauze-draped torsos (illus. 146). Elsewhere, it is possible to detect some of tartan's political and ideological transformations, such as the history of the 'all-weather' camouflaging properties of the traditional *fhéilidh-Mor*, which caused such consternation to the English after Culloden. Watanabe's Spring/Summer collection of 2000 presented waterproof, reversible plaids that disguised their chequerboard patterns beneath complex pleating and ruching, and dramatically resisted the showers raining down on the models. The Comme des Garçons collection of Autumn/Winter 2003 made even more explicit reference to tartan's history as a textile of dissent and opposition, presenting deconstructed tartan suits bearing slogans such as 'The majority is always wrong' and 'Conformity is the language of corruption' (illus. 146). In Autumn/Winter 2006, Kawakubo seemed to reference tartan's complex internal gendered history in a collection that consisted of different garments attached to other items of dress, one outfit featuring a model in masculine white shirt and black trousers with a vibrant red and blue ruffled tartan skirt 'sutured' on to the back of the trousers. This outfit seems to provide a demonstration of the gender possibilities already noted that exist in both kilt and kimono, but remain permanently elusive in the West's gendered fashion system.

As a significant historical and political textile, tartan finds its perfect utilization in the oppositional and radical clothing of the Japanese, its unique status as a banned textile aligning it to the confrontational Japanese philosophy that seeks to destabilize conventional fashion's functions. Whilst tartan's anti-Unionist histories relate directly to the nineteenth-century Europeanization of Japanese clothing that occurred after it had re-established contact with the West, a new generation of post-punk, street-informed designers led by Jun Takahashi and the Undercover label assimilated tartan's more recent British subcultural history. These designers are informed by, and are in turn informing, contemporary Japanese street fashion, especially that originally displayed in the Harajuku district of Tokyo, where the concept of *Wa-mono*, the merging of Japanese and Western styles, ruled. In Tokyo street fashion, home-made, second-hand and designer tartan garments often surface amongst a variety of other styles and garments in their wearers' subcultural *bricolage*; Takahashi, Naoto Hirooka (for the label H. Naoto), and Naoaki Mizuno amongst others, employ a 'cut and mix' aesthetic borrowed from contemporary music, where tartan is often 'dubbed' over other vestimentary references. British punk's use of the textile remains an abiding influence, as Takahashi confirmed when asked who had influenced him at the beginning of his career:

> When I was a student, I was very much struck by Vivienne Westwood's Seditionaries and Sex collections. That punk attitude was extremely exciting.[17]

This new generation of Japanese designers often recycle 'found' garments, many of them tartan, referencing both the 'do-it-yourself' aesthetic of early punk, and also the historical economy of the kilt handed down through successive generations. As has been said of Hirooka's ensembles, 'layers of time are born from this act of bleaching, applying friction and destroying each piece of ready-made clothing used to design something new'. The use of existing garments from the recent past produces a historical eclecticism of a different order from that of Westwood's or Galliano's historical 'pick and mix' tailored perfection, somehow more insistent and, if not for the high price tags, more accessible.

The original subversion implied by tartan and the punk aesthetic has united what could initially be perceived as different positions in contemporary Japanese fashion: the conceptual purist approach, where clothing is considered as 'design' rather than fashion, and modes of dress influenced by contemporary subcultural collisions. Rei Kawakubo's Spring/Summer 2006 collection for Comme des Garçons was critically maligned as being a redundant homage to Westwood and London; however, Kawakubo herself stated that the collection was about 'a lost empire' and 'cutting without a pattern' (the collection had been designed solely by draping on the stand rather than flat pattern cutting) (illus. 147). Whilst the use of Union Jacks and fabric crowns in conjunction with a myriad of tartan setts made it difficult to see past the Westwood influence, the collection also suggested a number of other interpretations. The complex use of draped, knotted, and swagged tartans referred again to an earlier period of tartan's history, and the crowns, whilst similar to those Westwood produced for her 'Harris Tweed' collection of Autumn/Winter 1997, also suggest the tension that is generated when one cultural system, be that Hanoverian royalty or punk/Westwood fashion 'royalty', impacts on other systems such as the Stuart monarchy or 'new wave' Japanese clothing. Also in 2006, Watanabe revisited punk in the spring, interpreting it through the lens of Japanese tradition and teaming tartan bondage with paper Mohicans reminiscent of origami, whilst in his Autumn/Winter collection of the same year he takes the notion of bondage to its extreme, overloading the punk references until they reach a fetishized excess (illus. 148).

In these recent Japanese collections, the shades of Westwood's early use of tartan are redrafted to make new outfits that outwardly display their sartorial references to punk and, it could be argued,

148 Junya Watanabe, Autumn/Winter 2004–5 and Autumn/Winter 2006–7

reach even further back by alluding to the recyclable properties of the kilt, acknowledging its original economical ability to be reworked, resewn and made 'new'. However, it is Takahashi's 'Melting Pot' of Autumn/Winter 2000, previously discussed in Chapter 10, *Supernatural Tartan*, which remains, for now at least, the quintessential Japanese tartan collection (illus. 123). Here tartan saturates clothing and body alike; garments of all types and periods are 'tartanized', reinforcing the pattern's ubiquity and reaching a mythological overload, a vestimentary demonstration of Barthes's 'reconstituted myth'.[18] However it is interpreted, contemporary Japanese fashion's utilization of tartan continues unabated, occurring regularly in both spring and autumn collections of all the major exponents – a phenomenon rare in designers from other countries, who continue to use tartan exclusively as a 'winter' fabric. Ultimately, it would seem that tartan remains an essential textile component in Akiko Fukai's formulation of the Japanese designer's 'proposal for a clothing of the future that will transcend ethnic and gender differences, and even the confines of an establishment called fashion'.[19]

> A translation issues from the original – not so much from its life as from its afterlife. For a translation comes later than the original, and since the important works of world literature never find their chosen translators at the time of their origin, their translation marks their stage of continued life.[20]

If tartan is considered as a text as well as a textile, then as Benjamin suggests, it will continue to survive via its translations, and these translations, as its history demonstrates, are absolutely necessary to ensure its continuing development. At the time of writing, there seems to be an unprecedented surge of interest in tartan. Whilst it is no surprise that Japanese designers continue to find inspiration in tartan's setts, designers elsewhere have taken it down a variety of vestimentary paths. In just one season, Autumn/Winter 2006, Alexander McQueen invoked his Jacobite ancestry in a meeting of exuberant *fheilidh-Mor* and etiolated tailoring, all in the McQueen sett; Bottega Veneta produced urbane tartan two-pieces for men and women; and Ralph Lauren continued his love affair with tartan's aristocratic lineage, showing silk taffeta patchwork tartan evening dresses. Moschino referenced the schoolgirl eroticism of silk tartans whilst DSquared² lampooned tartan's aristocratic leanings, creating tartan raincoats with oversized sporrans; in London, Peter Jensen paid homage to early 1960s America, using tartan for two-pieces, jodhpurs and tie-neck blouses complete with bouffant hair. Nicolas Ghesquière at Balenciaga used tartan's grids to revitalize the house archives and Westwood continued to deconstruct and reassemble her own seminal tartan moments. When journalists are not covering runway tartan, reports of its appearance in street fashion continue to accumulate, whilst outside the fashion industry, tartan's influence is increasingly noticeable in interior design, fine art and, as always, is eagerly donned by emerging talent in the entertainment industries.

Tartan's essentially heterogeneous properties, traced throughout this study, have emerged in the twenty-first century with a new emphasis. As tartan's prominence increases in the fields of fashion, fine and applied arts, the media and popular culture, there has been a simultaneous decline in importance in the areas associated with its more traditional functions. With the collapse and amalgamation of the Scottish regiments, and the increasing public disinterestedness in a royal family regarded as anachronistic and irrelevant, two of tartan's chief symbolic functions as a military and regal textile are in decline. Similarly the establishment of an independent parliament has meant that for many Scots, tartan's other central function as a symbol of 'Scottishness' should be dispensed with as being primarily an English nineteenth-century construction. As a sign of clanship it retains, if not academic credibility, at least a commercial value which continues to grow, fuelled by ever inventive manufacturing and cinema industries, feeding those who claim Scottish ancestry, but reside elsewhere.

The study of textiles as a cultural product can provide a wealth of material concerning the way in which society constructs meaning through its artefacts. The diversity that this study of tartan has attempted to encompass is an indication of the significant position that textiles occupy as visual representations of historical, political and economic shifts within society. Marked by wars and revolutions, modified by migrations and prohibitions, textiles are uniquely positioned to act as reminders of the past whilst clothing the present. The way textiles are produced, how they are utilized and how they signify meaning is never fixed, and so the interrogation of their established histories and process of continual repositioning within different cultural contexts is necessary in order to reveal their full potential. As tartan so richly demonstrates, textiles, from the smallest details

149 Alexander McQueen, Autumn/Winter 2006–7

of their construction to their global dissemination, provide maps with which we can understand historical transformations within society and developments in our own time. The intersections and spaces between warp and weft provide a textile template for the collisions, coincidences and ruptures that punctuate the development of any society, so that the merest fragment of cloth contains within its fibres 'the crystal of the total event'.[21]

150 Cheddar Gorgeous, 2017

13.
TARTAN UNDECIDED

Few men are of one plain, decided color; most are mixed, shaded, and blended; and vary as much, from different situations, as changeable silks do from different lights.[1]

Tartan's irresistible geometries, at once declamatory and subtle, limitless yet confining, unexpected whilst entirely familiar, transform its wearers into a set of possibilities: possibilities that have afforded traditional and fashionable items of dress alike a fluidity of signification for both wearer and viewer. Such is tartan's potential that both its most traditional and progressive products share a dazzling language that announces, interrogates and reconstructs existing ideological structures, while simultaneously trapping within its irresistible grids fragments of earlier histories and, as yet, undecided futures. Recently, in the field of dress, whether understood as fashion, anti-fashion or afashion, nowhere has tartan's mutability been more effectively deployed than in the contesting of masculinity.

The interrogation of established constructions of masculinity that occurred as a direct result of the Women's Liberation Movement and so-called second-wave feminism of the 1970s, led to the destabilizing of the traditional relationship between power and the construction of masculinity. This initial interrogation resulted in a shift from a belief in power, whether political, economic, physical or a combination of all, as the primary component of the masculine ideal, to the essential feminist understanding that masculinity was the result of oppressive and problematic negotiations with women that maintained those same dominant societal power positions. This major revision was swiftly followed (with unsurprising reactionary outbursts typified by 'men's liberation' groups and the promotion of a masculinity which called upon dubious anthropological arguments supporting male dominance) by an understanding of masculinity as being the product of impossible to maintain societal conventions and demands. Men were now seen as victims of the socio-cultural norms imposed upon them and expectations which they were increasingly unable to achieve or maintain.

This fundamental shift in the perception of critical masculinity set in motion a process of destabilization of fixed cohesive formations and ushered in a more complex masculinity that was mutable and in a state of continuous evolution. The gay liberation movement, what would become known as queer studies, and revisions both historical and contemporary of topics such as androgyny, all meant that by the late 1970s at a very basic level men and masculinity was now widely understood (if not necessarily accepted) to encompass both masculine and feminine traits. As has been suggested, 'There was a very general sense that some sea-change had come over the world of sexuality and gender in the age of women's liberation, and like it or not, we have to grapple with it.'[2]

That fifty-year old 'sea-change' is currently itself being questioned and masculinity is again under a similar level of critical scrutiny as before. Echoing masculinity's former dismantling, today's interrogation of 'toxic masculinity' and the rise and formation of ultra right-wing men's groups has been largely undertaken by the work of the Trans and LGBTQIA+ communities. Accompanying this project has been an increase in gender reassignment and a wholesale linguistic reassessment including the use of gender-neutral pronouns, and the establishment of new terminology to describe a range of non-binary gender identities such as genderfluid, agender, bigender, genderqueer, novigender, pangender and the identification of gender from which this chapter takes its name; undecided. Whilst this text is not intended to offer an account of the recent developments in gender politics, the linguistic richness which these debates have nurtured does relate to, and indeed prompted, the subject of this chapter.

That textiles and dress are a form of language is now widely accepted, the proximity of linguistic and vestimentary communication being a central concern and inspiration for both fashion thinkers and designers alike. Tartan as a universally intelligible textile communicator has been emphasized throughout this book, its chromatic complexities constituting a dazzling visual language uniquely its own. This, considered in tandem with its composite social, economic and political histories and, most relevant to this chapter, its apparent ability to transcend fixed gender positions, which fashion has always understood, make it the ideal pattern to reflect and, as I hope to demonstrate, promote contemporary masculinity (and here I refer to masculinity in all of its possible forms and gender positions). The recognition of this multivalency has meant that, for many wishing to find a suitable vestimentary option in which to explore the possibilities of gender, tartan can simultaneously acknowledge, interrogate and deploy its established signification to assemble new positions, new identities. Tartan has become, on and off the runway, the textile of choice for the gender pioneer, traversing and encountering the many landscapes that construct its patterns.

Since this book was originally published in 2008, tartan has not only continued to occupy the world's increasingly gender-challenged runways, but has been incorporated into a number of celebrated menswear and indeed non-gendered collections, specifically to assist in ever more courageous projections of masculinity. Similarly, within the museum, the last ten years has witnessed an unprecedented blossoming of exhibitions and displays devoted to menswear, and its function in constructions of masculinity both historical and contemporary.[3] Themes encountered in this book[4] find material correspondences on runways, in museums and art spaces where tartan takes centre stage in the twenty first century's growing critique of fixed identities. As noted previously, tartan beloved by the showman, the extrovert and the man of fashion, has always presented a chimerical ability to disguise, reveal and project multiple vestimentary signals, at once the cloth of the establishment and the textile of revolt. As Lord Chesterfield suggests in the extract from one of the numerous letters written to his son on matters of taste, social etiquette, personal hygiene and dress that opens this chapter, tartan much like the silk used in his comparison 'can vary as much, from different situations' especially when those situations are when it is worn, and then becomes inherently 'changeable'.[5] It is tartan's changeability and the possibilities that might suggest for wearer and cloth alike that will be the subject of this chapter.

A close inspection of traditionally woven tartan cloth reveals a breath-taking chromatic complexity, as warp and weft threads of different shades emerge, intersect and recede only to reemerge again as the sett is declared across the cloth. As discussed in the section of this book devoted to tartan's technical construction,[6] this chromatic dialogue can be direct and urgent when composed of only a few colours, or of almost unfathomable richness and shaded subtlety once further colours are introduced. These tonal discourses are revealed as a series of messages sometimes continuous and melodic, sometimes disruptive and strident. A chorus of tinted refrains arise, form phrases, harmonies and discords, that diminish only to resurface, in chromatic combinations that blend in seamless unison, or unfamiliar polychromatic tonalites. Looking closer still we can see the oblique lines of the twill weave forming a graphic language of sequences and interruptions, lengths, breaks and chords akin to the language of musical notation itself or even of more arcane coded languages.

> Your dress (as insignificant a thing as dress is in itself) is now become an object worthy of some attention; for, I confess, I cannot help forming some opinion of a man's sense and character from his dress; and I believe most people do as well as myself.[7]

The recent furore resulting from the appearance of a man wearing an orange tartan dress over ripped jeans as one of the looks for Gucci's Autumn/Winter 2020 Menswear collections can be considered as merely one of the latest, and arguably rudimentary, uses of tartan to question

151 Screenshot featuring dress from Gucci's Autumn/Winter 2020 collection

culturally determined masculine identity. Promoted on the brand's official website as 'disrupting the toxic stereotypes that mold masculine gender identity', the orange and white tartan cotton dress, described less adventurously perhaps as a 'tartan cotton long smock shirt', with satin drawstring belt and Peter Pan collar, pearl buttons and smock-stitched bodice, was part of a collection that featured a variety of tartans and checks, worn by both men and women.[8] These were made up into tailored coats, baggy 'grunge' style shirts and childlike dresses reminiscent of mid twentieth century infant clothing including the infamous orange and white dress. What is perhaps more noteworthy than Gucci's media-ready 'shock' sighting of a man in a dress, is its use of tartan. Whilst clearly aiming for full-on girl's party dress mode, it is neither the paring of it with ripped denim flares nor the grunge styling of long, lank hair and woolly bobble hat that registers the outfit as 'disruptive', rather it is the use of tartan itself. Because of tartan's essential duality, discussed throughout this book, especially its remarkable fluidity as a cloth worn by both sexes – and I would argue those that refuse to identify with either – it is the very act of producing an archetypally gendered garment, and indeed its atypical cloth and colour palette (we have been conditioned to 'understand ' this species of dress as indelibly associated with seasonal dressing up, Christmas party frocks made from darker hued traditional tartans of green, red, and blue in crisp, stiff cotton or taffeta (rather than the lighter weight orange and white of the Gucci version), that positions it as 'fancy dress' rather than truly disruptive. The Gucci dress suggests not so much an interrogation of gender stereotypes, but rather a reaffirmation of them by way of cisgender men dressing up in women's clothes on a stag night, albeit Gucci's reveller is fashionably waif-like.

For truly disruptive tartan fancy dress, we need to return to some of the themes encountered earlier in this book centred on masquerade, the figure of harlequin and the grotesque. Tartan's limiting, yet limitless grids, its multiple evolving histories, make it the textile of choice for those traditional upsetters of gender, the pantomime dame and the drag queen.

Allan Stewart, Scottish comedian, impressionist and perennial pantomime dame, has suggested that he becomes more comedically dangerous as a woman, and for the lavish centenary production of *Cinderella* at the King's Theatre Edinburgh in 2006, he effected his transformation into the Fairy Godmother with the aid of metres of tartan silk, draped and ruffled in a Baroque cacophony of clashing setts. His dame is engulfed in a universe of tartan possibilities, magical, transforming and pan gendered, oscillating between the recognizable comedian, the fabulous dame and an emerging silk tartan kitsch pastiche, part Queen Victoria part Queen Stewart.

Mikhail Bakhtin when considering the transgressive, grotesque body argued that it is a body 'in the act of becoming. It is never finished, never completed; it is continually built, created, and builds another body.'[9]

Drag artist, academic and unicorn Cheddar Gorgeous 'believes that life is too short to be only one person' and donned tartan, or perhaps more accurately an undecided tartan, given its atypical sett, to become the personification of the tartan pioneer.[10] Posed against a snowy Alpine landscape, Cheddar Gorgeous stands resplendent in a red, blue and white tartan suit designed by drag queen and costume maker Liquorice Black (see illus. 150). The tartan, which rather than repeating and reversing around pivot points, conforms to earlier tartans that repeat the sett across the cloth without reversing, producing an asymmetrical pattern. Recalling the

152 Allan Stewart as The Fairy Godmother in 'Cinderella'

romantic Alpine explorers of the painter Caspar David Friedrich, the puffed sleeves of the jacket echo the early nineteenth-century silhouette of Friedrich's visionary heroines, but, crucially, unlike the painter's enigmatic Alpine explorers who typically present their backs to the viewer, Gorgeous poses full frontal and fixes us with a triumphant non-binary gaze.[11] The possibilities of multiple genders are proclaimed by the irregular tartan, set free from the traditional dance of conventional setts, evoking an earlier, less regulated period in tartan's history. For Cheddar Gorgeous, tartan's vivid shades are not only fittingly spectacular and extravagant but offer a 'portal to other worlds'.[12] Gorgeous in this image evokes Bakhtin's grotesque body that 'can merge with various natural phenomena, with mountains, rivers, seas, islands, and continents', its blue and white at one with the snow-covered landscape and clear skies, while simultaneously its insistent red grids oppose this sublimation establishing a tension between dominance and recession.[13]

153 Vivienne Westwood, Autumn/Winter 1996

Fancy dress not only allows the assumption of alternative personae, but also exaggerates and transforms our sense of the past, creating a chronotopic (to use another Bakhtinian concept) body, where time, 'thickens, takes on flesh, becomes artistically visible; likewise space becomes charged and responsive to the movements of time, plot and history.'[14] The condensation that occurs with fancy dress in turn destabilizes traditional histories, emphasizes their fictional, remembered status and fosters a space constructed from clothing where new stories, new formations of power are possible. We have seen this process operating in a number of examples of tartan dress throughout this book and it is perhaps Vivienne Westwood who remains historical tartan's most ardent revisionist.

For her Autumn/Winter 1996 collection Westwood included a reincarnation of the dazzling beings who have performed variations on the theme of eighteenth-century Highland romanticism; from Bonnie Prince Charlie himself, in tartan exile at his court in Rome, via Lords Tullibardine and George Murray masquerading in 1897 and Bruce Forsythe with his fellow players at the London Palladium to Steve Linnard at the Blitz (all featured in this book). Westwood gilds these lilies with an added layer of pastiche hyper masculinity complete with bird of prey, an overabundance of patrician lace, bayonet-sharp epaulettes, 'man and a half' *fhéilidh beag* and re-gendered version of a woman's arisaid doubling as tartan travelling rug. Westwood uses tartan to establish multiple masculinities, at once foppish, rugged, aristocratic, colonizing and vulnerable.

I would rather have a young fellow too much than too little dressed[15]

Glasgow-born Charles Jeffrey, since the launch of his Loverboy label in 2015, has incorporated tartan into his collections. Multivalently experimental, Loverboy, originally a symbiotic relationship, part fashion brand, part club night, nourishing each other creatively, emotionally and financially, has proved fertile ground for tartan's continued development. In Jeffrey's work, tartan, including the eponymous instantly recognizable Loverboy sett with its distinctive red, blue and white check on a black ground, has been the conduit for a carnivalesque, gender free-for-all. In turn excessive, extravagant, elegant and determinedly permissive, the sartorial language of Loverboy celebrates tartan's fluidity, the ur-non-binary importance of the kilt, its confrontational history and above all its dazzling optical pleasure. Declaring his clothes to be typically 'about peacocking',[16] Jeffrey's use of tartan subverts, re-establishes, only to subvert fixed gender identities once more, a disordering of order, a celebration of diversity. Truly carnivalesque, Jeffrey's work encourages miscellany, misalliance and mischief, as Bakhtin suggested 'carnival is not a spectacle seen by the people; they live in it'.[17] The sustenance that Jeffrey's

154 Charles Jeffrey Loverboy, Spring 2018 and Autumn/Winter 2019

work receives from club culture is akin to carnival time when 'life is subject only to its laws, that is, the laws of its own freedom. It has a universal spirit; it is a special condition of the entire world, of the world's revival and renewal, in which all take part.'[18] Tartan's other worldly yet unifying tendencies discussed earlier in this book, in Jeffrey's work, find new purpose, from clan to club its setts allowing its wearer's entrance to a post-gender universe.

If Charles Jeffrey is one of the latest designers to explore the exuberance and excess of tartan, Rei Kawakubo, who is acknowledged throughout this work as celebrating tartan's potential, continues to find freedom, possibility and resistance to the accepted norms of fashion in its transgressive geometry.

Shades of Bakhtin's clowns and fools share the runway with the vestimentary disrupters of her Autumn/Winter 2020 collection, with its surfeit of setts, its cacophony of colour. Her former admiration for tartan as a sign of sedition and its function as a textile highway between feudal Japan and Scotland, has more lately evoked the disruptive power of the clown, a figure of the people, who hovers above fashion's runways. In the collection with its grotesque oversized spor rans transformed into necklace/chest wigs, skin-tight tartan leggings reminiscent of a jester's hose and braided Afro wigs instead of cap and bells, her pubescent fools 'represented a certain form of life, which was real and ideal at the same time. They stood on the borderline between

155 Comme des Garçons, Autumn/Winter 2020

life and art, in a peculiar mid-zone as it were; they were neither eccentrics nor dolts, neither were they comic actors.'[19] These 'real' lads play with an 'ideal' of masculinity here represented by the dislocation and exaggeration of the sporran, the traditional protection from, and rebuff to, the feminine potential of the kilt. Kawakubo's 'mid-zone' has always hovered between art and life, now it oscillates with potential masculinity, as yet undetermined, and assumed only as pantomime.

> Dress is of the same nature; you must dress; therefore, attend to it; not in order to rival or to excel a fop in it, but in order to avoid singularity, and consequently ridicule.[20]

While tartan acts as a textile catalyst for the revision of identity, in this instance a rethinking or enlargement of the territories which new perspectives of masculinity afford, it also signals a reaffirmation of traditional ideas of maleness. The kilt, as has been discussed at length in this book, affirms ideas of hyper masculinity, of a masculinity that can withstand a garment more readily associated with femininity. A masculinity that, as Eric Gill advocated in his polemic *Trousers & the Most Precious Ornament*, speaks of liberation and release from the oppression of gendered tailoring, of a return to original, 'gender-neutral' forms of dressing, which he finds in certain examples of traditional global dress, and Western ceremonial clothing 'the highlander in his kilt (beneath which he is normally naked) is not exposing his sex, but, on the other hand, neither is he dishonouring it'.[21] Contemporary kilt designers draw on this masculine tradition, relying on the popular collective understanding of its ancient heritage of rugged emancipation and indeed opposition, formulated by early English accounts of the kilt, that is the belted plaid or *fhéilidh-Mor*, rather than the later tailored version, as not only an affront to moral/English sensibilities, but as a symbol of primitive unlawfulness.

Dsquared2's Autumn/Winter 2016 menswear collection explored the potential relationship between Scotland and Japan via the respective traditional dress of each culture, a shared sartorial aesthetic centred on pleating according to the label's Dean and Dan Caten, linking the Highlander's kilt and the samurai's *hakama;* wide, pleated trousers. Amongst the label's signature mix of denim, punk-inspired bondage trousers and zipped black leather, a series of similarly pop culture inflected Black Watch tartan garments were presented including an immaculately tailored and pleated kilt, which replaced its absent sporran with black sequinned embroidery. The practical sporran, needed when wearing the pocketless kilt, a descendant of the medieval belt pouch, has, due to its emphatic positioning become along with the kilt itself, a sign of potent masculinity, typically oversized, embellished or constructed from animal fur and parts. In Dsquared2's design this exaggerated sign is replaced by ostensibly feminine decoration emasculating the wearer and, by removing the kilt's symbolic 'pocket', rendering it dysfunctional. Upon closer consideration, however, the sparkling black embellishment and its depiction of blossoming, fruit-laden stems, inspired in keeping with the show's inspiration by Japanese illustration, bearing what appear to bunches of grapes or cherries, speaks of abundant fecundity, of virile productivity emphasizing the wearer's potential potency.

Or is this an interrogation of entrenched gender positions and archetypes of masculinity in that 'fruit' is the pejorative slang term for a gay man, understood to date back at least to the 1930s and possibly to the nineteenth century, thus interrogating one of the most widely

156 DSquared², Autumn/Winter 2016

perceived vestimentary symbols of dominant masculinity (its use of Black Watch one of the original regimental setts, signifying order, authority and courage, emphasizing this further) and revealing an alternative understanding of both tartan and the kilt? Black Watch is the ideal tartan for the more reserved dresser, its conservative darker greens and blues a chromatic contrast to the vibrant reds and yellows of Royal Stewart arguably the other most popular tartan. In its sobriety we can understand Black Watch as the true dandy's tartan, if, following Baudelaire's formulation referenced previously in this book,[22] 'the perfection of his toilet will consist in absolute simplicity',[23] the reserved, 'quiet' shades of Black Watch provide the dandy's essential 'distinction'[24] but without undue display, 'in order to avoid singularity' as Chesterfield advocated.[25]

The detail is the true measure of the dandy's wardrobe, the subtle signs that communicate to the select few who can read and understand them, whilst going unnoticed by the crowd. In opposition to the showy tartan waistcoats and trousers beloved by the man of nineteenth-century fashion whose intention was to be noticed, today's man might opt instead for the more discreet tartan lining, providing pleasure mostly for himself, a pleasure received from the private physical proximity of dazzling tartan to his own body, hidden, except for the occasional glimpse, from the onlooker's gaze. The lining as tartan's secret hiding place in today's conventional tailored masculinity follows a tradition of quintessentially English abstinence from exhibitionism, here epitomized in an article extolling the praises of the London female couture trade, but expressive of the same tradition long established in men's tailoring: 'The luxury you find here is not the kind that flaunts itself in outward display, in brilliant colour or glitter. Rather, it's a controlled generosity in the handling of beautiful fabrics and furs, a refusal to skimp on workmanship or details, even unseen ones – a costume's lining maybe one of its chief attractions.'[26] The small immoderations of a brightly patterned lining to an immaculately cut suit or strident socks evoke Baudelaire's dandy in decline, a characteristic it could be argued not only of the modern conservative male wardrobe, but of conventional contemporary masculinity itself. 'Dandyism is a sunset; like the declining daystar, it is glorious without heat and full of melancholy.'[27]

Issey Miyake's Spring/Summer 1996 menswear collection exposed the tradition of hidden flamboyance, producing a collection that consisted of jackets and waistcoats made of silk tartan fabric reminiscent of linings (see illus. 157). Miyake, famous for his monochromatic menswear, in this collection literally turns the tradition of covert splendour inside out, revealing the libertarian potential for masculinity that lines its orthodox exterior. This revelation is costly, however, as many of the pieces in this collection were also suggestive of subalternity, alongside padded, fitted jackets that spoke of liveried footmen and bellboys, were tartan waistcoats worn over shirts – the off-duty butler – creating the impression of jackets literally turned inside out revealing the decorative, patterned body and plain sleeve linings. These newly exposed 'peacocks' are unsettled in their finery, forcibly revealed and parading a sartorial identity that now needs to be lived up to rather than secretly enjoyed, forced out from undercover these tartans speak of undecided, newly fashioned masculinities, not yet fully formed, its vivid colours still coalescing like butterflies newly emerged from the chrysalis drying their dazzling wings in preparation for their brief life of splendour.

157 Issey Miyake, Spring/Summer 1996 (left) Kenzo, Autumn/Winter 2017 (right)

… when they are dressed to go abroad, their clothes are contrived to conceal.[28]

More recently Kenzo has explored the concept of visibility, or, perhaps, ironically a visibility that blinds in the label's colour saturated, tartan/Argyle, multi-textured Autumn/Winter 2017 collection. Outfits consisting of leggings stolen from harlequin's wardrobe, tartan net skirts and thick work shirts in destabilized 45-degree tartans or gridded Argyle perhaps, were suggestive of the trickster or harlequin's ability to shape and gender shift, become visible or invisible in turn, and mediate between different realms. Colour gives way to black and white; tartans are translated, and textures overlap. Kenzo's tartan harlequins demand to be seen and yet resist easy optical registration, their clashing setts and Argyles unsettle and evoke the ability of harlequin to register successive emotions by indicating the different coloured diamonds of his traditional costume, waves of emotional intensity that accompany a constantly shifting gender identification. The tartaned body becomes a text that has multiple interpretations, multiple narrative possibilities.

Having invoked once more the figure of harlequin, and his ability to be seen or to become invisible by merely touching the black diamond on his costume, it is, ironically, the more sombre hued tartans such as Black Watch and Grey Douglas that have captured the imaginations of contemporary menswear designers and allowed them to explore issues of liberation and oppression. For Nicholas Daley's Autumn/Winter 2017 collection *Blackwatch* (see page 306), the designer drew on his Scottish Jamaican heritage to make visible the figure of George Rose. Rose, a former slave from Spanish Town, sergeant in the Black Watch regiment, Methodist minister and veteran of the Battle of Waterloo, played a significant role in the Napoleonic Wars, as did many other black servicemen of the period, and yet their presence remains largely unknown and unacknowledged. Daley lifts harlequin's finger to make the black soldier visible once more and yet, whilst his kilt proclaims his military prowess, the waxed tartan cagoule worn over it is suggestive of the need for protection, from the elements perhaps but also from the reassertion of imperialist military hegemony that would all too swiftly reinstate harlequin's diamond of invisibility.

Repression expressed in part via the use of somberly hued tartans also resides at the heart of Walter van Beirondonck's Spring/Summer 2013 collection *Silent Secrets* (see page 307). The collection which, according to the designer, was concerned with the need for secrecy in an age of global connectivity and contemporary society's saturation with information both trivial and critical, also referenced the ceremonial regalia of secret societies. Tartan with its hidden histories, its multiple languages that can speak of political allegiance, rebellion, conformity or subversion according to the wearer's allegiances, took centre stage in a collection that seemed as much about oppression as secrecy. The first look of the collection modelled by a contemporary harlequin, hesitates between visibility and disappearance, with top hats signifying the nineteenth-century industrialist, ring master or possibly magician's disappearing trick replacing the traditional *commedia dell'arte* two-pointed hat, and which were adorned with arcane symbols including a triangle (or perhaps open arrow) topped with the cross from the traditional female (Venus) sign, an amalgam suggestive of the newer symbology of alternative gender positions. If van Beirondonck's hats speak of potential, of new genders still coded, but nevertheless supplanting tradition, the tartan jacket with its padded white leather harness is evidence of a state of continued repression. The jacket is simultaneously restrained by the harness, keeping in check the potential for limitless self-expression that tartan can bestow, whilst overlaying its subdued, barely visible sett with a new insistent restraining grid. It is as if tartan's traditions, that have helped define established masculine ideals, are now in bondage, a bondage that we recognize from alternative sexualities, making both this tartan and its wearer undecided; subservient and dominant, invisible and visible.

Pray be not only well dressed, but shining in your dress; let it have 'du brillant'.[29]

Tartan continues to provide a textile arena in which those who wish to identify as non-binary can explore, assert and indeed promote multiple masculine possibilities. Its essential polyvalence explored throughout this book makes it the textile of choice in which to confront societal conventions, to be understood at once as an essential part of that same society if it is to continue to grow and develop and to represent alternatives to society's outmoded gender norms. RuPaul, actor, singer, entrepreneur and arguably America's most well-known and successful drag queen, regularly chooses tartan for his public appearances when not in drag. Tartan's flamboyance, its signalling of rebellion, defiance and strength made it the obvious

158 Nicholas Daley, 'Blackwatch', Autumn/Winter 2017

159 Walter van Beirondonck, 'Silent Secrets', Spring/Summer 2013

textile in which to receive his star on the Hollywood Walk of Fame, in 2018, the first drag queen to be honoured in this way. Whether attending awards ceremonies, participating on TV talk shows or indeed acting as judge and compere on his highly successful TV show *RuPaul's Drag Race*,[30] tartan both reaffirms his status as a global style icon and is suggestive of his even more extravagant on-stage personae. His use of tartan as simultaneously performative and sign of 'realness' as understood within the drag community as the ability to embody the most accurate version of a character, attitude or social convention, is akin to the use of clothing as performance by the nineteenth-century bohemian. As Elizabeth Wilson has suggested, 'bohemians used dress to signal inner authenticity and theatrical display simultaneously', and she goes on to propose that 'this accounts for the ambivalence of the bohemians and equally of the attitude of their audience towards them: they made of authenticity itself a performance.'[31]

Interestingly, while RuPaul reserves tartan primarily for when he is in 'mufti' (to borrow the military reference), for when not going to battle in drag, this is not the case for many of his most successful contestants. Raja Gemini, winner of season 3 of *RuPaul's Drag Race* who is perhaps most famous for top-to-toe tartan including Leigh Bowery-inspired full-face hood, makes of tartan a literal second skin, a protective performative layer between his multiple gender positions and the outside world. While Violet Chachki, season 7's winner, emphasized tartan's duality in his show-stopping 'tartan eleganza' look. Modelling a black sequinned gown that when unbuckled floated open to reveal its interior and was transformed into a spangled tartan jumpsuit, Chachki declared, 'I'm giving you tartan eleganza … Being able to serve two looks in one is a talent'.[32] While centred on the sartorial merits of tartan's ability to transform an outfit, Violet Chachki's comments address not only tartan's centrality to fashion, but more importantly its multivalency.

Tartan's history composed of multiple stories and a resistance to the occupation of definitive positions has meant that it has been prized by those who continue to challenge fixed identities. As Bowker and Starr have asserted, 'the indeterminacy of the past implies recovering multivocality; it also means understanding how standard narratives that appear universal have been constructed'.[33] Tartan's narratives make it at once preserver, conduit and declaration of contemporary masculinities, embracing ambiguity and unwilling to be decided.

160 RuPaul receiving his star on The Hollywood Walk of Fame, 2018

TARTAN TIMELINE

This timeline provides a list of the key events in Scottish history relevant to tartan, as well as specific cultural and economic tartan-related events referred to in the text. It is not intended to be either a complete chronology of Scottish history, or of the development of tartan manufacture. Rather, it is intended to demonstrate the relatively brief period during which tartan was transformed into the global cultural phenomenon we recognize today.

1124	King David the First takes the throne and introduces the feudal system of landholding to much of Scotland
1237	Southern border of Scotland established in the Treaty of York
1292	Edward I of England intervenes in Scottish affairs and grants the Scottish throne to John Balliol
1297	Andrew de Moravia and William Wallace lead the Scots to victory over England at Stirling Bridge
1314	Robert the Bruce defeats the English at Bannockburn
1328	Treaty of Edinburgh. England recognizes Scottish independence
1371	Robert II becomes the first Stuart/Stewart king
1513	James IV and thousands of Scots killed at Flodden
1578	James VI takes over government from his regent, James Douglas
1587	Mary, Queen of Scots is beheaded by the order of Queen Elizabeth I of England
1603	Union of the Crowns. James VI of Scotland becomes James I of England
1606	Around this date William Shakespeare's *Macbeth* is first staged
1621	Sir William Alexander establishes the colony of Nova Scotia
1676	Private archery club founded that would form the basis of the Royal Company of Archers – bodyguards to the British sovereign when in Scotland
1683	Portrait of Lord Mungo Murray painted by John Michael Wright
1689	Jacobite Highlanders defeat the army of William III at Killiecrankie, but are halted at Dunkeld
1692	Massacre of Glencoe
1695	Bank of Scotland created by Act of Parliament
1707	Act of Union between England and Scotland is passed
1715	First Jacobite uprising
1719	Second Jacobite uprising
1721	*Tartana* written by Allan Ramsay
1724	Field Marshal George Wade appointed as commander-in-chief in Scotland. Recruitment for the Highland regiments begins.
1725	General Wade's order requesting the provision of tartan uniform for the newly formed regiments

1727	Thomas Rawlinson establishes a factory near Invergarry, where the shorter kilt or *fhéilidh beag* is reputed to have been first developed as more practical wear for his workers
1739	43rd Regiment (The Black Watch) formed
1745	Final Jacobite uprising
1746	Culloden
1746	Act of Proscription passed, banning the wearing of tartan in the Highlands of Scotland
1749	*John Campbell of Ardmaddie* painted by William Mosman
1749	*Incident in the Scottish Rebellion, 1745* painted by David Morier
1760s	Beginning of European admiration for Ossian as 'The Celtic Homer'
1760s	Start of significant Highland emigration, which would reach its peak by the middle of the nineteenth century
1762	Land tenure reform leads to the Highland clearances and subsequent emigration
1766	Portrait of Colonel William Gordon of Fyvie painted by Pompeo Batoni
1766	Portrait of Sir James MacDonald of Sleat and Sir Alexander MacDonald, 'the MacDonald Boys', painted by Jeremiah Davison
1778	Founding of the Highland Society of London
1782	Repeal of the Act of Proscription
1790s	William Wilson & Son start exporting large quantities of tartan for clothing slaves in America and the Caribbean
1790	A regimental tailor sews box pleats into the shorter kilt, initiating the early phase of the tailored kilt
1795	Sir John of Sinclair of Ulbster is painted by Henry Raeburn in the uniform he designed for his regiment, the Caithness Fencibles
1810	*The MacNab* painted by Henry Raeburn
1812	Portrait of Colonel Alastair Macdonell of Glengarry painted by Henry Raeburn
1815	Following the Battle of Waterloo, the appearance of kilted Highland soldiers in Paris sees the beginning of the French admiration for tartan and the erotic speculation as to what is worn under the kilt
1817	*Rob Roy* by Walter Scott published
1819	William Wilson & Son of Bannockburn prepare their Key Pattern Book containing weaving instructions for over 240 tartans
1820	Celtic Society of Edinburgh founded by Stewart of Garth
1822	George IV visits Edinburgh
1829	The Sobieski Stuarts reveal that they have *The Vestiarium Scoticum* in their possession
1831	Publication of James Logan's *The Scottish Gaël*
1832	*La Sylphide* premiered in Paris
1835	Donizetti's opera, *Lucia di Lammermoor*, based on a Walter Scott novel, is premiered
1839	Eglinton Tournament staged
1840s	Smiths of Mauchline develop their tartan 'machine painting' process
1842	Publication of the first limited edition of *The Vestiarium Scoticum*
1844	Publication of the second edition of *The Vestiarium Scoticum*
1847	Sobieski Stuarts leave Scotland
1847	Queen Victoria purchases Balmoral
1851	Queen Victoria's children appear in Highland dress at the opening ceremony of the Great Exhibition
1855	The Prince of Wales's appearance in Highland dress causes a sensation during Victoria's state visit to Paris
1856	Thomas Burberry opens his first store in Basingstoke
1856	First artificial colour produced: aniline violet or 'mauveine'
1860s	Kilts made with knife pleats begin to replace the older box-pleated kilt.

1861	Death of Albert, the Prince Consort
1861	James Clerk Maxwell produces what is considered to be the first colour photograph; its subject is a tartan ribbon
1890s	Kilts pleated to sett rather than to stripe become the norm
1914–18	Kilted Highland regiments fighting in the First World War earn the German epithet 'ladies from Hell'
1920	Discovery of Gerumsberget Cloak in Sweden
1934	Discovery of the Falkirk Tartan
1936	*The Ghost Goes West*, directed by René Clair
1945	*I Know Where I'm Going!*, directed Michael Powell and Emeric Pressburger.
1946	'Reproduction' colours developed by D.C. Dalgleish Ltd
1947	*Brigadoon* by Lerner and Loewe premiered on Broadway
1950	Publication of Donald C. Stewart's *The Setts of the Scottish Tartans*
1954	*Brigadoon*, directed by Vincente Minnelli
1955	*Geordie*, directed by Frank Launder
1957	Scottish Television starts broadcasting
1957	*The Kilt is My Delight* broadcast until 1963
1958	*White Heather Club* broadcast until 1968
1961	Publication of Isabel Grant's *Highland Folk Ways*
1962	Publication of John Telfer Dunbar's *History of Highland Dress*
1967	*Casino Royale*, directed by John Huston et al.
1969	Dom Hans van der Laan presents his essay 'On a Scottish Tartan'
1971–3	Slade, with tartan-wearing Noddy Holder as front man, release a succession of chart-topping singles in the UK
1971	Idi Amin seizes control of Uganda and for a time dresses his army in kilts
1974–5	Peak of the Bay City Rollers' popularity, with two UK no.1 singles and a twenty-week UK television series: *Shang-a-Lang*
1976	Vivienne Westwood and Malcolm Maclaren open Seditionaries, selling tartan bondage wear
1981	Rei Kawakubo and Yohji Yamamoto show collections for the first time in Paris, heralding the so-called 'Japanese revolution in fashion'. Kawakubo and subsequent designers associated with Comme des Garçons regularly incorporate tartan in their designs
1983	Publication of Hugh Trevor-Roper's *The Invention of Tradition: The Highland Tradition of Scotland*
1994	*Rob Roy*, directed by Michael Caton-Jones
1994	*Highland Fling*, Matthew Bourne's ballet based on *La Sylphide*, is staged.
1995	*Braveheart*, directed by Mel Gibson
1995	Alexander McQueen's Autumn/Winter 'Highland Rape' collection presented
1997	Tartan Day resolution passed by US Congress
1998	Puett and Bocanegra's *Manhattan Tartan Project* developed
1999	Scottish parliament sits for the first time under the new constitutional arrangements
2000	Jun Takahashi, for the Undercover label, presents his Autumn/Winter collection: 'Melting Pot'
2000	New-found commercial success of Burberry (after the appointment of Rose Marie Bravo as chief executive in 1997) leads the company to register its Nova check as a trademark, and to stop production of the Burberry baseball cap due to its association with 'chavs'
2001	*The 51st State*, directed by Ronny Yu
2002	Matthew Barney completes the Cremaster Cycle with *Cremaster 3*, which includes the grand finale 'The Order', in which Barney appears as the Entered Apprentice
2002	Cao Fei produces *Rabid Dogs* video with a cast of 'dogs' dressed in fake Burberry
2004	Opening of the new Scottish Parliament Building
2004	Marc Jacobs's Autumn/Winter collection for Louis Vuitton
2006	Autumn/Winter collections of a large number of prominent fashion designers all feature tartan

2007	Start of the Great Recession, the most severe global economic and financial crisis since the Great Depression
2011	The Scottish National Party (SNP) gains overall majority of the Scottish Parliament
2012	The Scotland Act ratifies the largest transfer of financial powers to Scotland from Westminster since the creation of the United Kingdom
2014	Referendum on Scottish independence from the UK. 55.3% vote against while 44.7% are in favour
2016	European Union Membership referendum (BREXIT). The UK electorate vote to leave by a very narrow margin, although the majority (62% to 38%) of Scots vote to remain
2017	Scottish Jamaican designer Nicholas Daley presents his 'Blackwatch' collection
2018	Glaswegian born Charles Jeffrey first showcases his 'Loverboy' tartan in the Autumn/Winter collection 'Rampage'. Tartan continues to feature strongly in the designer's non-binary collections
2020	During the Covid-19 global pandemic Nicola Sturgeon, Scotland's First Minister, frequently wears the Shelter Scotland 'Homeless' tartan facemask
2020	For its Autumn/Winter menswear collection Gucci includes a man wearing a tartan dress in order to disrupt 'toxic stereotypes'

NOTES

INTRODUCTION

1. Gordon Teall of Teallach and Philip D. Smith Jr. (1992), *District Tartans*, London: Shepheard-Walwyn.
2. Donald C. Stewart (1974, 2nd edition), *The Setts of the Scottish Tartans*, London: Shepheard-Walwyn.
3. The term 'thread count' generally refers to the number of warps and wefts in a square inch of fabric. In tartan studies, however, there is a tradition (established by the majority of mid-twentieth century pioneering tartan historians, Stewart amongst them) to use the term to describe the actual sequence of colour changes and their widths in each individual tartan sett. Taken from descriptions found in the earliest nineteenth-century tartan manufacturers' pattern books, such as William Wilson and Son of Bannockburn, these 'thread counts' are an attempt to establish the correct ratio of width and colour necessary to produce any particular accredited tartan, and should not be confused with the contemporary meaning of the term.
4. James D. Scarlett (1985), *The Tartan Weaver's Guide*, London: Shepheard-Walwyn. James D. Scarlett (1990), *Tartan: The Highland Textile*, London: Shepheard-Walwyn.
5. I. F. Grant (1995 edition), *Highland Folk Ways*, Edinburgh: Birlinn.
6. J. Telfer Dunbar (1962), *History of Highland Dress*, Edinburgh: Oliver & Boyd.
7. Hugh Cheape (1991), *Tartan: The Highland Habit*, Edinburgh: National Museums of Scotland.
8. Hugh Trevor-Roper (1983), 'The Invention of Tradition: The Highland Tradition of Scotland', in Eric Hobsbawm and Terence Ranger (eds.), *The Invention of Tradition*, (1992 edition), Cambridge: Cambridge University Press.
9. Teallach and Smith, 1992, p. ix.
10. Walter Benjamin (1999 edition), 'N [On the Theory of Knowledge, Theory of Progress]' in *The Arcades Project*, Massachusetts: Belknap Press, p. 461.
11. Philippe Perrot (1994), *Fashioning the Bourgeoisie: A History of Clothing in the Nineteenth Century*, New Jersey: Princeton University Press, p. 7.
12. The ban on wearing tartan following the Act of Proscription will be discussed in detail later. These and other salient moments in tartan's history can also be visually contextualized by referring to the timeline on p. 293.
13. Michel Foucault, 'Of Other Spaces' in *Diacritics*, Spring 1986, p. 25. James Clifford (1988), *The Predicament of Culture: Twentieth-Century Ethnography, Literature, and Art*, Massachusetts: Harvard University Press, p. 236.
14. Catherine McDermott (2002), *Made in Britain: Tradition and Style in Contemporary British Fashion*, London: Mitchell Beazley, p. 60.
15. Roland Barthes (1973 edition), *Mythologies*, London: Collins, p. 133.
16. Gilles Deleuze and Félix Guattari (1992), *A Thousand Plateaus: Capitalism and Schizophrenia*, London: Athlone Press, 1992, p. 9.

1. TECHNICAL CONSTRUCTION

1. This oscillation between foreground and background will be discussed in further detail in Chapter 9, *Tartan, the Grid and Modernity*, but what is of primary importance here is to

understand that the intricacy and apparent contradictions inherent in tartan's actual construction also characterizes our broader sociocultural understanding of it. At almost every point in its many histories, it displays properties that reveal its intrinsic ambiguity and multivalency.

2. James Logan (1831), *The Scottish Gaël*, London: Smith, Elder & Co.

3. The process that produced the patterned papers and its significance to the blossoming nineteenth-century Scottish tourist industry will be discussed later in Chapter 8, *Balmoralization*.

4. Scarlett, 1990, pp. 6–7.

5. The pattern stick debate is just one of the many examples of obscure textile tributaries that typify the landscape of tartan studies and which the researcher can all too easily become immersed in. Based on early travellers' accounts of Highland ways of life and then elaborated upon in the nineteenth century, pattern sticks and other similar 'research' swiftly became part of the folklore of the fabric, adding to the growing mythology of tartan.

6. Aside from The Scottish Tartans Authority, many organizations exist that provide databases which make it possible to search for, and identify, existing tartans both old and modern. Others offer to help with the design and registration of new tartans. Much of this information is available electronically and a list of the more reliable and interesting is provided in the bibliography. To a large degree, the advent of these electronic databases has rendered the many published tartan dictionaries somewhat redundant, however information concerning the most widely available of these is also contained in the bibliography. The wealth of reliable material in both electronic and more traditional formats has meant that it was never the intention of this study to include a directory of tartan in any form, and instead specific patterns are referred to only when relevant to the subject under discussion.

7. Scarlett, 1990, p. 46.

8. The term 'plaid' here indicates a garment: a length of cloth that could act as a form of cloak and which, as a staple element of early Highland dress, will be discussed at length in succeeding chapters. However, the terminological confusion that is so characteristic of tartan studies is also noticeable, as for many readers (particularly those in North America), the term is more commonly associated with the tartan pattern itself rather than a specific garment; again this linguistic slippage will be commented upon in more detail in Chapter 2, *Early Appearances*.

9. Crowfoot, Grace, M., 'Two textiles from the National Museum, Edinburgh' *Proceedings of the Society of Antiquaries of Scotland*, vol. 82 (1947–48), pp. 225–231.

10. See Elizabeth Wayland Barber, *The Mummies of Urumchi* (1999), for an account of the Chinese mummies and their textiles. It includes her research linking the tartan-style cloth found with the mummies to textiles originating in Anatolia and the Caucasus. The discovery at Hallstatt, in 1846, of a prehistoric cemetery rich in artefacts including many textile specimens, remains arguably the most important proof of the cultural life of Central Europe during a period spanning from 1200 to 500 BC. Hallstatt Culture, as it has become known, sheds light on a period that saw the end of the Bronze Age and the dawn of the Iron Age, establishing the existence of the Celtic civilization alongside those of the Greeks and Romans in Europe during this period.

11. Grant, 1995, p. 227.

12. As with Note 9 above, the term 'plaid' is used to indicate a garment that will be discussed in detail later, not the checked pattern.

13. Grant, 1995, p. 232.

14. Many of these waulking songs were first collected and set down by Alexander Carmichael in his exhaustive four-volume work, *Carmina Gadelica* (Hymns and Incantations), first published in 1928. Carmichael was an antiquarian, a Gaelic scholar and a collector of early tartan specimens and oral literature gathered throughout the Highlands of Scotland, amongst which were the waulking songs included in *Carmina Gadelica*. Dunbar suggests that many waulking songs 'referred to old tales and traditions; others were based on the latest news or scandal'. John Telfer Dunbar (1983), *Highland Costume*, Edinburgh: The Mercat Press, p. 11.

15. The particular section of the Act of Proscription directly related to the ban on tartan is reproduced in full in Chapter 5, *Regulation Tartan*; the political ideologies embedded in the wearing

of tartan during its period of proscription are considered in Chaptr 4, *Transforming Tartan*. The notion of textiles as a sign of oppression is discussed in Chapter 11, *Colonization*. The Act of Proscription of 1746 can be historically situated with the aid of the timeline.

16. Quoted in Iain Zaczek and Charles Phillips (2004), *The Complete Book of Tartan*, London: Hermes House, p. 18.
17. Scarlett, 1990, p. 7.
18. Events such as George IV's visit to Edinburgh, the raising of the Highland regiments, and other seminal moments in tartan's history, will be discussed in detail in their relevant sections. The timeline referred to in Note 15 above places these tartan developments in their broader historical context.
19. Teallach and Smith, 1992, p. 196.
20. Dunbar, 1983, p. 8.
21. Quoted in Dunbar, 1962, p. 29.
22. Kok, A., 'Early Scottish Dyes' in Dunbar, 1962, pp. 222–40.
23. Ibid., p. 226.
24. Ibid., p. 232.
25. Ibid., p 229
26. Watson, J., 'Tartan's Not Dyed-in-the-Wool Scots', *Scotland on Sunday*, 11 January 2004.
27. Scarlett, 1990, p. 43.

2. EARLY APPEARANCES

1. Raphael Samuel (1996), *Theatres of Memory*, London: Verso, p. 8.
2. Dunbar also suggests the rare Irish *tuartan* as a possible source.
3. 2 Kings 18:17 reads: 'And the king of Assyria sent the Tartan, the Rabsaris, and the Rabshakeh with a great army from Lachish to King Hezekiah at Jerusalem.' Also: 'A small one-masted vessel with a large lateen sail and a foresail, used in the Mediterranean.' C.T. Onions (ed.) (1973), *The Shorter Oxford English Dictionary,* (3rd ed.), vol. II, Oxford: Oxford University Press, p. 2246.
4. Ibid., p. 2246.
5. Foucault's 'certain Chinese encyclopaedia' contains categories of animals including: '(a) belonging to the Emperor, … (h) included in the present classification, … (k) drawn with a very fine camelhair brush, … (j) innumerable, … [and] (n) that from a long way off look like flies,…'

amongst others. Michel Foucault (2002 edition), *The Order of Things*, London: Routledge, p. xvi.
6. Scarlett, 1990, pp. 9–10.
7. Quoted in Dunbar, 1962, p. 29.
8. Taylor is quoted in Dunbar, 1983, p. 24, and Martin Martin's celebrated account can be found in numerous works on tartan including Cheape, 1995, p. 20.
9. See Samuel, 1996, pp. 3–48 for a full exploration of the term 'unofficial knowledge'.
10. Ibid., p. 8.
11. Dunbar, 1983, p. 1.
12. *Braveheart*, 1995, dir. Mel Gibson. *Rob Roy*, 1994, dir. Michael Caton-Jones. Whilst other costume dramas set in the Highlands of Scotland have contributed to a late twentieth-century Hollywood Highland aesthetic, the impact of these two particular films, released in close proximity to one another, is undeniable. For a detailed examination of this cinematic effect see Colin McArthur, *'Brigadoon', 'Braveheart' and the Scots: Distortions of Scotland in Hollywood Cinema*, I. B. Tauris, 2003; and Lin Anderson, *Braveheart: From Hollywood to Holyrood*, Luath Press, 2004.
13. See Bibliography for a list of such sites.
14. Philippe Perrot, in the introduction to his *Fashioning the Bourgeoisie*, expresses this division as 'humanity sewn and humanity draped'. Perrot, 1994, p. 7.
15. Scarlett, 1990, p. 9.
16. Quoted in Teallach and Smith, 1992, p. 5.
17. A sept was a subdivision within the clan. It was formed of groups of people owing allegiance to, or somehow affiliated, to the clan. They typically shared a common surname different from that of the clan. These names often originated from the person's trade: Smith or Weaver, for example.
18. Teallach and Smith, 1992, p. 8.
19. The first meeting of the new Scottish parliament took place on 12 May, 1999, nearly 300 years after the original independent Scottish parliament had been swept away with the ratification of the Act of Union of 1707.
20. Dunbar, 1962, p. 55.
21. Nicholson, R., 'From Ramsay's *Flora MacDonald* to Raeburn's *MacNab*: The Use of Tartan as a Symbol of Identity', *Textile History*, 36, 2005, p. 149.
22. Ibid., p. 149.

23. Ibid., pp. 152–3.
24. Ibid., p. 152.
25. Hobsbawm and Ranger, 1992, p. 31.

3. FRAGMENTS AND FABRICATION

1. Raymond Bellour, 'System of a Fragment' in Bellour (2000), *The Analysis of Film*, Indiana: Indiana University Press, p. 29.
2. Ibid., p. 29.
3. Ibid., p. 29.
4. Ibid., p. 29.
5. Hayden White, 'The Fictions of Factual Representation' in Donald Preziosi and Claire Farago (eds.) (2004), *Grasping the World: The Idea of the Museum*, Hampshire: Ashgate, p. 26.
6. Quoted in Stephen Bann, 'Shrines, Curiosities, and the Rhetoric of Display', in Lynne Cooke and Peter Wollen (eds.) (1995), *Visual Display: Culture Beyond* Appearances, Seattle: Bay Press, p. 21.
7. Taken from the information panel accompanying the display at the Visitor Centre, Culloden Moor, Inverness, Scotland. At the time of writing it is expected that the new Culloden Battlefield Memorial, including the creation of a new Visitor Centre, will open in the latter part of 2007 as part of the Year of Highland Culture 2007. See the website of the National Trust for Scotland, www.nts.org.uk.
8. Taken from the information panel accompanying a display in the Scottish Tartans Museum, Keith, Scotland.
9. D. W. Stewart (1893), *Old and Rare Scottish Tartans*, Edinburgh: George. P. Johnston.
10. See Note 7.
11. Ibid.
12. The remarkable collection of the Queen's Own Highlanders is, like the aforementioned Seafield Collection, also housed at Fort George, Ardersier, near Inverness, Scotland.
13. I am especially grateful to Kelvin Hunter, curator of the Regimental Museum, Queen's Own Highlanders, Fort George, for showing me this last particular fragment. Whilst the date of the battle of Culloden was 1746 (rather than 1745), 1745 has become a generic date signifying not only the last Jacobite Rebellion, but all of its associated conflicts, including Culloden itself. Given the proximity of Fort George to Culloden Moor, it is fair to speculate that the fragment may well have been found at the site of that final confrontation.
14. Scarlett, 1990, p. 24.
15. Ibid. p. 187.
16. Elizabeth Wilson (1985), *Adorned in Dreams: Fashion and Modernity*, London: Virago. Mark Wigley (1995), *White Walls, Designer Dresses: The Fashioning of Modern Architecture*, Boston: MIT Press. Ulrich Lehmann (2000), *Tigersprung: Fashion in Modernity*, Boston: MIT Press. Caroline Evans (2003), *Fashion at the Edge: Spectacle, Modernity and Deathliness*, New Haven and London: Yale University Press.
17. From Vogue.com web page: www.vogue.co.uk/vogue_daily/story.asp?stid=16073.
18. The evolution of the kilt and its various transformations is discussed in detail in subsequent sections.
19. Samuel, 1996, p. 6.
20. Jean Baudrillard, 'The System of Collecting' in John Elsner and Roger Cardinal (eds.) (1994), *The Cultures of Collecting*, London: Reaktion, p. 8.
21. Dunbar, 1983, p. 4.
22. Guy Debord (1983 edition), 'Separation Perfected' No. 3 in *Society of the Spectacle*, Detroit: Black & Red (un-numbered).
23. See Hobsbawm and Ranger, 1992, pp. 17–18.
24. From Walter Scott's letters quoted in Trevor-Roper, 1983, p. 29.
25. Robertson Davies (1977), *Fifth Business*, London: W. H. Allen & Co., p. 242.
26. Both Dunbar (1962) and Trevor-Roper (1983) have extensive accounts of the activities of the Allen bothers.
27. See chapters seven to ten on the *Vestiarium Scoticum* in Dunbar, 1962.
28. Quoted in Dunbar, 1962, p. 119.
29. Ibid.p. 106.
30. Scarlett, 1990, pp. 195–6.
31. Dunbar, 1962, p. 111.
32. Hobsbawm and Ranger, 1992, p. 38.
33. Albert designed the 'Balmoral' tartan to be worn specifically at their Highland retreat. This is discussed further in Chapter 8, *Balmoralization*.

4. TRANSFORMING TARTAN

1. Roland Barthes (1990) *The Fashion System*, Berkeley: University of California Press, p. xi.
2. Ibid., p. xi.

3. Deleuze and Guattari, 1992, p. 12.
4. Hobsbawm and Ranger, 1992, p. 22.
5. Barthes, 1990, p. xi.
6. Barthes, 1990, p. xi.
7. Perrot, 1994, p. 8.
8. From 'Tartana: Or, The Plaid' (1721) by Allan Ramsay, quoted in Dunbar, 1962, p. 98.
9. From 'A Journey through Scotland (1723) in Dunbar, 1962, p. 97.
10. Nicholson, 2005, p. 150.
11. Quoted in Perrot, 1994, p. 196.
12. Nicholson, 2005, p. 149.
13. Shorter Oxford English Dictionary, 1990 edition, p. 1285.
14. *William West and the Regency Toy Theatre* (2004), London: Sir John Soane's Museum, p. 35.
15. *La Sylphide*, alongside other theatrical and cinematic productions, is discussed fully in Chapter 10, Supernatural *Tartan*.
16. Nicholson, 2005, p. 164.
17. *William West and the Regency Toy Theatre*, 2004, p. 54.
18. Tartan and other similar bold checks became a textile beloved of entertainers – whether comedians, popular musicians or other 'larger than life' personalities on stage and screen – throughout the twentieth century and on into the twenty-first. This reconfiguration of tartan as entertainment, with a new-found subversive resonance, is discussed in further detail in Chapter 7, *Tartan Toffs*.
19. Both long-running, Scottish-themed light entertainment programmes were produced by BBC Scotland; *The White Heather Club* ran from 1958 to 1968, and *The Kilt is My Delight* from 1957 to 1963.
20. It has also been suggested, by Lin Anderson amongst others, that the success of *Braveheart* in Britain was instrumental in hastening the eventual establishment of an independent Scottish parliament in 1999, nominally free from English influence at least in matters of specifically Scottish legislation.
21. Jon Savage (1992), *England's Dreaming: Sex Pistols and Punk Rock*, London: Faber and Faber, p. 230.
22. Ibid., p. 282.
23. Rarely sung sixth verse of 'God Save the King', written in 1745, which contrasts with the first verse of the Sex Pistols' 'God Save the Queen', written in 1977, see for example, at http://www.philjens.plus.com/pistols/pistols/pistols_lyrics.htm#GodSaveTheQueen, accessed 1 April 2008
24. Interestingly, there is a military precedent for the apron or 'nappy' kilt adopted by punks in the late 1970s. As Thomas Abler points out: 'In the Boer War, the sporran was abandoned while on service and the front of the kilt was covered with a kilt apron of khaki, which came equipped with a pocket to replace the sporran. The kilt apron initially covered only the front of the kilt, but Highland units in the Great War of 1914–18 wore a second apron to cover the rear of the kilt.' Thomas S. Abler (1999), *Hinterland Warriors and Military Dress: European Empires and Exotic Uniforms*, Oxford: Berg, p. 78.
25. Barthes, 1990, p. xi.
26. Savage, 1992, p. 230.
27. Quoted in Claire Wilcox (2004), *Vivienne Westwood*, London: V&A Publications, p. 15. The irony of an exhibition (at the Museum of London in 2000) devoted to the collection of Westwood's designs owned by Lady Romilly McAlpine, wife of the former treasurer of the Conservative Party, and one of Westwood's most 'established' patrons and collectors, is inescapable.
28. Mikhail Bakhtin (1984), *Rabelais and His World*, Bloomington: Indiana University Press, pp. 410–11.
29. Dunbar, 1962, p. 84.
30. C. Willett Cunnington (1990), *English Women's Clothing in the Nineteenth Century*, New York: Dover Publications, p. 1.

5. REGULATION TARTAN

1. Quoted in Dunbar, 1962, p. 3.
2. Ibid., p. 6.
3. Ibid.
4. Quoted in Dunbar, 1962, p. 155.
5. Quoted in Dunbar, 1962, p. 157.
6. Quoted in Phyllis G. Tortora and Keith Eubank (2005), *Survey of Historic Costume*, New York: Fairchild Publications, p. 232.
7. Perrot, 1994, p. 9.
8. Robert Walser (1999), *Jakob Von Gunten*, New York: New York Review Books, p. 4.

9. Elizabeth Ewing (1986), *History of Children's Costume*, London: Bibliophile, p. 85.

10. Brian J. McVeigh (2000), *Wearing Ideology: State, Schooling and Self-Presentation in Japan*, Oxford: Berg, p. 77.

11. *Battle Royale II*, 2003, dir. Kenta and Kinji Fukasaku. *Kill Bill*, 2003, dir. Quentin Tarantino.

12. *Coming to America*, 1988, dir. John Landis.

13. *Roseanne*, 1988–1997, ABC. *Frasier*, 1993–2004, NBC.

14. *The King of Queens*, 1998–2007, CBS (original network).

15. Antony Shugaar 'The Comedy of Errors: Gender Icons as Modular Components of Identity' in Giannino Malossi (ed.) (2000), *Material Man: Masculinity Sexuality Style*, New York: Harry N. Abrams, p. 67.

16. *Everybody Loves Raymond*, 1996–2005, CBS.

6. EROGENOUS ZONES

1. Nicholson, 2005, p. 161.

2. Quoted in Dunbar, 1962, p. 186.

3. Anne Hollander (2000), *Feeding the Eye*, Berkeley: University of California Press, p. 106.

4. Anne Hollander (1993), *Seeing Through Clothes*, Berkeley: University of California Press, p. 127.

5. Quoted in Nicholson, 2005, p. 165.

6. Hobsbawm and Ranger, 1992, pp. 27–28.

7. Ted Polhemus, 'The Invisible Man: Style and the Male Body' in Giannino Malossi (ed.) (2000), *Material Man: Masculinity Sexuality Style*, p. 44.

8. Sir Colin Campbell, Brigadier-General, The Queen's 93rd Sutherland Highlanders.

9. Taken from the copy accompanying an advert appearing on the web page www.topdrawers.com/underwear/gregg/a1104.html.

10. Jean Baudrillard (1983), *Simulations*, New York: Semiotext[e], p. 37.

11. From *Putting Pants on Philip*, 1927, dir. Clyde Bruckman.

12. Ibid.

13. From *Geordie*, 1955, dir. Frank Launder.

14. Bakhtin, 1984, p. 411.

15. From *The Battle of the Sexes*, 1955, dir. Charles Crichton.

16. The Highland clearances and their relationship to the global dissemination of tartan is discussed in Chapter 11, *Colonization*.

17. From *Braveheart*, 1995, dir. Mel Gibson.

18. From *Rob Roy*, 1994, dir. Michael Caton-Jones

19. *British Vogue*, April 1966.

20. Scarlett, 1990, p. 40.

21. From Vogue.com web page: www.co.uk/vogue_daily/story/story.asp?stid=16103.

22. Ibid.

7. TARTAN TOFFS

1. Quoted in Kenneth Baker (2005), *George IV: A Life in Caricature*, London: Thames and Hudson, p. 132. Dunbar, 1983, p. 42., also lists 17½ yards of 'Royal Plaid Casemere' and notes that when Hunter's opened a new shop in Princes Street, Edinburgh, queues formed from people wanting to see the king's accoutrements.

2. Prince William, Duke of Cumberland was the younger son of George II. Leading the government forces, he was responsible for finally crushing the Jacobite rebellion at Culloden on 16 April 1746. The savage reprisals he took against the remaining pockets of Highland resistance earned him the nickname of 'Cumberland the Butcher'.

3. This cartoon is included in Dunbar, 1983, p. 43.

4. See Hobsbawm and Ranger, 1992, p. 31.

5. In Dunbar, 1983, p. 32.

6. Quoted in Philip Mansel (2005), *Dressed to Rule: Royal and Court Costume from Louis XIV to Elizabeth II*, New Haven and London: Yale University Press, p. 144.

7. Ibid.

8. Giles Foden (1999), *The Last King of Scotland*, London: Faber and Faber, p. 192.

9. Abler, 1999, p. 81.

10. Foden, 1999, pp. 292–3.

11. R. S. Surtees (1986), *Mr. Sponge's Sporting Tour*, Oxford: Oxford University Press, p. 160.

12. Roland Barthes (2006), *The Language of Fashion*, Oxford: Berg, p. 66.

13. Surtees, 1986, p. 230.

14. Quoted in Hobsbawm and Ranger, 1992, p. 28.

15. Aileen Ribeiro (1986), *Dress and Morality*, London: B.T. Batsford, pp. 125–6.

16. Charles Baudelaire (2005), *The Painter of Modern Life and Other Essays*, London: Phaidon, p. 28.

17. Ibid., p. 28.

18. Ibid.

19. Nicholson, 2005, p. 149.

20. Bakhtin, 1984, p. 35.
21. Tom Wolfe (1990), *Mauve Gloves & Madmen, Clutter & Vine*, London: Picador, pp. 182 and 184.
22. Henry Louis Gates, Jr. (1987), *Figures in Black: Words, Signs, and the 'Racial' Self*, New York: Oxford University Press, p. 51.
23. Quoted in Gates, 1987, pp. 238–9.
24. One could perhaps argue that in contemporary popular music this is not the case, but even before the advent of television, early pop promos were made to be played on what amounted to 'video jukeboxes'.
25. Susan Stewart (1993), *On Longing: Narratives of the Miniature, the Gigantic, the Souvenir, the Collection*, Durham: Duke University Press, p. 106.
26. Wolfe, 1990, p. 182.
27. Surtees, 1986, p. 229.
28. From Colley Cibber's *Love's Last Shift* quoted in J.M. and M.J. Cohen (1971), *The Penguin Dictionary of Quotations*, Harmondsworth: Penguin Books, p. 111.

8. BALMORALIZATION

1. 'D [Boredom, Eternal Return]' in Benjamin, 1999, p. 116.
2. Ibid.
3. Ibid.
4. 'B [Fashion]' in Benjamin, 1999, p. 79.
5. Quoted in Dunbar, 1962, p. 11.
6. Quoted in Hobsbawm and Ranger, 1992, p. 20.
7. 'B [Fashion]' in Benjamin, 1999, p. 79.
8. Mansel, 2005, p. 136.
9. Jeanne Cannizzo (2005), *Our Highland Home: Victoria and Albert in Scotland*, Edinburgh: National Galleries of Scotland, p. 45.
10. Stewart, 1999, p. 68.
11. Quoted in *Balmoral: Highland Retreat of the Royal Family Since 1852 – Guide to the Castle and Estate* (2004), Derby: Heritage House Group, p. 6.
12. Quoted in Cannizzo, 2005, p. 48.
13. Ibid.
14. Quoted in the Spring/Summer 2005 Anta catalogue, p. 1. Quoted in April 2006 *World of Interiors* magazine, pp. 164–71.
15. See Joseph Holtzman (ed.) (2001), *Every Room Tells a Story: Tales from the Pages of Nest Magazine*, New York: D.A.P., pp. 148–65.

16. See particularly Chapter 11, 'Tartan Pattern Books', in Dunbar, 1962, which has been an invaluable resource whilst writing this section.
17. See Teallach and Smith, 1992, p. 28.
18. Quoted in Dunbar, 1962, p. 102.
19. Reported in the *Stirling Journal* and quoted in Dunbar, 1962, p. 150.
20. The relationship of the Burberry check to tartan is discussed in detail in Chapter 9, *Tartan, the Grid and Modernity*.
21. Jane Pavitt (ed.) (2000), *Brand.new*, London: V&A Publications, p. 16.
22. Quoted in Scarlett, 1990, p. 11.
23. Dunbar, 1962, p. 151.
24. Ibid.
25. Quoted in Zaczek and Phillips, 2004, p. 107.
26. This highly controversial development means that in effect the separate regimental tartans will be replaced by a new generic tartan based on that currently worn by the Argyll and Sutherland Highlanders and similar to that worn by the former Black Watch. Not only has the amalgamation of these individual Scottish regiments been highly controversial, but the possibility of a non-Scottish firm being selected to produce the tartan more cheaply abroad was a serious possibility when the contract was put out to tender. The recent decision to award Noble's the contract (whilst based, presumably, on the firm being able to produce the tartan at the most competitive rates), must also surely be a way of avoiding public outcry over this perceived final insult after the disbanding of the Scottish regiments. See *Edinburgh Evening News*, 30 March 2007, for a full report, also available online at http://edinburghnews.scotsman.com.
27. More information concerning Lochcarron, their history and products can be found on www.lochcarron.com. Lochcarron also have an outlet in London, Savile Row Kilts, which according to their website specializes in 'bespoke Highland Wear for Gentlemen and Ladies'. The site elsewhere suggests the logical sartorial connections between the kilt and Savile Row thus: 'Beau Brummel, born in 1778 and a close friend of the Prince of Wales (later King George IV) created a fashion for bespoke tailoring in wool – the essence of Savile Row today. By 1806 the first tailor was established in Savile Row. Almost 200 years later Savile Row tailoring is as

highly regarded as ever and has just taken a step in a new direction for the twenty-first century with the launch of Savile Row kilts.' See www.savilerowkilts.com.

28. Quoted on the website of the International Movie Database: www.imdb. Tartan Asia Extreme, the highly successful division of Tartan Films, became the first distribution label to deal specifically with East Asian films in the UK. The previously mentioned *Battle Royale II* is a typical Tartan production, and whilst there appears to be no direct connection, it is interesting to note that the Japanese obsession with tartan and the tartan-clad schoolgirl has no doubt become more embedded in the Western contemporary cultural psyche due to Tartan Asia Extreme's productions, making this particular Scottish/Japanese image recognizable to a Western audience.

9. TARTAN, THE GRID AND MODERNITY

1. Rosalind Krauss (1989), *The Originality of the Avant-Garde and Other Modernist Myths*, Boston: MIT Press, p. 9.
2. Scarlett, 1990, p. 46.
3. Krauss, 1989, p. 9.
4. Michel Nuridsany (2004), *China Art Now*, Paris: Éditions Flammarion, p. 95.
5. Krauss, 1989, p. 22.
6. Ibid., p. 12.
7. Ibid.
8. Quoted in the catalogue *Minimalism and After III* (2003), Berlin: DaimlerChrysler AG, p. 56.
9. Ibid.
10. Dom Hans van der Laan (1969), 'On a Scottish Tartan' in *Living and Correspondences* (2001), Henry Moore Foundation External Programmes, p. 13.
11. Ibid. Van der Laan.
12. Ibid.
13. Van der Laan, p. 17.
14. Ibid.
15. Van der Laan, p. 25.
16. Ibid.
17. Krauss, 1989, p. 10.
18. Quoted in Charles Harrison and Paul Wood (eds.) (1993), *Art in Theory 1900–1990*, Oxford: Blackwell, p. 278.
19. Ibid.

20. Krauss, 1989, p. 169.
21. Dunbar, 1983, p. 15.
22. Ted Polhemus and Lynn Procter (1978), *Fashion and Anti-Fashion: An Anthropology of Clothing and Adornment*, London: Thames and Hudson, p. 23.
23. Ibid., p. 20.
24. Nuridsany, 2004, p. 242.
25. Krauss, 1989, p. 169.

10. SUPERNATURAL TARTAN

1. Deleuze and Guattari, 1992, p. 320.
2. Dunbar, 1962, p. 95.
3. Dunbar, 1983, p. 11.
4. Nicholson, 2005, p. 157.
5. Quoted in Dunbar, 1962, p. 6.
6. Ibid., Nicholson.
7. Deleuze and Guattari, 1992, p. 320.
8. Ibid.
9. William Shakespeare, *Macbeth*, Act IV Scene 1. In *The Complete Works of William Shakespeare* (1904), London: Henry Frowde, p. 931.
10. Ibid.
11. Deleuze and Guattari, 1992, p. 314.
12. Nicholson, 2005, p. 148.
13. Deleuze and Guattari, 1992, p. 320.
14. It appears that from *Macbeth* to Maggie Smith's portrayal of the Scottish witchcraft expert Professor Minerva McGonagall (resplendent in a variety of tartan outfits in the *Harry Potter* films), a significant social group of the fictional Scottish landscape is the witch, tartan-clad or otherwise.
15. Deleuze and Guattari, 1992, p. 340.
16. Taken from the publicity material for the revival of *Highland Fling* presented at Sadler's Wells, London.
17. *Trainspotting*, dir. Danny Boyle, 1996. From Irvine Welsh's 1993 best-seller of the same name. *Tinsel Town* was a television drama produced by BBC Scotland, which ran for two series, and aired on BBC2 between 2000 and 2002. Created by Robbie Allen, Stuart Davis and Martin McCardie, the action centred on a Glasgow nightclub called Tinsel Town and the people who frequented it.
18. From *Dumbo*, dir. Walt Disney, 1941.
19. Quoted in Cannizzo, 2005, p. 41.
20. From *Brigadoon*, Vincente Minnelli, 1954. Incidentally, Lerner most probably used a real

Scottish landmark – the Bridge of Doon (or *Brig o' Doon*) – as the inspiration for the title of his village. According to legend, Tam o' Shanter fled across the same bridge whilst escaping the three witches (reminiscent of Macbeth's weird sisters) who were chasing him.

21. 'B [Fashion]' in Benjamin, 1999, pp. 63–4.
22. From *Brigadoon*, dir. Vincente Minnelli, 1954.
23. Quoted in *Balmoral: Highland Retreat of the Royal Family Since 1852 – Guide to the Castle and Estate*, 2004, p. 66.
24. From web pages http://www.highlandsnsw.com.au/Brigadoon.
25. Ibid.
26. From *I Know Where I'm Going!*, dirs. William Powell and Emeric Pressburger, 1945.
27. Carol Duncan (1995), *Civilizing Rituals: Inside Public Art Museums*, London: Routledge, p. 13.
28. From *I Know Where I'm Going!*, dirs. William Powell and Emeric Pressburger, 1945.
29. Deleuze and Guattari, 1992, p. 311.
30. Deleuze and Guattari, 1992, p. 320. Barney's bonnet is a version of the original Highland bonnet. As Abler informs: 'The blue Highland bonnet was sometimes decorated with feathers on the left side above the cockade. These feathers "grew" through time until by 1810 or so they covered the bonnet entirely. Soon after, and continuing to this day, the Highland bonnet consisted of black ostrich feathers over a wire frame, a form felt to have evolved from those few feathers originally worn at the side of the bonnet.' Abler, 1999, p. 74.

11. COLONIZATION

1. Hollander, 2000, p. 129.
2. The Royal Company of Archers is a ceremonial unit that serves as the British sovereign's bodyguard when in Scotland. Founded in 1676 as a private archery club, it established its protective function in 1822, when it formed the guard for George IV on his visit to Edinburgh.
3. Extract from a letter written by James Oglethorpe from Frederica, Georgia on January 22, 1740, to the Duke of Newcastle. From the website 'Letters form the Georgia Colony 1732–1742': http://msit.gsu.edu/dhr/gacolony/letters/JO_Newcastle_1740_January.htm.
4. Abler, 1999, p. 74.

5. Quoted from the 'Tartan Day in Canada' website: www.tartan-day.org.uk/tartan_day_canada.htm.
6. These and other events were obtained from the pages of 'Tartan Day Events' website: www.rampantscotland.com/features/tartanday.htm.
7. Abler, 1999, p. 79.
8. British *Vogue* November 1949, pp. 55–7.
9. Richard Martin and Harold Koda (1994), *Orientalism: Visions of the East in Western Dress* (catalogue), New York: Metropolitan Museum of Art, p. 11.
10. Abler, 1999, p. 67.
11. Mansel, 2005, p. 47–8.
12. Evans, 2003, p. 26.
13. From Steve Blamires, 'The Highland Clearances: An Introduction' on website: www.clannada.org/highland.php.
14. Hobsbawm and Ranger, 1983, p. 30.
15. Dunbar, 1962, p. 150.
16. Much work still needs to be done on this important aspect of tartan's (and indeed other textiles') historical association with the slave trade and other similarly oppressive institutions, such as textiles and garments produced by, and for, the penal system.
17. Dunbar, 1962, pp. 150–51 and 144.
18. Pavitt, 2000, p. 21.
19. Linda Nochlin (2001), *The Body in Pieces: The Fragment as a Metaphor of Modernity*, London: Thames and Hudson, p. 37.
20. Occasionally, tartan's conspicuousness could be a disadvantage to those in positions of authority, such as when the 78th Highlanders were fighting in the Boer War in 1897 – they were compelled to wear unembellished khaki uniforms as opposed to the regimental tartan, and to remove their rank distinctions as tartan decorations would have proved an easy target for the outstanding Boer marksmen.
21. Dunbar, 1962, p. 147.
22. Nicholson, 2005, p. 160.
23. Michel Pastoureau (1991), *The Devil's Cloth: A History of Stripes and Striped Fabric*, New York: Columbia University Press, p. 55.
24. From Adam Hochschild (2004), *Bury the Chains: Prophets and Rebels in the Fight to Free an Empire's Slaves*. Quoted on web pages: http://www.wnyc.org/books/42930.
25. From *The 51st State*, 2001, dir. Ronny Yu.

12. TARTAN'S TRANSLATION

1. Perrot, 1994, p. 2.
2. Barthes, 1973, p. 147.
3. Ibid.
4. Dunbar, 1962, p. 17.
5. Dunbar, 1962, p. 48.
6. Hollander, 2000, p. 129.
7. Oscar Wilde, 'The Decay of Lying', in *Complete Works of Oscar Wilde* (1971), London: Collins, p. 988.
8. The *daimyo* (literally 'big name') were feudal lords who exercised power in Japan from the tenth century until the nineteenth century. During the Tokugawa shogunate (1616–1867), Japan was divided into fiefs presided over by these *daimyo*, who were divided into three ranks according to the income received from their tenants, and whether or not they owned and maintained a castle. The *daimyo* were attended by the samurai, who acted as their retainers. In the eighteenth and early nineteenth centuries, the luxurious lifestyles of the *daimyo* became harder to support (mirroring the lives of Highland clan leaders in nineteenth-century Scotland, who became absentee landlords unable to support their southern lifestyles until they evicted their tenants and turned to more profitable sheep farming). The *daimyo's* role became increasingly redundant until finally, by 1871 and the establishment of the Meiji dynasty, they had lost all of their feudal privileges.
9. Colin McDowell (2000), *Fashion Today*, London: Phaidon, p. 134.
10. Both Yohji Yamamoto and Rei Kawakubo for Comme des Garçons showed for the first time in Paris in 1981. However, Issey Miyake, who can be considered the progenitor of so-called Japanese 'avant-garde' fashion, was already established in Paris. All three would remain firmly indebted to the pioneer of Japanese fashion in Paris, Kenzo (Kenzo Takada) who went to the city in the 1960s and staged his first show in 1970.
11. Barbara Vinken (2005), *Fashion Zeitgeist: Trends and Cycles in the Fashion System*, Oxford: Berg, p. 99.
12. Nicholson, 2005, p. 156.
13. 'B [Fashion]' in Benjamin, 1999, p. 80.
14. Yuniya Kawamura (2004), *The Japanese Revolution in Paris Fashion*, Oxford: Berg, p. 138.
15. Ibid., p. 131.
16. *Boro* are historic textiles that have been mended and patched over time, and which function as a kind of visual archive of fabrics from the Edo and Meiji eras. Literally meaning 'rags', *boro*, whilst indicative of the poverty of Japan's rural past, have been a fertile source of inspiration for designers such as Yamamoto and Kawakubo, who have discerned in their ragged, holey collages of different textiles, opportunities to reconsider how textiles are utilized in clothing and how to incorporate references to the past without resorting to a limited historicism.
17. Quoted in the catalogue *Jam: Tokyo-London* (2001), London: Booth-Clibborn Editions, p. 341.
18. Barthes, 1973, p. 147.
19. Quoted in Martin and Koda, *Orientalism: Visions of the East in Western Dress* (catalogue), 1994, p. 75.
20. Walter Benjamin 'The Task of the Translator' in *Illuminations*, (1992), London: Fontana, p. 72.
21. 'N [On the Theory of Knowledge, Theory of Progress]' in Benjamin, 1999, p. 461.

13. TARTAN UNDECIDED

1. *Lord Chesterfield's Letters*, London, 30 April, O.S. 1752. In Roberts, D. (ed.), 1992, p. 260.
2. Carrigan, T., Connell, B. and Lee J. 'Toward a New Sociology of Masculinity', in *Theory and Society*, vol.14, no.5, 1985, p. 569.
3. Since 2008 amongst an increasing number of exhibitions that have comprised totally, or in part, of men's clothing, those dealing specifically with menswear and the construction of sexual identity have included:
The Ideal Man: Fashion for Real Men. Kunstmuseum Den Haag, The Hague, 26/7–26/10/2008
The Dandy. Nordiska Museet, Stockholm, 22/10/2010–1/5/2011
The Peacock Male: Exuberance and Extremes in Masculine Dress. Philadelphia Museum of Art, Philadelphia, 22/1–18/9/2011
Manstyle. National Gallery of Victoria, Melbourne, 11/3–27/11/2011

A Queer History of Fashion: From the Closet to the Catwalk, F.I.T. Museum, New York, 13/9/2013–4/1/2014

Standing Tall: The Curious History of Men in Heels. Bata Shoe Museum, Toronto, 8/5/2015–17/5/2016

Mad About the Boy. Fashion Space gallery, London, 8/1–2/4/2016

Moses, Mods and Mr. Fish: The Menswear Revolution. The Jewish Museum, London, 31/3–19/6/2016

Reigning Men: Fashion in Menswear 1715-2015. LACMA, Los Angeles, 10/4–21/8/2016

Gender Bending Fashion. Museum of Fine Arts, Boston, 21/3–25/8/2019

Invisible Men: An Anthology from the Westminster Menswear Archive. University of Westminster, London, 25/10–24/11/2019.

At the time of writing the wave of exhibitions that seek to understand to what extent male clothing produces gender seems set to continue with shows including *Dandy Style* at the Manchester Art Gallery, Manchester (November 2021 to April 2022) and *Fashioning Masculinities* at the Victoria & Albert Museum, London (March–November 2022).

4. See 'Erogenous Zones' p. 131 and 'Tartan Toffs' p. 151

5. Roberts, 1992, p. 206.

6. See 'Technical Construction: Sett, Weave, Colour' p. 13

7. *Lord Chesterfield's Letters*, London, December 30th, O.S. 1748. Roberts, 1992, p. 127.

8. From the official Gucci website https://www.gucci.com/us/en/pr/men/ready-to-wear-for-men/shirts-for-men/tartan-cotton-long-smock-shirt-p-632536ZAFDL7261, accessed 1/11/2020.

9. Bakhtin, Mikhail, 'The Grotesque Image of the Body' in *Rabelais and his World*, 1984, p. 317.

10. Taken from the biography of Cheddar Gorgeous available on the TEDˣ Royal Tunbridge Wells site https://www.tedxroyaltunbridgewells.com/speakers/cheddar-gorgeous#:~:text=Cheddar%20Gorgeous%20is%20a%20drag,to%20only%20be%20one%20person, accessed 2/11/2020.

11. I am thinking here particularly of Friedrich's oil paintings *Woman Before the Rising Sun* of 1818–20 in the collection of the Museum Folkwang, Essen and *Chalk Cliffs on Rügen* 1818 in the Kunst Museum Winterthur.

12. Cheddar Gorgeous in conversation with the author 2/11/2020.

13. Bakhtin, 1984, p. 318.

14. Bakhtin, Mikhail, 'Forms of Time and of the Chronotope in the Novel' in *The Dialogic Imagination: Four Essays by M.M. Bakhtin*, Holquist, M., (ed.), 1981, p. 84.

15. *Lord Chesterfield's Letters*, London, 30 December, O.S. 1748. Roberts, 1992, p. 128.

16. From '5 Things To Know About The SS21 Charles Jeffrey Loverboy Collection' https://www.vogue.co.uk/news/gallery/charles-jeffrey-loverboy-ss21-everything-you-need-to-know, accessed 13/11/2020.

17. Bakhtin 1984, p. 7.

18. Ibid. p. 7

19. Ibid. p. 8

20. *Lord Chesterfield's Letters* Bath, 9 October, O.S. 1746. Roberts, 1992, p. 46

21. From Eric Gill Trousers & The Most precious ornament (1937) available at http://vestoj.com/trousers-the-most-precious-ornament/, accessed 14/11/2020.

22. See 'The Dandy, The Swell and The Gent' p. 161

23. Baudelaire, Charles, 'The Dandy' in *The Painter of Modern Life and Other Essays*, 1995, p. 27.

24. Ibid.

25. *Lord Chesterfield's Letters* Bath, 9 October, O.S. 1746. Roberts, 1992, p. 46.

26. From 'Couture Clothes: Are They Worth the Money?' *UK Vogue*, September 1960.

27. Baudelaire, 1995, p. 29.

28. *The Works of Lord Chesterfield: Including His Letters To His Son &C*. Greenwich, 6 June, O.S. 1751. In first complete American edition, 1838, p. 414.

29. *The Works of Lord Chesterfield: Including His Letters To His Son &c*. London, 14 November, 1749. In first complete American edition, 1838, p. 292.

30. Multi-award-winning American television programme *RuPaul's Drag Race*, first broad-

cast in 2009, in which RuPaul searches for the next drag superstar, has at the time of writing reached its twelfth season and spawned a number of spin offs including *RuPaul's Drag Race UK.*

31. Wilson, Elizabeth, 'Bohemian Dress and the Heroism of Everyday Life' in *Fashion Theory* 2:3, 1998, p. 239.

32. Jason Dardo (Violet Chachki) speaking on episode 1, season 7 of *RuPaul's Drag Race* first broadcast 2/3/2015.

33. Bowker, Geoffrey, C. and Star, Susan Leigh, *Sorting Things Out: Classification and its Consequences*, 2000, p. 41.

BIBLIOGRAPHY

Abler, T. S. (1999), *Hinterland Warriors and Military Dress: European Empires and Exotic Uniforms*, Oxford: Berg.

Anderson, B. (1991), *Imagined Communities*, London: Verso.

Anderson, L. (2004), *Braveheart: From Hollywood to Holyrood*, Edinburgh: Luath Press.

Anstey, H. and Weston, T. (1999), *Guide to Textile Terms*, Weston Publishing.

Bain, R. (1976), *The Clans and Tartans of Scotland*, London: Collins.

Baker, J. (2004), *Mauchline Ware*, Princes Risborough: Shire Publications.

Baker, K. (2005), *George IV: A Life in Caricature*, London: Thames and Hudson.

Bakhtin, M. (1984), *Rabelais and His World*, Bloomington: Indiana University Press.

Bakhtin, M. (2014), *The Dialogic Imagination*, Austin: University of Texas Press.

Barthes, R. (1973), *Mythologies*, London: Collins.

Barthes, R. (1983), *Empire of Signs*, New York: Hill and Wang.

Barthes, R. (1990), *The Fashion System*, Berkeley: University of California Press.

Barthes, R. (2006), *The Language of Fashion*, Oxford: Berg.

Baudelaire, C. (2005), *The Painter of Modern Life and Other Essays*, London: Phaidon.

Baudrillard, J. (1983), *Simulations*, New York: Semiotext[e].

Bellour, R. (2000), *The Analysis of Film*, Bloomington: Indiana University Press.

Benjamin, W. (1992), *Illuminations*, London: Fontana.

Benjamin, W. (1999), *The Arcades Project*, Cambridge, MA: Belknap Press.

Bills, M. (2006), *The Art of Satire: London in Caricature*, London: Philip Wilson.

Bolton, A. (2003), *Men in Skirts*, London: V&A Publications.

Bowker, G.C. and Star, S.L. (2000), *Sorting Things Out: Classification and Its Consequences*, Cambridge: Massachusetts Institute of Technology.

Breward, C. (2003), *Fashion*, Oxford: Oxford University Press.

Breward, C. and C. Evans (eds) (2005), *Fashion and Modernity*, Oxford: Berg.

Cannizzo, J. (2005), *Our Highland Home: Victoria and Albert in Scotland*, Edinburgh: National Galleries of Scotland.

Carrigan, T., Connell, B. and Lee J. (1985), 'Toward a New Sociology of Masculinity', in *Theory and Society*, vol. 14, no. 5, pp. 551–604.

Carter, M. (2003), *Fashion Classics from Carlyle to Barthes*, Oxford: Berg.

Casalis, L. (ed.) (1980), *Fashion in Paris: from the 'Journal des Dames at des Modes' 1912–1913*, London: Thames and Hudson.

Cheape, H. (1991), *Tartan: The Highland Habit*, Edinburgh: National Museums of Scotland.

Chesterfield, Lord. (1838), *The Works of Lord Chesterfield: Including His Letters To His Son &C* (First Complete American Edition), New York: Harper & Brothers.

Chesterfield, Lord. (1992), (Roberts, D. ed.), *Lord Chesterfield's Letters*, Oxford: Oxford University Press.

Clifford, J. (1988), *The Predicament of Culture: Twentieth-Century Ethnography, Literature, and Art*, Harvard: Harvard University Press.

Coates, N. (2003), *Guide to Ecstacity*, London: Laurence King.

Cohen, J. M. and M. J. Cohen (eds) (1971), *The Penguin Dictionary of Quotations*, Harmondsworth: Penguin Books.

Colley, L. (1992), *Britons, Forging the Nation, 1707–1837*, London: Macmillan.

Cooke, L and P. Wollen, (eds) (1995), *Visual Display: Culture Beyond* Appearances, Seattle: Bay Press.

Cosgrave, B. (ed.) (2005), *Sample: 100 Fashion Designers, 010 Curators*, London: Phaidon.

Davies, R. (1977), *Fifth Business*, London: W.H. Allen & Co.

Debord, G. (1983), *Society of the Spectacle*, Detroit: Black & Red.

Deleuze, G. and F. Guattari (1992), *A Thousand Plateaus: Capitalism and Schizophrenia*, London: Athlone.

Dunbar, J. T. (1962), *History of Highland Dress*, Edinburgh: Oliver & Boyd.

Dunbar, J. T. (1983), *Highland Costume*, Edinburgh: The Mercat Press.

Duncan, C. (1995), *Civilizing Rituals: Inside Public Art Museums*, London: Routledge.

Elsner, J. and R. Cardinal (eds) (1994), *The Cultures of Collecting*, London: Reaktion.

Evans, C. (2003), *Fashion at the Edge: Spectacle, Modernity and Deathliness*, New Haven and London: Yale University Press.

Ewing, E. (1986), *History of Children's Costume*, London: Bibliophile.

Foden, G. (1999), *The Last King of Scotland*, London: Faber and Faber.

Foreman, C. (2004), *Made in Scotland: Household Names that Began in Scotland*, Edinburgh: Berlinn.

Foucault, M. (1986), 'Of Other Spaces', *Diacritics*, spring 1986.

Foucault, M. (2002), *The Order of Things*, London: Routledge.

Gates, H. L. Jr. (1987), *Figures in Black: Words, Signs, and the 'Racial' Self*, New York: Oxford University Press.

Gow, I. (1992), *The Scottish Interior*, Edinburgh: Edinburgh University Press.

Grant, I. F. (1995), *Highland Folk Ways*, Edinburgh: Birlinn.

Grant, J. (1992), *Scottish Tartans in Full Color*, New York: Dover.

Grimble, I. (2004), *Scottish Clans and Tartans*, London: Octopus.

Harrison, C. and P. Wood (eds) (1993), *Art in Theory 1900–1990*, Oxford: Blackwell.

Hart, A. and North, S. (1998), *Historical Fashion in Detail: The 17th and 18th Centuries*, London: V&A Publications.

Hastreiter, K. and D. Hershkovits (eds) (2004), *20 years of Style: The World According to Paper*, New York: Harper Design International.

Hobsbawm, H. and R. Ranger (eds) (2004), *The Invention of Tradition*, Cambridge: Cambridge University Press.

Hollander, A. (1993), *Seeing Through Clothes*, Berkeley: University of California Press.

Hollander, A. (2000), *Feeding the Eye*, Berkeley: University of California Press.

Holtzman, J. (ed.) (2001), *Every Room Tells a Story: Tales from the Pages of Nest Magazine*, New York: D.A.P.

Innes of Learney, Sir T. (1964), *The Tartans of the Clans and Families of Scotland*, Edinburgh: Johnston & Bacon.

Jackson, A. (2000), *Japanese Textiles*, London: V&A Publications.

Johnston, L. (2005), *Nineteenth-Century Fashion in Detail*, London: V&A Publications.

Kawamura, Y. (2004), *The Japanese Revolution in Paris Fashion*, Oxford: Berg.

Krauss, R. (1989), *The Originality of the Avant-Garde and Other Modernist Myths*, Boston: MIT Press.

Kuchta, D. (2002), *The Three-Piece Suit and Modern Masculinity*, Berkeley: University of California.

Laver, J. (1968), *Dandies*, London: Weidenfeld and Nicolson.

Lehmann, U. (2000), *Tigersprung: Fashion in Modernity*, Boston: MIT Press.

Logan, J. (1831), *The Scottish Gaël*, London: Smith, Elder & Co.

Mackie, J. D. (1982), *A History of Scotland*, London: Penguin.

Maclean, F. (2000), *Highlanders: A History of the Highland Clans*, London: David Campbell.

Malossi, G. (ed.) (2000), *Material Man: Masculinity Sexuality Style*, New York: Harry N. Abrams.

Mansel, P. (2005), *Dressed to Rule: Royal and Court Costume from Louis XIV to Elizabeth II*, New Haven and London: Yale University Press.

McArthur, C. (2003), *'Braveheart', 'Brigadoon' and the Scots: Distortions of Scotland in Hollywood Cinema*, London: I.B. Tauris.

McDermott, C. (2002), *Made in Britain: Tradition and Style in Contemporary British Fashion*, London: Mitchell Beazley.

McDowell, C. (2000), *Fashion Today*, London: Phaidon.

McDowell, C. (2002), *Ralph Lauren: the Man, the Vision, the Style*, London: Cassell Illustrated.

McVeigh, B. (2000), *Wearing Ideology: State, Schooling and Self-Presentation in Japan*, Oxford: Berg.

Miller, L. (1993), *Cristóbal Balenciaga*, London: B.T. Batsford.

Nicholson, R. (2005), 'From Ramsay's *Flora MacDonald* to Raeburn's *MacNab*: The Use of Tartan as a Symbol of Identity', *Textile History*, 36(2), November 2005.

Nochlin, L. (2001), *The Body in Pieces: The Fragment as a Metaphor of Modernity*, London: Thames and Hudson.

Nuridsany, M. (2004), *China Art Now*, Paris: Éditions Flammarion.

Pantellini, C. and P. Stohler (eds) (2004), *Body Extensions*, Stuttgart: Arnoldsche.

Pastoureau, M. (1991), *The Devil's Cloth: A History of Stripes and Striped Fabric*, New York: Columbia University Press.

Pavitt, J. (ed.) (2000), *Brand.new*, London: V&A Publications.

Perrot, P. (1994), *Fashioning the Bourgeoisie: A History of Clothing in the Nineteenth Century*, Princeton: Princeton University Press.

Polhemus, T. and L. Procter (eds) (1978), *Fashion and Anti-Fashion*, London: Thames and Hudson.

Preziosi, D and C. Farago (eds) (2004), *Grasping the World: The Idea of the Museum*, Aldershot: Ashgate.

Ribeiro, A. (1986), *Dress and Morality*, London: B.T. Batsford.

Roberts, L. and J. Thrift (eds) (2002), *The Designer and the Grid*, Hove: RotoVision SA.

Rose, J. (2002), *The Intellectual Life of the British Working Classes*, London: Yale Nota Bene.

Rothenstein, N. (1994), *The Victoria & Albert Museum's Textile Collection: Woven Textile Design in Britain to 1750*, London: V&A Publications.

Rothstein, N. (ed.) (1984), *Four Hundred Years of Fashion*, London: V&A Publications.

Said, E. W. (2003), *Orientalism*, London: Penguin.

Samuel, R. (1996), *Theatres of Memory*, London: Verso.

Savage, J. (1992), *England's Dreaming: Sex Pistols and Punk Rock*, London: Faber and Faber.

Scarlett, J. D. (1985), *The Tartan Weaver's Guide*, London: Shepheard-Walwyn.

Scarlett, J. D. (1990), *Tartan: The Highland Textile*, London: Shepheard-Walwyn.

Scott, Sir W. (1995), *Rob Roy*, Ware: Wordsworth. ,

Shakespeare, W. (1904), *The Complete Works of William Shakespeare*, London: Henry Frowde.

Stewart, D. C. (1974), *The Setts of the Scottish Tartans*, London: Shepheard-Walwyn.

Stewart, D. W. (1893), *Old and Rare Scottish Tartans*, Edinburgh: George. P. Johnston.

Stewart, S. (1999), *On Longing: Narratives of the Miniature, the Gigantic, the Souvenir, the Collection*, Durham: Duke University Press.

Surtees, R. S. (1986) [1853], *Mr. Sponge's Sporting Tour*, Oxford: Oxford University Press.

Teal of Teallach, G. and P. D. Smith, Jr. (1992), *District Tartans*, London: Shepheard-Walwyn.

Thomas, A. (ed.) (1997), *Beauty of Another Order: Photography in Science*, London: Yale University Press.

Tortora, P. G. and E. Keith Eubank (2005), *Survey of Historic Costume*, New York: Fairchild.

Vinken, B. (2005), *Fashion Zeitgeist: Trends and Cycles in the Fashion System*, Oxford: Berg.

Walser, R. (1999), *Jakob Von Gunten*, New York: New York Review Books.

Way, G. and R. Squire (2000), *Clans and Tartans*, Glasgow: Harper Collins.

Wigley, M. (1995), *White Walls, Designer Dresses: The Fashioning of Modern Architecture*, Boston: MIT Press.

Wilcox, C. (2004), *Vivienne Westwood*, London: V&A Publications.

Wilcox, C. (ed.) (2001), *Radical Fashion*, London: V&A Publications.

Wilde, O. (1971), *Complete Works of Oscar Wilde*, London: Collins.

Willett Cunnington, C. (1990), *English Women's Clothing in the Nineteenth Century*, New York: Dover.

Wilson, E. (1985), *Adorned in Dreams: Fashion and Modernity*, London: Virago.

Wilson, E. (1998), 'Bohemian Dress and the Heroism of Everyday Life' in *Fashion Theory* vol. 2, no. 3, pp. 225–44.

Wolfe, T. (1990), *Mauve Gloves & Madmen, Clutter & Vine*, London: Picador.

Zaczek, I. and C. Phillips (eds) (2004), *The Complete Book of Tartan*, London: Hermes House.

CATALOGUES

Fashion 1900–1939 (1975), Scottish Arts Council.

Give & Take: 1 Exhibition 2 Sites (2001), Serpentine Gallery, London.

Jam: Tokyo-London (2001), Barbican Gallery, London.

Living and Correspondences (2001), Henry Moore Foundation External Programmes.

Minimalism and After III (2003), DaimlerChrysler Collection, Berlin.

Richard Martin and Harold Koda, *Orientalism: Visions of the East in Western Dress* (1994), Metropolitan Museum of Art, New York.

Rabid Dogs (2002), Sonic China.

Viktor & Rolf: Haute Couture Book (2000), Groninger Museum, The Netherlands.

William West & the Regency Toy Theatre (2004), Sir John Soane's Museum, London.

WEBSITES

Brigadoon in Bundanoon: http://www.highlandsnsw.com.au/brigadoon

Highland Clearances Information: http://www.clannada.org/highland.php

Internet Movie Database: http://www.imdb.com/

Locharron: http://www.locharron.com

Scottish Tartans Authority: http://www.tartansauthority.com

Scottish Tartans Museum, Keith: http://www.keithcommunity.co.uk

Scottish Tartans World Register: www.tartans.scotland.net/

Style.com: http://www.style.com/

Tartan Day Information: http://www.tartanday.gov.uk

Tartan Finder: http://www.house-of-tartan.scotland.net

Tartangenerator.com: http://www.tartangenerator.com

Tartans of Scotland: http://www.tartans.scotland.net

Vogue: http://www.vogue.co.uk

161 McDaddy tartan designed by Inez Laing-Faiers

ACKNOWLEDGEMENTS

This book is dedicated to Dell and Inez, whose unfailing encouragement, patience and love have been truly remarkable.

I am grateful to the many friends and colleagues at V&A Publications, V&A Enterprises and Berg who have been ever generous with their expertise and advice, in particular Kathryn Earle and Mary Butler for their initial belief in *Tartan* and their continued enthusiasm.

Particular thanks go to Jean Anderson and Deborah Smeaton at Blair Castle, Thomas Andrews, Matthew Barney, Niklas von Bartha, Robyn Beeche, Alistair and Andrew Buchan and Mary Aitken at Lochcarron, Rosemary Crill, Mark Croxford, Daisy de Villeneuve, Bridget Donahue, Volker Eichelmann, Stephen Ellcock, Jane England, Cao Fei, Brian and Linda Gorn and the Scottish Tartans Museum in Keith, Danny Heffer, Matthias Herrmann, Delisia Howard, Doris Hutton, Aiko Inoue, Jill Jacques, the Keith Kilt School, Lieutenant Colonel G. Latham and Kelvin Hunter at Fort George, Andrew Logan, Ruth Maclennan, Glen Marks at Rex, Frank McGarry, Niall McInerney, Lesley Miller, Chris Moore and Zoë Roberts at Catwalking. com, the National Dahlia Collection, Out of Joint and the Arcola Theatre, Linda Parry, Roxanne Peters, J. Morgan Puett, Isla Robertson, Corrine Ross, John Ross, Gill Saunders, Andrea Stern, Meriel Scott at Precious McBane, Saro Schwyzer, Peter Stubbs, Junko Tajima, Jun Takahashi and Yuka Nakamura at Undercover, Dieter Suls and finally, Linda Welters.

I am especially thankful for the support of the School of Fashion, Textiles and Jewellery, Central St Martins, University of the Arts, London.

Jonathan Faiers

ILLUSTRATION CREDITS

INTRODUCTION

1 Courtesy of England & Co. Gallery, London. © V&A Images/Victoria and Albert Museum.
2 Photo: Author.
3 Photo: Steve Wood/Rex Features.
4 © V&A Images/Victoria and Albert Museum.
5 Photo: Courtesy of the National Collection of Dahlias.

CHAPTER 1

6. Photo: Author.
7 Courtesy of Lochcarron.
8 Courtesy of Lochcarron.
9 Courtesy of Lochcarron.
10 © The Trustees of the National Museums of Scotland.
11 Courtesy of Lochcarron.
12 Courtesy of Lochcarron.
13 Courtesy of Lochcarron.
14 Courtesy of Lochcarron.

CHAPTER 2

15 Photo: Author.
16 Photo: Author.
17 Photo: Author. By kind permission of the Scottish Tartans Museum, Keith.
18 Courtesy of Lochcarron.
19 Photograph reproduced by kind permission of the Duke of Atholl, Blair Castle.
20 Photograph reproduced by kind permission of the Duke of Atholl, Blair Castle.
21 Image courtesy of the Royal Bank of Scotland Collection.
22 © V&A Images/Victoria and Albert Museum.

CHAPTER 3

23 © V&A Images/Victoria and Albert Museum.
24 Photo: Author. By kind permission of the Scottish Tartans Museum, Keith.
25 Photo: Author. By kind permission of the Regimental Museum, Queen's Own Highlanders (Seaforth and Camerons).
26 Photo: Dan Tuffs/Rex Features.
27 Photograph courtesy of MoMu, Antwerp.
28 Photo: Rex Features.
29 Photo: Photonews Scotland/Rex Features.
30 © V&A Images/Victoria and Albert Museum.
31 Courtesy of Lochcarron.
32 Photo: Author.
33 Photo: Author.
34 © V&A Images/ Victoria and Albert Museum.

CHAPTER 4

35 Photographs courtesy of Robyn Beeche.
36 Photo: George Konig/Rex Features.
37 © V&A Images/Victoria and Albert Museum.
38 Photo: Author.
39 Photo: Author.
40 Photograph reproduced by kind permission of the Duke of Atholl, Blair Castle.
41 Courtesy of Lochcarron.
42 Scottish National Portrait Gallery.
43 © V&A Images/Victoria and Albert Museum.
44 © V&A Images/Victoria and Albert Museum.
45 Photo: Author.
46 Image © Ruth Maclennan and Szuper Gallery.
47 Photo: Eugene Adebari/Rex Features.
48 Courtesy of Vivienne Westwood. Photographer unknown.

49 Photographs courtesy of Robyn Beeche.
50 © V&A Images/ Victoria and Albert Museum.
51 Photos: Niall McInerney.

CHAPTER 5

52 Photo: Author. By kind permission of the Regimental Museum, Queen's Own Highlanders (Seaforth and Camerons).
53 Courtesy of Lochcarron.
54 Photo: Chris Moore/Catwalking.com.
55 Photo: Author. By kind permission of the Regimental Museum, Queen's Own Highlanders (Seaforth and Camerons).
56 Photograph courtesy of Robyn Beeche.
57 © V&A Images/Victoria and Albert Museum.
58 © V&A Images/Victoria and Albert Museum.
59 Photo: Brian Rasic/Rex Features.
60 Photo: © Miramax/Everett/Rex Features.
61 Photo: Author.
62 Photo: Sharok Hatami/Rex Features.
63 Photo: Roger Bamber/Rex Features.
64 Photo: Ross McDairmant/Rex Features.

CHAPTER 6

65 Photo: Rex Features.
66 Photo: Author. By kind permission of the Regimental Museum, Queen's Own Highlanders (Seaforth and Camerons).
67 Photograph © The Trustees of the British Museum. Courtesy of the Department of Prints and Drawings.
68 Photo: Author. By kind permission of the Scottish Tartans Museum, Keith.
69 Photograph © Gregg Homme.
70 Photograph courtesy of Matthias Herrmann.
71 Photo: Author.
72 Photograph courtesy of Corinne Ross.
73 © V&A Images/Victoria and Albert Museum.
74 © V&A Images/Victoria and Albert Museum.
75 Photo: Chris Moore/Catwalking.com.

CHAPTER 7

76 By kind permission of the National Trust for Scotland Photo Library/Fyvie Castle Collection.
77 Scottish National Galleries.
78 © V&A Images/Victoria and Albert Museum.
79 Photo: Author. By kind permission of the Scottish Tartans Museum, Keith.

80 Photo: John Haynes. By kind permission of Out of Joint and the Arcola Theatre, London. © V&A Images/Victoria and Albert Museum.
81 Photo: Matt Baron/BEI/Rex Features.
82 © V&A Images/Victoria and Albert Museum.
83 Photo: Author.
84 Photo courtesy of Robyn Beeche.
85 © V&A Images/Victoria and Albert Museum.
86 By kind permission of the Trustees of the National Library of Scotland.
87 Photo: Brian Moody/Rex Features.
88 © V&A Images/Victoria and Albert Museum.
89 © V&A Images/Victoria and Albert Museum.
90 Photo: Patsy Lynch/Rex Features.
91 Photo: Ray Tang/Rex Features.
92 Courtesy of Lochcarron.

CHAPTER 8

93 © V&A Images/Victoria and Albert Museum.
94 © V&A Images/Victoria and Albert Museum.
95 Photo: Author. By kind permission of the Scottish Tartans Museum, Keith.
96 © V&A Images/Victoria and Albert Museum.
97 © V&A Images/Victoria and Albert Museum.
98 Photo: Michael Fresco/Rex Features.
99 © V&A Images/Victoria and Albert Museum.
100 © V&A Images/Victoria and Albert Museum.
101 Photo: Author.
102 Photograph reproduced by kind permission of the Duke of Atholl, Blair Castle.
103 © V&A Images/Victoria and Albert Museum.
104 Images by kind permission of Precious McBane.
105 Photo: Author. By kind permission of the Scottish Tartans Museum, Keith.
106 Photo: Author. By kind permission of the Scottish Tartans Museum, Keith.
107 Photographs by kind permission of J. Morgan Puett and Alexander Gray Associates, New York.
108 © V&A Images/Victoria and Albert Museum.
109 Courtesy of Lochcarron.
110 Photo: Author. By kind permission of the Scottish Tartans Museum, Keith.
111 Photo: Author.

CHAPTER 9

112 Experiment photograph © Peter Stubbs/www.edinphoto.org.uk.
113 © V&A Images/Victoria and Albert Museum.

114 Photo: Author. By kind permission of the Kilt School, Keith.
115 Courtesy Gallery Niklas von Bartha, London. © Beat Zoderer.
116 Courtesy of Lochcarron.
117 Photographer: John French. © V&A Images/ Victoria and Albert Museum.
118 Photo: Sipa Press/Rex Features.
119 © V&A Images/Victoria and Albert Museum. Photo: Rex Features.
120 © Cao Fei.
121 © The Estate of Edward Bawden. Scottish National Gallery of Modern Art.

CHAPTER 10
122 Photograph: Chris Winget. Courtesy Gladstone Gallery, New York.
123 Photographs: Mamoru Miyazawa. Courtesy of Jun Takahshi/Undercover.
124 Photo: Willi Schneider/Rex Features.
125 Photo: Author. By kind permission of the Regimental Museum, Queen's Own Highlanders (Seaforth and Camerons).
126 © V&A Images/Victoria and Albert Museum.
127 Photo: © John Ross.
128 Photo: © John Ross.
129 Photo: Everett Collection/Rex Features.
130 Photo: Author.
131 © V&A Images/ Victoria and Albert Museum.

CHAPTER 11
132 Photo: Author.
133 Courtesy of Lochcarron.
134 © The Trustees of the National Museums of Scotland.
135 Photograph reproduced by kind permission of the Duke of Atholl, Blair Castle.
136 © V&A Images/Victoria and Albert Museum.

137 Photograph: Niall McInerney.
138 Photo: Author. © V&A Images/Victoria and Albert Museum.
139 © V&A Images/Victoria and Albert Museum.
140 Photo: Charles Knight/Rex Features.
141 Photo: Author. By kind permission of the Regimental Museum, Queen's Own Highlanders (Seaforth and Camerons).
142 Photo: Author.
143 © V&A Images/Victoria and Albert Museum.

CHAPTER 12
144 © V&A Images/Victoria and Albert Museum.
145 © V&A Images/Victoria and Albert Museum.
146 Photos: Chris Moore/Catwalking.com.
147 Photos: Charles Knight/Rex Features.
148 Photos: Chris Moore/Catwalking.com.
149 Photo: Rex Features.

CHAPTER 13
150 Photo: Cheddar Gorgeous.
151 Photo: Author.
152 Photo by Gideon Mendel/Corbis via ©Getty Images.
153 Bloomsbury Fashion Photography.
154 © Getty images.
155 © Getty images.
156 © Getty images.
157 Bloomsbury Fashion Photography and © Getty images.
158 Photo: Nicholas Daley.
159 © Getty images.
160 © Getty images.

161 Photo: Author.

INDEX

Wilson, Janet 197
Wilson, Richard, *Flora MacDonald* **86,** 87
Wilson, William, & Son of Bannockburn 23, 66,
     66, 116, 154, 155, 195–200, 224, 270, 272
   letters addressed to **195**
   tartan swatches **197**
Wilson, Woodrow 261
woad 24
Wolfe, Tom 173, 175
women, clothing 37, 85–8, 132–4, 143–8, 181

wool 20–1, 24
World of Interiors magazine 192
wrapping paper **230**
Wright, John Michael, *Lord Mungo Murray* 40–2

Yamamoto, Yohji 284

Zoderer, Beat 217–18, 219
   Bandage No. 5 **217**
   TESA No. 2 **217,** 218